LSAT LOGIC GAMES SOLUTIONS MANUAL

Complete Solutions to All Analytical Reasoning Sections from PrepTests 1-50

Published by
Cambridge LSAT
225 W. Verdugo Ave., #302
Burbank, CA 91502

Author: Morley Tatro

Manufactured in the United States
June 2010

ISBN-10: 1453605096
ISBN-13: 978-1453605097

TABLE OF CONTENTS

PART 5: PREPTESTS 41-50

PART 6: BONUS SOLUTIONS

APPENDIX

The LSAT (Law School Admission Test) is one of the biggest factors affecting your potential acceptance to the law school of your dreams. Law school admission committees routinely place a huge emphasis on a person's LSAT score in making their decisions. Although the use of the LSAT in law school admissions decisions is not without controversy, one thing remains certain: to maximize your acceptance offers from the better schools, you must maximize your LSAT potential and score at or near your potential on test day. I hope you find this book to be invaluable to your preparation.

The Logic Games (formally known as Analytical Reasoning) section of the LSAT tends to be a polarizing element of the test. Some welcome the challenge while others view the section as a loss before even attempting any of the games. In terms of its initial foreignness, Logic Games, more so than Logical Reasoning and Reading Comprehension, can be "learned." The required thinking is not something that is readily taught in college, and takes a good deal of getting used to for the average student. While a perfect score on the section may not be essential to achieve a great LSAT score, strong games performance can make the difference between a good score and a 99th percentile score. Those who excel at games have systems which they've perfected through regular practice and they know how to adapt those systems to the curveball games LSAC can, and inevitably will, throw on test day.

This book is not meant to be an introduction to LSAT Logic Games. Rather, it is meant to complement your games practice. There are a number of instructive Logic Games strategy books on the market, among them books by PowerScore, Manhattan LSAT (formerly Atlas LSAT), and Brian Talbot. You can purchase these books at **www.cambridgelsat.com/bookstore**. This book presumes a certain amount of Logic Games diagramming familiarity and understanding of basic formal logic principles. For those unfamiliar with "LSAT speak," this means that I'm assuming you've already done your homework and have some kind of strategy guide which has exposed you to the fundamentals of LSAT Logic Games.

For those looking to maximize their LSAT potential, there is a wealth of practice material available. Including the LSAC SuperPrep book and the free PrepTest on LSAC's website, there are over 60 previously administered LSAT tests with which to practice. The only downside to all this material is that, with the exception of SuperPrep, the tests don't come with explanations. While reasoning through answers after correcting a test can have tremendous value as an exercise, it is helpful to have an authoritative source to get the most out of your review. Until now, there hasn't been a book with complete, clear solutions to the first 50 numbered LSAT PrepTests. This book was written over a lengthy period of time with great attention given to the quality and clarity of the explanations. It doesn't contain any of the actual games. You can purchase and print them at **www.cambridgelsat.com**. You can also purchase hard copies of our LSAT Logic Games by Type books through our bookstore or directly through Amazon.

It is important to attempt the games on your own before looking at the explanations. Once you have gone through the explanations, think about how you can incorporate the presented methods into your future games performance. You may want to revisit games after some time has elapsed to lock in the various concepts. Logic Games can be approached in numerous ways, as evidenced by the many different approaches presented by the various prep companies. The biggest benefit of using this book is that it can add new tools to your arsenal. I believe that the solutions presented are the most efficient means to solve the problems. However, you may find some methods more useful than others in regards to your overall system. As such, it may be in your best interest to mix and match different methods in developing your own comprehensive method. These solutions tend to "over diagram," in the interest of providing the most concrete illustrations. In the heat of battle, it is often advisable to create "bare bones" diagrams for the individual questions, so long as your master diagram includes the important information. While this approach might lead to some oversights in the early stages of your preparation, with practice, you'll find that it will help you save time on the section as a whole. The way in which you incorporate these methods into your own practice is completely up to you. To receive access to the most recent Logic Games solutions (for PrepTests numbered 51 and above), send an e-mail to info@cambridgelsat.com. Be sure to let us know if you come across any errors in the book.

Part 1:
PrepTests 1-10

Questions 1-7

Setup:
- six trade representatives: K L M N O P
- six chairs evenly spaced around a circular table
- chairs: 1 2 3 4 5 6
- each chair is occupied by exactly one representative

Conditions:

#1: 

#2: LM or LN or MLN

#3: KM

#4: MOP

Overview:
None of the conditions address the issue of seat numbers, so we can leave them off our diagram. Additionally, the issue of direction is not addressed, so any acceptable solution will have a symmetrical solution with the variables going in the opposite direction which is also acceptable. The pieces given by the first two conditions can either be separate or connected through N. We can use this information to set up three molds.

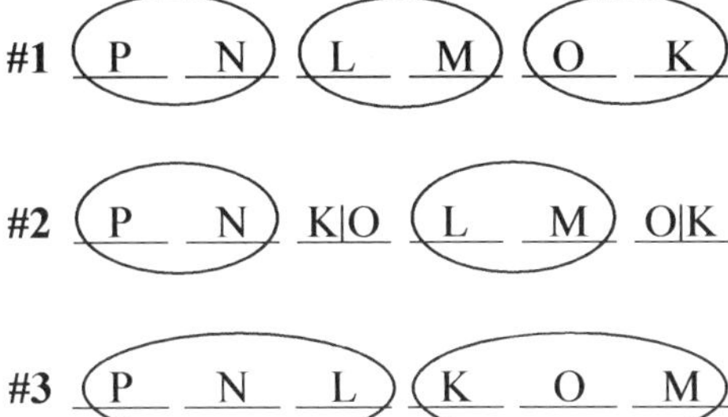

Mold #1: The PN and LM pieces can flank each other.

Mold #2: The PN and LM pieces can be separated by K and O individually.

Mold #3: Creating a PNL piece from the first two conditions, we're left with K, M, and O. Due to the third condition, O must be the middle variable in this three-variable piece.

1. (A) violates the second condition
   (B) Correct – see mold #1
   (C) violates the fourth condition
   (D) violates the third condition
   (E) violates the first condition

2. **(A)** This could only be true of mold #1. Thus, we know that K and O must sit next to each other, and choice A is correct.

   N P L M O K

3. **(B)** This could only be true of mold #2. Locking the variables into place reveals that M must be flanked by both L and O, and choice B is therefore correct.

   N P K L M O

4. **(E)** This could only be true of mold #1. Fixing the PN and LM pieces in place leaves two options for K. K could sit between P and O, and choice E is thus correct.

   P N M L K|O O|K

5. **(E)** This is true of molds #1 and #2. In mold #1, L could be next to any one of K, N, O, and P, and choice E is therefore correct.

6. **(C)** This is true of molds #1 and #3. By fixing P, N, and L in place, we are left with K, M, and O. The third condition dictates that K must be separated from M by O, and there are two acceptable solutions. Since O is flanked by both K and M, choice C must be false.

   P N L K|M O M|K

7. This is true of molds #1 and #3. Comparing the choices to these two molds allows us to eliminate those that are incorrect.
   (A) could be true of mold #1
   (B) could be true of mold #3
   (C) could be true of either mold
   (D) could be true of mold #1
   (E) Correct – this cannot be true of mold #1 since L is flanked by M on one side and it cannot be true of mold #3 since O is flanked by both K and M

Questions 8-13

Setup:
- four offices: 1 2 3 4
- each office ⟶ one computer (C) and one printer (P)
- each machine was bought in one of three years
- years: 7 8 9

Conditions:
#1: C ≤ P
#2: C2 = P1
#3: C3 = P4
#4: C2 ≠ C3
#5: C1=8 and P3=8

Overview:
From the first and fifth conditions, we can deduce some limitations. The printer in office 1 must have been bought in either 1988 or 1989. We also know that the computer in office 3 must have been bought in either 1987 or 1988. Applying the second and third conditions, we know that the computer in office 2 was bought in either 1988 or 1989 and that the printer in office 4 was bought in either 1987 or 1988. Revisiting the first condition, we can further deduce that the printer in office 2 was bought in either 1988 or 1989 and that the computer in office 4 was bought in either 1987 or 1988.

	1	2	3	4
P	8|9	8|9	8	7|8
C	8	8|9 ≠	7|8	7|8

From the various options, we can create three distinct molds.

#1

	1	2	3	4
P	8	8|9	8	7
C	8	8	7	7

#2

	1	2	3	4
P	9	9	8	7
C	8	9	7	7

#3

	1	2	3	4
P	9	9	8	8
C	8	9	8	7|8

Mold #1: If the printer in office 1 and the computer in office 2 were both bought in 1988, the fourth condition dictates that the computer in office 3 must have been bought in 1987. Applying the first and third conditions, we have two acceptable solutions.

Mold #2: If the printer in office 1 was bought in 1989, and the computer in office 3 was bought in 1987, there is one acceptable solution.

Mold #3: If the printer in office 1 was bought in 1989, and the computer in office 3 was bought in 1988, the first and third conditions combined dictate that the computer in office 4 was bought in either 1987 or 1988.

8. **(B)** This could only be true of the first mold. Accordingly, the printer in office 2 must have been bought in 1989. Therefore, choice B must be true, and the other choices must be false.

9. **(D)** Comparing the choices to our molds reveals that only D could be true (under mold #3), and it is therefore correct.

10. **(A)** Mold #3 allows for a solution in which none of the machines were bought in 1987. Thus, choice A is correct.

11. **(B)** This could only be true of mold #3. Thus, it must be true that the printer in office 1 was bought in 1989, and choice B is correct.

12. **(D)** This is only true of mold #3. Comparing the choices to this mold reveals that only D could be true.

13. **(C)** Since our initial diagram included the fourth condition only symbolically, we can still use it for this question. Applying this new condition to our initial diagram, we know that the computers in offices 2 and 3 were purchased in 1988. We can further deduce that the printers in offices 1 and 4 were both purchased in 1988. The only machine that could have been bought in 1989 is the printer in office 2, and choice C is therefore correct.

P	8	8|9	8	8
C	8	8	8	7|8
	1	2	3	4

Questions 14-18

Setup:

- eight partners: G H I J K M N O
- eight years: 1 2 3 4 5 6 7 8
- in each year, exactly one partner joined

Conditions:
#1: H – N
#2: K – J
#3:

#4: N – O
#5: J – M
#6: G – I

Overview:
Combining the conditions yields the following sketch.

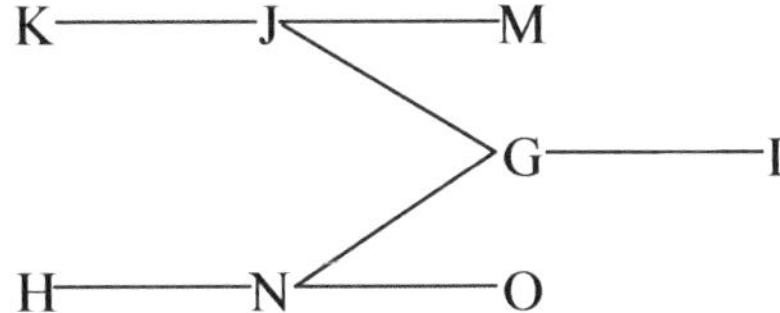

14. **(C)** Comparing the choices to our diagram reveals that C cannot be true. Since G must follow at least four others (K, J, H, and N), G cannot be fourth.

15. Combining this with our sketch, we know that K is first.

K	J						
1	2	3	4	5	6	7	8

(A) H can occupy the first open slot
(B) M can occupy the first open slot
(C) H would be preceded by M, which would occupy the third slot
(D) N would be preceded by H, which would occupy the third slot
(E) Correct – O must be preceded by at least two others (H and N), meaning that earliest slot O can occupy is the fifth

16. **(D)** Since J must be followed by at least three other variables (G, I, and M), the latest slot J can occupy is the fifth. Therefore, choice D is correct.

17. **(B)** With O and M placed, were left with the following sketch for the remaining six slots:

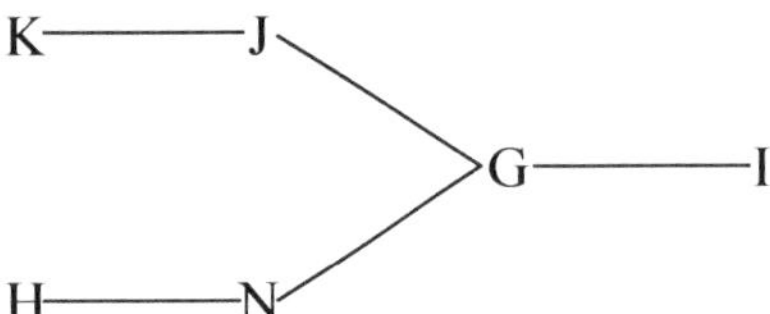

Accordingly, G and I must fill the sixth and eighth slots, respectively, and choice B is correct.

				O	G	M	I
1	2	3	4	5	6	7	8

18. **(D)** We can redraw our sketch to incorporate this information. Since M must be preceded by at least five variables (K, J, H, N, and O), the earliest slot M could fill is the sixth. Thus, choice D is correct.

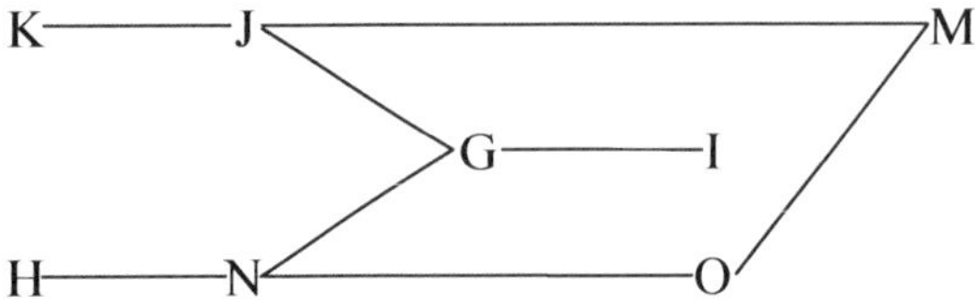

Questions 19-24

Setup:
- three lines: 1 2 3
- two months: J F
- one set of tickets for each line for each of the two months

Conditions:
#1: four colors: G P R Y
#2: J1 ≠ F1; J2 ≠ F2; J3 ≠ F3
#3: J1 ≠ J2 ≠ J3; J1 ≠ J3; F1 ≠ F2 ≠ F3; F1 ≠ F3
#4: exactly one R_J
#5: J3=G or F3=G (but not both)
#6: J2=P
#7: F ≠ P

Overview:
From the first, third, and seventh conditions, we can deduce that there will be tickets of the following three colors in February: G, R, and Y. We can set up two molds based on the fifth condition.

#1					**#2**				
	F	R|Y	Y|R	G		F	____	____	R|Y
	J	____	P	R|Y		J	R	P	G
		1	2	3			1	2	3

Mold #1: With a G placed in F3, the seventh dictates that F1 and F2 must be occupied by R and Y, in either order. The second and third conditions dictate that J3 must be occupied by either R or Y.

Mold #2: With a G placed in J3, the fourth condition dictates that R must occupy J1. From the second and seventh conditions, we can deduce that F3 must be occupied by either R or Y.

19. **(E)** This could only be true of mold #1. Thus, G must occupy F3, and choice E is correct. We also know that J1 must be occupied by either G or Y, due to the third condition.

F	R|Y	Y|R	G
J	G|Y	P	R
	1	2	3

20. **(A)** This could only be true of mold #2. The second condition dictates that we must place a Y in F1, which leaves R to occupy F3. Only choice A must be true, and it is therefore correct. Choices B through E must be false.

F	Y	G	R
J	R	P	G
	1	2	3

21. **(A) Correct – see the following diagram, derived from mold #1**

F	Y	R	G
J	R	P	Y
	1	2	3

(B) violates either the third or the seventh condition
(C) violates either the fourth or the sixth condition
(D) violates either the fourth or the sixth condition
(E) violates either the sixth or the seventh condition

22. (A) this is incompatible with either mold
    (B) Correct – this could be true of our diagram for #19
    (C) this is incompatible with either mold
    (D) this is incompatible with either mold
    (E) violates either the second or the fourth condition

23. **(E)** This could only be true of mold #2. Since we must place a G and an R in the two remaining February slots, and the second condition precludes an R from occupying F1, we must place the G and R into F1 and F2, respectively. Thus, choice E must be false, and it is correct.

F	Y	R	Y
J	R	P	G
	1	2	3

24. **(C)** We can redraw our molds to incorporate this information. From the third condition, we know that both months will have tickets of all three colors. Irrespective of where we place the second G, all remaining slots must be occupied by either R or Y. Applying the second and third conditions reveals that only choice C could be true, as illustrated by two of the diagrams.

F	R|Y	Y|R	G
J	G	R|Y	Y|R
	1	2	3

F	R|Y	Y|R	G
J	Y|R	G	R|Y
	1	2	3

F	G	R|Y	Y|R
J	R|Y	Y|R	G
	1	2	3

F	R|Y	G	Y|R
J	Y|R	R|Y	G
	1	2	3

Questions 1-5

Setup:

- nine new workers: B C D E F G H I J

Conditions:

#1: [F I] and no others
#2: [C G] and no others
#3: on each of the other days ⟶ exactly one worker
#4: E – B
#5: H – D
#6: I – D – E
J > G
B > G
B – J

Overview:
Combining all the conditions yields the following sketch.

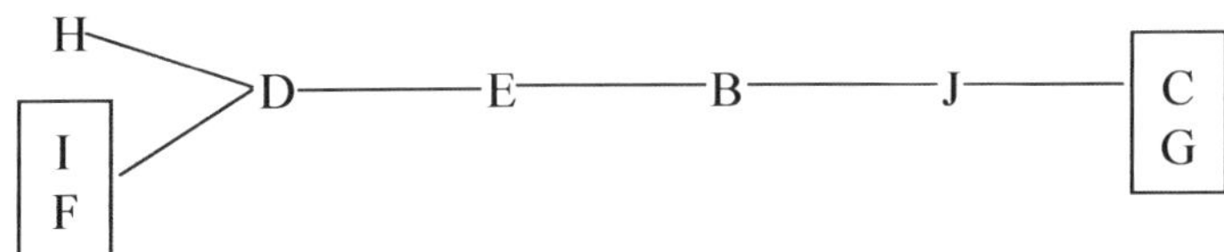

1. **(D)** As our sketch clearly illustrates, C and G are the last two to be hired. Thus, choice D is correct.

2. **(A)** There are three hiring days preceding E, and choice A is therefore correct.

3. **(A)** J is preceded by six workers, and choice A is thus correct.

4. **(E)** Comparing the choices to our sketch reveals that only E must be true, and it is therefore correct.

5. **(D)** Since at least two hiring days must take place between E and G, we can infer that G could have been hired on Thursday at the earliest. Thus, choice D is correct.

			C
E	B	J	G
M	T	W	Th

Questions 6-12

Setup:
- five floors: 1 2 3 4 5
- each floor has one or two apartments
- exactly eight apartments in the building
- eight residents: J K L M N O P Q
- each resident lives in exactly one apartment

Conditions:

#1: 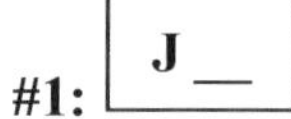

#2: 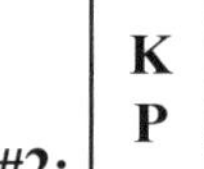

#3: floor 2 ⟶ only one apartment

#4: 

#5: 

#6: **L**

#7: ~Q_1 and ~Q_2

Overview:
Combining the third and fourth conditions, we know that neither M nor N can be on the second floor. From the first and third conditions, we can deduce that J cannot live on the second floor. From the second condition, we can deduce that K cannot live on the first floor, and P cannot live on the fifth floor.

```
        ~P 5 ____ ------
           4 ____ ------
           3 ____ ------
~M ~N ~J ~Q 2 ____
     ~K ~Q 1 ____ ------
```

6. **(D)** As we inferred, N cannot live on the second floor, and choice D is therefore correct.

7. **(E)** We inferred that P cannot live on the fifth floor, and choice E is thus correct.

8. **(A)** Applying the second condition, we know that P lives on the fourth floor. Due to the third condition, the MN piece must be placed on either the first or the third floor. If the MN piece is on the first floor, Q could be on the third or the fifth floor. If the MN piece is on the third floor, Q could be on the first or the fifth floor. Only choice A is compatible with either scenario (the second one), and it is therefore correct.

5	K	|Q		5	K	|Q
4	P	J		4	P	J
3	Q|			3	M	N
2				2		
1	M	N	or	1	Q|	

9. **(E)** Combining this with the second and third conditions, we must place the KP piece on either the third and fourth floors or the fourth and fifth floors. Since either K or P lives on the fourth floor, the sixth condition precludes L from living on that floor. Thus, choice E is correct.

5	K			5	|M	|N
4	P			4	K	
3	|M	|N		3	P	
2	O			2	O	
1	M|	N|	or	1	M|	N|

10. **(C)** Combining this with the second and fourth conditions, we can deduce that the KP piece must span either the first and second floors or the second and third floors. Due to the sixth condition, L must be on one of the first, third, and fifth floors. Therefore, choice C must be false, and it is correct.

5	|L			5	|L	
4	M	N		4	M	N
3	L|			3	K	
2	K			2	P	
1	P		or	1	L|	

11. Since each answer choice is presented as a conditional statement, we'll use our previous work to eliminate the incorrect choices.

    (A) see #8
    (B) Correct – due to the third and sixth conditions, there would be no way to place the KP piece
    (C) see the first diagram for #10
    (D) could be true of the second diagram for #10

5	O	J
4	M	N
3	K	Q
2	P	
1	L	

    (E) see the first diagram for #9

12. **(C)** Applying the second condition, we know that K is on the third floor. The MN piece can be placed either on the first or the fifth floor. Whichever of the two floors the MN piece does not occupy must be occupied by L, due to the sixth condition. Since the fifth, sixth, and seventh conditions preclude Q from being on any other floor than the third, choice C must be true. J can only be placed on the fourth floor under either scenario.

5	L			5	M	N
4	O	J		4	O	J
3	K	Q		3	K	Q
2	P			2	P	
1	M	N	or	1	L	

Questions 13-17

Setup:
- o 14 days, exclusive of travel time
- o six cities

Conditions:
#1: three countries: X Y Z
#2: each of the three countries has many cities
#3: 1^+ city in each of the three countries
#4: 2^+ days in each city she visits
#5: only whole days in any city

Overview:
Since there are six cities, and she must visit at least one city in each country, there are three possible allocations of cities to countries:
4, 1, 1
3, 2, 1
2, 2, 1

Combining the fourth condition with the setup conditions, we can infer two possible allocations of days to cities:
4, 2, 2, 2, 2, 2
3, 3, 2, 2, 2, 2

We'll use slots to represent individual cities, and numbers to represent the number of days she spends in each particular city.

X Y Z

13. **(A)** Combining this with our days to cities allocations, we can deduce three combinations of days which total eight: 4, 2, 2; 3, 3, 2; and 2, 2, 2, 2. Since she must visit at least three cities in country X, choice A must be false.

14. **(D)** Combined with the fact that she visits six cities, we know that she visits two cities in each country. To maximize the number of days she spends in country X, she must spend either four days in one city and two days in the other, or three days in each of the two cities. Thus, choice D is correct.

X	Y	Z		X	Y	Z
4	2	2		3	2	2
2	2	2	or	3	2	2

15. **(D)** This triggers the second allocation of days to cities. Since she spends seven days in Z, she must spend three days in one of the cities and two days in each of the other two. With two cities remaining, they must be assigned to X, and our days to cities allocation dictates that she must visit each one for two days. Thus, choice D must be false, and it is correct.

X	Y	Z
		3
2		2
2	3	2

16. **(B)** The maximum number of days she can spend in any particular city, according to our days to cities allocations, is four. Therefore, we know that she spends four days in Nomo and at least four days in country X. We cannot infer anything concrete about the cities to countries allocation. The only thing we know for certain is that she can visit four cities in country X, and choice B is therefore correct.

X	Y	Z
2		
2		
2		
4	2	2

17. **(C)** Since we need to maximize the number of days she spends in country Y, we should maximize the number of cities she visits in country Y. Under this scenario, the third condition limits the maximum number of cities she could visit in country Y to three. Maximizing the number of days she spends in country Y using the two allocations of days to cities yields the same number: eight. Thus, choice C is correct.

X	Y	Z
	2	
	2	2
2	4	2

or

X	Y	Z
	2	
	3	2
2	3	2

Questions 18-24

Setup:

- six dogs: P Q R S T U
- four ribbons: 1 2 3 4
- each ribbon is awarded to exactly one dog

Conditions:

#1: each dog ⟶ G or L (but not both)

#2: F F M M M M

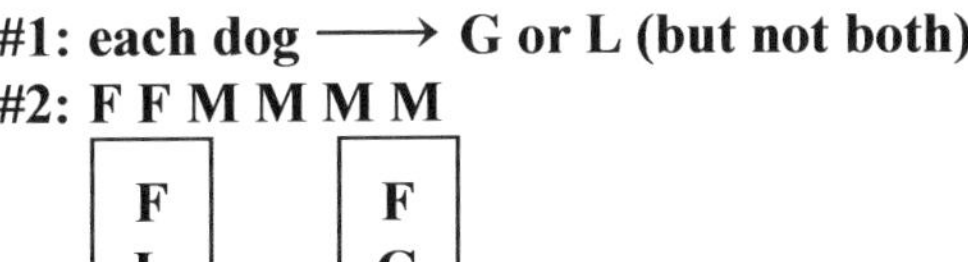

#3: [F L] and [F G] ⟶ ribbons

#4: exactly 1 L wins a ribbon

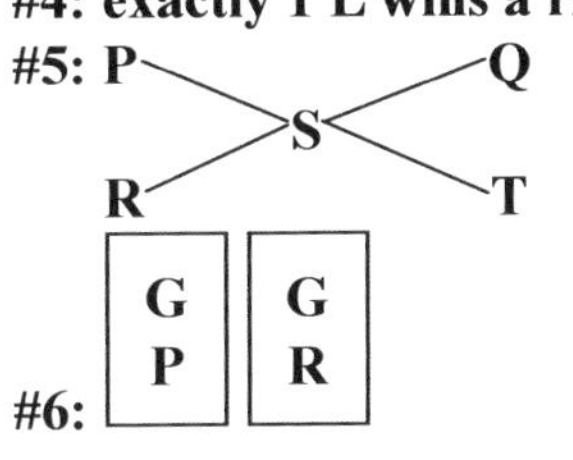

#5: P, R ⟶ S ⟶ Q, T

#6: [G P] [G R]

#7: [L S] [L U]

Overview:

From the fifth condition, and the fact that there are six dogs, we can deduce that S can be preceded by a maximum of three dogs. Accordingly, S must receive a ribbon. Combining this with the fourth and seventh conditions, we know that U doesn't receive a ribbon. Since S is only preceded by two dogs (P and R), we can definitively place S in the third slot. Since both Q and T follow S (fifth condition), one of the two must occupy the fourth slot, and the other dog must be unranked. Combining the second and third conditions, we know that both unranked dogs are male. Due to the fourth condition, the fourth slot must be occupied by a greyhound.

		F		M	M
G	G	L	G	L	
P|R	R|P	S	Q|T	U	T|Q
1	2	3	4		

18. **(E)** A glance at our diagram reveals that in addition to P and R, which must be greyhounds (sixth condition), Q and T can be greyhounds. Thus, choice E is correct.

19. **(B)** Comparing the choices to our diagram reveals that B is incompatible with our deductions. The dog that wins the second place ribbon must be a greyhound.

20. **(E)** We inferred that both unranked dogs are male, and L is unranked. Therefore, choice E is correct.

21. **(A)** Among the answer choices, all must be true with the exception of A. Although we know that P and R both precede S (fifth condition), the relative ordering of P and R is left undetermined by the setup and conditions.

22. **(E)** In order for Q to be female, Q must win the fourth place ribbon. Accordingly, T must be unranked. With two females placed, we can deduce that P and R are both male, due to the second condition. The only one of the choices that need not be true is E, and it is therefore correct.

M	M	F	F	M	M
G	G	L	G	L	
P|R	R|P	S	Q	U	T
1	2	3	4		

23. **(B)** According to our deductions, one of Q and T must be unranked. Since T wins the fourth place ribbon, Q must be unranked. Since both unranked dogs must be male, choice B is correct.

		F		M	M
G	G	L	G	L	
P|R	R|P	S	T	U	Q
1	2	3	4		

24. **(D)** Comparing the choices to our diagram reveals that only D could be true. The previous question further validates choice D.

Questions 1-7

Setup:
- three couples: J and K, L and M, N and O
- women: K M O
- men: J L N
- each orders exactly one of five entrees
- entrees: P R S T V

Conditions:
#1: J ≠ K; L ≠ M; N ≠ O
#2: J ≠ L ≠ N; J ≠ N
#3: S_M
#4: $\sim S_J$ and $\sim T_J$; $\sim S_N$ and $\sim T_N$
#5: R_O

Overview:
From the first and fourth conditions, we can infer that N must order either P or V. Due to the first condition, L cannot order S.

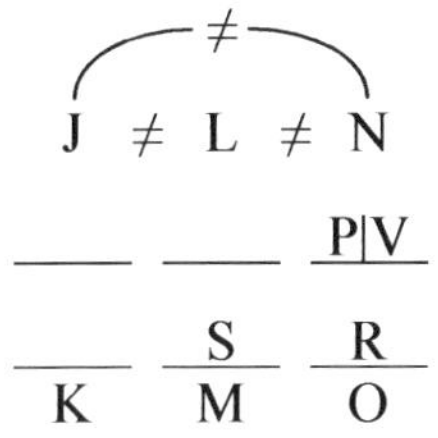

J ≠	L ≠	N (J ≠ N)
____	____	P|V
____	S	R
K	M	O

1. **(D)** As we inferred, L cannot order S, and choice D is therefore correct.

2. (A) the combination of the third and fourth conditions precludes this
   (B) Correct
   (C) violates the second condition
   (D) violates one of the third and fifth conditions
   (E) violates the first condition

3. **(A)** Scanning the choices reveals that A must be true. As we inferred, N must order either P or V.

4. **(E)** Applying the second condition to our initial diagram, we know that N must order P. Due to the first and second conditions, L can order either R or T. Thus, choice E is correct.

J	L	N
V	R|T	P
	S	R
K	M	O

5. **(C)** From this, we can infer that N orders V. Due to the second and fourth conditions, J must order R. The first and second conditions, combined with the condition that none of the men orders P, dictate that L must order T. Therefore, choice C is correct.

J	L	N
R	T	V
	S	R
K	M	O

6. **(A)** Combining this with our initial diagram, we know that N must order V. J cannot order P or V due to the second condition, and J cannot order S or T, due to the fourth condition. Therefore, J must order R, and choice A is correct.

J	L	N
R	P	V
	S	R
K	M	O

7. **(D)** Combining this with the third and fifth conditions, we know that L orders S, and N orders R. The second and fourth conditions dictate that J must both order either P or V. Thus, only choice D could be true, and it is therefore correct.

J	L	N
P|V	S	R
P|V	S	R
K	M	O

Questions 8-13

Setup:

- seven houses on a street
- seven families: K L M N O P R
- all the houses are on the same side of the street
- runes from west to east

Conditions:

#1: ~R_1 and ~R_7

#2: K_4

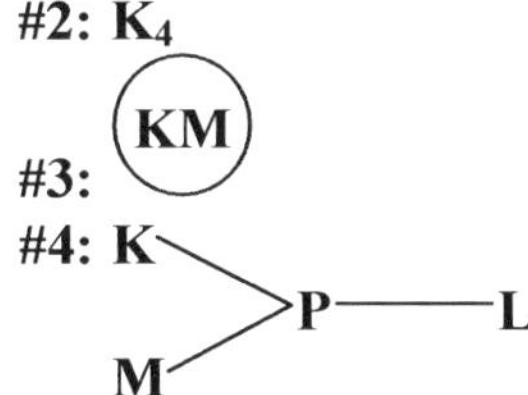

Overview:

Since K is featured in three of the conditions, we can anticipate that it will play a large role in the game. The third condition allows for two placements of M: third and fifth. We can create four molds based on these two options: one with M fifth, and three with M third.

	1	2	3	4	5	6	7
#1		R|	|R	K	M	P	L
#2		R|	M	K	|R	P	L
#3		R|	M	K	P	|R	L
#4	N|O	R	M	K	P	L	O|N

Mold #1: If M is fifth, the sixth and seventh slots must be filled by P and L, due to the fourth condition. Due to the first condition, R must be either second or third.

Mold #2: If M is third, and P is sixth, the fourth condition dictates that L must be seventh. Due to the first condition, R must be either second or fifth.

Mold #3: If M is third, and P is fifth, L can be seventh. The first condition dictates that R must be either second or sixth.

Mold #4: If M is third, and P is fifth, L can be sixth. The first condition dictates that R must be second, leaving N and O to occupy the first and seventh slots, in either order.

8. **(C)** Our molds indicate that one of L, O, and N must be seventh. Only N is listed among the choices, and C is therefore correct.

9. **(A)** Due to the fourth condition, K and L cannot be adjacent to one another. Thus, choice A is correct.

10. **(C)** This is true of molds #2, #3, and #4. Accordingly, R must be next to exactly one of M and P, and choice C is thus correct.

11. **(A)** This could only be true of mold #1. The first condition dictates that we must place R second, leaving O to occupy the first slot. Accordingly, choice A must be false, and it is correct.

O	R	N	K	M	P	L
1	2	3	4	5	6	7

12. **(A)** This could only be true of molds #2, #3, and #4. Therefore, we know that M precedes K, and choice A is correct.

13. **(D)** This could only be true of molds #2, #3, and #4. We can quickly complete the solutions to answer this question. Since N and R must occupy the first two slots, choice D is correct.

N	R	M	K	O	P	L
N	R	M	K	P	O	L
N	R	M	K	P	L	O
1	2	3	4	5	6	7

Questions 14-19

Setup:
- three floors: 1 2 3
- each floor: F or S; N or U; P or R

Conditions:
#1: F and S ⟶ S
|
F
#2: R ⟶ N; U ⟶ P
#3: R ⟶ F; S ⟶ P
#4: 1 ⟶ N
#5: 3 ⟶ U

Overview:
From the second and fifth conditions, we can deduce that there are production cars on the third floor.

3 ____ _P_ _U_

2 ____ ____ ____

1 ____ ____ _N_

F⟵R⟶N
S⟶P⟵U

14. **(A)** Applying the first condition, we know that sports cars are displayed on floors 2 and 3, and that family cars are displayed on floor 1. Applying the third condition, we know that the sports cars on floor 2 are production models. Only choice A is compatible with this scenario, and it is therefore correct.

    3 _S_ _P_ _U_

    2 _S_ _P_ ____

    1 _F_ ____ _N_

15. (A) violates the third condition
    (B) violates the second condition
    (C) violates the third condition
    (D) Correct – this could be true of our diagram for #14
    (E) we have inferred that production models must be displayed on floor 3

16. **(D)** As we initially inferred, production models must be displayed on floor 3, and choice D is therefore correct.

17. **(E)** Combining this with our diagram, we know that research models must be displayed on floors 1 and 2. Applying the second and third conditions, we know that the cars on floors 1 and 2 are new family cars. The cars on floor 3 can be either family or sports, and choice E is the only choice that need not be true.

    3 _F|S_ _P_ _U_

    2 _F_ _R_ _N_

    1 _F_ _R_ _N_

18. **(D)** Combined with the second condition, this creates a biconditional between N and R, and between P and U. Due to the fourth condition, we can infer that the cars on floor 1 are research models, and the third condition dictates that they are also family cars. Under this scenario, the N ⟷ R ⟶ F chain ensures that any new cars are also family cars, and choice D is therefore correct.

```
3  ____  _P_  _U_

2  ____  ____  ____

1  _F_   _R_   _N_
   F⟵R⟷N
   S⟶P⟷U
```

19. **(A)** Combined with the second condition, this creates a biconditional between U and P and between N and R. As we deduced in question eighteen, the cars on floor 1 must be family cars, and choice A is thus correct.

Questions 20-24

Setup:
- four planes: 1 2 3 4

Conditions:
#1: pilots (P): A B C
#2: copilots (Co): D E F
#3: plane flies ⟶ 1^+ P
#4: only Ps and Cos fly in the show
#5: A_1 or A_4
#6: D_2 or D_3

Overview:
Since the fifth and sixth conditions preclude A and D from flying together, the third condition dictates that D must fly with at least one of B and C. The conditions leave open the possibility that some of the planes don't fly in the show, but we can deduce from the fifth and sixth conditions that at least two of the planes fly. Further, the number of people aboard the planes that fly is also left open. A scenario in which five people are aboard one plane and one person (a pilot) is aboard another plane is acceptable.

```
_____  D|   |D  _____

A|   _____  _____  |A   A B C
1     2      3      4
```

20. **(B)** Since D must fly with at least one of B and C (third condition), if one of B and C flies in a plane other than plane 2, the other must fly in plane 2. Thus, choice B is correct.

21. **(C)** As we inferred, D must fly with at least one of B and C. Since B flies with A, and A cannot fly in the same plane as D (fifth and sixth conditions), we can infer that D flies with C. Therefore, choice C is correct.

22. **(D)** This precludes B and C from flying together. Applying the same logic as in the previous question, we know that D must fly with B. Thus, choice D is correct.

23. **(B)** From the sixth condition, we know that D cannot be included in the list, and we can therefore eliminate choices D and E. Further, since D must fly with at least one of B and C, we can eliminate choices A and C, leaving B as the correct answer. The following diagram proves the validity of choice B.

1	2	3	4
A			
B			
E	C|	|C	
F	D|	|D	

24. **(C)** Since D cannot fly in plane 1 (sixth condition), and D must fly with at least one of B and C (third condition), the largest number of people who can fly in plane 1 is four, and choice C is correct.

Questions 1-6

Setup:

- nine partners: F G H I J K L M N

Conditions:

#1:

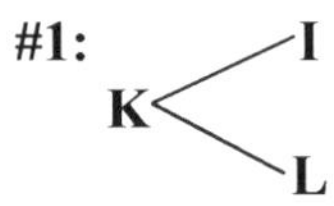

#2: L – N
#3: I – F
#4: F – M
#5: M – G
#6: G – J
#7: J – H

Overview:
Combining all the conditions yields the following sketch.

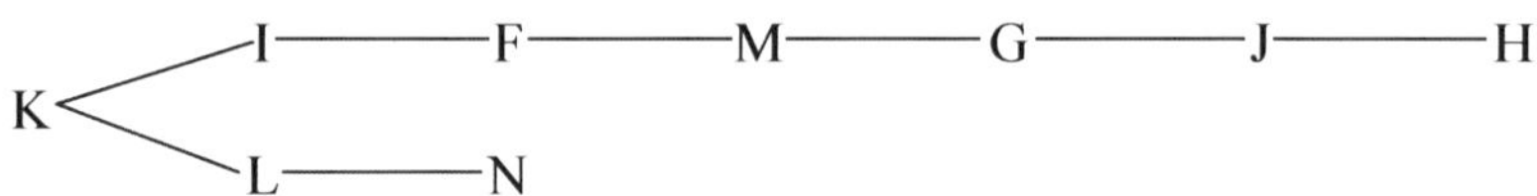

1. **(D)** Since M must be preceded by at least three variables (K, I, and F), it cannot be third, and choice D is therefore correct.

2. **(C)** Sketching a new diagram to incorporate this information reveals that L must precede five other variables (M, N, G, J, and H). Thus, choice C is correct.

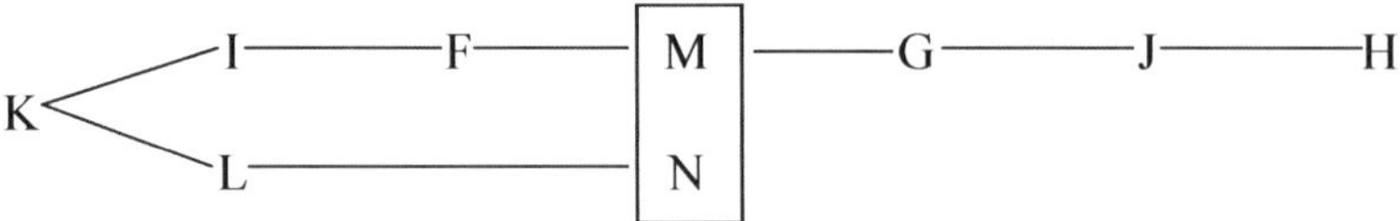

3. (A) the relative ordering of I and L is left uncertain as well as N's position
   (B) N's position is left uncertain
   (C) the relative ordering of I and L is left uncertain
   (D) Correct – see the following diagram

K	L	N	I	F	M	G	J	H
1	2	3	4	5	6	7	8	9

   (E) L's position in relation to I and F is left uncertain

4. (A) N could have the same salary as I, F, M, G, J, or H
   (B) N could have the same salary as I, F, M, G, J, or H
   (C) N could have the same salary as M, G, J, or H
   (D) Correct – this would produce the following solution

K	I	F	M	G	J	H	L	N
1	2	3	4	5	6	7	8	9

   (E) N could have the same salary as J or H

5. **(C)** To produce the minimum number of salaries, we must pair each of L and N with one other variable. Thus, the minimum number of different salaries is seven, and choice C is correct.

6. **(D)** G is only constrained by the number of variables which must precede it and the number of variables which must follow it. Since those numbers are four and two, respectively, we can conclude that G can be fifth, sixth, or seventh, and choice D is therefore correct.

Questions 7-11

Setup:
- five illnesses: J K L M N
- each one characterized by at least one of three symptoms
- symptoms: F H S
- none of the illnesses has any symptom other than these three

Conditions:
#1: J ⟶ H and S
#2: J ≠ K
#3: J and L share 1⁺ symptom
#4: $L_{\#} > K_{\#}$
#5: L ≠ N
#6: $M_{\#} > J_{\#}$

Overview:
Combining the first and sixth conditions, we know that M is characterized by F, H, and S, and that J is characterized by only H and S. From the second condition, we can deduce that K is characterized by only F. From the fourth and fifth conditions, we can deduce that L is characterized by exactly two symptoms, and N is characterized by exactly one symptom.

						F
H				___		H
S	≠	F	H|S	≠	___	S
J		K	L		N	M

Since the symptom that characterizes N is only one of three, and the fifth condition precludes it from being one of L's two symptoms, we can draw up a total of three acceptable solutions.

#1

J	K	L	N	M
				F
H		H		H
S	F	S	F	S

#2

J	K	L	N	M
				F
H		F		H
S	F	S	H	S

#3

J	K	L	N	M
				F
H		F		H
S	F	H	S	S

7. **(E)** Comparing the choices to the solutions reveals that E must be false.

8. **(C)** This could only be true of solution #1. Of the pairs JL and KN, only KN is listed among the choices, and C is therefore correct.

9. **(A)** This is true of solutions #2 and #3. In both solutions, F is a symptom of L. Thus, choice A is correct.

10. **(E)** Since M is characterized by all three symptoms, it must share exactly one symptom with each of K and N. The MN pair is the only one listed among the choices, and E is thus correct.

11. **(E)** There are two pairs of illnesses which, if he had both, would require him to have all three symptoms: JK and LN. Only LN is listed among the choices, and E is therefore correct.

Questions 12-17

Setup:

- work days: M T W Th F
- one street ⟶ entire morning or entire afternoon
- eight streets: 1 2 3 4 5 6 7 8

Conditions:
#1: F_A ⟶ no street
#2: W_P ⟶ no street
#3: 4_{TA}
#4: 7_{ThA}
#5: 4 – 6 or [6 / 4]; 8 – 4 or [4 / 8]
#6: 2_P; 5_P; 8_P

Overview:
Since there are eight streets and ten slots, and the first and second conditions give us two slots that won't have street numbers in them, we know that all the remaining slots will be filled. Combining the third, fifth, and sixth conditions, we can deduce that 8 must be cleaned on Monday afternoon. Applying the fifth condition, we know that 6 cannot be cleaned on Monday morning. Since 3 and 5 are both cleaned in the afternoon (sixth condition), we can infer that exactly one of streets 1, 3, and 6 is also cleaned in the afternoon.

	M	T	W	Th	F	
P	8		X			2 5 1|3|6
A		4		7	X	

12. **(B)** Since there is only one afternoon slot preceding 7 (Tuesday), the sixth condition dictates that we place 2 in that slot. Thus, choice B is correct.

	M	T	W	Th	F
P	8	2	X	5|	|5
A		4		7	X

13. **(C)** Building on our diagram from the previous question, the fifth condition, combined with the stipulation that 6 be cleaned in the morning, dictates that we place 6 in the Wednesday morning slot. Since we cannot deduce the respective slots for streets 1, 3, and 5, choice C is correct.

	M	T	W	Th	F
P	8	2	X	5|	|5
A		4	6	7	X

14. **(E)** None of the conditions preclude any of the remaining variables (1, 2, 3, 5, and 6) from occupying the Friday afternoon slot. Since there are five variables left to place, choice E is correct.

15. **(A)** One of three streets (1, 3, and 6) must occupy the remaining afternoon slot. If the street to occupy the remaining afternoon slot were 1, the question would dictate that 3 be assigned to the Wednesday morning slot. This would only leave the Monday morning slot for street 6, which violates the fifth condition. Thus, choice A is correct. One of streets 3 and 6 must fill the remaining afternoon slot.

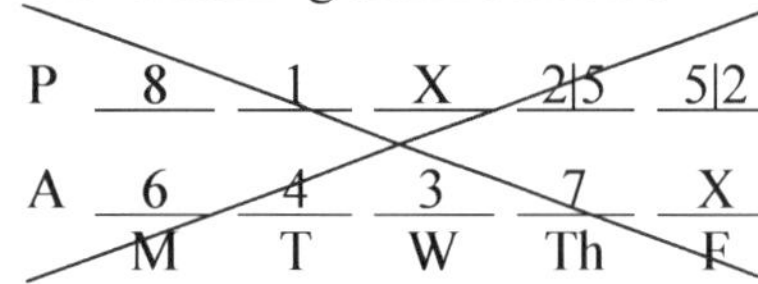

P	8		X				P	8		X		
A	1	4	6	7	X	or	A	1	4	3	7	X
	M	T	W	Th	F			M	T	W	Th	F

16. **(D)** Since the Tuesday afternoon slot is the only afternoon slot which precedes 7, the sixth condition dictates that we assign 5 to it. Wednesday morning is the only available slot in between 5 and 7, so we must assign 6 to it. We still need to place streets 1, 2, and 3. Since street 2 must be assigned to an afternoon slot (sixth condition), we can assign either street 1 or street 3 to the Monday morning slot, each of which creates two schedules. Thus, there are four acceptable schedules, and choice D is correct.

P	8	5	X	2|3	3|2		P	8	5	X	1|2	2|1
A	1	4	6	7	X	or	A	3	4	6	7	X
	M	T	W	Th	F			M	T	W	Th	F

17. **(B)** Since street 8 must be cleaned in the afternoon (sixth condition), we must leave it in the Tuesday afternoon slot. We must assign the remaining afternoon streets (2 and 5) to Thursday and Friday, in either order. Since there's only one open slot following 4, (Wednesday morning) the fifth condition dictates that we assign street 6 to it. This leaves streets 1 and 3 to occupy the Monday morning and Tuesday morning slots, in either order. Only choice B need not be true, and it is therefore correct.

P	8	4	X	2|5	5|2
A	1|3	3|1	6	7	X
	M	T	W	Th	F

Questions 18-24

Setup:

- o ski chalets: J K L M N O
- o positioned in two straight rows as pictured
- o J and M are directly opposite each other
- o K and N are directly opposite each other
- o L and O are directly opposite each other
- o a single continuous path connects all the chalets

Conditions:

#1: five straight segments; each segment connects exactly two chalets
#2: each chalet is connected to at least one other chalet
#3: each chalet ≤ 2 direct connections
#4: no two segments cross each other
#5: J and N are directly connected; K and L are directly connected

Overview:

From the second condition, we know that M must be connected to either J or N. If M were connected to both J and N, there would be only one remaining segment to connect both O and one of K and L. Therefore, this cannot be true, and we can deduce that M must be connected to exactly one of J and N. If M is connected to N, there are two ways to connect J to the remaining chalets: JK and JO. If M is connected to J, there are two ways to connect N to the other chalets: NK and NO.

#1 J K L / M N O

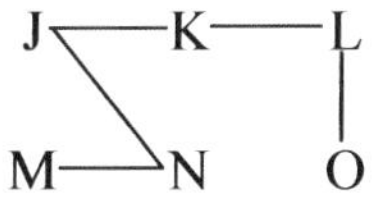

#2 J K L / M N O

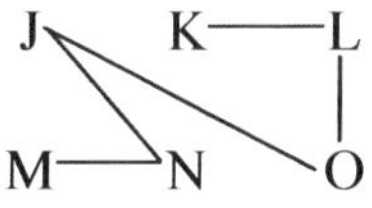

#3 J K L / M N O

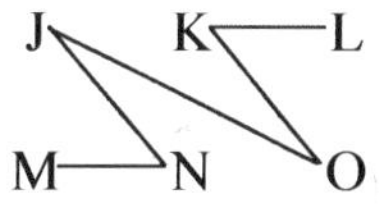

#4 J K L / M N O

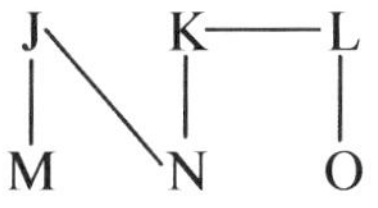

#5 J K L / M N O

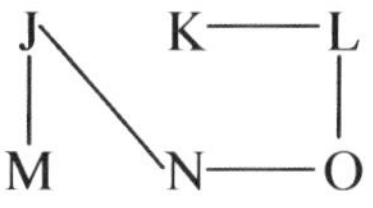

#6 J K L / M N O

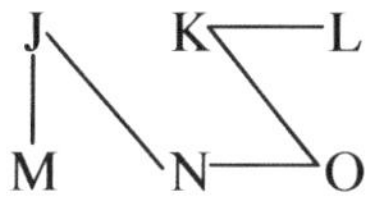

Solution #1: Given MN and JK, O cannot be connected to J or K (third condition). It must therefore be connected to L.

Solution #2: Given MN and JO, O can be connected to L.

Solution #3: Given MN and JO, O can be connected to K.

Solution #4: Given JM and NK, O cannot be connected to N or K (third condition). It must therefore be connected to L.

Solution #5: Given JM and NO, O can be connected to L.

Solution #6: Given JM and NO, O can be connected to K.

18. (A) violates the fourth condition
    (B) violates the fourth condition
    (C) that segment would also cross N, violating the first condition
    (D) violates the fourth condition (KM)
    (E) Correct – see solution #5

19. **(C)** This triggers solution #4. We know that a segment must connect L and O, and choice C is thus correct.

20. **(D)** This triggers solution #1. We know that a segment must connect L and O, and choice D is therefore correct.

21. **(A)** This is true of solutions #3 and #6. Only choice A could be true (solution #6), and it is correct.

22. **(A)** M and N are directly connected in solutions #1, #2, and #3, so we need to look for something that is not true of the other three solutions. J and K are only connected in solution #1, and choice A is therefore correct.

23. **(C)** As we initially inferred, M must be connected to exactly one other chalet (J or N), and choice C is thus correct.

24. **(B)** This is only true of solution #3. Choice B contradicts our diagram, and it is therefore correct.

Questions 1-6

Setup:
- one grade for each of six courses
- courses: Ec G H I P R
- possible grades: A B C D E
- E is the only failing grade
- adjacent in the alphabet ⟷ consecutive letter grades

Conditions:

#1: 

#2: 

#3: Ec – H
#4: G – P

Overview:

From the first and fourth conditions, we can deduce the following piece: [GP]. The third condition dictates that he cannot receive an E in economics and he cannot receive an A in history. None of the conditions specifies that he must have received each grade at least once, but we do know that there must be at least three pairs of variables which are assigned to different grades. As such, we can deduce four acceptable allocations of classes to grades:
3, 3, 0, 0, 0
3, 2, 1, 0, 0
3, 1, 1, 1, 0
2, 1, 1, 1, 1

A	B	C	D	E
~H				~Ec
~P				~G

1. **(C)** Applying the second condition, we know that he must receive a D in Italian. The scenario given by the question dictates that he must receive a D in economics, and applying the third condition, we know that he must receive an E in history. Therefore, choice C is correct.

A	B	C	D	E
			Ec	H
			I	R

2. **(D)** Combining this with the first, second, and fourth conditions, we have:

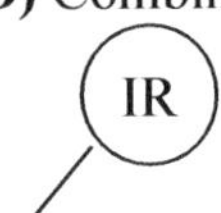

. To accommodate these variables, we need at least three different grades, and since we're told that none of his grades were Es, the GP piece can either span A and B or B and C. If the GP piece spans A and B, then one of I and R must be assigned to C. If the GP piece spans B and C, the IR pair must occupy slots above C and D. Thus, it must be true that he receives at least one B and at least one C, and choice D is correct.

G	P	I|R		X
A	B	C	D	E

or

		I|R		
	G	P	R|I	X
A	B	C	D	E

3. Combining this with the conditions gives the following:

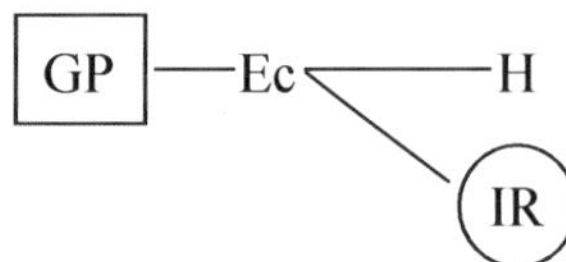

(A) the grades for I and R are left undetermined
(B) the grade for H could be D or E
(C) the HI piece could be assigned to either D or E
(D) the HR piece could be assigned to either D or E
(E) Correct – since the grade for H can be D at the highest, this forces R into an E slot, and the second condition dictates, that I occupy a D slot

			H	
G	P	Ec	I	R
A	B	C	D	E

4. **(E)** Combining this with the conditions gives the following:

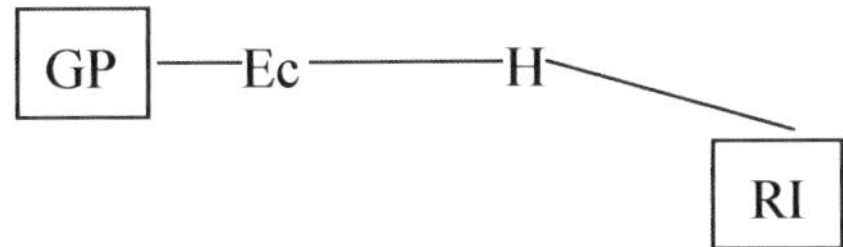

Since there are only five grades, this scenario forces H to occupy a D slot, and forces the variables in front of it into the A, B, and C slots, respectively. I must be assigned to an E slot, and the second condition dictates that R must be assigned to a D slot. Thus, all six grades are determined, and choice E is correct.

			H	
G	P	Ec	R	I
A	B	C	D	E

5. **(C)** Combining this with the conditions gives the following piece: [GPIR]. With five different grades, this piece must span A through D or B through E. Thus, he must receive both a B and a D, and choice C is correct.

G	P	I	R	
	G	P	I	R
A	B	C	D	E

6. **(E)** Combining this with the conditions, we can deduce the following chain:

[GP] – Ec – H. This ensures that he receives at least four of the five grades. In order to ensure that he failed a course, we would need to either place a variable in front of G, or place a variable behind H. Choice E does so, and it is therefore correct. Our diagram for question three, choice E illustrates this scenario.

<ins>Questions 7-11</ins>

Setup:

- three shirt sizes: S M L
- three shirt colors: R Y B
- Casey buys exactly three shirts

Conditions:
#1: shirt type ⟶ a size and a color
#2: no two shirts of the same type
#3: S ⟶ ~L; L ⟶ ~S (contrapositive)
#4: ~SR
#5: ~LB

Overview:
From the conditions, we can deduce the following allocation table:

S	M	L
2	1	0
1	2	0
0	3	0
0	2	1
0	1	2

We'll use the following diagram to represent the different shirts that can be selected.

SY	MR	LR
SB	MY	LY
	MB	

7. **(A)** Choice A violates the fourth condition. Since he buys three shirts, if two were small and two were red, at least one would have to be both small and red.

8. **(B)** Using our allocations as a guide, we know that he buys either one or two small shirts. Since there is only one red shirt between the two sizes (small and medium), choice B must be false.

9. **(B)** Since Casey must buy at least one medium shirt (allocation table), we know that either an MR or an MB must be selected. Thus, choice B is correct.

10. **(B)** From this, we can deduce two acceptable allocations: 2, 1, 0 and 0, 1, 2. Since both colors must be selected from either the small or the large options, and the question dictates that the medium shirt be of a different color, the medium shirt must be either red or blue. Therefore, choice B is correct.

SY

SB MR or MB LY

LR

11. **(D)** This question narrows down the selection considerably. Casey can either select all three medium shirts, or two medium shirts and one small or large shirt. Since Casey must select two of the three medium shirts at a minimum, he must select at least one of RM and BM, and choice D is therefore correct.

SY MR LY
MY
MB

<u>Questions 12-17</u>

Setup:
- three different fish species
- two species of plants
- fish: G H J K L
- plants: W X Y Z

Conditions:
#1: G ⟶ ~H; H ⟶ ~G (contrapositive)
G ⟶ ~Y; Y ⟶ ~G (contrapositive)
#2: H ⟶ K; ~K ⟶ ~H (contrapositive)
#3: J ⟶ W; ~W ⟶ ~J (contrapositive)
#4: K ⟶ X; ~X ⟶ ~K (contrapositive)

Overview:
We can use the following diagram to make any necessary inferences.

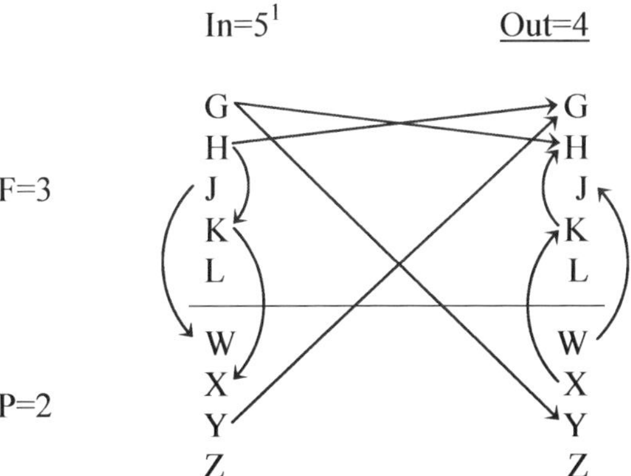

[1] Visit Manhattan LSAT (http://www.manhattanlsat.com) to learn more about using this diagram.

12. (A) violates the first condition
    (B) Correct
    (C) violates the third condition
    (D) violates the second condition
    (E) violates the second condition

13. **(B)** Following the chain from H selected, we know that K and X are also selected. Thus, choice B is correct.

14. **(C)** Since W is not selected, we know that J is not selected. We can therefore eliminate choices B, D, and E. Choice A violates the first condition, leaving choice C as the correct answer.

15. **(C)** Without additional information, we must scan the choices for violations. Choice C triggers the second condition, but there are already three fish species selected. Therefore, it is correct.

16. **(D)** Combining this with the first condition, we know that she does not select a G. Since we must select three from among H, J, K, and L, and not selecting X would preclude both K and H from being selected (contrapositives of the fourth and second conditions), we can infer that X must be selected. With W out, the contrapositive of the third condition tells us that J must also be out. Thus, H, K, and L must all be selected, and choice D is correct.

H	
L	X
K	Y
F	P

17. We can use our previous work to disprove some of the choices.
    (A) see #12
    (B) Correct – Y ⟶ ~G (first condition); ~X ⟶ ~K (contrapositive of the fourth condition) ⟶ ~H (contrapositive of the second condition); only two fish (J and L) could be selected under this scenario
    (C) we cannot infer anything directly from W and Z being selected
    (D) we can only infer that G is not selected (first condition)
    (E) see #14

Questions 18-24

Setup:
- five towns: P Q R S T
- ranked from first (best) to fifth (worst)
- three criteria: C L F

Conditions:

#1: each ranking is occupied by exactly one town
#2: T_{C3}; S_{C4}
#3: Q_{L2}; R_{L3}; P_{L4}
#4: $T_F - P_F$; Q_{F4}; S_{F5}
#5: $R_C - R_F$

≠

#6: $Q_C \neq Q_L \neq Q_F$

Overview:
The fourth condition leaves the first three friendliness slots open. Due to the fifth condition, R can be ranked no higher than second in friendliness. The fourth condition also precludes P from occupying the first friendliness slot, so we can definitively place T there. From the third condition, we know that S and T must occupy the first and fifth slots in location, in either order. Revisiting the fifth condition, we can infer that R must be ranked either first or second in climate. Since T occupies the third climate slot (second condition), the sixth condition dictates that Q must be ranked either first or fifth in climate.

	1	2	3	4	5
F	T	P|R	R|P	Q	S
L	S|T	Q	R	P	T|S
C	R|P|Q	P|R	T	S	Q|P

18. **(B)** As we inferred, R must be ranked either first or second in climate, and choice B is therefore correct.

19. **(C)** Our deductions regarding R tell us that it cannot be ranked fifth in any one of the three criteria. Thus, choice C is correct.

20. (A) T is first in friendliness
    (B) violates the sixth condition
    (C) Correct – see the following diagram

	1	2	3	4	5
F	T	P	R	Q	S
L	S|T	Q	R	P	T|S
C	R	P	T	S	Q

    (D) violates the third condition
    (E) T is first in friendliness

21. **(D)** With Q first in climate, R must be second in climate, leaving P to occupy the fifth slot. Applying the fifth condition, we know that R is third in friendliness, leaving P to occupy the second slot. Choice D is therefore correct.

F	T	P	R	Q	S
L	S|T	Q	R	P	T|S
C	Q	R	T	S	P
	1	2	3	4	5

22. **(A)** With P second in climate, R must occupy the first slot. Due to the sixth condition, Q must be ranked fifth in climate. Choice A is the only one that can be true under this scenario, and it is thus correct.

F	T	P|R	R|P	Q	S
L	S|T	Q	R	P	T|S
C	R	P	T	S	Q
	1	2	3	4	5

23. **(E)** Combining this with the third condition, we know that S is ranked fifth in location. With R ranked second in friendliness, P is forced into the third slot. Due to the fifth condition, R must be ranked first in climate. Applying the sixth condition, we know that Q occupies the fifth climate slot. Since we have deduced all three rankings for all five towns, choice E is correct.

F	T	R	P	Q	S
L	T	Q	R	P	S
C	R	P	T	S	Q
	1	2	3	4	5

24. **(E)** Comparing the choices to our initial diagram reveals a contradiction in E. We deduced that T must be ranked first in friendliness, and choice E is therefore correct.

Questions 1-6

Setup:
- fourteen animals: G G G H H H L L L S S S S S
- four separate cages: W X Y Z

Conditions:
#1: each cage ⟶ 2, 4, or six animals

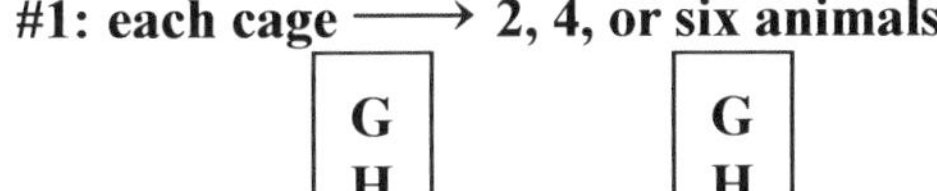

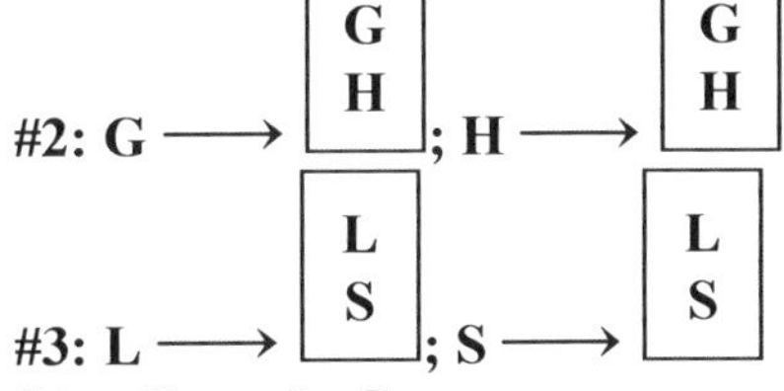

#4: ~G_Y and ~G_Z
#5: ~L_W and ~L_X

Overview:
From the second and fourth conditions, we can deduce that all the Gs and Hs are allocated among cages W and X. From the third and fifth conditions, we can deduce that all the Ls and Ss are allocated among cages Y and Z. Combining this information with the first condition gives two possible allocations of animals to cages for W and X (4, 2) and two possible allocations of animals to cages for Y and Z (6, 2 and 4, 4). The second and third conditions dictate that each cage must hold animals of each of their respective species (G and H to W and X; L and S to Y and Z). Due to the first condition, the G and H that haven't yet been placed must be assigned as a pair to either cage W or cage X.

W	X	Y	Z
		___	___
		___	___
G|	|G	___	___
H|	|H	___	___
G	G	L	L
H	H	S	S
W	X	Y	Z
4	2	6	2
or		or	
2	4	4	4
		or	
		2	6

1. **(A) Correct – see the following diagram**

W	X	Y	Z
	G	L	L
	G	L	S
G	H	S	S
H	H	S	S

(B) violates the first condition
(C) violates the first condition
(D) violates the third condition (cage Z would have four Ss and no Ls)
(E) cage Y cannot have any Hs

2. **(D)** We have established that the GH pair must be assigned to one of cages W and X. For this question, we must assign it to cage W. Since cage X has one G, the question dictates that cage Y must have one S. Therefore, the four remaining Ss are in cage Z, and choice D is correct. Since the cages cannot have an odd number of animals (first condition), the remaining L must be placed in cage Z.

W	X	Y	Z
			L
			L
G			S
H			S
G	G	L	S
H	H	S	S

3. **(C)** This question focuses solely on the YZ aspect of the game. With three Ls to assign in total, the question dictates that we assign two to cage Z and one to cage Y. With three additional Ss to assign, we can allocate none to Y and three to Z or two to Y and one to Z. Only choice C is compatible with either diagram (the second one), and it is therefore correct.

W	X		Y	Z
	L			
	L			
	S		L	L
	S		S	L
L	S		S	S
S	S	or	S	S

4. **(D)** According to the allocations we derived, W and Z can either have four animals each or two animals each. In the first option the number of Ls and Ss in cages Y and Z is left uncertain, but in the second option, Z must have one of each, thereby ensuring that the remaining Ls and Ss are assigned to cage Y. Choice D is compatible with the first option, and it is correct.

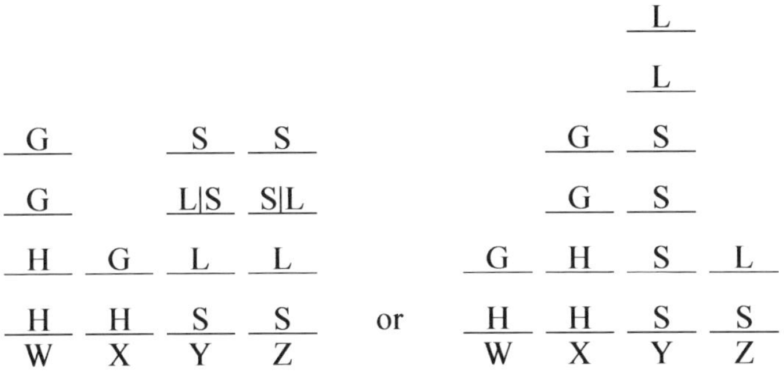

W	X	Y	Z
G		S	S
G		L|S	S|L
H	G	L	L
H	H	S	S

or

W	X	Y	Z
		L	
		L	
	G	S	
	G	S	
G	H	S	L
H	H	S	S

5. **(E)** According to our allocations, Z must have two animals. Since it must have one L and one S (third condition), the remaining Ls and Ss must all be assigned to cage Y. Our second diagram for question four illustrates this, and choice E is correct.

6. **(D)** Since cage Z must have one L and one S at a minimum (first and third conditions), the greatest number of Ss that can occupy cage Y is four, and choice D is therefore correct.

Questions 7-12

Setup:
- seven proposed names: J K L M N O P
- ranked according to the number of votes
- the name with the most votes was ranked first
- every name received a different number of votes

Conditions:
#1: J – O
#2: O – K
#3: K – M
#4: ~N_7
#5:
L — P < O, N (P branches to O and N)

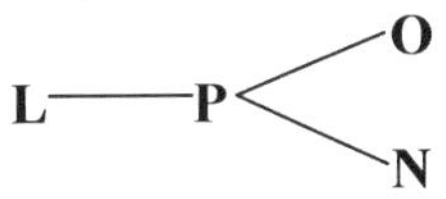

Overview:
Combining the conditions yields the following sketch:

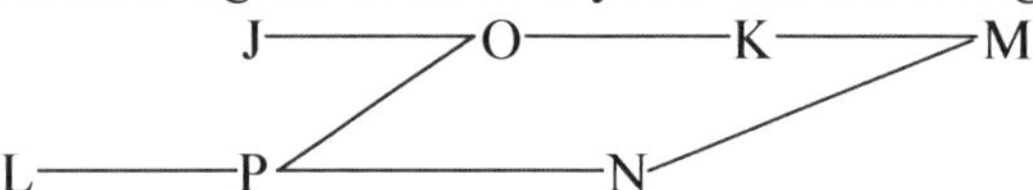

Connecting N and M serves as a reminder of the fourth condition, and we can deduce that M must be seventh. One of J and L must be first.

J|L						M
1	2	3	4	5	6	7

7. (A) violates the second condition
   (B) violates the fourth condition
   (C) Correct
   (D) violates the fourth condition
   (E) violates the fifth condition

8. **(E)** Checking the choices against our diagram reveals that only E must be true, and it is therefore correct.

9. **(C)** Our sketch confirms that for P, O, and K to be consecutive, they must be in that exact order. Retaining the ordering connections from our original sketch, we can infer the following relative ordering, and choice C must be false.

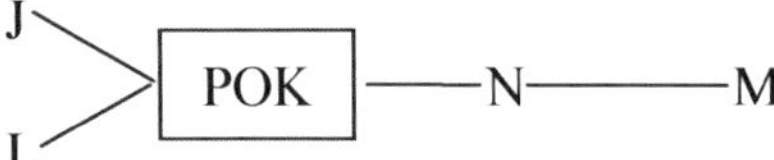

10. **(A)** As we inferred, M must be seventh, and choice A is therefore correct.

11. **(B)** Variables that must be preceded by at least three others cannot be ranked in the top three. Thus, we can eliminate O, K, and M, leaving L, P, N, and J, any of which could be among the top three. Accordingly, choice B is correct.

12. **(B)** Creating a new sketch to incorporate this scenario reveals that exactly three positions can be determined: L_1, P_2, and M_7. Thus, choice B is correct.

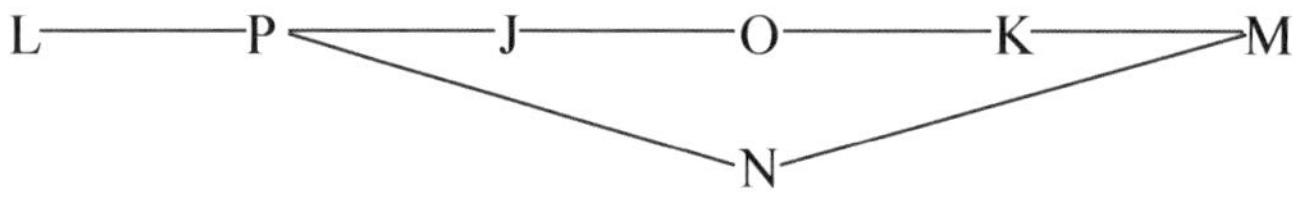

<u>Questions 13-19</u>

Setup:

- eight benches: J K L T U X Y Z
- arranged along the perimeter as pictured

Conditions:

#1: green (G): J K L
red (R): T U
pink (P): X Y Z

#2: (JKL) in any order

#3: (XYZ) in any order

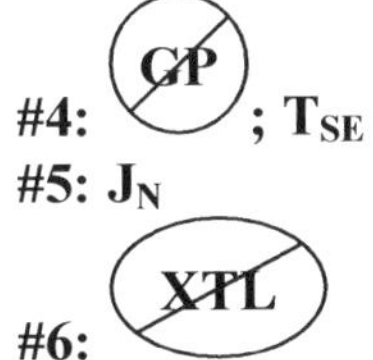

Overview:

Combining the second, third, and fourth conditions, we can infer that the two red benches must both act as buffers between the pink and green benches. Therefore, the two red benches must be separated from each other by three benches in each direction. From the second, fourth, and fifth conditions, we can deduce that the remaining green benches must be in the northeast and east positions. This leaves U to act as a buffer in the northwest position, and the pink benches must occupy the west through the south positions.

U / R	J / G	K|L / G
___ / P		L|K / G
___ / P	___ / P	T / R

13. **(E)** We inferred that K or L must occupy the northeast position. Only L is listed among the choices, and E is therefore correct.

14. **(A)** Comparing the choices to our diagram reveals that only choice A need not be true. In fact, it must be false, and A is thus correct.

15. **(D)** As we initially inferred, U must be assigned to the northwest corner, due to the fourth condition, and choice D is correct.

16. **(A)** Each of K and L has exactly two positions to which it can be assigned. Only K is listed among the choices, and A is therefore correct.

17. **(D)** This could only happen if Z and Y occupy the west and southwest positions, respectively. This leaves X to occupy the south position. To satisfy the sixth condition, K must occupy the east position, leaving L to occupy the northeast position. Hence all the choices aside from D must be false.

U / R	J / G	L / G
Z / P		K / G
Y / P	X / P	T / R

18. **(B)** Assigning Y to the west position means that X and Z must occupy the southwest and south positions, in either order. If Z were assigned to the southwest corner and K were assigned the northeast corner, the sixth condition would be violated. Thus, choice B is correct.

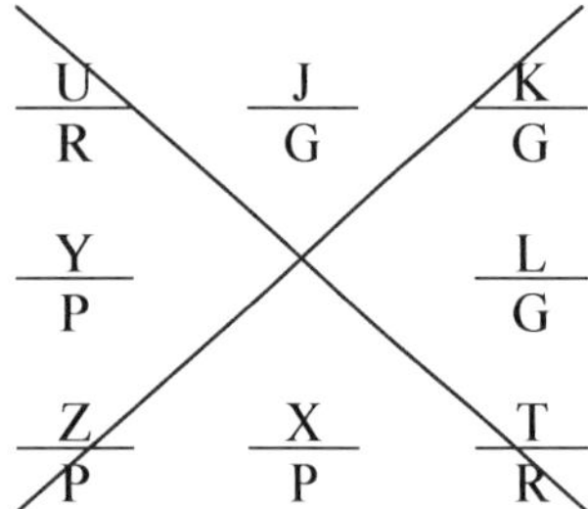

19. **(C)** Applying this information to our diagram, we know that Y must be assigned to the west position, and L must be assigned to the northeast position, leaving K to fill the east slot. Since the placement of X and Z is uncertain, T and X need not be next to each other, and choice C is therefore correct.

U / R	J / G	L / G
Y / P		K / G
X|Z / P	Z|X / P	T / R

Questions 20-24

Setup:
- o five islands: J K L M O
- o they are unconnected by bridges
- o contractors will build a network of bridges

Conditions:
#1: each bridge connects exactly two islands; no two bridges intersect
#2: any two islands can only be connected by one bridge
#3: each island ≤ 3 bridges
#4: JM or JO; KM or KO; LM or LO
#5: J ⟶ connected to 2 islands
#6: K ⟶ connected to 1 island
#7: J connected to O; M connected to O

Overview:
Since none of the conditions specify that the bridges must be straight, and an overhead diagram might cause difficulty (due to the first condition), we'll focus solely on the pairings and not on the physical relationships between the individual islands. Combining the fourth and sixth conditions, we can deduce that K cannot be connected to J or L. Writing out the ten possible pairings (prior to the application of the conditions) is a good first step. Reorganizing them to better represent the conditions proves useful in this case. We can asterisk those connections which are specified by the conditions and cross out those which the conditions preclude.

Initial		Reorganized
JK	1 {	JL
JL		JM
JM		JO*
JO	1^+ {	KM
KL		KO
KM	1^+ {	LM
KO		LO
LM		~~JK~~
LO		~~KL~~
MO		MO*

We can further refine our diagram to get a clear picture of how many connections are allowed by the conditions. Due to the third condition, we can deduce that at least one of the KO and LO pairs must not be selected. Therefore, the total number of connections must be either five or six.

	------	------	JO
____	____	____	MO
JL	KM	LM	JO
JM	KO	LO	MO

(KO and LO: not both)

20. **(D)** As our diagram illustrates, L can be connected to any one of J, M, and O. Therefore, choice D is correct.

21. **(C)** Comparing the choices to our diagram reveals that only C could be true.

	------	------	JO
JL	____	LM	MO
JL	KM	LM	JO
~JM	KO	LO	MO

22. **(B)** Applying the third condition, we know that LO is not possible under this scenario. To satisfy the fourth condition, LM must be selected. Only choice B is compatible with our diagram, and it is therefore correct.

	------		JO
____	KO	LM	MO
JL	KM	LM	JO
JM	KO	~LO	MO

23. **(B)** Applying the third condition, we know that KO is not possible under this scenario. To satisfy the fourth condition, KM must be selected. Therefore, choice B is correct.

		LM	JO
____	KM	LO	MO
JL	KM	LM	JO
JM	~KO	LO	MO

24. **(A)** Since J is connected to O, this scenario precludes JM. To satisfy the fifth condition, we must select JL. Thus, choice A is correct. We also know that the number of connections under this scenario must be five.

			JO
JL	____	____	MO
JL	KM	LM	JO
~JM	KO	LO	MO

Questions 1-7

Setup:
- o seven consecutive time slots: 1 2 3 4 5 6 7
- o six song tapes: G H L O P S
- o one news tape: N
- o each tape is assigned to a different slot
- o all the tapes are of the same length

Conditions:

#1: 

#2: L – N

#3: **G|P __ __ P|G**

Overview:
We can combine the first and second conditions into the following: LO – N. From this, we can infer that N cannot be placed first or second, L cannot be placed sixth or seventh, and O cannot be placed seventh.

1	2	3	4	5	6	7
~N	~N				~L	~L ~O

1. **(C)** Applying the third condition, we know that P must be fifth. Since we need two slots for the LO piece, and L cannot sixth, we must place it in the third and fourth slots. Thus, choice C is correct.

	G	L	O	P	N|	|N
1	2	3	4	5	6	7

2. **(A)** As we inferred, N cannot be first, and choice A is therefore correct.

3. **(C)** Since none of the conditions govern H and S, we can place them in the first and seventh slots, in either order. We need a minimum of five slots to satisfy the first three conditions. We can do this by placing the LO piece with the GP span and placing N sixth. Only choice C is compatible with this diagram, and it is thus correct.

H|S	G|P	L	O	P|G	N	S|H
1	2	3	4	5	6	7

4. **(C)** Applying the third condition, we know that G must be second. Everything about this scenario matches our diagram for question #1, and choice C is therefore correct.

5. **(E)** Since N can be seventh, and none of the conditions governs the placement of S, we can place S first to achieve the maximum spread between the two. Borrowing from our question one diagram, we can create the following diagram to prove choice E correct.

S	G	L	O	P	H	N
1	2	3	4	5	6	7

6. **(C)** We have inferred that L can be neither sixth nor seventh. Can L be fifth? The first and second conditions would dictate that we place O and N in the sixth and seventh slots, respectively. G and P would have to span the first through the fourth slots (in either order), leaving H and S to fill the second and third slots. Thus, L can be fifth, and choice C is correct.

G|P	H|S	S|H	P|G	L	O	N
1	2	3	4	5	6	7

7. **(D)** G and P are made effectively interchangeable by the third condition. Therefore, placing one or the other in one particular slot will have the same effect. In questions one and four, G and P spanned the second through the fifth slots, forcing L and O to occupy the third and fourth slots. If we reverse the order of G and P, such that P occupies the second slot, and G occupies the fifth slot, the effect is identical, and L must still be placed third. Thus, choice D is correct.

	P	L	O	G	N|	|N
1	2	3	4	5	6	7

<u>Questions 8-12</u>

Setup:
- work days: M T W F S
- four different activities: L O T R
- each day: A P

Conditions:
#1: exactly 3 O_As
#2: $O_M \longrightarrow \sim O_T$; $O_T \longrightarrow \sim O_M$ (contrapositive)
#3: [LL]$_P$

#4: exactly 1 T_A and exactly 3 T_Ps
#5: exactly 1 R_A
#6: $\sim L_S$ and $\sim O_S$

Overview:
The third and fourth conditions provide the five activities the doctor performs in the afternoons: L, L, T, T, and T. The first, fourth, and fifth conditions give us the five activities she performs in the mornings: O, O, O, R, and T. Although she doesn't work on Thursdays, we need to include it in our diagram since the third condition pairs two Ls on consecutive days. From the third and sixth conditions, we can deduce that Ts must be placed in the afternoon slots on both Friday and Saturday. Since the double L piece will either span the Monday and Tuesday, or the Tuesday and Wednesday slots, we can place an L in the Tuesday afternoon slot. Due to the sixth condition, the Saturday morning slot must be filled by either R or T. Since O cannot fill both the Monday morning and the Tuesday morning slots, we must place Os in the Wednesday and Friday morning slots.

```
P   L|T   L    T|L   X    T    T     T T T  [LL]

A   O|    |O   O     X    O    R|T   O O O R T
    M     T    W     Th   F    S
  [O   O] (crossed out)        ~L
                               ~O
```

8. **(B)** As we inferred, an L must be placed on Tuesday afternoon, and choice B is therefore correct.

9. **(C)** We have established that she must operate in the morning. The only two variables that could be placed in the Wednesday afternoon slot are L and T. Thus, only choice C could be true, and it is correct.

10. **(E)** Comparing the choices to our diagram reveals that only E must be true. If we place the remaining L in the Monday afternoon slot, L and O will be paired on either Monday or Tuesday. If we place the remaining L on Wednesday, L and O will be paired on Wednesday.

11. From this information, we can deduce that either R or T must fill the Monday morning slot. Placing O on Tuesday doesn't affect the placement of the remaining T

```
P   L|T   L    T|L   X    T    T

A   R|T   O    O     X    O    T|R
    M     T    W     Th   F    S
```

(A) she operates on Friday morning
(B) she must treat patients on either Monday afternoon or Friday afternoon
(C) she operates on Wednesday morning
(D) she operates on Wednesday morning
(E) Correct

12. **(E)** We initially inferred that Ts must occupy the Friday and Saturday afternoon slots, and choice E is therefore correct.

Questions 13-18

Setup:
- seven judges
- each votes for or against
- is judge is one of three: C M L
- C C M M L L L

Conditions:

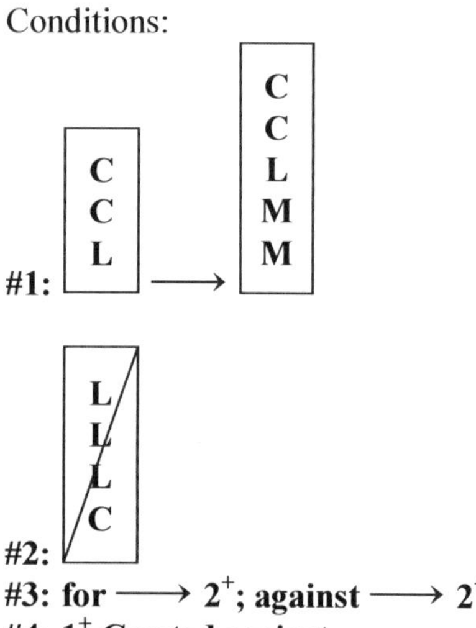

#3: for ⟶ 2⁺; against ⟶ 2⁺
#4: 1⁺ C voted against

Overview:
If the first condition is triggered, the fourth condition dictates that the CCLMM piece must be assigned to the 'against' side. If the second condition is triggered, the fourth condition dictates that the LLL pieces must be assigned to the 'for' side.

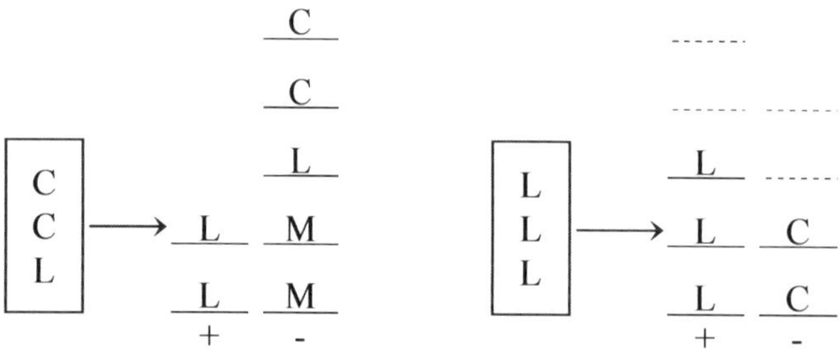

Since the second and fourth conditions establish that all three Ls could not have voted against Datalog, we can infer that at least one L voted for Datalog.

13. **(B)** Since both Ms did not vote the same way, we can infer that the first condition cannot be triggered. Thus, if both Cs voted against Datalog, then all three Ls must have voted for Datalog. If only one C voted against Datalog, then the second condition precludes the possibility of all three Ls having voted the same way, and we know that either one L or two Ls voted against Datalog. Only choice B is compatible with either diagram, and it is correct.

M			L|	|L
L	M		M	M
L	C		L	L
L	C	or	C	C
+	-		+	-

14. **(C)** As we initially inferred, at least one L voted for Datalog, and choice C is therefore correct.

15. **(E)** We have drawn a diagram which represents the triggering of the second condition, and only choice E must be true according to it.

16. **(A)** Since one of the 'against' slots is already filled (fourth condition), we only need to fill one additional slot to satisfy the condition given by the question. We cannot fill the second slot with an M, since the second condition would be triggered and violated on the 'for' side. Thus, the remaining 'against' slot must be filled with either a C or an L, and choice A is therefore correct.

M			M	
M			M	
L			L	
L	C		L	L
L	C	or	C	C
+	-		+	-

17. **(E)** Scanning the answer choices reveals that E violates the second condition. It is thus correct.

18. **(B)** This question triggers the first condition. Comparing the choices to our diagram above reveals that choice B must be false, and it is therefore correct.

Questions 19-24

Setup:

- five runners: L N O P S
- parallel lanes: 1 2 3 4 5
- each runner represents a different charity
- charities: F G H J K

Conditions:

#1: K$_4$

#2:

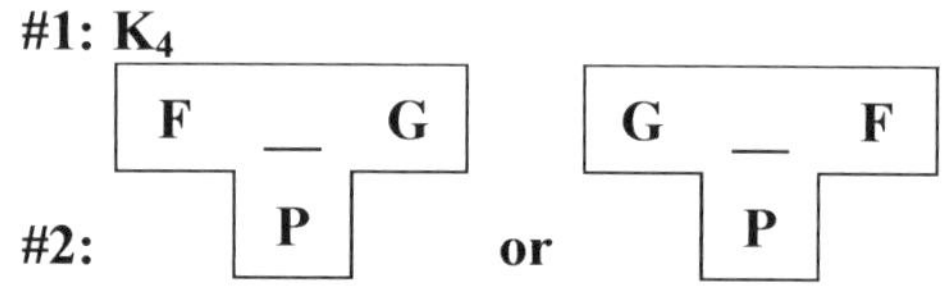

#3:

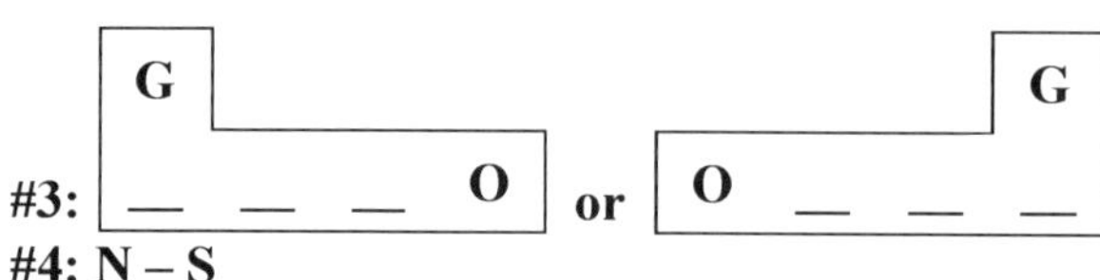

#4: N – S

Overview:
Combining the second and third conditions with the fact that there are five lanes, we can create two larger pieces:

Further, since charity K is assigned to the fourth lane (first condition), each piece can only fit into our main diagram in one way. This is an excellent opportunity to set up molds.

#1				
___	___	F	K	G
N|	O	|N	P	___
1	2	3	4	5

#2				
G	___	F	K	___
N|	P	|N	O	___
1	2	3	4	5

In both molds, the fourth condition dictates that N must be assigned to either the first or the third lane.

19. (A) F must be third
    (B) F must be third
    (C) violates the first condition
    (D) F must be third
    (E) Correct – this could be true of mold #1

20. **(D)** Our molds establish that P and O must be separated by exactly one lane, and choice D is therefore correct.

21. **(B)** This triggers mold #1. Since G must be fifth, choice B is correct.

22. **(D)** Since F must be third, and L, N, and S have all yet to be placed in either mold, we can infer that any one of them can occupy the third slot. Thus, choice D is correct.

23. **(B)** N must represent either G or F under mold #2. Therefore, this question requires that we use mold #1. The JN piece cannot be third, so we must place it first. With J assigned to the first lane, H must be assigned to the second lane. Therefore, choice B is correct.

J	H	F	K	G
N	O	L|S	P	S|L
1	2	3	4	5

24. **(A)** The only lane with slots open for both a runner and a charity are lane 1 under mold #1 and lane 5 under mold #2. Filling in the remaining charity (H) and applying the fourth condition, we can draw up two acceptable solutions under this scenario. Only choice A matches up with one of the options (the first one), and it is therefore correct.

J	H	F	K	G		G	H	F	K	J
L	O	N	P	S	or	N	P	S	O	L
1	2	3	4	5		1	2	3	4	5

Questions 1-5

Setup:
- weekly schedule: M T W Th F
- six students: H I K O U Z
- exactly one student each day except for one day with two consecutive sessions

Conditions:

#1: H – Z or [Z over H]
#2: I_{Th}
#3: (KO)
#4: M and W ⟶ 1 student each

Overview:
The third condition allows for four possible placements of the KO pair: M and T, T and W, W and Th, Th and F. Since the last two options require that Thursday be the day with two consecutive sessions scheduled, we can use these four options to create a set of molds.

#1

M	T	W	Th	F
K|O	O|K		I	

#2

M	T	W	Th	F
	K|O	O|K	I	

#3

M	T	W	Th	F
			O|K	
H|U		K|O	I	U|Z

#4

M	T	W	Th	F
			K|O	
H|U		U|Z	I	O|K

Mold #1: Since the day with two sessions is undetermined, we cannot infer anything about the assignments of H, U, and Z.

Mold #2: Since the day with two sessions is undetermined, we cannot infer anything about the assignments of H, U, and Z.

Mold #3: With Thursday's slots filled up, the first condition dictates that one of U and Z must fill the Friday slot, and that one of H and U must occupy the Monday slot.

Mold #4: With Thursday's slots filled up, the first condition dictates that one of U and Z must fill the Thursday slot, and that one of H and U must occupy the Monday slot.

1. **(D)** For this question, we can narrow our focus to the first two molds. Since K or O must be scheduled for Tuesday, we can eliminate choices A, B, and E. Due to the third condition, we can also eliminate choice C, leaving D as the correct answer.

2. **(B)** This could only happen under the first two molds. To ensure that Z is scheduled for the earliest day, we must assign H to the earliest possible day (first condition). With O scheduled for Monday, H could be scheduled for Tuesday, and Z could be scheduled for Wednesday. With O scheduled for Wednesday, H could be scheduled for Monday, and Z could be scheduled for Tuesday. Therefore, choice B is correct.

	H			
O	K	Z	I	U
M	T	W	Th	F

or

	Z			
H	K	O	I	U
M	T	W	Th	F

3. Since each answer choice is phrased as a conditional statement, we must check to see if the first half of each statement guarantees the second half.

   (A) this is true of molds #3 and #4, but not necessarily true of mold #2
   (B) U could be scheduled for Tuesday under any of the molds
   (C) this is true of mold #4, but not necessarily true of mold #1
   (D) Correct – U could only be scheduled for Thursday under either of the first two molds, and the first condition dictates that Z must fill the Friday slot

			U	
K|O	O|K	H	I	Z
M	T	W	Th	F

or

			U	
H	K|O	O|K	I	Z
M	T	W	Th	F

   (E) mold #3 disproves this choice

4. (A) Z cannot be scheduled for Monday due to the first and fourth conditions
   (B) U would be scheduled for Friday under mold #2 and Wednesday under mold #4
   (C) U could be scheduled for either Monday or Tuesday under mold #4
   (D) Correct – this could only happen under either mold #1 or mold #2; the first condition would place H on Wednesday or Monday, respectively, leaving U to occupy the Friday slot

			Z	
K|O	O|K	H	I	U
M	T	W	Th	F

or

			Z	
H	K|O	O|K	I	U
M	T	W	Th	F

   (E) Z could be scheduled for Friday under any one of molds #1, #2, and #3

5. Combining this with the first condition, we have either [UH] – Z or [H / U] – Z. Due to the fourth condition, the second configuration is not compatible with any of the molds. Thus, we can eliminate choices C through E. Assuming the first configuration, we can check choices A and B against the molds and conditions.

   (A) **Correct – this could be true of either mold #3 or mold #4**

		O|K							K|O	
U	H	K|O	I	Z	or	U	H	Z	I	O|K
M	T	W	Th	F		M	T	W	Th	F

   (B) U could only be scheduled for Thursday under either mold #1 or mold #2, and the first condition would require Friday to have two sessions

Questions 6-12

Setup:
- square parking lot
- eight lights: 1 2 3 4 5 6 7 8
- situated as pictured

Conditions:
#1: three consecutively numbered lights cannot all be on
#2: 8_{on}
#3: $1_{on} \longrightarrow 2_{off}$; $2_{on} \longrightarrow 1_{off}$ (contrapositive)
$1_{on} \longrightarrow 7_{off}$; $7_{on} \longrightarrow 1_{off}$ (contrapositive)
#4: 1^{+} light on each side is on
#5: exactly 1 light on (one particular side) ⟶ center light
#6: two of 1, 2, and 3 are on

Overview:
Since lights 1 and 2 cannot both be on (third condition), the sixth condition dictates that either 1 and 3 or 2 and 3 are both on. Thus, light 3 must be on. From the fifth condition, we can deduce that if a corner light is off, the center lights on the two sides it touches must both be on. Since lights 4 and 5 cannot both be on (first condition), exactly one of 4 and 5 must be on.

___ 1	___ 2	+ 3
+ 8		+|- 4
___ 7	___ 6	-|+ 5

We can further establish two molds to represent what must be true when each of lights 1 and 2 is on.

#1

+	-	+
1	2	3
+		+|-
8		4
-	+	-|+
7	6	5

#2

-	+	+
1	2	3
+		-
8		4
+|-	-|+	+
7	6	5

Mold #1: With light 1 on, the third condition dictates that light 7 must be off. Due to the fifth condition, light 6 must be on.

Mold #2: With light 2 on, the first condition dictates that light 4 must be off. Due to the fifth condition, light 5 must be on. The fifth condition and the first condition together dictate that exactly one of lights 6 and 7 is on.

From these molds, we can infer four acceptable solutions.
#1: 1, 3, 4, 6, 8
#2: 1, 3, 5, 6, 8
#3: 2, 3, 5, 6, 8
#4: 2, 3, 5, 7, 8

6. (A) violates the third condition
   (B) violates the sixth condition
   (C) Correct – see solution #3
   (D) violates the first and sixth conditions
   (E) violates the third condition

7. **(B)** As we inferred, light 3 must be on, and choice B is therefore correct.

8. **(B)** This triggers mold #2, and choice B is thus correct.

9. (A) see solution #3
   (B) see solutions #1 and #2
   (C) see solution #1
   (D) Correct – we deduced this initially
   (E) See solution #4

10. This is true of solutions #2, #3, and #4.

    (A) Correct – see solution #4
    (B) violates the third condition
    (C) violates the first condition (lights 3, 4, and 5)
    (D) at least one of lights 2 and 6 must be on
    (E) violates the first condition (lights 5, 6, and 7)

11. **(B)** This question triggers solution #1. Choice B must be false, and it is therefore correct.

12. **(E)** Applying the fifth condition, we know that light 2 is on. Since light 3 is off, we can deduce from the fifth condition that light 4 must be on. From the first condition, we know that light 6 cannot be on in addition to one of the corner lights (5 and 7). Thus, there are two options: one with lights 5 and 7 on, and one with light 6 on. Only choice E need not be true, and it is correct.

- 1	+ 2	- 3		- 1	+ 2	- 3
+ 8		+ 4		+ 8		+ 4
+ 7	- 6	+ 5	or	- 7	+ 6	- 5

Questions 13-17

Setup:
- o seven children
- o seven chairs arranged in a row from west to east
- o all seven children face north
- o four boys (B): F H I J
- o three girls (G): R S T

Conditions:
#1: exactly one child in each chair

#2: 

#3: I_5, I_6, or I_7
#4: I – S

#5: FR

Overview:
Combining the second condition with the fact that there are four boys and seven chairs, we can deduce that no two girls will sit next to each other. Thus, since the seventh chair is occupied by a boy, the third and fourth conditions dictate that we must place I and S in the fifth and sixth chairs, respectively. F cannot occupy the seventh chair, due to the fifth condition. Combining this with our deductions about the boys and girls, we know that F must sit in either the first or the third chair.

	B	G	B	G	B	G	B	
West	F|		|F		I	S		East
	1	2	3	4	5	6	7	
							~F	

We can create two molds to represent the placement options for F.

#1	F	R	H|J	T	I	S	J|H
#2	H|J	R|T	F	T|R	I	S	J|H
	1	2	3	4	5	6	7

Mold #1: With F sitting in the first seat, the fifth condition dictates that R must sit in the second seat, leaving H and J to occupy the third and seventh seats, in either order.

Mold #2: With F sitting in the third seat, the fifth condition dictates that R must sit in either the second or the fourth seat. Since T is the only girl left to place, she must sit in whichever of the second or fourth seat unoccupied by R. This leaves H and J to sit in the first and seventh seats, in either order.

Since the first mold has two options, and the second mold has two sets of two options each, we can draw out a set of six solutions to represent all the acceptable outcomes.

#1	F	R	H	T	I	S	J
#2	F	R	J	T	I	S	H
#3	H	R	F	T	I	S	J
#4	J	R	F	T	I	S	H
#5	H	T	F	R	I	S	J
#6	J	T	F	R	I	S	H
	1	2	3	4	5	6	7

13. **(C)** As the solutions illustrate, F and R could occupy any of the seat pairs between the first and fourth seats. This amounts to three individual pairs, and choice C is therefore correct.

14. (A) see solutions #1 and #2
    (B) see solutions #1 and #2
    (C) Correct – since only two boys sit in the first four chairs, and F must be among them, this must be false
    (D) see solution #3
    (E) see solutions #1 and #2

15. **(E)** This scenario is true of solutions #3 and #4. Only choice E is compatible with either of the solutions (#4), and it is therefore correct.

16. **(B)** This is only true of solutions #1 and #2. Choice B is the only one that is compatible with either solution (#2), and it is thus correct.

17. **(D)** This is true of solutions #3 and #4. As such, I and R must be separated by F and T, and choice D is correct.

<u>Questions 18-24</u>

Setup:
- organisms: W X Y Z
- antibiotics: F G H

Conditions:
#1: organism ⟶ 1^+ antibiotic
#2: each organism ≤ 2 antibiotics
#3: F ⟶ 2-3 organisms
#4: F_W ⟶ F_X; G_W ⟶ G_X; H_W ⟶ H_X
#5: F ⟶ G; ~G ⟶ ~F (contrapositive)
#6: F_Y

Overview:
From the fifth and sixth conditions, we can infer that Y responds to G. Applying the second condition, we know that Y does not respond to H. None of the organisms can respond to F and H, since the fifth condition would be triggered, and the second condition precludes any of the organisms from responding to all three antibiotics. From the third and fifth conditions, we can infer two to three FG pieces. Thus, at least one of X and Z must respond to both F and G.

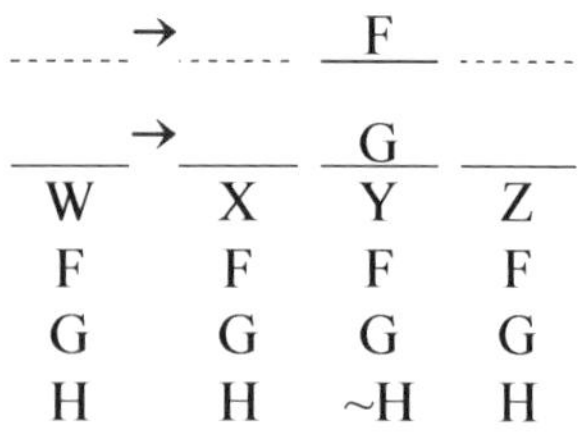

W		X	Y	Z
-------	→	-------	F	-------
____	→	____	G	____
W		X	Y	Z
F		F	F	F
G		G	G	G
H		H	~H	H

18. **(D)** As we inferred, Y cannot respond to H, and choice D is correct.

19. (A) due to the fourth condition, all four organisms would respond to F, violating the third condition
    (B) Correct – see question #24
    (C) X would respond to G, due to the fourth condition, but Y also responds to G
    (D) violates the fourth condition
    (E) violates the fifth condition

20. (A) violates the third condition
    (B) Y cannot respond to H
    (C) violates either the second or the fifth condition
    (D) that organism would have to respond to F (first condition), which triggers and violates the fifth condition
    (E) Correct – see questions #21 and #24

21. **(D)** Combining this with the fourth condition, we know that W does not respond to F. To satisfy the third and fifth conditions, we must assign a FG piece to Z. To satisfy the first condition, at least one of G and H must be assigned to both W and X. Only choice D must be true, and it is therefore correct.

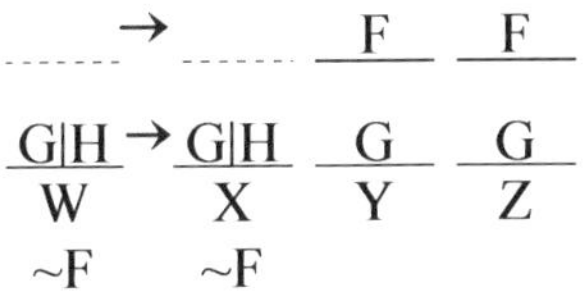

......	→	F	F
G|H	→ G|H	G	G
W	X	Y	Z
~F	~F		

22. **(B)** As we have inferred, one particular organism cannot respond to both F and H. Therefore, if one organism responds to two antibiotics, those antibiotics must be either F and G or G and H. Since both pairs contain G, choice B is correct.

23. **(E)** Combining this with the first condition, we know that each organism must respond to at least one of F and G. Due to the fifth condition, we can infer that all four organisms respond to G. Thus, choice E is correct.

24. **(C)** We have previously inferred that there must be at least two FG pieces. Combined with the information that three of the organisms respond to the same set of antibiotics and the fact that there are four organisms in total, we know that the three organisms which respond to the same set must respond to both F and G. To satisfy the first condition, Z must respond to either G or H. Thus, choice C is the only one that need not be true, and it is correct.

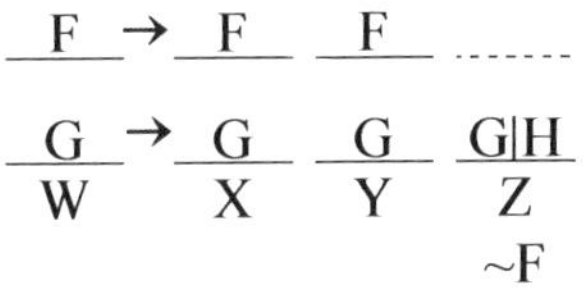

F	→ F	F	......
G	→ G	G	G|H
W	X	Y	Z
			~F

Questions 1-7

Setup:
- three corsages: 1 2 3
- four types of flowers: G O R V
- each corsage ⟶ exactly three flowers
- nine flowers must include 1+ of each type
- R ≥ 2O

Conditions:
#1: Corsage 1 ⟶ exactly two types
#2: Corsage 2 ⟶ 1^+ R
#3: Corsage 3 ⟶ 1^+ G, ~O

Overview:
From the setup condition that at least twice as many Rs as Os will be in the corsages, we can make some deductions about possible allocations. If there's one O, the number of Rs could between two and six. If there are two Os, the number of Rs could be four or five. Note that it would not be possible for there to be six Rs under this scenario, since that would only leave one flower remaining, which would have to be both G and V.

G + V	R	O
6	2	1
5	3	1
4	4	1
3	5	1
2	6	1
3	4	2
2	5	2

We can box two of the slots over corsage 1 as a reminder of the first condition.

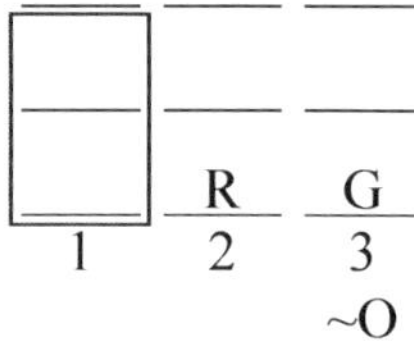

1. (A) violates the third condition
   (B) violates the setup condition regarding Os and Rs
   (C) Correct
   (D) violates the first condition
   (E) violates the second condition

2. **(D)** As we inferred, the maximum number of Rs is six, and choice D is therefore correct.

3. **(B)** We only have two allocations that have two orchids. Since we need to maximize the number of Vs, we must use the 3, 4, 2 allocation. Thus, we can have two Vs and one G among the corsages. Therefore, choice B is correct.

4. **(A)** From the second and third conditions, we can deduce that corsages 2 and 3 must contain at least one G and at least one R. The remaining flower will be one of G, R, and V, due to the third condition. In both of the first two scenarios, corsage 1 must contain a V. Since the second scenario contains four Rs, we can assign two Os to corsage 1. Only choice A is compatible with the diagrams, and it is therefore correct.

O	G	G		O	R	R		O	V	V
V	G	G		O|V	G	G			G	G
V	R	R	or	V	R	R	or		R	R
1	2	3		1	2	3		1	2	3

5. **(C)** Due to the third condition, we can deduce that there must be one O in corsage 1, and one O in corsage 2. In combination with the second condition, we know that corsage 2 includes at least one O and one R. Thus, choice C is correct.

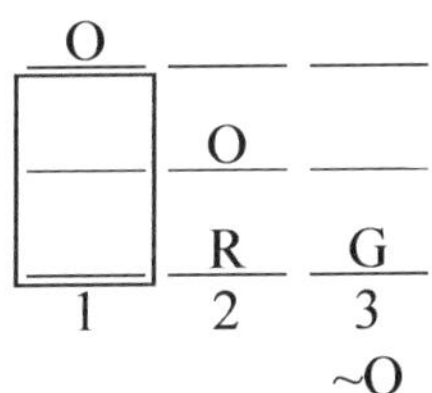

6. **(D)** To maximize the number of Vs, we must use the 6, 2, 1 allocation. Therefore, we know that there will be two Rs in the three corsages, and choice D is correct.

7. **(A)** Applying the third condition, we know that corsage 3 contains one V, one R, and one G. There are two acceptable configurations for corsage 1: one V and two Gs, two Vs and one G. Since the corsages can contain a maximum of three Rs, the setup conditions dictate that there is no more than one O. Only choice A contains one O, and it is therefore correct.

V		V		V		V
G	R	R		V	R	R
G	O	G	or	G	O	G
1	2	3		1	2	3

Questions 8-13

Setup:

- o seven people: J K L M N P Q
- o exactly four will be selected

Conditions:

#1: J or K (but not both) must be selected
#2: N or P (but not both) must be selected
#3: N ⟶ L; ~L ⟶ ~N (contrapositive)
#4: Q ⟶ K; ~K ⟶ ~Q (contrapositive)

Overview:
The following diagram will serve as a visual representation of the conditions.

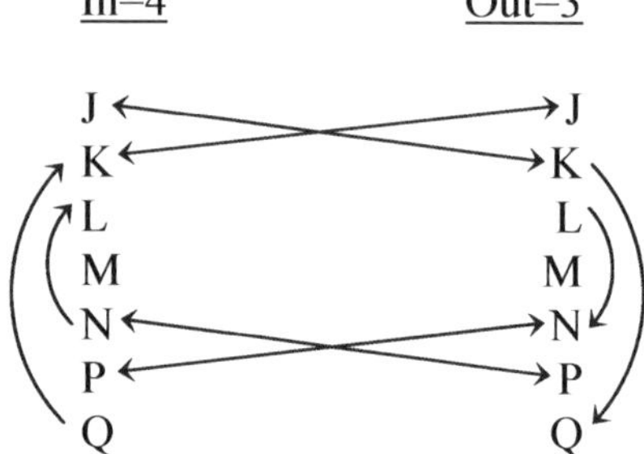

From the first two conditions, we can infer that exactly two of L, M, and Q will be selected.

J|K N|P ___ ___
L M Q

We can create three distinct molds, each one representing a different one of the three not being selected.

#1 J|K N|P L M

#2 K N|P L Q

#3 K P M Q

Mold #1: When L and M are selected, we cannot make any inferences about the other two people selected.

Mold #2: With L and Q selected, the fourth condition dictates that K must also be selected.

Mold #3: With M and Q selected, the fourth condition dictates that K must be selected, and the contrapositive of the third condition dictates that N cannot be selected.

---

[2] Visit Manhattan LSAT (http://www.manhattanlsat.com) to learn more about using this diagram.

8. (A) violates the first condition
   (B) violates the fourth condition
   (C) violates the third condition
   (D) Correct – see mold #3
   (E) violates the second condition

9. **(B)** Comparing the pairs to our molds reveals that L and M are the only pair of which at least one must be selected. Therefore, choice B is correct.

10. **(B)** Comparing the choices to our molds reveals that all of the pairs are acceptable with the exception of J and Q. Thus, choice B is correct.

11. **(B)** This triggers the second mold. Therefore, choice B is correct.

12. **(C)** This could only be true of the first two molds. Since N must be selected, we can infer three unique selections, and choice C is correct.

    _J_ _N_ _L_ _M_

    _K_ _N_ _L_ _M_

    _K_ _N_ _L_ _Q_

13. **(E)** Since we created mold #3 from M and Q being selected, choice E is correct.

Questions 14-18

Setup:
- three boys: K L M
- three girls: R S T
- three dances: 1 2 3
- each dance ⟶ three pairs of children
- each pair ⟶ a boy and a girl

Conditions:
#1: K and S in either 1 or 2
#2: _ and R in 2 ⟶ _ and S in 3
#3: one pair cannot partner each other more than once

Overview:
From the third condition, and the fact that there are three dances, we know that each boy will partner with each girl once. We can therefore infer from the second condition that whoever partners with R in dance 2 and S in dance 3 will partner with T in dance 1. Due to the first condition, we know that K cannot partner T in dance 1 <u>and</u> R in dance 2. Therefore, the person to do so must be either L or M.

	1	2	3
R		L|M	
S	K|	|K	L|M
T	L|M		

Since K can partner with S in either of the first two dances, and either L or M can satisfy the second condition, we can create four distinct solutions which represent all the acceptable pairings.

#1

	1	2	3
R	M	L	K
S	K	M	L
T	L	K	M

#2

	1	2	3
R	L	M	K
S	K	L	M
T	M	K	L

#3

	1	2	3
R	K	L	M
S	M	K	L
T	L	M	K

#4

	1	2	3
R	K	M	L
S	L	K	M
T	M	L	K

14. **(D)** This is true of solutions #1 and #3. Thus, M could partner R (solution #1) or S (solution #3), and choice D is correct.

15. **(B)** This is true of solutions #2 and #4. Only choice B could be true (solution #2), and it is therefore correct.

16. **(B)** This is only true of solution #3. Thus, choice B is correct.

17. **(C)** This is only true of solution #2, and we know that L and R must be partners in dance 1. Therefore, choice C is correct.

18. **(D)** This is only true of solution #1, and choice D is therefore correct.

Questions 19-24

Setup:
- six cities located as pictured
- within the six-city area are eight institutions: H H H H J J U U

Conditions:
#1: each institution ⟶ exactly one city
#2: ~JJ and ~UU
#3: J ⟶ ~U; U ⟶ ~J(contrapositive)
J ⟶ H; ~H ⟶ ~J (contrapositive)
#4: cities containing the two Us don't share any boundaries
#5: city 3 ⟶ U; city 6 ⟶ J

Overview:
From the fourth and fifth conditions, we can deduce that the second U must be in either city 2 or city 6. Combining the third and fifth conditions, we know that the second U must be in city 2, and that city 6 also contains an H. Combining our deduction that U is in city 2 with the third condition, we know that A J cannot be located in city 2. With two Us, a J and an H placed, there are only four variables left to assign: H, H, H, J. From the third condition, we know that there will be one JH pair among the four (assigned to city 1, city 4, or city 5), and that the two other Hs will be placed elsewhere.

	1	___	U	2 ~J
~J	3	U	___	4
	5	___	J H	6 ~U

19. **(E)** Comparing the choices to our deductions reveals that only choice E could be true.

20. **(A)** Comparing the choices to our diagram reveals that only choice A could be true.

21. **(D)** Cities 2 and 3 are the only ones to which the second J can be assigned. Thus, the second J can be in city 1, city 4, or city 5, and choice D is correct.

22. **(D)** Since we have two Hs and an HJ pair left to assign, and there are three cities without any assigned institutions (1, 4, and 5), the question dictates that an H must be placed in each one of those cities. Thus, choice D is correct.

1	H	U	2
3	U	H	4
5	H	J H	6

23. **(B)** To answer the question, we need to figure out which of the cities can have three Hs. City 6 could be assigned two more Hs, so choice E is eliminated. We could assign both the two Hs and the HJ pair to any one of cities 1, 4, and 5. Thus, choices A, C, and D are incorrect, leaving B as the correct answer. Since one of the Hs is paired up with a J, we cannot assign all four remaining variables to city 2, as this would violate the third condition.

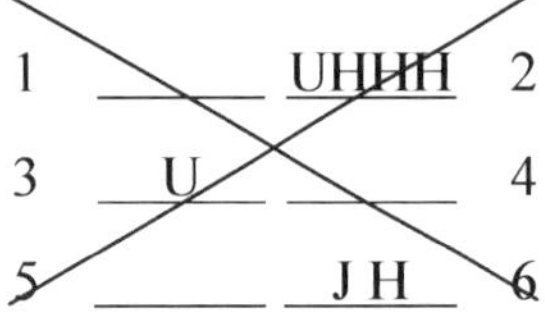

24. **(A)** Only city 2 or city 3 could contain two Hs and a U. We have established previously that the HJ pair must be assigned to one of cities 1, 4, and 5. Thus, the three cities without an H must be two of 1, 4, and 5, and one of either city 2 or city 3. Only choice A meets these criteria, and it is therefore correct.

1	______	U	2		1	______	H H U	2
3	H H U	______	4		3	U	______	4
5	______	J H	6	or	5	______	J H	6

Questions 1-5

Setup:
- nine students: F G H I J K L M N
- each placed in one of three classes
- three highest scorers ⟶ level 1 class
- three lowest scores ⟶ level 3 class
- remaining three ⟶ level 2 class
- each class has exactly three students

Conditions:
#1: I – G
#2: **G** < **J**, **K**
#3: J – M
#4: M – H
#5: H – N
#6: **K** < **F**, **L**

Overview:
We can combine the conditions to create the following sketch:

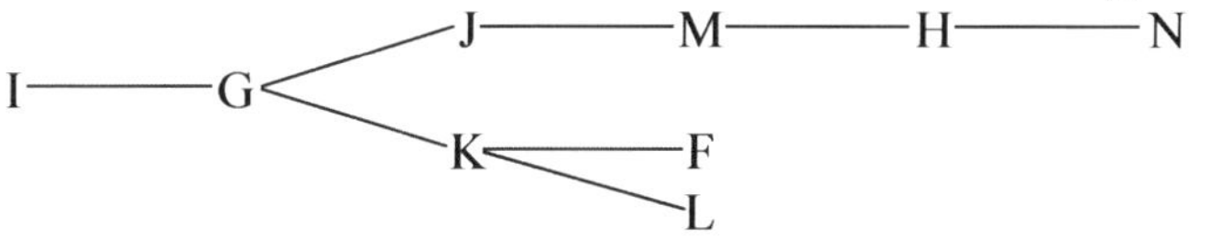

Since I and G both precede all the other variables, they must be assigned to the level 1 class. One of J and K will fill the remaining slot in the level 1 class.

1	2	3
J|K	___	___
I	___	___
G	___	___

1. **(B)** Since the only uncertainty about the level 1 class is which one of J and K fills the third slot, there are two possible combinations of students, and choice B is therefore correct.

2. **(C)** Because J must be followed by at least three variables (M, H, and N), J cannot be in the level three class. J could be in the level 2 class, if K filled the third slot in the level 1 class. Thus, choice C is correct.

3. **(C)** Since K only has to be preceded by at least two variables (I and G), and only has to be followed by at least two variables (F and L), K could be assigned to any one of the three classes. Therefore, choice C is correct.

4. (A) L could be assigned to either the level 2 class or the level 3 class
   (B) this doesn't establish which of J and K occupies the third slot in the level 1 class
   (C) Correct – since M is in between J and H, M must also be in the level 2 class, allowing us to create a complete solution

K	J	F
I	M	L
G	H	N
1	2	3

   (D) F could be assigned to either the level 2 class or the level 3 class
   (E) this doesn't establish which of J and K occupies the third slot in the level 1 class

5. (A) all three could be together in the level 3 class
   (B) all three could be together in the level 2 class
   (C) all three could be together in either the level 2 class or the level 3 class
   (D) all three could be together in the level 2 class
   (E) Correct – this couldn't be true of the level 2 class, since J and K would both have to be in the level 1 class, and it couldn't be true of the level 3 class, since H and N both follow M

Questions 6-12

Setup:
- six reviewers: F G H J K L
- four movies: M R S W

Conditions:
#1: each reviewer ⟶ exactly one movie; each movie ⟶ 1^+ reviewer

#2: [H / F]

#3: 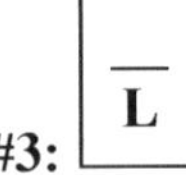

#4: G_M
#5: J_M or J_W
#6: $\sim H_W$

Overview:
We can use the second and third conditions to establish the acceptable allocation of reviewers to movies. Applying the second condition leaves four reviewers to spread among three movies. Thus, one of the three remaining movies must be reviewed by two of the reviewers, and we have the following allocation: 2, 2, 1, 1. Accordingly, H and F cannot be grouped with any other variables. The fourth condition precludes the HF piece from being assigned to M. The sixth condition precludes the HF piece from being assigned to W. With only two movies (R and S) to which the HF piece can be assigned, we can establish two distinct molds to efficiently represent these options. The allocation, combined with the fourth condition, precludes J from reviewing M. Therefore, J must always be assigned to review W.

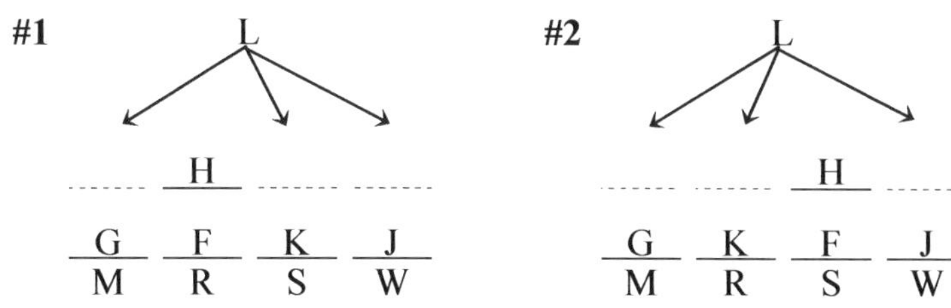

Mold #1: With the HF piece assigned to R, K must be assigned to S, and L can be assigned to any one of M, S, and W.

Mold #2: With the HF piece assigned to S, K must be assigned to R, and L can be assigned to any one of M, R, and W.

6. **(A)** This could only be true of the first mold. Thus, H must be assigned to R, and choice A is correct.

7. **(E)** This is only true of the second mold. Accordingly, F and H are assigned to review S, and choice E is correct.

8. **(E)** Since L can be assigned to review any one of the movies, choice E is correct.

9. **(E)** Comparing the choices to our molds reveals that only E could be true (under mold #2).

10. (A) see mold #1 and mold #2
    (B) Correct
    (C) see mold #2
    (D) see mold #1
    (E) see mold #1 and mold #2

11. **(C)** If K is paired with another reviewer, it has to be L. K and L can both be assigned to either S (mold #1) or R (mold #2). Thus, choice C is correct.

12. (A) violates the fifth condition
    (B) Correct – see mold #1
    (C) violates the fifth condition
    (D) violates the third condition
    (E) violates the second and fourth conditions

<u>Questions 13-18</u>

Setup:
- "words" ⟶ any combination of 4+ letters
- "sentence" ⟶ exactly five words

Conditions:
#1: the five words are written from left to right in alphabetical order
#2: a sentence is started by any word
each successive word is formed by performing one of three operations to the word immediately preceding it
operations: delete one letter; add one letter; replace one letter with another letter
#3: words that begin with the same letter ≤ 3
#4: the same operation cannot be applied to two consecutive words

Overview:
Since none of the conditions specifies any particular words, our time is best allocated in working on the individual questions.

13. (A) violates the first condition
    (B) Correct
    (C) violates the second condition
    (D) violates the fourth condition
    (E) violates the third condition

14. **(D)** This question tests our grasp of the third condition. Can we start a sentence with a word that begins with the letter z? This would violate the third condition, since the first condition precludes a sentence with five words, each beginning with the letter z. We can start a sentence with a word that begins the letter y. We would have either two or three words beginning with y, and the remaining words would begin with z. Thus, choice D is correct.

15. **(C)** The letter b is changed to s in over two operations. Since nothing else about the word is different, and we can't replace a letter in two consecutive words (second condition), the only way this could happen is if the letter b were deleted by the first operation, and the letter s were added by the second operation. Therefore, choice C is correct.

    blender ⟶ lender ⟶ slender

16. **(D)** For this question, we know that three operations will be performed. A maximum of two of them can delete one letter, due to the second condition. Thus, the fourth word must have at least seven letters, and choice D is correct.

17. **(E)** To determine how far apart the words learn and clean can be in a sentence, we must first note the differences between the two words. Clean contains an added c and a deleted r. Getting from one to the other would require at least two operations. Since it could be done in two operations (delete r ⟶ add c; add c ⟶ delete r), we can eliminate the choices that contain second or don't contain third. This leaves choices B and E to analyze. Could clean be the fourth word? Rather than deleting r and adding c immediately, we could change r prior to deleting it, or add a letter other than c and then change it to c. Thus, by process of elimination, we know that choice E is correct.

    learn ⟶ leasn ⟶ lean ⟶ clean
    learn ⟶ lean ⟶ blean ⟶ clean

18. **(C)** For this question, we know that four operations will be performed. A maximum of two of those operations could consist of adding a letter. For instance, the following two patterns of operations would be acceptable:

    add ⟶ replace ⟶ add ⟶ replace
    replace ⟶ add ⟶ replace ⟶ add

    Attempting to add a letter in three of the operations would violate the fourth condition. We can therefore infer that the fifth word could contain a maximum of six letters, and choice C is correct.

Questions 19-24

Setup:

- six different concertos
- six consecutive Sundays: 1 2 3 4 5 6
- two of three Giuliani (G): H J K
- two of four Rodrigo (R): M N O P
- two of three Vivaldi (V): X Y Z

Conditions:

#1: N ⟶ J; ~J ⟶ ~N (contrapositive)
#2: M ⟶ ~J; J ⟶ ~M (contrapositive)
M ⟶ ~O; O ⟶ ~M (contrapositive)
#3: X ⟶ ~Z; Z ⟶ ~X (contrapositive)
X ⟶ ~P; P ⟶ ~X (contrapositive)
#4: J and O ⟶ J – O
#5: X_5 ⟶ R_1; ~R_1 ⟶ ~X_5 (contrapositive)

Overview:
We can use the following diagram to deduce any chains.

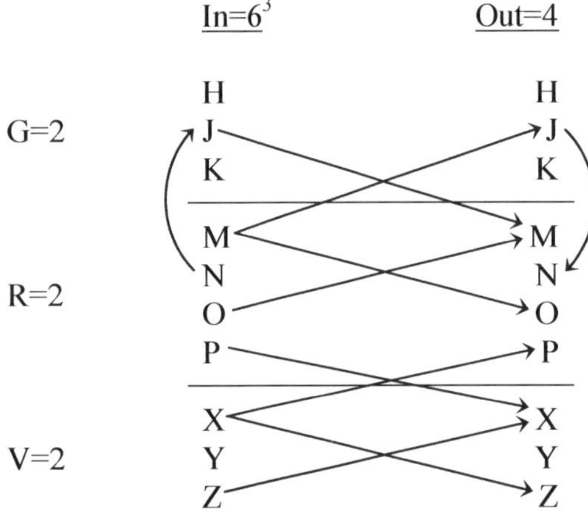

From the second condition and the setup condition that two Rs are selected, we can deduce that if either one of N or P is not selected, the other must be selected. The third condition, combined with the setup condition that exactly two Vs are selected, tells us that Y must be selected in any acceptable solution.

____	____	X|Z
____	N|P	Y
H	M	X
J	N	Y
K	O	X
	P	

19. (A) violates the first condition
    (B) Correct
    (C) violates the second condition
    (D) violates the third condition
    (E) violates the third condition

20. **(C)** This triggers the fourth condition. Since O cannot precede J, O cannot be second, and choice C is correct.

N	____	____	____	____	____
1	2	3	4	5	6
	~O				~J

[3] Visit Manhattan LSAT (http://www.manhattanlsat.com) to learn more about using this diagram.

21. **(E)** This triggers the fourth condition, and we know that either J or Y will be first. Due to the contrapositive of the fifth condition, X cannot be fifth, and choice E is correct.

1	2	3	4	5	6
J	O	Y			
J	Y	O			
Y	J	O			
~O				~X	

22. **(B)** Applying the fourth condition, we know that J is not selected. To satisfy the setup condition that two Gs are selected, both H and K must be selected. Thus, choice B is correct.

H	O	X|Z
K	N|P	Y
~J		

23. **(D)** As we inferred from the third condition, Y must always be selected. Therefore, choice D is correct.

24. **(A)** Following the chain from N selected, we are led to M not being selected, and choice A is therefore correct.

Part 2:
PrepTests 11-20

Questions 1-6

Setup:
- eight camp counselors: F G H J K L N O
- each is assigned to supervise exactly one of three activities
- activities: S T V

Conditions:
#1: each activity ⟶ 2-3 supervisors
#2: H_S
#3: ~K_T and ~O_T
#4: 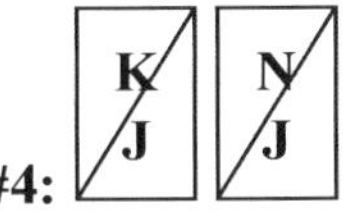
#5: G_S ⟶ N_V and O_V; ~N_V or ~O_V ⟶ ~G_S (contrapositive)

Overview:
Combining the number of counselors with the first condition, we can deduce one acceptable allocation of counselors to sports: 3, 3, 2.

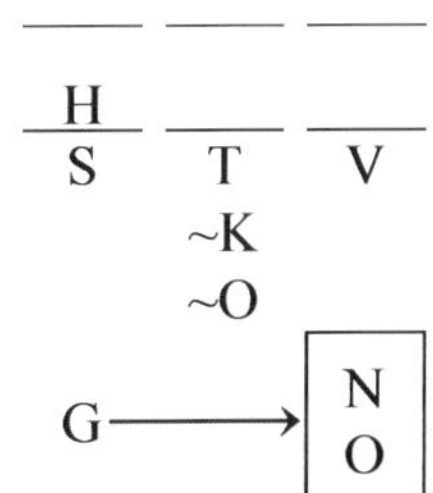

1. **(A) Correct**
   (B) violates the fifth condition
   (C) violates the first condition
   (D) violates the fourth condition
   (E) violates the third condition

2. (A) triggers and violates the fifth condition
   (B) triggers and violates the fifth condition
   (C) violates the fourth condition
   (D) violates the fourth condition
   (E) Correct

3. (A) violates the third condition
   (B) Correct
   (C) violates the second condition
   (D) violates the fourth condition
   (E) violates the third condition

4. **(D)** This triggers the fifth condition, and we can assign N and O to volleyball. Since swimming has no remaining slots, the fourth condition dictates that we must assign J to tennis. Only choice D is compatible with this diagram, and it is therefore correct.

```
 G   ------ ------
 K   ____   N
 H    J     O
 S    T     V
```

5. **(C)** With all the swimming slots filled, the third condition stipulates that we must assign K and O to volleyball. Applying the fourth condition, we must assign J to tennis. The fourth condition dictates that we must assign N to volleyball, leaving G to supervise tennis.

```
 F          N
 L    G     K
 H    J     O
 S    T     V
```

6. **(B)** Due to the third condition, the JO piece must be assigned to either swimming or volleyball. If it is assigned to swimming, the third condition forces K to supervise volleyball. If the JO piece is assigned to volleyball, the fourth condition precludes N from being assigned to volleyball. Due to the contrapositive of the fifth condition, G cannot be assigned to volleyball. Choice B is incompatible with either scenario, and it is therefore correct.

```
 J   ____  ____          N|  ____  ____
 O   ____  ____          K   ____   J
 H   ____   K     or     H   |N     O
 S    T     V            S    T     V
                        ~G         ~N
                                   ~K
```

Questions 7-11

Setup:
- five firefighters: F G H I J

Conditions:
#1: exactly one of the firefighters works each day (M T W Th Fr)
#2: each firefighter ≤ 2 days

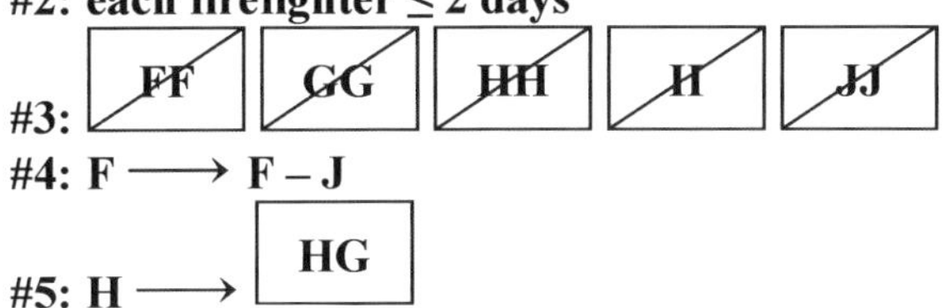

Overview:
From the fourth and fifth conditions, we can deduce that neither F nor H can be assigned to work on Friday. Four of the five questions provide additional conditions, so we'll head straight to the questions.

M	T	W	Th	Fr
				~H
				~F

7. **(B)** As we inferred, F cannot be assigned to work on Friday, and choice B is correct.

8. We can use the additional constraint along with the conditions to eliminate the incorrect choices.
   (A) H only has one day off in between assigned workdays
   (B) violates the third condition
   (C) violates the third condition
   (D) Correct
   (E) violates the fourth condition

9. **(B)** Applying the fourth condition, we know that J cannot be assigned to work on Monday. Thus, choice B is correct.

10. **(B)** Due to the fourth condition, the two Fs must precede the assigned J. The third condition dictates that we must assign the two Fs to Monday and Wednesday. With the Wednesday slot filled, we can infer that H cannot be assigned to work on Tuesday, due to the fifth condition. Only choice B is compatible with this scenario, and it is therefore correct.

F		F	J	
M	T	W	Th	Fr
	~F			~H
	~H			~F

11. **(D)** Due to the fifth condition, H cannot be assigned to work during the week. With three firefighters remaining (F, I, and J), the second condition dictates the following allocation of workdays to firefighters: 2, 2, 1. F and J cannot each be assigned to work on two days, due to the third and fourth conditions. This would require a minimum of six slots. Thus, we can infer that I must be assigned to work two days, and choice D is correct.

<u>Questions 12-19</u>

Setup:
- committee to consist of exactly five representatives
- one representative will be the chairperson
- five tenants (T): F G J K M
- four homeowners (H): P Q R S

Conditions:
#1: 2^+ T and 2^+ H
#2: chairperson ⟶ group with two representatives
#3: F ⟶ Q; ~Q ⟶ ~F (contrapositive)
#4: G ⟶ K; ~K ⟶ ~G (contrapositive)
#5: J ⟷ M
#6: M ⟶ ~P; P ⟶ ~M (contrapositive)

Overview:
For the purpose of making inferences, we can use the following diagram:

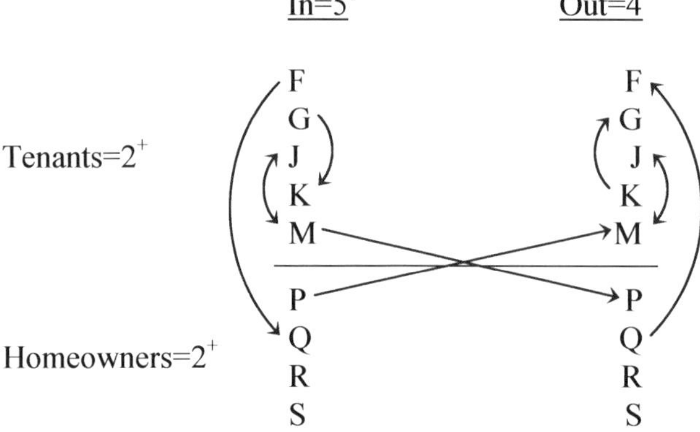

[1] Visit Manhattan LSAT (http://www.manhattanlsat.com) to learn more about using this diagram.

Using the numerical conditions, we can create five different acceptable molds with which to answer the questions.

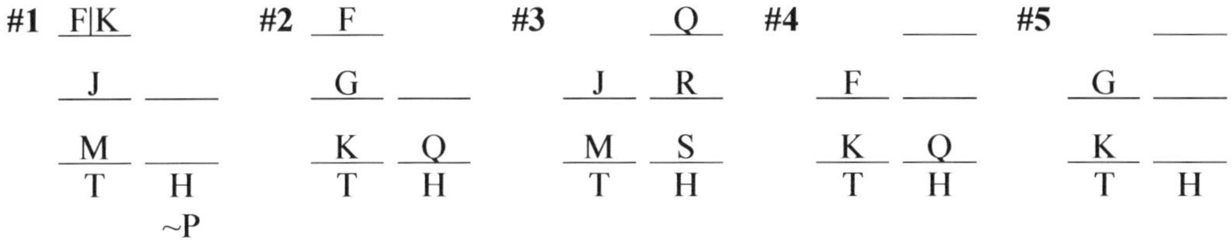

Mold #1: If there are three tenants on the committee including either J or M, the other must be on it, due to the fifth condition. With only one slot remaining, the fourth condition precludes G from being on it, leaving F or K to occupy the final slot.

Mold #2: If there are three tenants on the committee and neither J nor M is on it, F, G, and K must all be representatives. The third condition dictates that Q must also be on the committee.

Mold #3: If there are two tenants on the committee including either J or M, the other must also be on it, due to the fifth condition. Since the sixth condition precludes P from being a representative, Q, R, and S must all be on the committee.

Mold #4: If there are two tenants on the committee, and they are F and K, the third condition dictates that Q must also be on the committee.

Mold #5: If there are two tenants on the committee, and they are G and K, we cannot infer anything about the three homeowner representatives.

12. (A) violates the fourth condition
    (B) violates the fifth condition
    (C) violates the first condition
    (D) Correct – see mold #1
    (E) violates the sixth condition

13. (A) the fifth condition is triggered, which would lead to four tenants
    (B) the fifth condition is triggered, which would lead to four tenants
    (C) Correct – see mold #1
    (D) the fifth condition is triggered, which would lead to four tenants
    (E) the fourth condition is triggered, which would lead to four tenants

14. **(E)** This could only be true of mold #3, and choice E is therefore correct.

15. **(B)** This could only be true of mold #4, choice B is therefore correct.

16. **(A)** For this question, we can narrow our focus to molds #1, #2, and #4. G cannot be the chairperson in any of these scenarios, since G isn't selected in the scenario with two homeowners (mold #4). Thus, choice A is correct.

17. **(C)** This is only true of mold #3, and we know that either J or M must be the chairperson. Therefore, choice C is correct.

18. **(A)** This could only be true of mold #1 or mold #2. Mold #2 proves choice A to be correct.

19. We can check the pairs against our molds and eliminate the incorrect answers.
    (A) see molds #1, #3, and #5
    (B) see mold #4
    (C) Correct – this is true of mold #1, due to the third condition
    (D) see molds #2, #4, and #5
    (E) see mold #2

Questions 20-24

Setup:
- four apprentices: L M N O
- initially assigned respectively to projects: Q R S T
- two reassignments of apprentices to projects will be made
- each reassignment will be according to a different plan

Plans:

#1: Q ⟷ S R ⟷ T

#2: S ⟷ T

#3: L ⟷ M

Overview:
Since only two reassignments are to be made, and they must be made according to different plans, there are six different reassignment patterns:
1 followed by 2
1 followed by 3
2 followed by 1
2 followed by 3
3 followed by 1
3 followed by 2

We can chart out these patterns, thus eliminating all the uncertainty in the game.

Projects	Q	R	S	T
Initial	L	M	N	O
1	N	O	L	M
2	N	O	M	L
1	N	O	L	M
3	N	O	M	L
2	L	M	O	N
1	O	N	L	M
2	L	M	O	N
3	M	L	O	N
3	M	L	N	O
1	N	O	M	L
3	M	L	N	O
2	M	L	O	N

20. **(E)** This is true of the 2-3 and the 3-2 patterns. In both cases, O is assigned to project S after the second reassignment, and choice E is therefore correct.

21. **(E)** Checking the choices against the patterns reveals that only choice E could be true. N and O remain assigned to the same projects after one reassignment if the first reassignment is made according to plan 3.

22. **(A)** This is true of the following three patterns: 2-3, 3-1, and 3-2. Only choice A could be true (after the first reassignment according to the 2-3 pattern), and it is therefore correct.

23. **(B)** Comparing the choices to the acceptable patterns reveals that only B could be true.

24. **(A)** We can narrow our focus to the 1-2 and 1-3 patterns for this question. In either case, L is assigned to project T after the second reassignment, and choice A is therefore correct.

Questions 1-6

Setup:
- six students: G H J S T U
- exactly one lesson per student
- one lesson per day
- six consecutive days

Conditions:
#1: J – H
#2: S – U
#3: **G __ __ S** (boxed)
#4: $\mathbf{J_1}$ **or** $\mathbf{J_3}$

Overview:
Combining the second and third conditions gives the following: G _ _ S – U. Since these variables span at least five slots, we must place G in either the first or the second slot. When G is placed first, the fourth condition dictates the J must be placed third. When G is placed second, J can be placed either first or third. We can set up three molds to efficiently represent these options, for a total of five unique solutions.

	1	2	3	4	5	6
#1	G	T	J	S	H|U	U|H
#2	J	G	H|T	T|H	S	U
#3	T	G	J	H	S	U

Mold #1: The first two conditions stipulate that H and U must occupy the last two slots, leaving T to occupy the second slot.

Mold #2: The second condition dictates that we place U sixth, leaving H and T to occupy the second and third slots, in either order.

Mold #3: The second condition dictates that we place U sixth, and the first condition forces us to place H fourth, leaving T to occupy the first slot.

1. **(E)** This triggers the first mold, and we know that U must be scheduled for the sixth day. Thus, choice E is correct.

2. **(B)** A glance at our molds reveals that H is the only variable which meets this criteria (mold #1 and mold #2). Therefore, choice B is correct.

3. **(C)** According to our molds, only G or T could occupy the second slot, and choice C is thus correct.

4. **(B)** This could only be true of the second mold, and choice B is correct.

5. **(C)** This is true of mold #1 and mold #3. Checking the choices against the two molds leaves C as the correct answer (under mold #1).

6. **(D)** Our molds reveal that T could be scheduled for any slot aside from the last two. Thus, choice D is correct.

Questions 7-11

Setup:
- five children (C): F G H J K
- four adults (A): Q R S T
- three groups: 1 2 3

Conditions:
#1: each canoe ⟶ 1^+ A

#2: 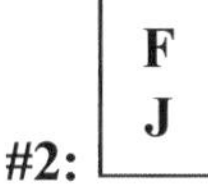

#3: 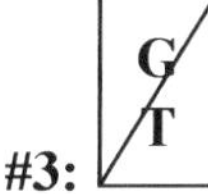

#4: 

#5: $\sim H_2$ and $\sim T_2$

Overview:
Every question supplies an additional condition, so we can keep our diagram sparse and head to the questions.

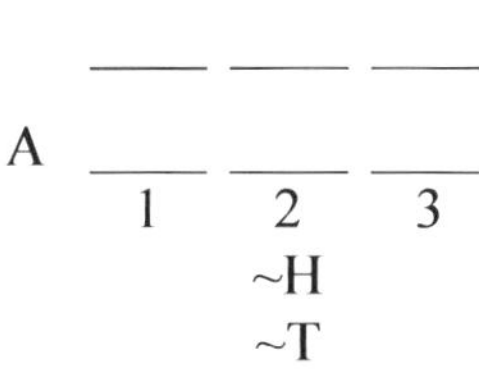

7. The second condition dictates that J must also be assigned to group 1. Since group 1 hasn't yet been assigned an adult, H cannot be assigned to it. Combining this with the fifth condition, we know that H must be assigned to group 3. Applying the fourth condition, we know that R cannot be assigned to group 3. We can eliminate the incorrect choices using the conditions in conjunction with our deductions.

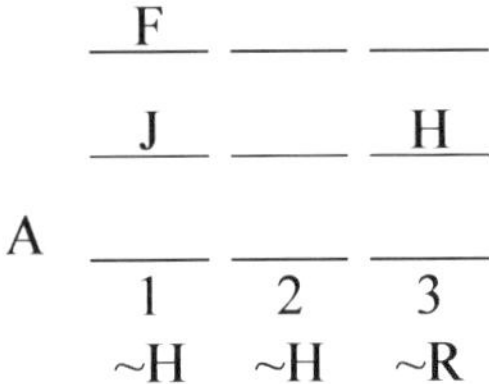

(A) violates the first condition
(B) violates the fourth condition
(C) violates the second condition
(D) group 1 only has one remaining slot
(E) Correct – R would have to be assigned to group 1 (fourth condition), leaving T to fill the adult slot in group 3

8. **(A)** Due to the second condition, J must also be assigned to group 3. Since H cannot be assigned to group 2 (fifth condition), it must be assigned to group 1. The fourth condition forces us to assign R to group 2, and the fifth condition forces us to assign T to group 1. Due to the third condition, G must be assigned to group 2, leaving K and Q to fill the remaining two slots. Only choice A must be true, and it is therefore correct.

	K|Q	Q|K	J
	H	G	F
A	T	R	S
	1	2	3
	~R	~H	~R

9. **(E)** Since group 3 hasn't yet been assigned an adult, H cannot be assigned to it. The fifth condition forces us to assign H to group 1. The third and fifth conditions dictate that we must assign T to group 1. Group 2 is the only one of the three with two or more slots remaining, and the second condition stipulates that we must assign F and J to it. Only choice E must be true, and it is therefore correct.

		F	G
	H	J	K
A	T		
	1	2	3
	~R	~H	~H
		~T	~T

10. **(D)** Since group 2 still requires an adult (first condition), and T cannot be assigned to it (fifth condition), we must assign R to group 2. T must be assigned to either group 1 or group 3, and choice D, therefore, must be false.

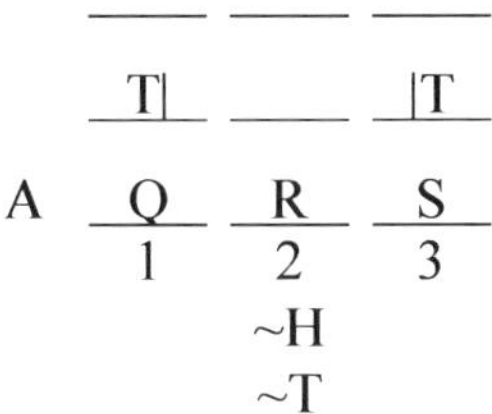

11. **(B)** Combining this with the fifth condition, we know that H must be assigned to group 3. The third and fifth conditions dictate that T must be assigned to group 3. Since only group 2 has two slots remaining for children, the second condition dictates that we assign both F and J to it. The remaining adults (Q, R, and S) can be assigned in three different ways to groups 1 and 2. Only choice B must be true, and it is therefore correct.

	1	2	3
	G	F	H
		J	K
A			T
		~H ~T	

Questions 12-17

Setup:

- Three people: L M N
- each buy at least one kind of food
- foods: F H P S

Conditions:

#1: each person buys no more than one portion of each kind

#2: 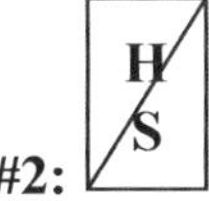

#3: 1^+ H and 1^+ P

#4: S_M

#5: F_N

#6: $\sim P_L$ and $\sim P_N$

#7: M ≠ N

Overview:
The conditions give us enough information to make some deductions regarding the number of items that each person purchases. Due to the second and sixth conditions, L can purchase a maximum of two kinds of food. Combining the third and sixth conditions, we know that M must buy P. Combining the fourth, fifth, sixth, and seventh conditions, we can deduce that M purchases two kinds and that N purchases no more than two kinds.

```
------  _P_  --|H--

_H|_   _S_   _F_
 L      M ≠  N
~P     ~H    ~P
       ~F
```

12. **(D)** As we inferred, M must buy P, and choice D is therefore correct.

13. **(B)** To minimize the number of purchased items, we must assign H to L (L must purchase at least one item). This solution satisfies all the conditions, and choice B is thus correct.

```
       _P_

_H_   _S_   _F_
 L     M     N
```

14. **(B)** Since each person can purchase a maximum of two items, the maximum that they could spend in total is $6, and choice B is correct.

15. **(A)** Due to the second and sixth conditions, L must purchase one of H and S along with F. Therefore, choice A is correct.

```
_H|S_  _P_  ------

_F_    _S_   _F_
 L      M     N
```

16. **(C)** Applying the second condition, we know that L does not buy H. Since one of L and N must buy H (third condition), we can deduce that N buys H. Choice C is therefore correct.

```
------  _P_  _H_

_S_    _S_   _F_
 L      M     N
~P
~H
```

17. **(C)** This question prompts us to reconsider our numerical deductions, but other than that, our direct placement of variables remains valid. From the seventh condition, we can deduce two possible allocations of items between M and N respectively: 3, 1 and 2, 2. Due to the sixth condition, L can purchase at a maximum F, H, and S. The only uncertainty remaining is which of M and N purchases H, and there are two acceptable solutions that maximize the number of purchased items. The maximum number of items purchased is seven, and choice C is therefore correct.

F	H				F		
H	P				H	P	H
S	S	F	or		S	S	F
L	M	N			L	M	N

Questions 18-24

Setup:

- four flasks: 1 2 3 4
- original respective colors: R B G O
- experiment consists of emptying one flask into another

Conditions:

#1: product of an experiment cannot be used in further experiments
#2: 1 + 2 ⟶ R
#3: 2 + 3 ⟶ O
#4: 1 + 3 ⟶ B; 3 + 4 ⟶ B
#5: 1 + 4 ⟶ G; 2 + 4 ⟶ G

Overview:
The first condition combined with the setup condition that there are four flasks limits the number of experiments to two. Since two flasks are mixed completely in one experiment, the second experiment (if there is one), must consist of the remaining two flasks. We can chart out the six possible initial experiments, and follow each scenario to its logical completion, assuming two experiments are performed.

Flasks:	1	2	3	4
Colors:	R	B	G	O

	Experiment 1	Product	Remaining	Experiment 2	Products
#1	1 + 2	R	G, O	3 + 4	R, B
#2	1 + 4	G	B, G	2 + 3	G, O
#3	1 + 3	B	B, O	2 + 4	B, G
#4	3 + 4	B	R, B	1 + 2	B, R
#5	2 + 3	O	R, O	1 + 4	O, G
#6	2 + 4	G	R, G	1 + 3	G, B

Note that there are only three unique outcomes following two experiments, since the end products are solely determined by which experiments are performed, not the order in which they are performed.

18. **(D)** We can compare the answer choices to our chart, and only choice D matches with one of the solutions (#6).

19. **(C)** Checking the choices against the chart reveals that only C could be true (solutions #1 and #4).

20. **(B)** This could only be true of solutions #2 and #3. Thus, choice B is correct (solution #2).

21. **(A)** Scanning the chart reveals that this is only true of solution #2. Therefore, we know that the other two flasks both contain green chemicals, and choice A is correct.

22. **(E)** This scenario matches solutions #1 and #3. Thus, the only possible combinations for the second experiment are 3 & 4 and 2 & 4. Choice E is the only one that presents one of the pairs, and it is correct.

23. **(E)** This is true of solutions #2, #4, and #6. Thus, we know for certain that flask 4 was mixed with one of the other flasks, and choice E is correct.

24. **(D)** This is true of solutions #2 and #5. Thus, the other nonempty flask must contain a green chemical, and choice D is correct.

Questions 1-6

Setup:

- o eight consumers: F G H J K L M N
- o divided into exactly two 4-person groups
- o groups: 1 2

Conditions:

#1: 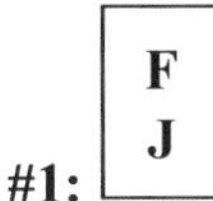

#2: 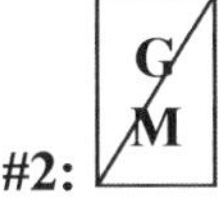

#3: $H_1 \longrightarrow L_1$; $L_2 \longrightarrow H_2$ (contrapositive)
#4: $N_2 \longrightarrow G_1$; $G_2 \longrightarrow N_1$ (contrapositive)

Overview:
The interaction of the first and second conditions allows us to create two distinct molds.

#1		
	____	____
	F	____
	J	H
	G|M	M|G
	1	2
	G←	N
	N←	G

#2		
	____	____
	____	F
	L	J
	G|M	M|G
	1	2
	G←	N
	N←	G

Mold #1: Placing the FJ piece in group 1 leaves too few slots for both H and L in group 1, so the third condition dictates that we place H in group 2.

Mold #2: Placing the FJ piece in group 2 leaves too few slots for both H and L in group 2, so the contrapositive of the third condition dictates that we place L in group 1.

1. (A) violates the third condition
   (B) violates the first condition
   (C) violates the fourth condition (N is in group 2)
   (D) Correct
   (E) violates the second condition

2. **(B)** Plugging this information into our two molds yields two diagrams. Using the first mold, the fourth condition dictates that we place G in the first group. In either case, H must be in group 2, and choice B is therefore correct.

<table>
<tr><td>L</td><td>K</td><td></td><td>K</td><td>H</td></tr>
<tr><td>F</td><td>N</td><td></td><td>N</td><td>F</td></tr>
<tr><td>J</td><td>H</td><td></td><td>L</td><td>J</td></tr>
<tr><td>G</td><td>M</td><td>or</td><td>G|M</td><td>M|G</td></tr>
<tr><td>1</td><td>2</td><td></td><td>1</td><td>2</td></tr>
</table>

3. **(C)** We can recycle our second diagram for question number two to eliminate the incorrect answer choices. Only choice C must be true of this diagram, and it is thus correct.

4. **(E)** This could only be true of the first mold. After placing G, L, and M into their respective groups, only the placement of K and N is uncertain. Since K is the only one of the two listed in the choices, E is correct.

<table>
<tr><td>K|N</td><td>N|K</td></tr>
<tr><td>F</td><td>L</td></tr>
<tr><td>J</td><td>H</td></tr>
<tr><td>G</td><td>M</td></tr>
<tr><td>1</td><td>2</td></tr>
</table>

5. (A) see #4
   (B) Correct – the first, second, and third conditions interact in such a way that group 1 would need five slots to accommodate F, H, J, L, and one of G and M
   (C) see the first diagram for #2
   (D) could be true of mold #2
   (E) could be true of mold #2

6. **(D)** This could only be true of the first mold. After placing L in group 2, we can explore the possible placements of K and N. When N is in group 2, the fourth condition dictates that we assign G to group 1. When N is in group 1, G could be assigned to either group. Only choice D is incompatible with these two diagrams, and it is therefore correct.

<table>
<tr><td>K</td><td>N</td><td></td><td>N</td><td>K</td></tr>
<tr><td>F</td><td>H</td><td></td><td>F</td><td>H</td></tr>
<tr><td>J</td><td>L</td><td></td><td>J</td><td>L</td></tr>
<tr><td>G</td><td>M</td><td>or</td><td>G|M</td><td>M|G</td></tr>
<tr><td>1</td><td>2</td><td></td><td>1</td><td>2</td></tr>
</table>

Questions 7-11

Setup:
- five people: H I K N V
- one contestant per day
- five consecutive days: M T W Th F

Conditions:
#1: ~N_M
#2: H_M ⟶ N_F; ~N_F ⟶ ~H_M (contrapositive)
#3: N_T ⟶ I_M; ~I_M ⟶ ~N_T (contrapositive)
#4: [VK]

Overview:
From the fourth condition, we can infer that V cannot be scheduled on Friday and that N cannot be scheduled on Monday.

M	T	W	Th	F
~N				~V
~K				
H⟶				⟶N
I⟵	N			

7. **(E)** As we inferred, V cannot be scheduled for Friday, and choice E is correct.

8. **(E)** This question gives us another piece to place: [HI]. Accordingly, H cannot be scheduled for Friday. The HI piece cannot occupy the Tuesday and Wednesday slots, since the VK piece would have to occupy the Thursday and Friday slots, forcing N to violate the first condition. H can be placed Monday, Wednesday, or Thursday, as proved by the following diagrams. Therefore, choice E is correct.

H	I	V	K	N
V	K	H	I	N
V	K	N	H	I
M	T	W	Th	F

9. **(C)** Applying the fourth condition, we know that V must be scheduled for Tuesday. With H, I, and N left to place, the first condition dictates that one of H and I must fill the Monday slot. If H is scheduled for Monday, the second condition is triggered, and N must be scheduled for Friday, leaving I to occupy the Thursday slot. If I is scheduled for Monday, H and N must fill the Thursday and Friday slots, in either order. Only choice C could be true, and it is therefore correct.

H	V	K	I	N
I	V	K	H|N	N|H
M	T	W	Th	F

10. **(C)** Applying the fourth condition, we must assign V to the Thursday slot. The contrapositive of the second condition precludes H form being scheduled on Monday. The first condition also precludes N from occupying the Monday slot, we must assign it to I. H and N must occupy the Tuesday and Wednesday slots, in either order. Thus, choice C is correct.

I	H|N	N|H	V	K
M	T	W	Th	F

11. **(C)** With I scheduled for the middle slot, we must decide where to place the VK piece. If we placed it in the Thursday and Friday slots, the second condition would preclude H from being scheduled for Monday. Since N cannot be scheduled for Monday (first condition), this scenario is not acceptable. If we place the VK piece in the Monday and Tuesday slots, H and N must occupy the Thursday and Friday slots, in either order. Only choice C must be true, and it is therefore correct.

V	K	I	H|N	N|H
M	T	W	Th	F

Questions 12-17

Setup:

- six of eight lectures
- lectures: F H L N O P S W
- three days: 1 2 3
- two lectures each day: M A

Conditions:
#1: O ⟶ O_2
#2: ~S_{PM} and ~W_{PM}

#3: 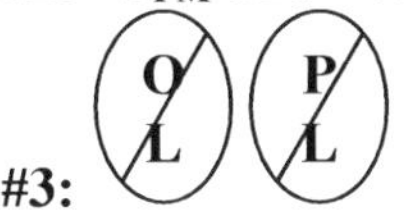

#4: P_1 ⟶ (F H)$_2$; P_2 ⟶ (F H)$_3$

Overview:
The fact that five of the six questions impose additional conditions is a big clue that this game doesn't have any major upfront deductions.

A ____ ____ ____ ~S ~W

M ____ ____ ____
1 2 3
~O ~O

12. (A) violates the third condition
    (B) Correct
    (C) violates the first condition
    (D) violates the second condition
    (E) violates the fourth condition

13. Applying the third condition, we know that O is not assigned to any of the slots. We can use the other conditions to eliminate the incorrect choices.

    (A) Correct – see the following diagram

    A H L F

    M N S P
    1 2 3

    (B) violates the first condition
    (C) violates the fourth condition
    (D) violates the second condition
    (E) violates the second condition

14. **(E)** Applying the third condition, we know that O cannot be assigned to any of the slots. Since one of S and W must be given (there must be six lectures), the second condition dictates that S or W must occupy the morning slot of day 1. Since only S is listed among the choices, E is correct.

```
A  ____  ____  ____

M  S|W    L     H
    1     2     3
   ~O    ~O    ~O
         ~P
```

15. **(D)** Applying the third condition, we know that P cannot be given on the third day. The fourth condition, in combination with the O and L assignments, precludes P from being assigned to either of the first two days. Thus, choice D is correct.

```
A  ____  ____  ____

M  S|W    O     L
    1     2     3
   ~P    ~P    ~P
```

16. **(B)** Since the difference between morning and afternoon only affects S and W, and the question dictates that both S and W must be scheduled, we can focus on assigning the lectures to their respective days without worrying about what time of day each lecture is given. Since F won't be given, the fourth condition stipulates that we must assign P to day 3. With O and L occupying slots on day 2 and day 3, the third condition forces L to be given on day 1. Thus, choice B is correct.

```
____  ____  ____

 L     O     P
 1     2     3
      ~L    ~L
```

17. **(E)** Combining this information with the second condition reveals that neither S nor W will be scheduled for any of the three days. Since all three morning slots are filled, O must occupy the afternoon slot on Tuesday, due to the first condition. F and H cannot be given, so the fourth condition forces us to assign P to the afternoon slot on day 3, leaving N to fill the afternoon slot on day 1. The third condition precludes L from being assigned to day 3. L must be assigned to either day 1 or day 2, and choice E is the only one that could be true.

```
A   N    O    P              A   N    O    P

M   L   F|H  H|F      or     M  F|H   L   H|F
    1    2    3                  1    2    3
             ~L                            ~L
```

Questions 18-24

Setup:
- five clans: N O P S T
- exactly three of the five clans participates each year

Conditions:

#1: each clan ⟶ 1^{+} in two consecutive years

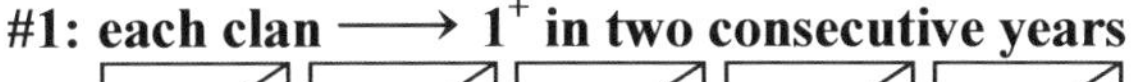

#2:

#3: one cycle ⟶ each clan participates three times

#4: one cycle ⟶ each clan ≤ 3 times

Overview:
From the third condition and the setup condition that there are five clans, we can infer that one cycle is comprised of fifteen clan participations. Since every clan must participate at least once in any two consecutive years (first condition), we can deduce a limited number of acceptable year combinations for any particular clan.

1st	2nd	3rd
1	3	5
1	2	4
1	3	4
2	3	5
2	4	5

The fact that this chart contains three of each number is not a coincidence. If we try to construct a sample solution with more than one clan participating in the same set of three years, we'll see that it results in a contradiction of the conditions. What follows are test solutions with both N and O participating in the first, third, and fifth years. Applying different patterns to the next two clans leads to a scenario in which the final clan to be assigned has to fill two slots during one particular year.

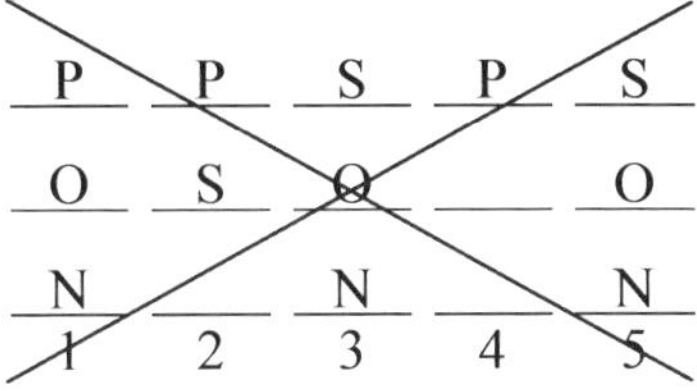

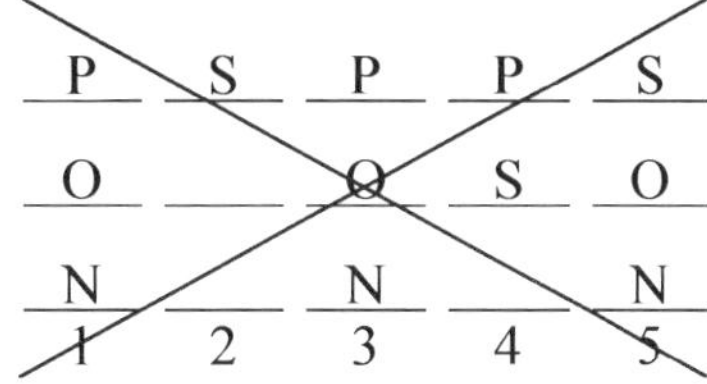

Since the conditions do not reference any of the clans in particular, they are completely interchangeable with one another. By assigning a letter to each combination, we can use the acceptable combinations in our table to construct a general solution, to which all specific solutions will conform.

C	D	C	C	E
B	B	D	B	D
A	E	A	E	A
1	2	3	4	5

18. **(E)** Since S and T are not participating in the first year, they must be participating in the second year. S and T correspond to letters D and E in our general solution. Thus, choice E is correct.

19. (A) violates the second condition
    (B) violates the second condition
    (C) Correct – this is true of A and C in our general solution
    (D) only one clan can fulfill the 1st, 3rd, 5th pattern
    (E) only one clan can fulfill the 1st, 3rd, 5th pattern

20. **(A)** As we inferred, one cycle is comprised of fifteen clan participations. Since three clans participate each year, one cycle lasts five years. Therefore, choice A is correct.

21. **(A)** Comparing the answer choices to our general solution reveals that only choice A must be true. Letters A and C in the diagram illustrate this concept. Choices B through E are not only incorrect, but each one of them must be false.

22. **(D)** A glance at our combination table reveals that any clan not participating in the first year must participate in both the second and fifth years. Thus, choice D is correct. We cannot infer anything concrete about N and O (choices A through C), since we don't know which pattern either of these two clans follows.

N				
O	P			P
S	T			T
1	2	3	4	5

23. **(C)** Applying the same logic as in the previous question, we know that both P and S participate in the second and fifth years. Since the question specifies that P also participates in the fourth year, the first condition precludes it from participating in the third year. Thus, choice C is correct.

N				
O	P		P	P
T	S		O	S
1	2	3	4	5
		~P		

24. **(E)** Similar to the previous two questions, we're given the three clans that participate in the first year. Our chart tells us that both P and T must participate in each of the second and fifth years. Only choice E contains both P and T, and it is therefore correct.

N		O		
O	P	S		P
S	T	T		T
1	2	3	4	5

Questions 1-6

Setup:
- five employees: F G H K L
- each employee holds exactly one position
- three positions: P M T
- only the president is not supervised
- other positions are supervised by exactly one employee (president or manager)
- each supervised employee holds a different position than his or her supervisor

Conditions:
#1: exactly one P
#2: P supervises 1^+ M
#3: each M supervises 1^+ employee
#4: F does not supervise any employee
#5: G supervises exactly two employees

Overview:
With five employees in total, we can make some inferences regarding the allocation of employees to positions. The first condition leaves four employees to allocate between manager and technician positions. Due to the second condition, there must be at least one manager. There cannot be three managers, since this would violate the third condition. Therefore, the acceptable allocations are the following:

P	M	T
1	2	2
1	1	3

The fourth condition tells us that F is a technician, and the fifth condition dictates that G must be either the president or a manager. Combining these with our allocations allows us to create three distinct molds.

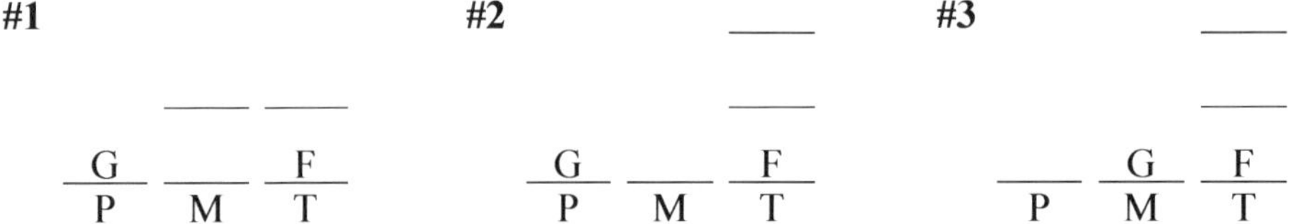

Note that G cannot be a manager under the first allocation since the fifth condition would leave no technician for the second manager to supervise, which would violate the third condition.

1. (A) does not match either of the acceptable allocations
   (B) Correct
   (C) violates the fourth condition
   (D) violates the first condition
   (E) does not match either of the acceptable allocations

2. **(A)** This question directly tests our command of the allocations. As we inferred, there can be at most three technicians, and choice A is therefore correct.

3. **(E)** The fourth condition allows us to eliminate choices A and B. If there are two managers, we know that G must be the president (third and fifth conditions). We can thus eliminate choices C and D, leaving E as the correct answer.

```
     K   H
 G   L   F
 P   M   T
```

4. (A) there must be two or three technicians
   (B) Correct – see mold #1
   (C) only the president is not supervised (setup conditions), and there is exactly one president (first condition)
   (D) violates the third condition
   (E) violates the third condition

5. **(D)** Under the 1, 2, 2 allocation, the president cannot supervise any technicians, since each manager supervises one technician. Thus, this scenario could only happen under the 1, 1, 3 allocation, and choice D is correct.

6. **(C)** Since K supervises other employees, K must be either the president or a manager. G and K cannot both be managers, as we have previously deduced that G cannot be a manager under the 1, 2, 2 allocation. Therefore, one of G and K must be the president, and choice C is correct.

```
                                L
      L|M  M|L                  M
 G    K    F     or    G|K  K|G  F
 P    M    T           P    M    T
```

Questions 7-12

Setup:
- two pieces of china (C): M P
- two pieces of glassware (G): W J
- three utensils: F K S
- [CC] [GG] [UUU]

Conditions:
#1: each object ⟶ exactly once
#2: C – G – U or U – G – C
#3: [FKS] or [KFS] or [KSF]; [MP]
#4: no two objects at the same time

Overview:
Combining the second and third conditions allows us to create six distinct molds, which works out to twelve unique solutions. To conserve space, we won't draw out each solution for the two orderings of the pieces of glassware.

	1	2	3	4	5	6	7
#1	M	P	J|W	W|J	F	K	S
#2	M	P	J|W	W|J	K	F	S
#3	M	P	J|W	W|J	K	S	F
#4	F	K	S	J|W	W|J	M	P
#5	K	F	S	J|W	W|J	M	P
#6	K	S	F	J|W	W|J	M	P

7. (A) see mold #4
   (B) see mold #5
   (C) see the first, second, and third molds
   (D) see the first, second, and third molds
   (E) Correct – with M and P occupying the second and third slots, the first slot would have to be occupied by an object of one of the other two types, which violates the setup condition that objects of the same type are washed consecutively

8. **(A)** Checking the choices against our molds reveals that only choice A could be true (mold #4), and it is therefore correct.

9. (A) see mold #5
   (B) Correct – violates the third condition
   (C) see mold #4
   (D) see mold #4
   (E) see the first, second, and third molds

10. **(C)** According to our molds, K can be placed first, second, fifth, or sixth. Choice C is thus correct.

11. **(E)** For this question, we can narrow our focus to mold #3 and mold #6. The only one of the choices that can be true is E, and it is therefore correct.

12. **(A)** This could only happen under mold #2 or mold #3. Choice A must, therefore, be false.

Questions 13-18

Setup:
- ten birds classified as shown
- breeder exhibits pairs consisting of one male and one female of the same kind
- at most two pairs are exhibited at a time
- the remaining birds are distributed between two cages

Conditions:
#1: each cage ≤ 4 birds
#2: birds of the same type and same sex cannot be caged together
#3: $J_E \longrightarrow S_C$; $S_E \longrightarrow J_C$ (contrapositive)
$W_E \longrightarrow S_C$; $S_E \longrightarrow W_C$ (contrapositive)

Overview:
Combining the second condition with the fact that there are two cages, we can infer that one of the male parakeets is exhibited. Since each exhibited bird must be paired with a bird of the same type and the opposite sex (setup conditions), one of the female parakeets must also be exhibited. We can use the setup conditions along with the first condition to establish three acceptable allocations of birds.

Exhibit	Exhibit	Cage	Cage
2	2	2	4
2	2	3	3
2	–	4	4

13. (A) violates the second condition (J and K)
    (B) violates the third condition
    (C) violates the second condition (T and W)
    (D) Correct
    (E) is not an acceptable allocation of birds

14. **(D)** Since we have inferred that a pair of parakeets must be exhibited, we can eliminate choices A and C. Choices B and E both violate the third condition, leaving, D as the correct answer.

15. **(D)** S is the only remaining male parakeet, so it must be exhibited. Applying the contrapositive of the third condition, we know that J cannot be exhibited. Therefore, choice D is correct.

16. **(D)** With T assigned to one of the cages, W must be exhibited, since at least one parakeet pair has to be exhibited. The male parakeet to be paired with W cannot be S, due to the third condition. Therefore, it must be R, and choice D is correct.

17. **(B)** This question directly tests our inference regarding a parakeet pair being exhibited. Choice B must be false, and it is correct.

18. **(E)** S must be paired with T, since the third condition precludes both S and W from being exhibited. Since W must be assigned to a cage, none of the other parakeets can be exhibited (only males remain), and both Q and R must be caged. Thus, choice E is correct.

<u>Questions 19-24</u>

Setup:
- four seasons: F W Sp Su
- two children: N O
- each will participate in exactly one of five sports during each season
- sports: H K M R V

Conditions:
#1: each child ⟶ exactly four different sports
#2: F ⟶ M, R, or V
#3: W ⟶ H or V
#4: Sp ⟶ K, M, R, or V
#5: Su ⟶ K, M, or V
#6: OF ≠ NF, OW ≠ NW, etc.
#7: V_{OSu}

Overview:
We can deduce from the first, third, and seventh conditions that Otto plays hockey in the winter. Accordingly, the third and sixth conditions dictate that Nikki must play volleyball in the winter. From the sixth and seventh conditions, we know that Nikki must participate in one of kayaking and volleyball during the summer. Since both children are participating in volleyball (Otto in the summer and Nikki in the winter), the second and sixth conditions dictate that each of Otto and Nikki participate in one of mountaineering and running.

```
O  _R|M_  _H_  ____  _V_    H K M R V (one out)

N  _M|R_  _V_  ____  _K|M_  H K M R V (one out)
     F     W    Sp    Su
     M     H    K     K
     R     V    M     M
     V          R     V
                V
```

19. **(B)** As we inferred, Nikki's winter sport must be volleyball, and choice B is correct.

20. **(A)** Since the children can only participate in hockey during the winter (third condition), and Otto participates in hockey during that season, the sixth condition precludes Nikki from participating in hockey. Thus, choice A is correct.

21. **(C)** Applying this information to our diagram, we know that Otto's fall sport is mountaineering, due to the sixth condition. This is the only thing that must be true, since Otto's and Nikki's spring sports are both undetermined. Therefore, choice C is correct.

```
O  _M_  _H_  _R|K_  _V_

N  _R_  _V_  _M|K_  _K|M_
    F    W    Sp     Su
```

22. **(B)** Comparing the answer choices to our initial inferences and diagram reveals that only choice B could be true. Nikki's spring sport would be kayaking.

23. **(B)** This condition sets off a chain of inferences. Since Otto only has two options for fall, his fall sport must be mountaineering. The sixth condition dictates that Nikki's fall sport must be running. We have previously inferred (in number twenty) that Nikki cannot participate in hockey, so her spring and summer sports must be kayaking and mountaineering, in either order. Thus, choice B must be false.

```
O  _M_  _H_  _K_    _V_

N  _R_  _V_  _M|K_  _K|M_
    F    W    Sp     Su
```

24. We can use our inferences and diagram to disprove the incorrect choices.

(A) Otto's fall sport would also be running, violating the first condition
(B) Otto's fall sport would also be running, violating the first condition
(C) Correct – see the following diagram

O	M	H	K|R	V
N	R	V	M	K
	F	W	Sp	Su

(D) Nikki's fall sport would also be mountaineering, violating the sixth condition
(E) Nikki and Otto would both participate in running in the fall, violating the sixth condition

Questions 1-5

Setup:
- six students: H J K R S T
- speeches delivered one at a time, consecutively

Conditions:

#1:  **in any order**

#2: 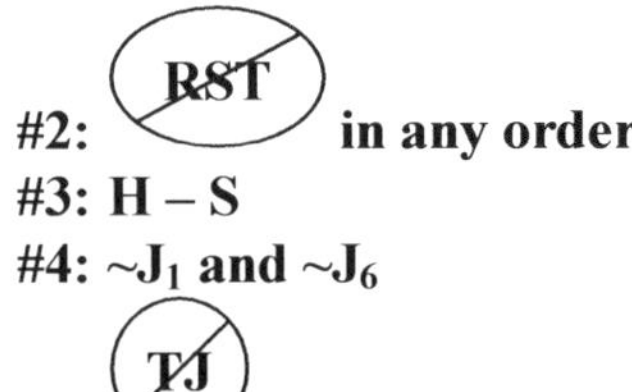 **in any order**

#3: H – S

#4: ~J_1 and ~J_6

#5:

Overview:
The first, second, and fifth conditions don't allow us to make any concrete deductions as far as our sketch. We can deduce from the third condition that H cannot be last, and S cannot be first.

1	2	3	4	5	6
~J					~J
~S					~H

1. (A) violates the second condition
   (B) violates the fourth condition
   (C) violates the fifth condition
   (D) Correct
   (E) violates the third condition

2. **(B)** Combining this with the fourth and fifth conditions, we know that J must be fifth. Therefore, choice B is correct.

		T		J	
1	2	3	4	5	6
~J	~J		~J		~J

3. **(C)** Applying the fourth and fifth conditions, we know that J must be placed second. Due to the third condition, H must occupy the first slot. The second condition precludes R from occupying the fifth slot, so K must be placed there, leaving R to fill the sixth slot. Thus, choice C must be true.

H	J	S	T	K	R
1	2	3	4	5	6
~J				~J	~J
				~R	

4. **(A)** Due to the third condition, S must be sixth. Since T and J cannot occupy consecutive slots, they must fill the second and fourth slots, in either order. This leaves R to occupy the third slot, and choice A is therefore correct.

K	J|T	R	T|J	H	S
1	2	3	4	5	6

5. **(D)** Combining this with the third condition, we have the following chain: H – SRK.

From the second condition, we know that T cannot precede this piece. We can split up J and T (fifth condition) in two different ways: flanking H or flanking the SRK piece. J and T cannot flank both H and the SRK piece since this would violate the fourth condition. Only choice D could be true, and it is correct.

T	H	J	S	R	K
H	J	S	R	K	T
1	2	3	4	5	6

6. **(A)** We haven't placed K third in any of the previous questions. From the fourth condition, we can deduce that J must be second, fourth, or fifth. Each of these options presents a potential violation of the first condition, and choice A completes the violation. With H fourth, J could only be second or fifth, violating the first condition either way. Therefore, choice A is correct.

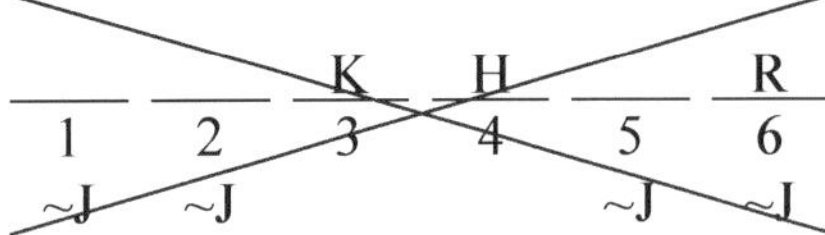

Questions 7-13

Setup:
- o four detection areas: R S T U
- o each detection area is circular and falls within Zendu
- o R intersects T
- o S intersects T
- o R does not intersect S
- o U is completely within R and completely within T
- o four planes: J K L M

Conditions:
#1: each plane is in 1^+ area
#2: J is in S; K and J are not in the same area
#3: L and M are not in the same area
#4: M is in exactly one area

Overview:
From the second condition, we can deduce that K must be in either R or T (or both). The fourth condition precludes M from being in area U, since area U is within both R and T. Combining the setup conditions yields the following diagram.

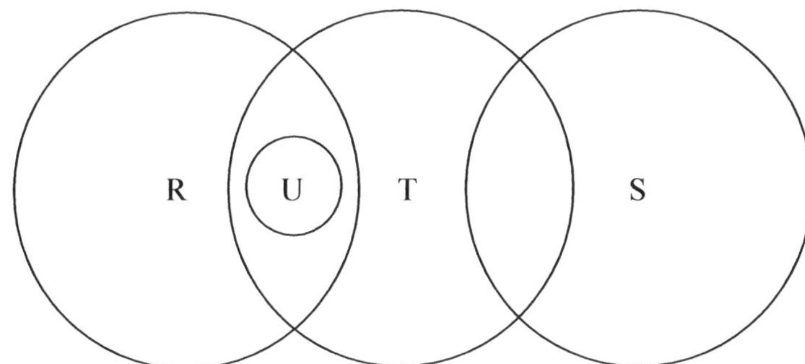

7. (A) violates the first condition (K is not within any of the areas)
   (B) violates the second condition
   (C) violates the fourth condition; since M is in U, it is also in R and T
   (D) Correct
   (E) violates the second condition

8. **(A)** K could be in one of two pairs of areas: R and T or S and T. In either case, since K is within T, the second condition precludes J from being in T, and choice A is correct.

9. **(E)** To answer this question, we can try placing each plane in area T and see if doing so leads to any of the conditions being contradicted.

   J: would be in the overlapping area of S and T; K would have to be in R
   K: J would be in the portion of S that doesn't overlap area T
   L: M would be in either R or S
   M: L would be in either R or S

   Placing any of the variables in area T doesn't lead to any contradictions, and choice E is therefore correct.

10. **(E)** As we inferred, M cannot be within U (fourth condition), and choice E is correct.

11. **(D)** This question tests our ability to properly map out the conditions. Since areas S and U do not overlap, choice D is correct.

12. **(E)** Combining this with the fourth condition, we know that M is not within the overlapping portion of S and T. Applying the third condition, we can infer that L must be in either R or S, in a portion that doesn't overlap with T. Since L cannot be in an overlapping area, choice E is correct.

13. This could only happen if L is within area U. Since area U is within R and T, the third condition dictates that M must be in a portion of S that doesn't overlap area T. K could be in areas R, T, or U (second condition).

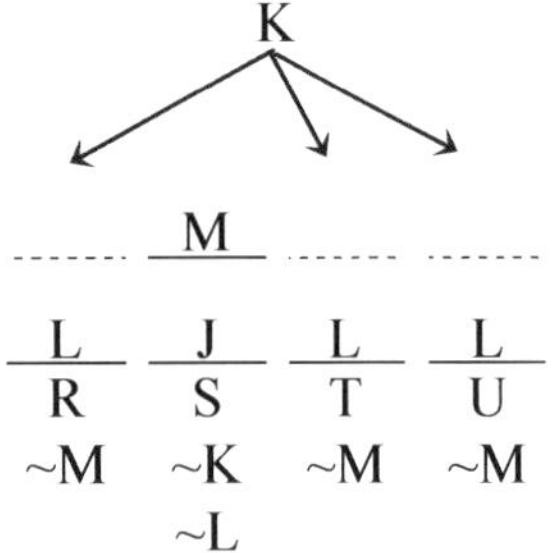

(A) Correct – J could be in the overlapping portion of S and T
(B) area S only overlaps with area T
(C) violates the second condition
(D) M must be in area S only
(E) M must be in area S only

Questions 14-19

Setup:
- four people: F G H J
- six days: M T W Th F S
- each day, exactly one person drives

Conditions:
#1: each person drives 1^+ day
#2: 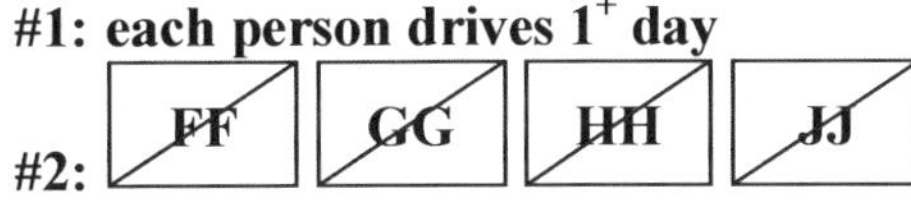

#3: ~F_M
#4: J_W or J_S (or both); J can also drive on other days
#5: $G_M \longrightarrow$ ~J_S; $J_S \longrightarrow$ ~G_M (contrapositive)

Overview:
Since the number of slots is greater than the number of people, at least one person will have to drive on more than one day. The following two allocations of days to drivers are possible:
3, 1, 1, 1
2, 2, 1, 1

We can also infer that if the fifth condition is triggered, J must drive on Wednesday, due to the fourth condition.

M	T	W	Th	F	S
~F					
G ⟶					~J

14. (A) violates the second condition
    (B) violates the fifth condition
    (C) violates the fourth condition
    (D) Correct
    (E) violates the first condition

15. (A) violates the fourth condition
    (B) this triggers the fifth condition, in turn violating the fourth condition
    (C) since J must also drive either Wednesday or Saturday (fourth condition), this would violate the second condition
    (D) this triggers the fifth condition; J would have to drive on Wednesday, but this would violate the second condition
    (E) Correct

16. **(C)** Due to the contrapositive of the fifth condition, we know that G doesn't drive on Monday. With J accounted for, and F precluded from that slot (third condition), the only person who can drive on Monday is H. Thus, choice C is correct.

H		J			J
M	T	W	Th	F	S
~F					
~G					

17. **(A)** Since G drives on exactly two days, this triggers the second allocation (2, 2, 1). Thus, choice A is correct. The fourth condition dictates that we place J on Wednesday. Due to the second condition, we also know that one of F and H must drive on each of Tuesday and Thursday.

G	F|H	J	F|H		G
M	T	W	Th	F	S
	~G		~G	~G	
	~J		~J		

(B) the fourth condition leaves this as a possibility
(C) H could drive on Tuesday and Friday
(D) the only person who cannot drive on Friday is G
(E) F could drive on Tuesday

18. **(B)** Choice B presents the same contradiction as number fifteen, choice D. GM triggers the fifth condition. The fourth condition dictates that J must drive on Wednesday, but this violates the second condition. Choice B is therefore correct.

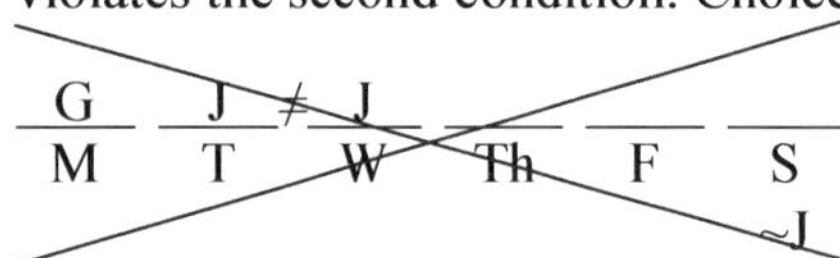

19. **(E)** Since F drives exactly twice, we can deduce the 2, 2, 1, 1 allocation. In combination with the third condition, the question prompts us to place two Fs in the last three slots. The second condition dictates that we place them in the Thursday and Saturday slots. Applying the fourth condition, we must place J in the Wednesday slot. Only choice E is compatible with this diagram, and it is therefore correct.

		J	F		F
M	T	W	Th	F	S
~F	~F	~F			

Questions 20-24

Setup:
- five experienced plumbers (E): F G J K M
- four inexperienced plumbers (I): R S T V
- four teams of exactly two plumbers each

Conditions:
#1: each plumber assigned to ≤ 1 team
#2: 1^+ E on each team

#3: 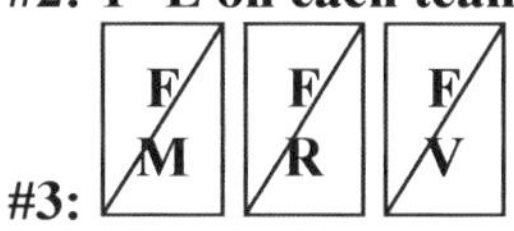

#4: T ⟶ 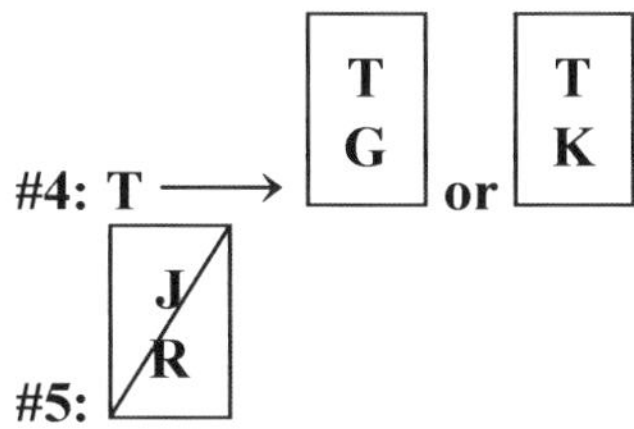

#5: J / R (crossed out)

Overview:
Combining the second, third, and fourth conditions reveals that if F is on one of the teams, F must be paired with either S or one of the other experienced plumbers (excluding M).

____ ____ ____ ____

E ____ ____ ____ ____ F G J K M

20. **(C)** As we inferred, the only inexperienced plumber F can be paired with is S, and choice C is correct.

21. (A) violates the third condition
    (B) violates the third condition
    (C) Correct
    (D) violates the fourth condition
    (E) violates the second condition

22. **(B)** Combining this information with the fourth condition, we have two possible pairings:
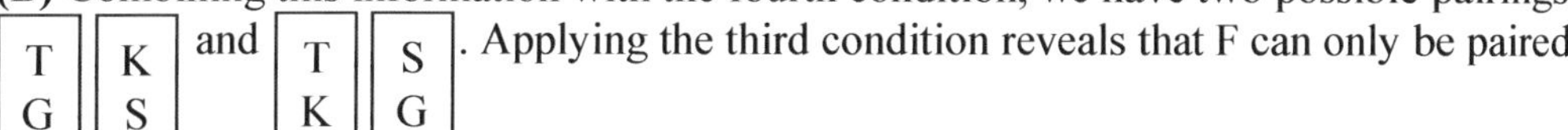

. Applying the third condition reveals that F can only be paired with J under this scenario, and choice B is correct.

23. **(A)** With G not assigned to any of the teams, we know that all eight of the other plumbers must be paired in teams, each team consisting of one experienced plumber and one inexperienced plumber. Applying the fourth condition, we know that T must be paired with K. Placing the remaining experienced plumbers directly into the diagram provides the strongest visible connection to the conditions. F cannot be paired with R or V (third condition), so F must be paired with S. J cannot be paired with R (fifth condition), so J must be paired with V. Choice A is therefore correct.

	S	V	T	R
E	F	J	K	M
	~R	~R		
	~V			

24. **(A)** For this question, we will directly place all the inexperienced plumbers into the diagram and apply the conditions. The fourth condition dictates that T be paired with K. Since R cannot be paired with G, and the third and fifth conditions preclude R from being paired with F or J, R must be paired with M. Since V cannot be paired with G, and the third condition precludes V from being paired with F, V must be paired with J. Only F and G are unassigned at this point, so one of them must be paired with S. Choice A is therefore correct.

I	R	S	T	V
E	M	F|G	K	J
	~F	~J		~F
	~J			~G
	~G			

Questions 1-6

Setup:

- o eight new students: R S T V W X Y Z
- o to be divided into three classes: 1 2 3
- o classes 1 and 2 will gain three new students
- o class 3 will gain two new students

Conditions:

#1: R_1

#2: S_3

#3: 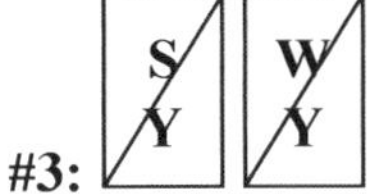

#4: 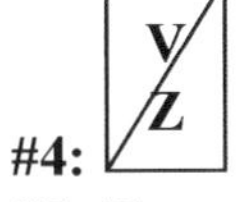

#5: $T_1 \longrightarrow Z_1$; $\sim Z_1 \longrightarrow \sim T_1$ (contrapositive)

Overview:

Building the conditional into our diagram, we have the following:

```
____  ____

____  ____  ____

_R__  ____  _S__
 1     2     3
 T          ~Y
 ↓
 Z
```

If the fifth condition is triggered, we can infer a complete solution.

```
        _T__  _V__

        _Z__  _X__  _W__

T1 ⟶  _R__  _Y__  _S__
         1     2     3
```

With class 1's slots filled, applying the third condition, we know that Y must be assigned to class 2, and W must be assigned to class 3. Only two slots remain, and we must assign V and X to class 2.

1. (A) violates the fifth condition
   (B) violates the second condition
   (C) violates the fourth condition
   (D) Correct
   (E) violates the third condition

2. **(E)** In our complete solution, V is assigned to class 2. We can therefore eliminate choices A through C. The only uncertainty remaining is whether V can be assigned to class 1. The only condition governing V's assignment is the fourth condition. Thus, V can be assigned to class 1, so long as Z isn't also assigned to class 1, and choice E is correct.

3. **(A)** With only one slot remaining in class 1, the fifth condition cannot be triggered. Class 3 also has only one slot remaining. The interaction of the third and fourth conditions is such that one of V and Z and one of W and Y must occupy the two open slots in class 2. The other member of each pair must be assigned to either class 1 or class 3, thus filling up all classes except class 2. We have to assign T to this open slot, and choice A is therefore correct.

___	V|Z	
X	W|Y	___
R	T	S
1	2	3

4. **(E)** With class 3's slots filled, the interaction of the third and fourth conditions creates two options for each of the two pairs (VZ and WY). With only one slot remaining in class 2, it must be filled by T. Only choice E cannot be true, and it is correct.

V|Z	Z|V	
W|Y	Y|W	X
R	T	S
1	2	3

5. **(C)** This scenario creates the same dynamic between the third and fourth conditions. The difference is that the open slot in class 2 has to be filled by X. Choice C is thus correct.

V|Z	Z|V	
W|Y	Y|W	T
R	X	S
1	2	3

6. We can use our previous work to eliminate the incorrect answers.
   (A) see the following diagram

V	Y	
W	T	Z
R	X	S
1	2	3

   (B) see #4
   (C) see #4
   (D) Correct – with class 1's slots filled, the third condition dictates that we assign Y to class 2; the third condition further dictates that we assign W to class 3

V	T	
X	Y	W
R	Z	S
1	2	3

   (E) see #4

Questions 7-12

Setup:
- four lions (L): F G H J
- two tigers (T): K M
- assigned to six stalls
- one animal per stall
- arranged as pictured
- stalls facing each other: 1 and 4, 2 and 5, 3 and 6

Conditions:

#1: 

#2: stall 1 ⟶ L
#3: H_6
#4: J = K + 1

#5: 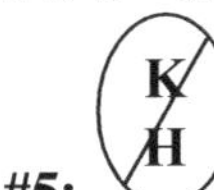

Overview:
The second and third conditions restrict the KJ pair (fourth condition) to one of the following pairs: 2 and 3, 3 and 4, 4 and 5. Due to the fifth condition, we can eliminate stalls 3 and 4 as an option. We can set up molds to efficiently represent the two remaining options.

#1

1	2	3
L	T K	L J
T M	L	L H
4	5	6

#2

1	2	3
L	M|	|M
T K	L J	L H
4	5	6

Mold #1: With KJ assigned to stalls 2 and 3, the first condition dictates that we assign M to stall 4.

Mold #2: With KJ assigned to stalls 4 and 5, M can only be assigned to either stall 2 or stall 3.

7. **(E)** This question directly tests the inference regarding the KJ pair. K must be assigned to either stall 2 or stall 4, and choice E is correct.

8. **(B)** Comparing the choices to the molds reveals that only B could be true, and it is therefore correct.

9. **(C)** According to both molds, K and M are in different rows, and choice C is thus correct.

10. **(E)** This is only true of the second mold. G must be in the same row as M, and choice E is correct.

11. **(C)** This question triggers the first mold. The only uncertainty is which of F and G is assigned to stall 1, and choice C could be true.

12. **(B)** Comparing the choices to our molds reveals that only B must be true.

<u>Questions 13-18</u>

Setup:
- four houses on one side: 1 3 5 7
- four houses on the opposite side: 2 4 6 8
- houses facing each other: 1 and 2, 3 and 4, 5 and 6, 7 and 8
- each house is one of three styles: R S T

Conditions:

#1: 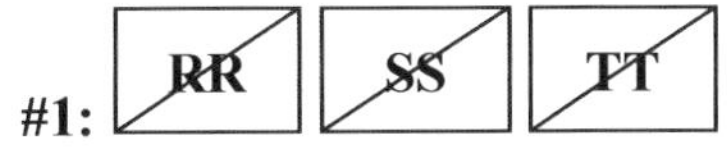

#2: 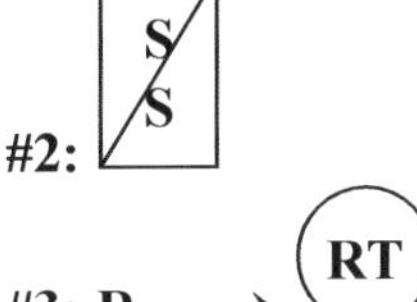

#3: R ⟶ (RT)
#4: R_3
#5: S_6

Overview:
Combining the first and fifth conditions, we know that house 8 cannot be a split-level. The third condition precludes it from being a Ranch. We can therefore place a T in the eighth slot. In combination with houses 3 and 6, the first and second conditions allow us to deduce that slot 5 must be filled by a T. The first condition excludes one style each for houses 1, 4, and 7.

1	3	5	7
S|T	R	T	R|S
	R|T	S	T
2	4	6	8

13. **(D)** Houses 3, 6, and 7 cannot be Tudor houses. Only house 7 is listed, and choice D is therefore correct.

14. **(B)** The only two houses opposite each other that could both be Ranch houses are 3 and 4. Applying the third condition, we know that house 2 must be a Tudor house. Only choice B could be true under this scenario, and it is correct.

1	3	5	7
S|T	R	T	R|S
T	R	S	T
2	4	6	8

15. **(A)** Applying the first condition, we know that house 2 must be either a Ranch house or a split-level house. The only choice that is compatible with this scenario is A, and it is correct.

1	3	5	7
S|T	R	T	R|S
R|S	T	S	T
2	4	6	8

16. **(A) Correct – only house 3 must be a Ranch house**

1	3	5	7
S|T	R	T	S
S|T	T	S	T
2	4	6	8

(B) houses 5 and 8 are both Tudors
(C) houses 5 and 8 are both Tudors, and either house 2 or house 4 must also be a Tudor (third condition)
(D) at most, there could be three Ranch houses (3, 7, and one of 2 and 4)
(E) see choice D

17. **(E)** Applying this to our master diagram reveals that house 4 would have to be a Tudor house, and choice E is therefore correct.

18. **(A)** The inferences we made in the beginning don't apply to this question, so we must check the remaining conditions against the choices. Choice A violates the third condition, and it is therefore correct.

Questions 19-24

Setup:
- each of five teams occupies one of five positions
- positions (highest to lowest): 1 2 3 4 5
- initial order (1 through 5): R J S M L R
- teams change positions ⟶ lower-positioned team defeats a higher-positioned team

Conditions:
#1: rounds are alternatively odd-position and even-position
#2: odd-position round: 2 and 3; 4 and 5
#3: even-position round: 1 and 2; 3 and 4
#4: when a lower-positioned team defeats a higher-positioned team, the two switch

Overview:
Since we don't know how many rounds there are going to be, and we don't know what kind of round begins the matches, we'll have to note the conditions and head to the questions.

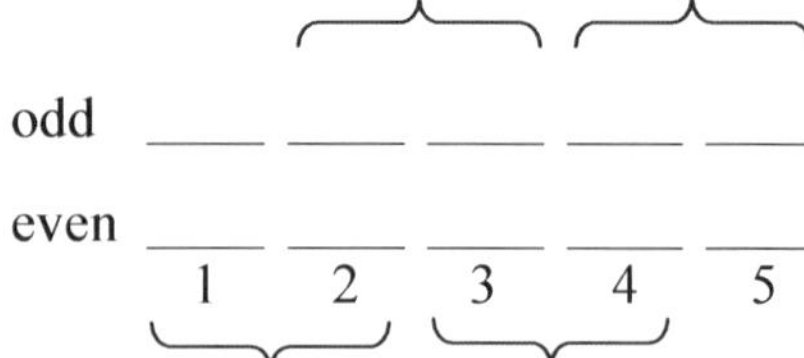

19. **(D)** Since the first round is even-position and the team ranked fifth won't be playing, it must stay in fifth. Only choice D has L in fifth position, and it is therefore correct.

20. **(E)** This question allows us to infer with certainty the positions of all five teams after the second round. Because each pair switches positions, all the choices aside from E (which cannot be true) must be true.

odd (1)	R	S	J	L	M
even (2)	S	R	L	J	M
	1	2	3	4	5

21. **(A)** **Correct – J could beat S in the first round (odd) and beat R in the second round (even)**
    (B) since L starts in fifth position and the matches are alternately even and odd, L can only play one match in the first two rounds
    (C) by the same logic as choice B, R can only play one match in the first two rounds
    (D) L's only match would have to be against either M or S
    (E) this would require two even-position matches in a row, violating the first condition

22. **(C)** Since J starts out in second position, it will play either two or three matches. In either case, winning all its matches ensures that it will be in first place after three rounds. Depending on whether the first round is even or odd, L will play either two or three matches. If it plays two matches (even – odd – even) and wins both, it will move up two positions to third. If it plays three matches (odd – even – odd) and wins all three, then it will move up to second place. Since L could be in second, choice C is correct. Choice E is the only one that isn't immediately incorrect based on our diagram. If S were in third, R would have to be in last. However, this would require R to lose four matches when only three rounds have been played.

even – odd – even ⟶	J	R	L	M	S
odd – even – odd ⟶	J	L	R	M	S
	1	2	3	4	5

23. **(A)** Depending on whether the first round is even-position or odd-position, M will advance either three positions or two positions. Since the other teams are in the same relative order, we can infer two possible solutions. In either case, J is in third after the third round, and choice A is correct.

even – odd – even ⟶	M	R	J	S	L
odd – even – odd ⟶	R	M	J	S	L
	1	2	3	4	5

24. The fourth condition precludes any team from increasing or decreasing its rank by more than one position in any one round. Given the team positions following the third round, we can eliminate incorrect choices by looking for individual changes of greater than one position.

    (A) L would have to advance two positions in one round
    (B) R would have to increase its rank by four positions in one round
    (C) Correct – only L and S switch places
    (D) J would have to advance three positions in one round
    (E) J would have to advance three positions in one round

Questions 1-5

Setup:

- o seven patients: P Q R S T U V
- o one patient per appointment
- o seven appointments: 1 2 3 4 5 6 7

Conditions:

#1: Q – W

#2: U – P

#3: R_3 or T_3

#4: 

Overview:

The first two conditions establish that W and U cannot be last, and that Q and P cannot be first.

		R|T				
1	2	3	4	5	6	7
~W						~Q
~P						~U

1. (A) violates the second condition
   (B) violates the third condition
   (C) violates the fourth condition
   (D) violates the first condition
   (E) Correct

2. **(E)** Applying the first condition, we know that Q occupies the first slot. Due to the second condition, the SR piece cannot be placed in the third and fourth slots. With R and S occupying the last two slots, the third condition dictates that we place T third, leaving U to occupy the fourth slot. Thus, choice E is correct.

Q	W	T	U	P	R|S	S|R
1	2	3	4	5	6	7

3. **(B)** This condition establishes the following piece: TURS. We can plug this in to the two options for the third slot (third condition), to obtain two diagrams. With the piece spanning the first four slots, the last three slots will be occupied by W, Q, and P. With the piece spanning slots three through six, the second condition dictates that we place P seventh, leaving Q and W to occupy the first two slots, respectively (first condition). In either case, S precedes P, and choice B is correct.

T	U	R	S			
Q	W	T	U	R	S	P
1	2	3	4	5	6	7

4. **(B)** Combining this with the fourth condition, we have the following piece: PSR. R cannot be third, since this would violate the second condition. Therefore, T must be third, and the PSR piece can span the fourth through the sixth slots or the fifth through the seventh slots. With the piece spanning slots four through six, the first two conditions dictate that Q and U occupy the first two slots, leaving W to fill the seventh slot. With the PSR piece spanning slots five through seven, the first condition stipulates that W cannot be first and Q cannot be fourth. Thus, choice B is correct.

Q|U	U|Q	T	P	S	R	W
		T		P	S	R
1	2	3	4	5	6	7
~W			~Q			

5. **(D)** Combining this with the first condition, we have: Q – PTW. If T were third, the second condition would be violated. Therefore, R must be third. We cannot span the PTW piece across the fourth through the sixth slots, since this would violate either the first, second, or third condition. Thus, the only acceptable placement of the piece is spanning the fifth through the seventh slots, and only choice D must be true.

	S|	R	|S	P	T	W
1	2	3	4	5	6	7

Questions 6-12

Setup:
- exactly six employees
- three officers (O): F G H
- three supervisors (S): K L M
- employees will be assigned to committees
- three committees: P Q S

Conditions:

#1: at least one O assigned to each committee

#2: each employee ⟶ 1^+ committee

#3: F, G, and H are assigned to P

#4: 

#5: K_S

Overview:

The setup and conditions don't lend themselves to inferences, so we'll make our sketch and head to the questions.

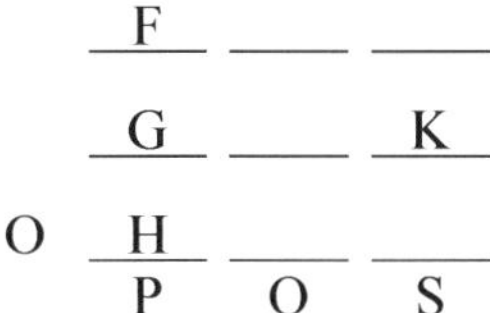

6. (A) violates the fifth condition
   (B) violates the fifth condition
   (C) violates the fourth condition
   (D) Correct
   (E) violates the first condition

7. **(C)** From this, we can deduce that one of F and G must be assigned to each of Q and S. Due to the second and fourth conditions, G can be assigned to a maximum of one of Q and S. The condition that F and M cannot be on the committee creates the same restriction with F. The only employee who can fill the open slot on Q is K, and choice C is therefore correct.

F	G|L	L|G
G	K	K
H	F|M	M|F
P	Q	S

8. (A) F can be assigned only to P
   (B) Correct – violates either the second condition (L must be assigned to at least one committee) or the fourth condition
   (C) the conditions don't preclude H from being grouped with any particular employee
   (D) K need not be assigned to more than one committee
   (E) the fourth condition would dictate that G be assigned to neither Q nor S

9. **(E)** Combining this scenario with the fourth condition, we have two options for the placements of G and L. When G is assigned to Q, L must be assigned to S, and vice versa. Since we still need to assign M to one of the committees (second condition), we must assign M to Q, and choice E is correct.

```
   _F_  _G_  _L_             _F_  _L_  _G_

   _G_  _M_  _K_             _G_  _M_  _K_

O  _H_  _F_  _F_    or   O   _H_  _F_  _F_
    P    Q    S               P    Q    S
```

10. We can check the choices against the conditions to eliminate those that are incorrect.
    - (A) the second condition would dictate that K, L, and M be assigned to S, violating the first condition
    - (B) L and M would have to be assigned to S (second condition) along with K (fifth condition), violating the first condition
    - (C) L and M would have to be assigned to S (second condition) along with K (fifth condition), violating the first condition
    - (D) violates the fourth condition
    - **(E) Correct – see the following diagram**

```
   _F_  _L_  ___

   _G_  _M_  _K_

O  _H_  _H_  ___
    P    Q    S
```

11. **(E)** In combination with the fourth condition, this precludes G from being assigned to either Q or S. Thus, the officer slot on each of Q and S must be filled by either F or H. This leaves only one open slot on Q, and we must assign M to that slot. Choice E is therefore correct.

```
   _F_  _L_  _L_

   _G_  _M_  _K_

O  _H_  F|H  F|H
    P    Q    S
```

12. We can use our previous work to eliminate the incorrect answer choices.
    - (A) see #11
    - **(B) Correct – G would have to be assigned to all three committees, violating either the second condition or the fourth condition**
    - (C) see #11
    - (D) this could be true of our diagram for #10, choice E
    - (E) see #7

Questions 13-17

Setup:
- two people: V W
- four separate meals: B L D S

Conditions:
#1: $V \neq W$ at any meal
#2: neither person eats the same food more than once
#3: B options: H P O
#4: L options: F H M O
#5: D options: F H M O
#6: S options: F O
#7: O_{WL}

Overview:
Combining the second, sixth, and seventh conditions, we know that W must eat fish for snack. Applying the first and sixth conditions, we know that Vladimir eats an omelet for snack. Since both Wendy and Vladimir eat an omelet during one of their meals, the first, second, and third conditions dictate that one must eat hot cakes and the other must eat poached eggs for breakfast. We can also infer that neither one will eat an omelet for dinner, due to the second condition.

	B	L	D	S
W	H|P	O	___	F
V	P|H	___	___	O
	H	F	F	F
	P	H	H	O
	~O	M	M	
		O	~O	

13. **(E)** As we have inferred, Wendy must eat fish for her snack, and choice E is therefore correct.

14. **(D)** As we have inferred, Vladimir must eat an omelet for his snack, and choice D is therefore correct.

15. **(D)** The only meal during which Wendy could eat macaroni is dinner. Applying the first condition, we can deduce that Vladimir would have to eat macaroni at lunch. This leaves only two food possibilities for Vladimir's dinner: fish and hot cakes. Only choice D could be true under this scenario.

	B	L	D	S
W	H|P	O	M	F
V	P|H	M	F|H	O

16. **(B)** Both Wendy and Vladimir have five foods total to select from. Applying the second condition to this question, we know that Wendy eats all four of the other foods. The only meal during which she can eat macaroni is dinner, and the second condition dictates that she must eat poached eggs for breakfast. Applying the first condition, we know that Vladimir eats hot cakes for breakfast. The second condition limits him to one of fish and macaroni for lunch and dinner. The only choice compatible with this diagram is B, and it is therefore correct.

W	P	O	M	F
V	H	F|M	M|F	O
	B	L	D	S

17. **(B)** Applying the first condition, we know that Vladimir eats hot cakes for breakfast. From the second condition, we can deduce the following meal possibilities:

W_{dinner}: H M
V_{lunch}: F M
V_{dinner}: F M

Only choice B is incompatible with our diagram, and it is therefore correct. Alternatively, we could have used our diagram from number sixteen to narrow down the choices to B and D.

W	P	O	M	F
V	H	F|M	M|F	O
	B	L	D	S

Questions 18-24

Setup:
- eight people: J K L M N O P R
- two four-person teams: X Y
- relay race is run in four consecutive legs: 1 2 3 4
- each team member runs exactly one of the legs
- exactly one team member runs in each leg

Conditions:
#1: J and K are on the same team
#2: K and N are not on the same team
#3: R – P regardless of which team each is on
#4: M_Y and N_Y
#5: ~J_3 and ~M_3
#6: K_2 and L_2
#7: O_4

Overview:
Combining the second and fourth conditions, we know that K must be on team X. Applying the first condition, we know that J is also on team X. Combining the sixth condition with our first deduction reveals that K must be assigned the second leg for X, and L must be assigned the second leg for team Y.

	1	2	3	4	
X		K		O|	J K
Y		L		|O	L M N
	~P		~J ~M	~R	

Since O must run fourth, we can set up two molds: one with O on team X, and one with O on team Y.

#1	1	2	3	4
X	J	K	P|R	O
Y		L		

#2	1	2	3	4
X	R|	K	|R	
Y	M	L	N	O

Mold #1: With O on team X, the fifth condition dictates that J must run first. Since both M and N are on team Y, one of P and R must fill the third slot on team X.

Mold #2: With O on team Y, the fifth condition dictates that M must run first, leaving N to occupy the third slot on team Y.

We can take things one step further and draw out four acceptable solutions from these two molds.

#1	1	2	3	4
X	J	K	P	O
Y	R	L	N	M

#2	1	2	3	4
X	J	K	R	O
Y	M	L	N	P

#3	1	2	3	4
X	R	K	P	J
Y	M	L	N	O

#4	1	2	3	4
X	J	K	R	P
Y	M	L	N	O

Solution #1: Using mold #1, if we place P in the third slot on team X, R must run first for team Y (third condition). Due to the fifth condition, M must run fourth, leaving N to occupy the third slot on team Y.

Solution #2: Using mold #1, if we place R in the third slot on team X, P must run fourth for team Y (third condition). Due to the fifth condition, M must run first, leaving N to occupy the third slot on team Y.

Solution #3: Using mold #2, if we place R first on team X, the fifth condition dictates that J must run fourth for team X. This leaves P to occupy the third slot on team X.

Solution #4: Using mold #2, if we place R third, P must be fourth on team X (third condition). This leaves J to occupy the first slot on team X.

18. **(A) Correct – the sufficient condition triggers mold #1**
    (B) see solutions #1 and #4
    (C) see solution #3
    (D) this cannot be true (solutions #3 and #4)
    (E) this cannot be true (solution #1)

19. **(D)** R is assigned to team X in solutions #2, #3, and #4. Thus, she can run either first or third, and choice D is correct.

20. **(E)** This is only true of solution #4. Therefore, choice E is correct.

21. (A) see solutions #1, #2, and #4
    (B) see solution #1
    (C) Correct
    (D) see solutions #1 and #3
    (E) see solutions #2 and #4

22. **(C)** This triggers mold #2. Accordingly, N must run third, and choice C is correct.

23. (A) see solution #3
    (B) Correct
    (C) see solutions #2 and #4
    (D) see solutions #1 and #3
    (E) see solutions #2 and #4

24. **(B)** This triggers solutions #1 and #3. Since R runs first in both solutions, choice B is correct.

Questions 1-6

Setup:
- five students: H L P R S
- each will visit exactly one of three cities
- cities: M T V

Conditions:

#1: 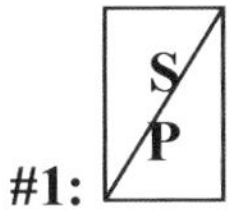

#2: 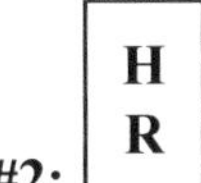

#3: L_M or L_T
#4: $P_V \longrightarrow H_V$; $\sim H_V \longrightarrow \sim P_V$ (contrapositive)
#5: none of the students visits a city alone

Overview:
The fifth condition allows for only one allocation of students to cities: 3, 2, 0. Therefore, we know that one of the cities won't be assigned any of the students. Using the allocation, we can further deduce that one of S and P will have to be grouped with the HR piece, due to the first condition. Thus, there are two acceptable groupings of students:

P	H	or	S	H
L	R		L	R
	S			P

If the fourth condition is triggered, we must use the second set of groupings, and the third condition dictates that the SL piece must be assigned to Toronto.

$P_V \longrightarrow$

M	T	V
		H
	S	R
	L	P

1. (A) violates the second condition
   (B) violates the fifth condition
   (C) Correct
   (D) violates the third condition
   (E) violates the first condition

2. **(D)** This question triggers the first acceptable grouping. Since P cannot visit Vancouver under this scenario, we can eliminate choice E. We can also eliminate choices A through C because they don't match the appropriate grouping, leaving D as the correct answer.

```
          _H_           _H_
     _P_  _R_           _R_  _P_
     _L_  _S_    or     _S_  _L_
 M    T    V             M    T    V
```

3. **(D)** Since L cannot visit Vancouver (third condition), L cannot be paired with S under this scenario. Therefore, we must use the first acceptable grouping. Choice D is thus correct.

4. **(A)** Since the four incorrect answer choices must be true, we can compare them to our deductions. We've already drawn up a diagram for P visiting Vancouver (above), and it shows that choice A not only could be false, but must be false.

5. **(C)** Combining this with the second condition, we know that H also visits Toronto. Since L must be paired with one of P and S, and this pair must visit either Montreal or Toronto (third condition), we must assign L to Montreal. The only uncertainty is which of the two groupings of students is used, and choice C is the only one that could be true.

```
         _S|P_
 _P|S_   _H_
  _L_    _R_
   M      T     V
```

6. We can use our previous work to eliminate the incorrect choices.
   - (A) see #2
   - (B) see #2
   - (C) see #2
   - (D) see #2
   - **(E) Correct – since the group of two includes L, the third condition precludes this group from being assigned to Vancouver**

Questions 7-13

Setup:
- three subjects: M N O
- each course offered once in each semester: F S
- book orders are kept in six folders: 1 2 3 4 5 6

Conditions:
#1: each folder contains orders for exactly one course
#2: $subject_1 = subject_2$
#3: $subject_3 \neq subject_4$
#4: FM_1 or FM_4
#5: SO_1 or SO_4
#6: $\sim SN_5$

Overview:
The interaction of the fourth and fifth conditions allows us to set up two distinct molds with which to answer the questions.

	1	2	3	4	5	6
#1	FM	SM	N	SO	FO|	|FO
#2	SO	FO	N	FM	SM|	|SM
					~SN	

Mold #1: With FM in the first slot, the second condition dictates that we place SM in the second slot. The fifth condition stipulates that SO must be fourth. Due to the third condition, the third slot must be occupied by either FN or SN. FO must fill one of the two open slots (5 and 6).

Mold #2: With SO in the first slot, the second condition dictates that we place FO in the second slot. The fifth condition stipulates that FM must be fourth. Due to the third condition, either FN or SN must occupy the third slot. SM must fill one of the open slots (5 and 6).

7. (A) violates the fifth condition
   (B) violates the second condition
   (C) violates the fourth condition
   (D) Correct
   (E) violates the third condition

8. **(A)** We have established that either FN or SN must be placed third, and choice A must therefore be false.

9. This question triggers the second mold. We can check the answer choices against the mold.
   (A) FM occupies the fourth slot
   (B) Correct – see the following diagram

SO	FO	SN	FM	FN	SM
1	2	3	4	5	6

   (C) FM occupies the first slot
   (D) violates the sixth condition
   (E) either FN or SN must occupy the third slot

10. (A) the first slot must be occupied by FM or SO
    (B) the first slot must be occupied by FM or SO
    (C) the fourth slot must be occupied by FM or SO
    (D) Correct – see the following diagram
    (E) either FN or SN must occupy the third slot

11. **(B)** This question triggers the second mold. According to our mold, there are two other courses for which the placements are certain: SO and FM. Thus, choice B is correct.

12. **(E)** By combining the second and third conditions, we can deduce that the fifth and sixth folders must contain orders for different subjects. Therefore, choice E is correct.

13. Armed with our molds and the conditions, we can quickly dispense with the incorrect answer choices.

    (A) FM and SO must be separated by two slots
    (B) violates the sixth condition
    (C) Correct – see the following diagram two diagrams

FM	SM	SN	SO	FN	FO
SO	FO	SN	FM	FN	SM
1	2	3	4	5	6

    (D) violates the second condition
    (E) this would have to happen under mold #1, but it would force SN to occupy the fifth slot, violating the sixth condition

<u>Questions 14-19</u>

Setup:
- exactly five subway lines: L1 L2 L3 L4 L5
- trains run in both directions along each line
- trains stop at every station

Conditions:
#1: L1 connects seven stations in this order: R – T – F – S – U – Q – P – R
#2: L2 connects T with S
#3: L3 connects R with U
#4: L4 connects three stations in this order: Q – G – R
#5: L5 connects Q with T, and no other stations

Overview:
Combining all the conditions, we obtain the following sketch:

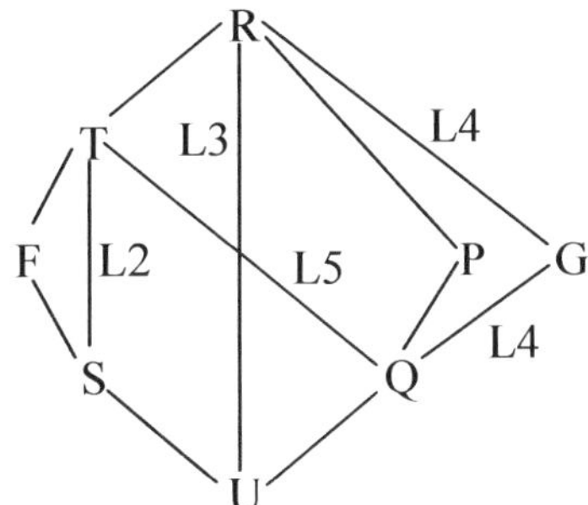

For the sake of clarity, any unlabeled line corresponds to a segment of L1.

14. **(C)** There are four lines leading away from R. A traveler could reach G, P, U, and T directly from R, without making any intermediate stops, and choice C is therefore correct.

15. **(C)** There are a number of ways a traveler can go from G to S by making three stops: G – Q – U – S, G – Q – T – S, G – R – U – S, and G – R – T – S. However, only one of these routes includes only two different lines: G – Q – U – S. Therefore, a traveler would have to make a stop at Q, and choice C is correct.

16. **(A)** Aside from using L3, a traveler can choose from the following four routes to get from U to R in the fewest possible stops:

    U – S – T – R
    U – Q – T – R
    U – Q – P – R
    U – Q – G – R

    Only choice A lists two intermediate stops from one of these four routes, and it is therefore correct.

17. **(C)** In order to go from F to G in as few stops as possible, a traveler can choose from the following two routes:

    F – T – R – G
    F – T – Q – G

    In either case, there must be two intermediate stops, and choice C is correct.

18. **(E)** With the UQ segment unavailable, a traveler could choose from among the following three routes to go from S to P in as few stops as possible:

    S – U – R – P
    S – T – Q – P
    S – T – R – P

    In all three routes, a traveler would pass through one of R and T, and choice E is therefore correct.

19. **(A)** A glance at our diagram reveals that these three stations are each connected to one line: F (L1), P (L1), and G (L4). Thus, choice A is correct.

Questions 20-24

Setup:

- partners$_0$: H R
- associates$_0$: O
- assistants$_0$: G J L S T W
- during each review, each assistant and associate is considered for promotion
- at least one person is promoted from each of the lower ranks
- assistant promoted to associate ⟶ a majority of higher-ranking staff votes for promotion
- associate promoted to partner ⟶ a majority of partners vote for promotion

Conditions:

#1: O never votes for promoting G, J, or T
#2: R never votes for promoting L or S
#3: H never votes for promoting J or W

Overview:
Due to the fifth setup condition, we know that O will be promoted to partner during the first annual review. Combining the first and third conditions, we know that J will not be promoted during the first annual review. In order for either L or S to be promoted at the first annual review, either one would have to get votes from both H and O.

	Initial	Year 1	Year 2
Partners	H R	H R O	
Associates	O		
Assistants	G J L S T W	J	

20. (A) J cannot be promoted during the first annual review (first and third conditions)
    (B) O must be promoted during the first annual review
    (C) S cannot be promoted from assistant to partner during one annual review (setup conditions)
    (D) one of the assistants must be promoted (setup conditions)
    (E) Correct

21. **(D)** Combining this information with the conditions, we can put together the following voting profile:

	G	J	L	S	T	W
H	-	-	+	+	-	-
R	+	-	-	-	-	+
O	-	-			-	

Thus, we know that G, J, and T will not be promoted during the first annual review, and we can eliminate choices A, B, C, and E, leaving D as the correct answer.

22. **(B)** From the conditions, we know that J has two votes against promotion (O and H). Therefore, J will require three votes for promotion in order for it to happen. R can vote for J's promotion, leaving two additional required votes. Thus, two assistants would have to be promoted to associates during this year's review, and choice B is correct.

23. **(E)** This question directly tests our grasp of the setup condition that at least one person from each rank is promoted during each annual review. Assuming the minimum number of promotions at each rank, we can make the following inferences about the numbers following the first two annual reviews:

	Initial	Year 1	Year 2
Partners	2	3	4
Associates	1	1	1
Assistants	6	5	4

Therefore, choice E is correct.

24. **(B)** From question number twenty-three, we know that there can be one associate following the second annual review. Can there be zero? This would violate the setup condition that at least one of the people from the lower ranks is promoted during each annual review. Thus, choice B is correct.

Questions 1-7

Setup:

- six consecutive days: 1 2 3 4 5 6
- six factories: F G H J Q R
- each factory will be inspected exactly once
- one factory per day

Conditions:
#1: F_1 or F_6
#2: J – Q
#3: [QR]
#4: G_3 ⟶ Q_5; ~Q_5 ⟶ ~G_3 (contrapositive)

Overview:
If G is not third, then we'll apply the conditions to our standard diagram. The second and third conditions can be combined into the following chain:

J—— [QR]

F|					|F
1	2	3	4	5	6
		G ⟶		Q	

If G is third, we can deduce a number of the other placements. Due to the fourth condition, Q must be fifth, and the third condition dictates that we place R sixth. Finally, since R is sixth, F must be first, due to the first condition.

G_3 ⟶

F	J|H	G	H|J	Q	R
1	2	3	4	5	6

1. (A) violates the second condition
   (B) Correct
   (C) violates the third condition
   (D) violates the first condition
   (E) violates the fourth condition

2. **(E)** The chances are good that the correct answer will violate our chain inference. Only choices D and E contain variables in our chain. If R were inspected second, we wouldn't have room for both J and Q, thus violating either the second or the third condition. Therefore, choice E is correct.

3. **(C)** We can narrow our focus to choices C, D, and E, since they contain the variables in our chain inference (J, Q, and R). If J were fifth, we wouldn't have room for both Q and R, thus violating either the second or the third condition. Choice C is therefore correct.

4. (A) violates the fourth condition
   (B) violates the fourth condition
   (C) the QR piece could only be placed in the first and second slots, violating the second condition
   (D) since Q and R constitute a piece (third condition), R must also follow J (second condition)
   (E) Correct – see the following diagram

J	Q	R	G	H	F
1	2	3	4	5	6

5. **(D)** Combining this information with the first condition, we know that R must be fifth and F must be sixth. Applying the third condition, we know that Q must be fourth. Finally, since Q is not fifth, due to the contrapositive of the third condition, only H or J could occupy the third slot. Thus, choice D is correct.

		H|J	Q	R	F
1	2	3	4	5	6

6. **(D)** Due to the first condition, we cannot place both G and H in the end slots. If we place F first, G and H can occupy the second and sixth slots, not necessarily in that order. If we place F sixth, G and H can occupy the first and fifth slots, not necessarily in that order. Thus, the only three variables that can fill the first slot are F, G, and H. Therefore, choice D is correct.

F	G|H	J	Q	R	H|G
G|H	J	Q	R	H|G	F
1	2	3	4	5	6

7. **(C)** Combining this with our original chain inference, we have: J – [GQR]. Since we cannot trigger the fourth condition (R would have to be placed fifth), the GQR piece has limited placements. With F first, the piece must span the fourth through the sixth slots. With F last, the piece must span the second through the fourth slots. Thus, only choice C could be true.

F	J	H	G	Q	R
J	G	Q	R	H	F
1	2	3	4	5	6

Questions 8-12

Setup:
- o four two-day workshops: L L P P R R S S
- o five days: M T W Th F

Conditions:

#1: 

#2: 1-2 workshops each day

#3: 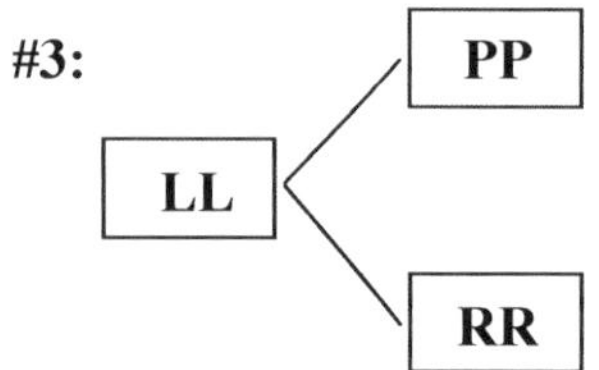

Overview:
Due to the third condition, P and R can each be placed on Wednesday at the earliest, and L can be placed on Wednesday at the latest. Since the PP piece and the RR piece must each span either Wednesday and Thursday or Thursday and Friday, both P and R must be in session on Thursday. To satisfy the second condition, at least one of L and S must occupy a slot on Monday and Tuesday. We can set up three distinct molds to represent the possible placements of the LL and SS pieces.

#1

	S	S	R	
L	L		P	
M	T	W	Th	F

#2

S	S		R	
L	L		P	
M	T	W	Th	F

#3

S	S		R	R
	L	L	P	P
M	T	W	Th	F

The LL piece and the SS piece cannot both span Tuesday and Wednesday, since that would violate the second condition. In mold #3, the third condition forces the PP piece and the RR piece to span Thursday and Friday.

8. (A) both P and R must be in session on Thursday
   (B) Correct – see the following diagram
   (C) an R can be placed on Wednesday at the earliest
   (D) the two Thursday slots are already filled with P and R
   (E) this would leave Friday with no sessions, violating the second condition

9. (A) violates the third condition
   (B) both P and R must be in session on Thursday
   (C) Correct – see mold #3
   (D) both P and R must be in session on Thursday
   (E) violates the third condition

10. **(A)** This could only be true of the first two molds. Accordingly, L must be in session on Monday, and choice A is correct.

11. **(A)** This could only be true of the first two molds. We know that L must be in session on Monday and Tuesday, and choice A must, therefore be false.

12. This is only true of the first mold, and we can check the answer choices against it.

    (A) R cannot be in session on Tuesday
    (B) S must be in session on Tuesday
    (C) Correct – see the following diagram

	S	S	R	R
L	L		P	P
M	T	W	Th	F

    (D) Wednesday only has one remaining slot
    (E) S cannot be in session on Thursday

<u>Questions 13-19</u>

Setup:
- two boats: 1 2
- each will be assigned exactly four people
- three adults (A): F G H
- five children (C): V W X Y Z

Conditions:
#1: each boat has 1^+ A
#2: $F_2 \longrightarrow G_2$; $G_1 \longrightarrow F_1$ (contrapositive)
#3: $V_1 \longrightarrow W_2$; $W_1 \longrightarrow V_2$ (contrapositive)

#4: 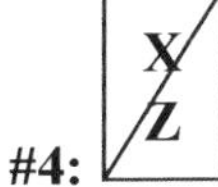

Overview:
It's easy to misinterpret the second and third conditions to mean that F and G are always in the same boat and that V and W are never in the same boat. However, if F is in boat 1, G could be in either boat, and if V is in boat 2, W could be in either boat.

X|Z Z|X

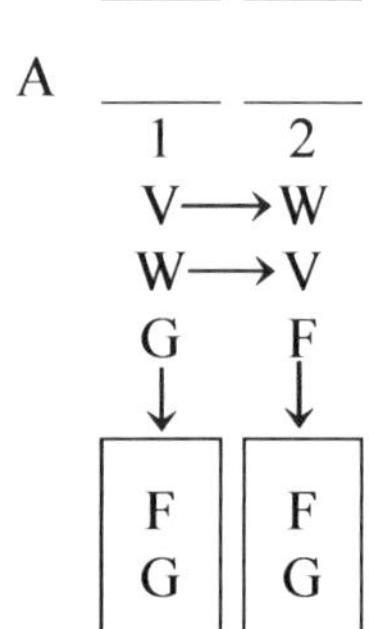

13. (A) violates the first condition
    (B) violates the fourth condition
    (C) Correct
    (D) violates the third condition
    (E) violates the fourth condition

14. **(E)** This triggers the second condition. With F and G assigned to boat 2, we must assign H to boat 1, in order to satisfy the first condition. With only one remaining slot in boat 2, one of V and W will be assigned to boat 1. Therefore, either the third condition or its contrapositive will be triggered, and one of V and W must be assigned to boat 2. Of the pairs given, only Y and Z could be assigned to the same boat, and choice E is correct.

	1	2
	X|Z	Z|X
	Y	W|V
	V|W	F
A	H	G

15. **(C)** Combining this with the first condition, we can infer that two adults are assigned to boat 2. G cannot be assigned to boat 1, since this would trigger the contrapositive of the second condition, and both F and G (two adults) would be assigned to boat 1. Thus, we have two possible pairs of adults who could be assigned to boat 2: FG and GH. We have already drawn the FG scenario for number fourteen. Since none of the choices match up with that diagram, we'll have to draw the scenario with GH in boat 2. As there is no overlap between the conditions governing the children and the conditions governing the adults, the same placement options exist for the children as did in number fourteen. Only choice C could be true, and it is therefore correct.

	1	2
	X|Z	Z|X
	Y	W|V
	V|W	H
A	F	G

16. **(A)** This triggers the contrapositive of the second condition, and F must also be assigned to boat 1. To satisfy the first condition, H must be assigned to boat 2, and choice A is correct.

	1	2
	X|Z	Z|X
	F	
A	G	H

17. **(B)** V and W can only be assigned to the same boat if they're assigned to boat 2. With three of boat 2's slots occupied by children, the open slot must be assigned to one of the adults (first condition). Assigning F to that slot would trigger and violate the second condition, so the slot must be filled by either G or H. Y must fill the remaining open slot in boat 1, and choice B is correct.

	1	2
	X|Z	Z|X
	Y	V
	G|H	W
A	F	G|H

18. **(A)** With this condition, we can account for two slots on each boat. The placements of F, G, W, and Y are uncertain, so we'll have to draw up some options to ascertain the answer. If V and W are assigned to the same boat, they would have to be assigned to boat 2. F and G would fill the two remaining slots in boat 1, and the first condition would dictate that H be assigned to boat 2. If V and W are assigned to different boats, F and G must also be assigned to different boats. Due to the second condition, we would have to assign F to boat 1 and G to boat 2. In either case, F is assigned to boat 1, and choice A is correct.

```
     X|Z  Z|X            X|Z  Z|X
      Y    W             H|Y  Y|H
      F    V             V|W  W|V
A     G    H     or   A   F    G
      1    2              1    2
```

19. **(B)** According to the contrapositive of the second condition, G cannot be assigned to boat 1 if boat 1 is only assigned one adult. Therefore, choice B is correct. Alternatively, we could recycle our work from questions 14, 15, and 18 by checking the answer choices against those diagrams.

Questions 20-24

Setup:

- nine students: F G H J K L M N P
- each student will be assigned to exactly one of three panels
- panels: O R W
- exactly three students will be assigned to each panel

Conditions:

#1: | **F** |
| --- |
| **G** |

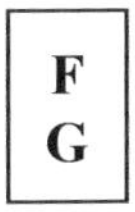

#2: | **K** |
| --- |
| **M** |

#3: | **F** |
| --- |
| **P** |

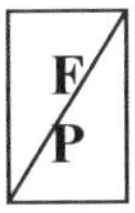

(slashed: F and P not together)

#4: | **G** |
| --- |
| **H** |

(slashed: G and H not together)

#5: | **J** |
| --- |
| **K** |

(slashed: J and K not together)

#6: ~P_O ⟶ ~H_O; H_O ⟶ P_O (contrapositive)

Overview:
The first condition can be combined with the third and the fourth conditions to produce two inferences: G/P (slashed) F/H (slashed)

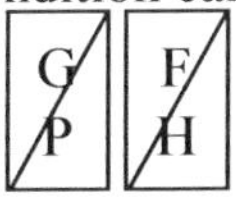

In addition, the second condition can be combined with the fifth condition to deduce that M cannot be assigned to the same panel as J: J/M (slashed)

____	____	____
____	____	____
____	____	____
O	R	W
H ↓ P		

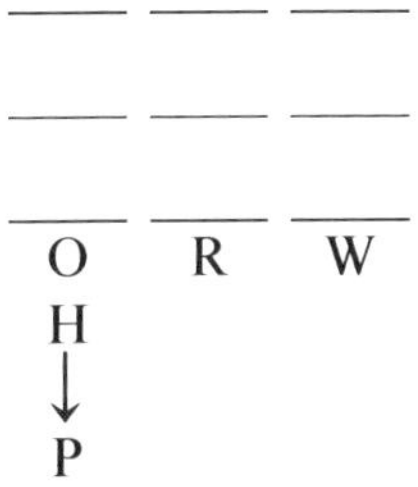

20. (A) violates the second condition
    (B) violates the first condition
    (C) violates the sixth condition
    (D) violates the fifth condition
    (E) Correct

21. **(A)** Combining this with the second condition, we must place K on Wetlands, which completely fills its slots. Applying the sixth condition, we can deduce that H is not on Oceans. Therefore, we must assign H to Recycling. The first and fourth conditions dictate that we assign both F and G to Oceans. Only choice A must be true, and it is therefore correct.

___	___	K
F	___	P
G	H	M
O	R	W

22. Applying the conditions individually as well as using our deductions, we can eliminate the incorrect choices.

    (A) violates the combination of the first and fourth conditions
    (B) violates the combination of the first and third conditions
    (C) Correct
    (D) violates the combination of the first and second conditions
    (E) violates the combination of the second and fifth conditions

23. **(D)** Combining this with the second condition, we know that the Recycling panel consists of K, M, and P. Due to the sixth condition, H must be assigned to the Wetlands panel. Applying the fourth condition, we know that G must be assigned to the Oceans panel, and the first condition dictates that F must also be assigned to the Oceans panel. Using these inferences, we can eliminate choices A, B, C, and E, leaving D as the correct answer.

L|N	M	N|L
F	K	J
G	P	H
O	R	W

24. **(A)** Scanning the choices reveals that A presents a problem. Since each panel consists of exactly three students, the first and second conditions preclude G and K from being assigned to the same panel. Thus, choice A is correct.

Questions 1-5

Setup:
- seven travelers: N O P R S T U
- each assigned to exactly one of nine seats
- arranged as pictured
- only seats in the same row are immediately beside each other

Conditions:
#1: O_L
#2: (XPR)
#3: N_M and R_L or N_F and R_M
#4: (SN crossed out) (UN crossed out)

Overview:
Combining the first two conditions, we know that the XPR piece cannot be placed in the last row. Applying the third condition, it becomes apparent that it can only be placed in the middle row, and we can definitively place N in the front row. We can further infer that if either one of S and U occupies a seat in the front row, it would have to be seat 1 or seat 3. S and U cannot both occupy seats in the front row, as this would violate the fourth condition. Therefore, at least one of them must be seated in the last row.

```
F  ____ ____ ____  N
    1    2    3

M  ____ _P__ ____  R X
    4    5    6

L  ____ ____ ____  O
    7    8    9
```

1. (A) Correct
   (B) violates the first condition
   (C) P must be in the middle row
   (D) R must be in the middle row
   (E) violates the fourth condition

2. **(A)** If S and U are not in the same row as each other, one of them must be in the front row. As a result, N must occupy either seat 1 or seat 3, due to the fourth condition. Therefore, choice A is correct.

3. **(D)** S and U can only occupy seats in the same row if the seats are in the last row. This allows us to infer which passengers occupy seats in the respective rows. Accordingly, besides P, only N or T could occupy a seat next to the empty seat. Only T is listed among the choices, and D is correct.

	1	2	3	
F	___	___	___	N T X
M	___	P	___	R X
L	___	___	___	O S U

(Seats numbered 1–3 in row F, 4–6 in row M, 7–9 in row L.)

4. **(A)** We know that only two of the seats are unoccupied. If T along with the unoccupied seat were in the last row, both S and U would be in the front row, violating the fourth condition. Therefore, T must be in the front row, and the row allocation matches that of question number 3. Thus, choice A is correct.

5. **(B)** Since one of the seats in the last row is unoccupied, one of S and U must be assigned to a seat in the front row. We must assign T to seat 2 in order to satisfy the fourth condition. Therefore, choice B is correct.

	1	2	3	
F	___	T	___	N S|U
M	___	P	___	R X
L	___	___	___	O U|S X

(Seats numbered 1–3 in row F, 4–6 in row M, 7–9 in row L.)

<u>Questions 6-12</u>

Setup:
- o five of eight will be reduced
- o areas of expenditure: G L M N P R S W

Conditions:
#1: G and S ⟶ W; ~W ⟶ ~G or ~S (contrapositive)
#2: N ⟶ ~R; R ⟶ ~N (contrapositive)
N ⟶ ~S; S ⟶ ~N (contrapositive)
#3: P ⟶ ~L; L ⟶ ~P (contrapositive)
#4: exactly two of L, M, and R are reduced

Overview:
Due to the fourth condition, we can establish three acceptable pairs from among L, M, and R (LM, LR, and MR). These pairs have bearing on which three of the other five areas will also be reduced, so it makes sense to set up molds which represent these options.

#1			#2			#3			#4		
		W			W			G			___ } 2 of G P S
	L	G		L	G		L	S		M	___ }
	M	N		M	S		R	W		R	W ~N

Mold #1: With L being reduced, P cannot be reduced (third condition). With N being reduced, S cannot be reduced (second condition).

Mold #2: With L being reduced, P cannot be reduced (third condition). With S being reduced, N cannot be reduced (second condition).

Mold #3: With L being reduced, P cannot be reduced (third condition). With R being reduced, N cannot be reduced (second condition).

Mold #4: With R being reduced, N cannot be reduced (second condition). Due to the contrapositive of the first condition, W must be reduced. Otherwise, one of G and S would also not be reduced, leaving only two of the five areas.

6. **(A) Correct**
   (B) violates the third condition
   (C) violates the second condition
   (D) violates the first condition
   (E) violates the fourth condition

7. This is true of all four molds, so we must check the answer choices against them to eliminate those that are incorrect.
   (A) if G, P, S, and W were all reduced, only one of L, M, and R could be reduced, violating the setup condition that exactly five areas are reduced
   (B) violates the third condition
   (C) violates the third condition
   (D) if N, P, S, and W were all reduced, only one of L, M, and R could be reduced, violating the setup condition that exactly five areas are reduced
   (E) Correct – this matches mold #4

8. **(B)** This could only be true of the fourth mold. We know that M and R must be reduced, and choice B is therefore correct.

9. **(A)** This could be true of either the second mold or the third mold. Choice A presents a pair that is reduced under the second mold, and it is thus correct.

10. **(A)** This is true of the first two molds. In both cases, G is reduced, and choice A is correct.

11. **(C)** This is only true of the fourth mold. Accordingly, L and N are not reduced, and choice C is correct.

12. **(E)** Our molds reveal that in any scenario, W must be reduced, and choice E is therefore correct.

Questions 13-18

Setup:
- single strand of beads
- beads threaded in a single direction from a clasp
- each bead is one of five colors: G O P R Y

Conditions:

#1: (PY) ⟶ R (PY) R

#2: two consecutive beads ⟶ [GG]

#3: (~~OR~~)

#4: 8 consecutive beads ⟶ at least one bead of each color

Overview:
The setup and conditions preclude any major deductions, and every question imposes an additional condition, so we'll head straight to the questions.

13. (A) violates the third condition
    (B) violates the second condition
    (C) Correct
    (D) violates the third condition
    (E) violates the fourth condition

14. **(D)** Applying the second condition, we know that the third bead cannot be orange. The fourth condition dictates that the third bead cannot be red. We can therefore eliminate choices A and B. Choice C violates the second condition and choice E violates the first condition, leaving D as the correct answer.

	Y	G	O
1	2	3	4
		~O	
		~R	

15. **(C)** We can use the second and third conditions to rule out some placements on the strand. Since neither the first nor the eighth bead can be orange, the fourth condition dictates that we place an O fifth. Thus, choice C is correct.

	R	G	Y	O	P	R	
1	2	3	4	5	6	7	8
~O				~P			~O
~R				~Y			~R

16. **(E)** Applying the second and third conditions, we know that the fourth bead cannot be orange or red. Further, the fifth and sixth beads cannot be purple and yellow (in either order), since this would trigger and violate the first condition. Therefore, choice E is correct.

P	Y	R			
1	2	3	4	5	6
			~O		
			~R		

17. **(E)** Applying the first condition, we know that the third and sixth beads must be red. To satisfy the fourth condition, we must place a G and an O in the seventh and eighth slots. O cannot be assigned to the seventh slot, since this would violate the third condition. Since the beads from the second through the eighth satisfy the fourth condition, the ninth bead can be any color besides orange and red (second and third conditions). Therefore, only choice E could be true.

P	Y	R	P	Y	R	G	O	
1	2	3	4	5	6	7	8	9
								~O
								~R

18. **(D)** This question is essentially a repeat of number 16, albeit with a longer strand. To satisfy the fourth condition, we must place a P and an O within the last four slots. If P and Y occupied the fifth and sixth slots (in either order), then the seventh slot would have to be occupied by R, due to the first condition. The third condition would preclude the eighth bead from being orange, thus violating the fourth condition. Choice D is therefore correct.

R	Y	G	R				
1	2	3	4	5	6	7	8
				~O			
				~R			

Questions 19-24

Setup:
- six songs (S): O P T X Y Z
- three vocalists (V): G H L
- songs will be sung consecutively, each performed exactly once

Conditions:

#1:

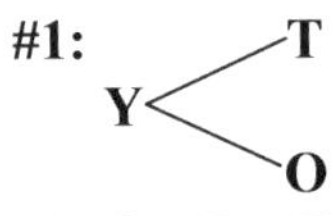

#2: O – P – Z
#3: G can perform only X, Y, and Z
#4: H can perform only T, P, and X
#5: L can perform only O, P, and X
#6: $V_1 \neq V_6$

Overview:
We can create a chart to track which songs each vocalist can sing:

G	H	L
X	T	O
Y	P	P
Z	X	X

Only two of the songs (P and X) can be performed by more than one of the vocalists, so we can infer a number of vocalist/song pairings:

G	G	H	L
Y	Z	T	O

We can combine the first and second conditions into the following chain:

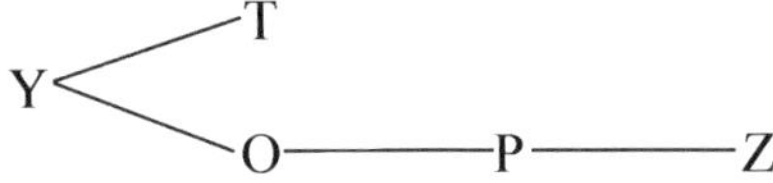

Other than X, all the songs must follow Y, so we can infer that the first song must be either X or Y.

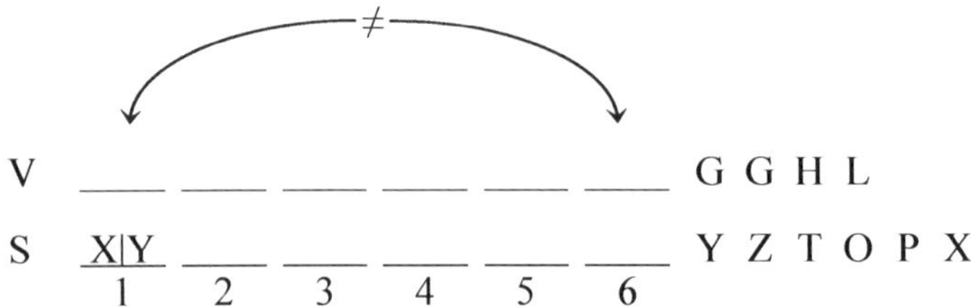

19. (A) violates the first condition
    (B) violates the second condition
    (C) violates the sixth condition
    (D) violates the second condition
    (E) Correct

20. **(C)** As we inferred, H must perform T, and choice C is correct.

21. **(D)** According to our ordering chain, P, O, and Y must each be followed by at least one variable. Therefore, none of them can be last. This leaves T, X and Z, and choice D is correct.

22. **(D)** Since Y must precede the other four variables, it must be second. Either T or Z must be placed sixth. Choice D is therefore correct.

X	Y				T|Z
1	2	3	4	5	6

23. **(B)** Although the question doesn't ask about the vocalists, we have paired four of the songs with vocalists, so we must make sure that each answer choice doesn't violate the sixth condition. Since G must perform both Y and Z, choice B presents an unacceptable list, and it is therefore correct.

24. With Y first, we know that T or X must be last. Since G performs both Y and Z, Z cannot be last, since this would violate the sixth condition. We can check the choices against the conditions and this inference to eliminate those that are incorrect.

Y					T|X
1	2	3	4	5	6

    (A) one of T and X must be last
    (B) violates the second condition
    (C) Correct – see the following diagram

Y	X	O	P	Z	T
1	2	3	4	5	6

    (D) O must precede P (second condition)
    (E) one of T and X must be last

Part 3: PrepTests 21-30

Questions 1-6

Setup:

- seven students are being assigned to dorm rooms
- fourth-year: K L
- third-year: P R
- second-year: S T V
- each room must have one (single), two (double), or three (triple) students assigned to it

Conditions:

#1: ~K_{triple}; ~L_{triple}

#2: ~S_{single}; ~T_{single}; ~V_{single}

#3: [L / R box, crossed out]

#4: [K / P box]

Overview:

Combining the first and fourth conditions, we know that K and P are assigned to a double together. We also know that a maximum of two students (L and R) can be assigned to singles. We can create three acceptable allocations of students to rooms using this information:

3, 2, 2

3, 2, 1, 1

2, 2, 2, 1

The nature of the relationships is such that we can create three distinct molds based on these allocations.

#1

___		
___	K	___
R	P	L
3	2	2

#2

S			
T	K		
V	P	L	R
3	2	1	1

#3

K	___	___	
P	___	___	L|R
2	2	2	1

Mold #1: Since R and L cannot share a room (third condition), and L cannot occupy a triple (first condition), R must be assigned to a triple and L must be assigned to a double.

Mold #2: L and R are the only two who can occupy singles, so S, T, and V must be assigned to the triple.

Mold #3: One of L and R must occupy the single.

1. **(C)** This question directly tests our command of the possible allocations. Only choice C matches with our molds (#3), and it is therefore correct.

2. For this question, we'll narrow our focus to mold #2 and mold #3.
   - (A) if there's exactly one double (mold #2), it cannot have a second-year student assigned to it
   - **(B) Correct – this is true of mold #2**
   - (C) P cannot be assigned to a triple
   - (D) the possible allocations preclude this arrangement
   - (E) the number of doubles must be either one (mold #2) or three (mold #3)

3. **(B)** As we inferred from the setup and conditions, K and P must share a double, and choice B is therefore correct.

4. **(C)** We can check the answers against mold #1. Only choice C must be true under this scenario.

5. **(A)** This could only be true of mold #3. Since we know that one room is a single, choice A is correct.

K	___	___	
P	T|V	V|T	L|R
2	2	2	1

6. (A) violates the fourth condition
   - (B) K and P must both be assigned to the same double
   - **(C) Correct – this could be true of the mold #1 and mold #3**
   - (D) L and R cannot share a room (third condition), and K must share a double with P
   - (E) K must share a double with P

Questions 7-11

Setup:
- three light sockets: 1 2 3
- three green bulbs: G G G
- three purple bulbs: P P P
- three yellow bulbs: Y Y Y

Conditions:

#1: $P_1 \longrightarrow Y_2$; $\sim Y_2 \longrightarrow \sim P_1$ (contrapositive)
#2: $G_2 \longrightarrow G_1$; $\sim G_1 \longrightarrow \sim G_2$ (contrapositive)
#3: $P_3 \longrightarrow P_2$; $\sim P_2 \longrightarrow \sim P_3$ (contrapositive)
$Y_3 \longrightarrow P_2$; $\sim P_2 \longrightarrow \sim Y_3$ (contrapositive)

Overview:
From the contrapositive of the third condition, we can infer that if light 2 is not purple, light three must be green: $\sim P_2 \longrightarrow G_3$.

___	___	___
1	2	3

P⟶Y
G⟵G
  P⟵P
  P⟵Y

7. (A) violates the third condition
   (B) violates the first condition
   (C) violates the first condition
   (D) Correct
   (E) violates the third condition

8. **(A)** From the contrapositive of the second condition, we know that light 2 cannot be green, and choice A is therefore correct.

9. We must use apply the conditionals to the choices to see which one results in a completed diagram.

   (A) Correct – $P_1 \longrightarrow Y_2$ (first condition) $\longrightarrow G_3$ (contrapositive of the third condition)

P	Y	G
1	2	3

   (B) we cannot infer anything about the other two lights
   (C) we cannot infer anything about the other two lights
   (D) we only know that light 2 is purple (third condition)
   (E) we only know that lights 2 is purple (third condition)

10. **(B)** Since we inferred in the previous question that if light 1 is purple, then light 3 is green, for this question, we know that light 1 cannot be purple. Since it cannot be green either, it must be yellow. We also know that light 2 must be purple due to the third condition, since no green bulbs are selected. Therefore, the only uncertainty is whether light 3 is purple or yellow, and choice B is correct.

Y	P	P|Y
1	2	3

11. Since we know that one of each color must be selected, and each choice presents two light colors, we only need to determine if the unlisted light could be the unlisted color.

	1	2	3	
(A)	**G**	**P**	**Y**	**Correct**
(B)	G	Y	P	violates the third condition
(C)	P	G	Y	violates the third condition
(D)	Y	G	P	violates the third condition
(E)	Y	G	P	violates the third condition

Questions 12-17

Setup:
- Monday through Saturday
- two full consecutive days reserved for hostile witnesses
- nonhostile witnesses: Q R U X Y Z
- each interviewed exactly once for a full morning or afternoon
- Q and R are the only witnesses interviewed simultaneously

Conditions:

#1: X_{ThA}

#2: Q – X or [X / Q]

#3: U – R or [R / U]

#4: X and Y before Z

Overview:
From the placement of X, we can deduce possible placements for the hostile piece. It must occupy a full two consecutive days, so we can place it on Monday and Tuesday, Tuesday and Wednesday, or Friday and Saturday. We can set up three distinct molds to represent these options efficiently.

#1

	M	T	W	Th	F	S
P	H	H	QR			
A	H	H	U	X		
				~Z		

#2

	M	T	W	Th	F	S
P	QR	H	H			
A	U	H	H	X		
				~Z		

#3

	M	T	W	Th	F	S
P				Z	H	H
A				X	H	H

Mold #1: The second and third conditions allow us to definitively place Q, R, and U on Wednesday. Due to the fourth condition, Z cannot be placed on Thursday.

Mold #2: The second and third conditions allow us to definitively place Q, R, and U on Monday. Due to the fourth condition, Z cannot be placed on Thursday.

Mold #3: Due to the fourth condition, we must place Z on Thursday afternoon.

Although our diagrams contain a vertical element, we can still combine the conditions to show a relative ordering of the interviews:

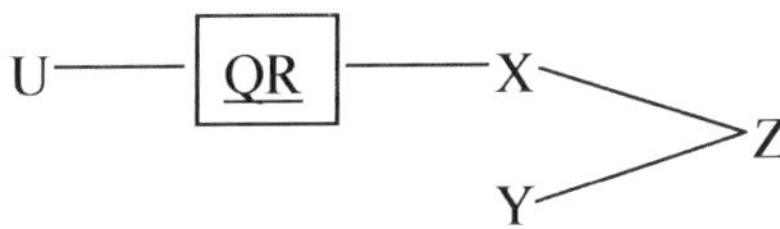

12. (A) violates the third condition
    (B) Q must be interviewed simultaneously with R (setup conditions)
    (C) violates the second condition
    (D) Correct – this could be true under the third mold
    (E) violates the second condition

13. Since the answer choices don't mention hostile witnesses for any of these slots, we know to use the third mold.

    (A) Q must be interviewed simultaneously with R (setup conditions)
    (B) Q must be interviewed simultaneously with R (setup conditions)
    (C) the QR piece must be between U and X
    (D) Correct – see the following diagram

	M	T	W	Th	F	S
P	___	Y	QR	Z	H	H
A	___	U	___	X	H	H

    (E) Z cannot be scheduled for Tuesday afternoon under the third mold

14. **(B)** From this condition, we can deduce the following chain: U – [QR] – X – Y – Z. Since this could not be true under mold #3, we must narrow our focus to the first two molds. Hostile witnesses are reserved for Tuesday in each case, and choice B is correct.

15. **(E)** From this condition, we can deduce the following chain:

    U, Y — [QR] —— X

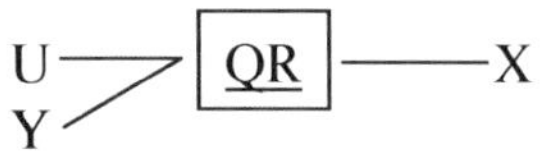

    Since this ordering is only possible under mold #3, we know that Friday and Saturday will be reserved for hostile witnesses, and choice E therefore is correct.

16. **(E)** This could only be true under mold #3. Comparing the choices to the mold reveals that only E must be true in this scenario.

17. **(A)** Since this cannot be true under the mold #3, we must compare the choices to the first two molds. Only choice A could be true (mold #2) in this scenario, and it is therefore correct.

Questions 18-24

Setup:
- seven previously unadvertised products: G H J K L M O
- a different pair will be advertised each week
- exactly one of the products will be a member of two of the pairs

Conditions:

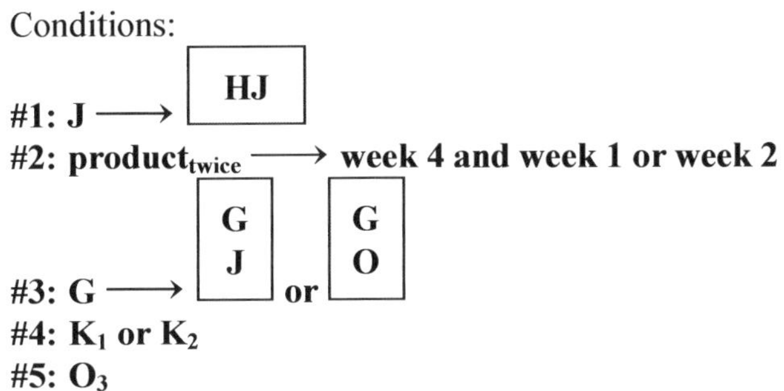

Overview:
In terms of the product which will be advertised twice, we can eliminate J and O from consideration. If J were advertised twice, H would also be advertised twice (first condition), but this contradicts the setup conditions. O cannot be advertised twice due to the second and fifth conditions. Since G must be paired with either J or O (third condition), it cannot be advertised twice. We can also infer that J cannot be advertised during the first week, due to the first condition.

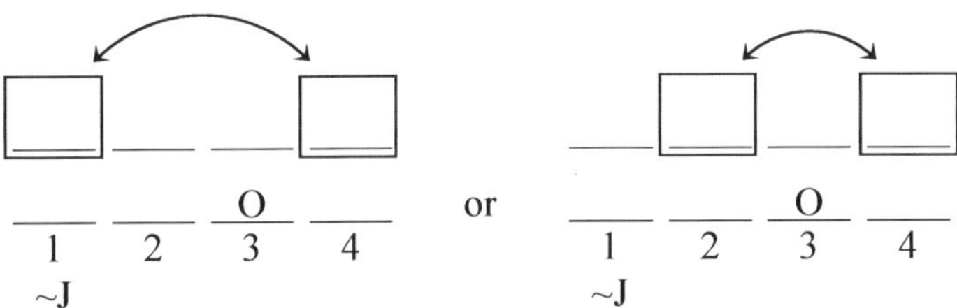

once: G J O
possibly twice: H K L M

18. (A) violates the first condition
    (B) Correct
    (C) violates the third condition
    (D) violates the fourth condition
    (E) violates the first condition

19. To test the pairs completely, you would have to generate complete solutions. Another approach is to come back to this question after completing those that generate diagrams.

    (A) see #22
    (B) see the following diagram

M	K	G	K
H	J	O	L
1	2	3	4

    (C) Correct – since G must be paired with either J or O, and none of the three can be advertised more than once, this would violate the third condition
    (D) see #22, choice E
    (E) see #22

20. This question can be quickly solved after working through all the questions which generate diagrams.

    (A) see #22
    (B) Correct
    (C) see #18
    (D) see #18
    (E) see #18

21. **(A)** As we initially inferred, G, J, and O cannot be advertised twice. G is the only one of the three listed among the choices, and A is correct.

22. **(E)** After placing two Ls, we have to analyze the remaining variables. We're left with the following five: G [HJ] K M. With Ls placed in the second and fourth weeks, in order to satisfy the third condition, we must pair G with O during the third week. This leaves the first and second weeks as the only placement for the HJ piece. We must place K in the first week to satisfy the fourth condition, leaving H to occupy the second fourth-week slot. With Ls placed in the first and fourth weeks, the HJ piece can only be placed in the first two weeks. Otherwise, either the third or the fourth condition would be violated. Since K must be advertised during the first two weeks (fourth condition), it must be placed in week 2, leaving M to occupy the open slot in week 4. In either case, M must be paired with L, and choice E is correct.

H	J	G	H
K	L	O	L
1	2	3	4

or

H	J	G	M
L	K	O	L
1	2	3	4

23. **(D)** Fortunately, we can use our previous work to find the correct answer without having to test all the choices. In number 18, L was advertised during the third week. In number 23, we have two completed diagrams which prove that it could be advertised during the other three weeks as well. Therefore, choice D is correct.

24. Chances are, the correct pair will not be one that we have come across in the other questions, so we'll have to check the choices against the conditions.

    (A) violates the third condition

    (B) this would have to happen during week 2 or week 4, violating the second condition in both cases

    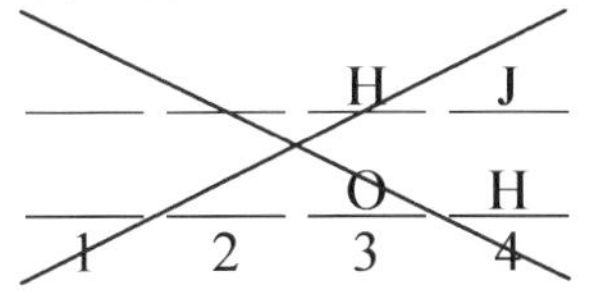

    or

    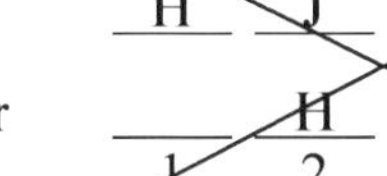

    (C) G would have to be paired with J (third condition); this couldn't happen in the fourth week, since neither G nor J can be advertised twice, and it couldn't happen in the second week, since H would have to be advertised twice (first condition), violating the second condition

    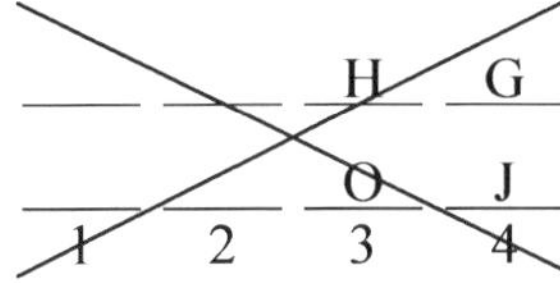

    or

    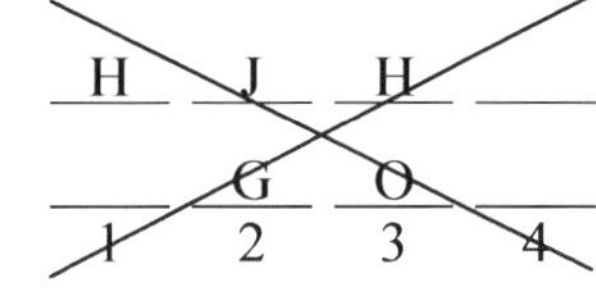

    (D) violates the fourth condition

    (E) Correct – see the following diagram

K	G	M	L
H	J	O	K|H
1	2	3	4

Questions 1-7

Setup:
- seven sponsors: K L M P Q V Z
- three tables: 1 2 3
- only three will receive honors (H): K L M
- only three will give a speech (S): M P Q

Conditions:
#1: at least two sponsors per table; each sponsor sits at exactly one table
#2: K, L, and M must each sit at table 1 or table 2
#3: 

Overview:
Combining the second and third conditions, we know that the only sponsors who can sit at table 3 are P, Q, and Z. Therefore, if one of the three is not at table 3, the first condition dictates that the remaining two must be. The first condition precludes the possibility that any one of the three tables could have four sponsors seated at it. As a further consequence of the first condition, exactly one of the tables must have three sponsors seated at it.

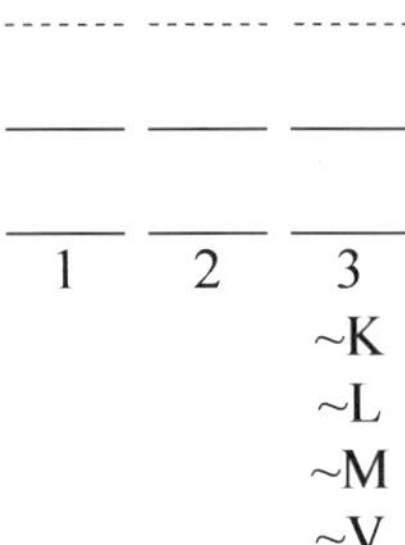

1. (A) violates the second condition
   (B) violates the second condition
   (C) violates the third condition
   (D) Correct
   (E) violates the first condition

2. **(C)** As we have already inferred, P, Q, and Z are the only sponsors who can be seated at table 3. Thus, choice C is correct.

3. **(E)** With K and M occupying a slot in each of the first two tables, we still need to place the LV piece on one of the two. Since the first two tables must have three and two sponsors, not necessarily in that order, we know that table 3 must have two sponsors. Therefore, choice E is correct.

<table><tr><td>L</td><td></td><td></td></tr><tr><td>V</td><td>____</td><td>____</td></tr><tr><td>K|M</td><td>M|K</td><td>____</td></tr><tr><td>1</td><td>2</td><td>3</td></tr></table>

or

<table><tr><td></td><td>L</td><td></td></tr><tr><td>____</td><td>V</td><td>____</td></tr><tr><td>K|M</td><td>M|K</td><td>____</td></tr><tr><td>1</td><td>2</td><td>3</td></tr></table>

4. **(B)** The LV piece must be placed at one of the first two tables, due to the second and third conditions. When it is at table 1, K and M must be seated at table 2 (second condition), leaving P and Z to sit at table 3. When the LV piece is at table 2, K and M must be seated at table 1 (second condition), again leaving P and Z to be assigned to table 3. Thus, it could be true that K and Q are seated at the same table, and choice B is correct.

<table><tr><td>L</td><td></td><td></td></tr><tr><td>V</td><td>K</td><td>P</td></tr><tr><td>Q</td><td>M</td><td>Z</td></tr><tr><td>1</td><td>2</td><td>3</td></tr></table>

or

<table><tr><td>K</td><td></td><td></td></tr><tr><td>M</td><td>V</td><td>P</td></tr><tr><td>Q</td><td>L</td><td>Z</td></tr><tr><td>1</td><td>2</td><td>3</td></tr></table>

5. **(E)** According to this question, exactly one of P and Q must be seated at table 3. Therefore, Z has to fill table 3's second slot. Since Z has been definitively assigned to table 3, choice E is correct.

<table><tr><td>-------</td><td>-------</td><td></td></tr><tr><td>____</td><td>____</td><td>Z</td></tr><tr><td>____</td><td>____</td><td>P|Q</td></tr><tr><td>1</td><td>2</td><td>3</td></tr></table>

6. **(B)** Placing the LV piece at the table 1 prompts us to assign K and M to table 2. Placing the LV piece at table 2 prompts us to assign one of K and M to table 2, since we need two sponsors who receive honors to be seated at table 2. The remaining slot on table 1 would be filled by one of P, Q, and Z. Therefore, it could be true that K and Z are seated at table 1, and choice B is correct.

<table><tr><td></td><td>____</td><td></td></tr><tr><td>L</td><td>K</td><td>____</td></tr><tr><td>V</td><td>M</td><td>____</td></tr><tr><td>1</td><td>2</td><td>3</td></tr></table>

or

<table><tr><td></td><td>M|K</td><td></td></tr><tr><td>____</td><td>L</td><td>____</td></tr><tr><td>K|M</td><td>V</td><td>____</td></tr><tr><td>1</td><td>2</td><td>3</td></tr></table>

7. This is a unique question, and we must analyze how the answer choices affect the possible outcomes.
   (A) see the diagrams for #6
   (B) Correct – in combination with the existing conditions, this would lock K, L, M, P, Q, and V to tables 1 and 2, leaving only Z to sit at table 3, violating the first condition
   (C) see the first diagram for #6
   (D) see #3 and #4
   (E) see #3 and #4

<u>Questions 8-14</u>

Setup:
- o four medical training sessions: M O R S
- o four consecutive days: 1 2 3 4
- o one session each day
- o six professionals
- o three nurses (N): F J L
- o three psychologists (P): T V W
- o each session ⟶ 1N and 1P

Conditions:
#1: each professional ⟶ 1^+ session
#2: L_3

#3: 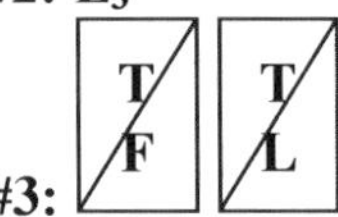

#4: 

#5: **SM**

Overview:
We can combine the fourth and fifth conditions into a bigger piece:

J	
S	M

. Since L is assigned to session 3, this piece can only occupy sessions 1 and 2, or sessions 2 and 3. We also know that J must be paired with T, due to the third condition. Since we know that J is assigned to only one session (fourth condition), we know that T is only assigned to one session. Setting up two molds allows us to represent these options efficiently. Note that once we have assigned J and T, the open nurse slots must be filled by either F or L, and the open psychologist slots must be filled by either V or W.

#1

1	2	3	4
T	V|W	V|W	V|W
J	F|L	L	F|L
S	M	O|R	R|O

#2

1	2	3	4
V|W	T	V|W	V|W
F|L	J	L	F|L
O|R	S	M	R|O

8. **(B)** This could only be true of the first mold. Accordingly, we must assign F to sessions 2 and 4. F must be paired with either V or W for session 2, and choice B is therefore correct.

1	2	3	4
T	V|W	V|W	V|W
J	F	L	F
S	M	R	O

9. **(B)** Checking the answer choices against the molds reveals that choice B must be false. As we previously deduced, S must be scheduled for either day 1 or day 2.

10. **(D)** According to both molds, either O or R must be scheduled for day 4. We can therefore eliminate choices A and E. Since T cannot be assigned to the session on day 4, we can also eliminate choices B and C, leaving D as the correct answer.

11. **(B)** This condition triggers the second mold, and we know that L must be paired with M. Thus, choice B is correct.

12. **(B)** This is only true of the first mold. The possible pairs of professionals for day 2 are FV, FW, LV, and LW. Only FW is presented in the answer choices, and B is therefore correct.

13. Comparing the choices with both our molds and the conditions allows us to eliminate the incorrect choices.

    (A) Correct – could be true under mold #2
    (B) J cannot be assigned to day 4's session
    (C) violates the fourth condition
    (D) violates the fourth condition
    (E) violates the first condition (J is not assigned to any of the four sessions)

14. **(A)** Since this could only be true under the first mold, we know that session R must be scheduled for day 4. Hence, choice A is correct.

Questions 15-19

Setup:

- six paintings hang as pictured

Conditions:

#1: each painting is one of two: O W

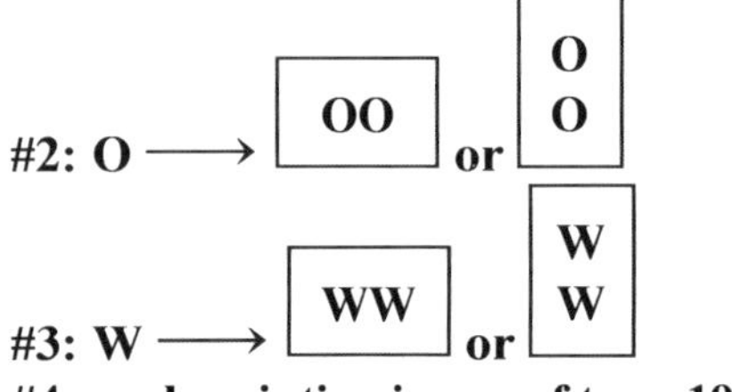

#4: each painting is one of two: 19 20

#5: 19 ⟶ [19 19] or [19 / 19]

#6: 19_2
#7: O_3
#8: 20_5

Overview:
Due to the fifth condition, we know that one of 1 and 3 must be from the nineteenth century. Due to the second condition, we know that one of 2 and 6 must be oil.

1	2	3
___	19	O
___	20	___
4	5	6

15. **(E)** This condition gives us 19 ⟶ W and its contrapositive O ⟶ 20. Since painting 3 is an oil, due to the fifth condition, painting 1 must be from the nineteenth century. Since both 3 and 5 are from the twentieth century, the fifth condition dictates that painting 6 must be from the twentieth century. Therefore, choice E is correct.

1	2	3
W 19	O 19	O 20
	20	20
4	5	6

16. **(D)** This question directly tests our command of the third condition. Only choice D presents an arrangement that is consistent with this condition, and it is therefore correct.

17. **(C)** For this question, the century of each painting is irrelevant, and we need to focus on satisfying the second and third conditions. We can create three scenarios: one with 2 and 6 as oils, one with 6 as an oil, and one with 2 as an oil. Note that if painting 2 is an oil, painting 5 cannot be an oil, as this would violate the third condition. In all three scenarios, painting 4 is a watercolor, and choice C is correct.

1	2	3		1	2	3		1	2	3
W	O	O		W	W	O		O	O	O
W	W	O	or	W	O	O	or	W	W	W
4	5	6		4	5	6		4	5	6

18. **(E)** Mapping out complete solutions would be very time consuming, so instead, we can focus on the painting types and the centuries separately. Applying the second condition, we have two scenarios, and applying the fifth condition, we have two scenarios. Together, these scenarios represent four unique solutions. Since painting 4 cannot be from the nineteenth century, choice E is correct.

1	2	3		1	2	3
W	O	O		W	W	O
W	W	W	or	W	W	O
4	5	6		4	5	6

1	2	3		1	2	3
19	19	20		20	19	19
20	20	20	or	20	20	20
4	5	6		4	5	6

19. Each of the answer choices presents centuries in a two of exactly three format, which tells us that the fifth condition is being tested. Using our initial diagram, we can eliminate the incorrect answer choices.

    (A) Correct – see our diagram for #15
    (B) painting 4 would violate the fifth condition
    (C) painting 6 would violate the fifth condition
    (D) painting 4 would violate the fifth condition
    (E) paintings 2, 4, and 6 would violate the fifth condition

<u>Questions 20-24</u>

Setup:

- six of seven jugglers to be assigned
- seven jugglers: G H K L N P Q
- each of the six is assigned to one of three positions: F M R
- two teams: 1 2
- one juggler is assigned to each position on each team

Conditions:

#1: G_1 or $G_2 \longrightarrow G_F$; H_1 or $H_2 \longrightarrow H_F$
#2: K_1 or $K_2 \longrightarrow K_M$
#3: $\sim L_2$

#4: 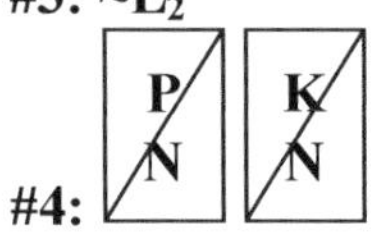

#5: 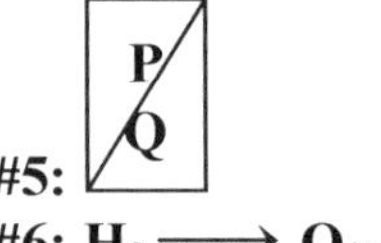

#6: $H_2 \longrightarrow Q_{1M}$

Overview:
With G, H, K, and L precluded from the rear position of team 2, that slot can only be occupied by N, P, or Q.

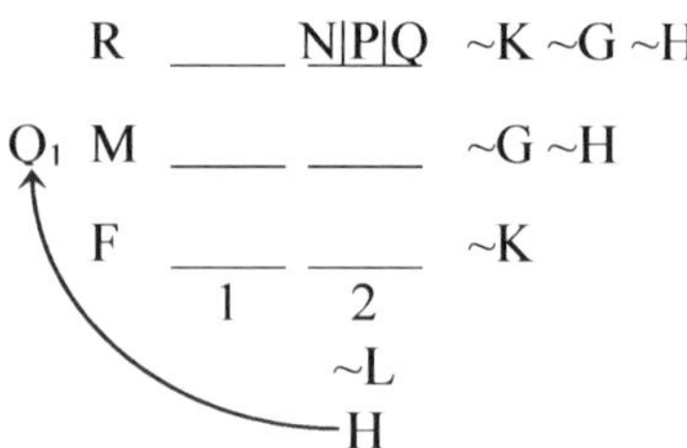

20. (A) violates the fourth condition
    (B) violates the second condition
    (C) violates the third condition
    (D) violates the fifth condition
    (E) Correct – the selection for team 1 would consist of three of H, K, L, and P. The following diagram represents one possible solution.

	1	2
R	L	P
M	K	Q
F	H	G

21. **(E)** This question triggers the sixth condition. Due to the first condition, H must be assigned to the front position. Since Q is assigned to team 1, one of N and P must occupy the rear slot on team 2. Accordingly, we can eliminate choices A through C. Choice D violates the first condition, leaving E as the correct answer. With N assigned to team 1, P would have to occupy the rear slot on team 2. Since G cannot be assigned to the middle position (first condition), K must occupy that slot.

	1	2
R	N	P
M	Q	K
F	L	H

22. Although the question asks about team 1, we must also monitor the possible arrangements for team 2.
    (A) team 2: H, N, and one of P and Q (fifth condition); this triggers and violates the sixth condition
    (B) team 2: H, N, and Q; this triggers and violates the sixth condition
    (C) team 2: one of G and H (first condition) and one of N and P (fourth condition), leaving team 2 with only two members
    (D) team 2: N and one of G and H (first condition), leaving team 2 with only two members
    (E) Correct – see the following diagram

	1	2
R	N	P
M	L	K
F	Q	G

23. This question is essentially a repeat of #22, with pairs of jugglers listed as opposed to complete teams. Due to the first condition, we must place G in the front position of team 1. We must analyze the choices with an eye on the possible arrangements for team 2.

    (A) violates the first condition
    (B) team 2: three of H, N, P, and Q; H cannot be assigned to team 2 since the sixth condition would be triggered and violated, and the other three cannot all be assigned to the same team (fourth condition)
    (C) team 2: three of L, N, P, and Q; L cannot be assigned to team 2 (third condition), and P and Q cannot both be assigned to team 2 (fifth condition)
    (D) team 2: three of H, K, P, and Q; P and Q cannot both be assigned to team 2 (third condition), and H cannot be assigned to team 2, as this would trigger and violate the sixth condition
    (E) Correct – team 2: H, K, and P

R	L	P
M	Q	K
F	G	H
	1	2

24. **(D)** This triggers the fourth condition, and we know that N cannot be on team 2. The options for the rear position on team 2 are now P and Q. If we assign P to this position, we can assign Q to the front position on team 2. On the other hand, if we assign Q to the rear position on team 2, one of H and P would have to be assigned the front position. Assigning H to this position would trigger and violate the sixth condition. We cannot assign P to this position, due to the fifth condition. Thus, choice D is correct.

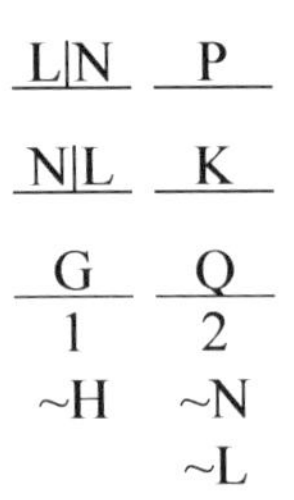

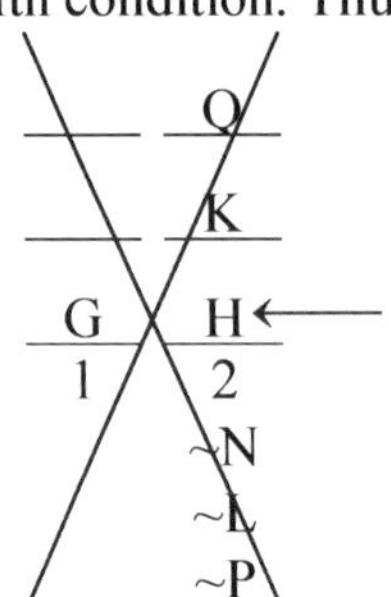

Questions 1-5

Setup:
- seven music pieces: F G H J K L M
- each will fill exactly one of the seven sequential tracks

Conditions:
#1: F_2
#2: ~J_7
#3: 
#4: H – L
#5: L – M

Overview:
We can combine the fourth and fifth conditions to make the following chain: H – L – M.

1	2	3	4	5	6	7
	F					
						~J

1. (A) violates the first condition
   (B) Correct
   (C) violates the second condition
   (D) violates the third condition
   (E) violates the fourth condition

2. **(D)** Combining this information with our chain, we have:

   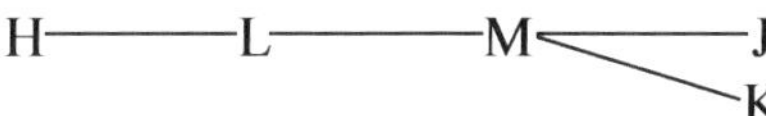

   Since H is followed by four variables, it must be either first or third. Therefore, choice D is correct.

1	2	3	4	5	6	7
H|	F	|H				

3. **(B)** From our chain, we know that neither L nor M can be first. We also know that F cannot be first, due to the first condition. All the other variables could be first, and choice B is correct.

4. **(C)** Our chain indicates that M must be preceded by at least two other variables. However, it cannot be third, since F occupies the second slot, leaving only one slot for H and L. Therefore, the earliest track M can fill is the fourth, and choice C is correct.

H	F	L	M			
1	2	3	4	5	6	7

5. **(D)** Combining this with our chain, we have: [GH] – L – M. With F occupying the second slot, the GH piece can occupy the third and fourth or the fourth and fifth slots. These four variables must follow F, which means that one of J and K must occupy the first slot. Therefore, K cannot immediately precede J, and choice D is correct.

J|K	F	G	H			
J|K	F	K|J	G	H	L	M
1	2	3	4	5	6	7

Questions 6-11

Setup:

- seven applicants: F G J K L M O
- hired ⟶ interviewed; ~interviewed ⟶ ~hired (contrapositive)

Conditions:

#1: $G_I \longrightarrow J_I$; $\sim J_I \longrightarrow \sim G_I$ (contrapositive)
#2: $J_I \longrightarrow L_I$; $\sim L_I \longrightarrow \sim J_I$ (contrapositive)
#3: F_I
#4: $F_H \longrightarrow K_I$; $\sim K_I \longrightarrow \sim F_H$ (contrapositive)
#5: $K_H \longrightarrow M_I$; $\sim M_I \longrightarrow \sim K_H$ (contrapositive)
#6: M_H and $L_I \longrightarrow O_H$; $\sim O_H \longrightarrow \sim M_H$ or $\sim L_I$ (contrapositive)

Overview:
We can combine the first two conditions into the following chains:
$G_I \longrightarrow J_I \longrightarrow L_I$
$\sim L_I \longrightarrow \sim J_I \longrightarrow \sim G_I$ (contrapositive)

6. (A) violates the first condition
   (B) violates the second condition
   (C) Correct
   (D) violates the first condition
   (E) violates the second condition

7. (A) violates the third condition
   (B) violates the second condition
   (C) from our chain, we know that J and L must also be interviewed, along with F (third condition)
   (D) from our chain, we know that J and L must also be interviewed, along with F (third condition)
   (E) Correct – from our chain, we know that J and L must be interviewed, and F must also be interviewed (third condition)

8. **(E)** Applying this information to the contrapositive of the fifth condition, we know that K is not hired. Since all the choices feature F and K, we should focus on these variables. Other than the fact that F is interviewed (third condition) we cannot infer anything else, and choice E is therefore correct.

9. **(E)** Since there are seven applicants in total, we know that only one of them is not interviewed. From our chain, we know that J and L must be interviewed, and the third condition dictates that F is interviewed. Therefore, exactly two of K, M, and O must be interviewed. Three of the answer choices (A, B, and D) contain M. If M were hired, the sixth condition would be triggered, but the choices don't contain O. Thus, we can eliminate choices A, B, and D. Choice C triggers the fifth condition, and since it contains O, all three of K, M, and O would have to be interviewed, which violates the condition given in the question. The following diagram proves the validity of choice E.

I	H
___ } 2 of K M O	
___	
F	
G	G
J	J
L	L

10. **(B)** In combination with the setup condition, we now have the following biconditional: interviewed $\longleftrightarrow$ hired. We can infer that F must be hired, due to the third condition. This triggers the fourth and fifth conditions: $F_H \longrightarrow K_I \longrightarrow K_H \longrightarrow M_I \longrightarrow M_H$. Since M is hired and L is interviewed, the sixth condition is triggered, and we know that O is both interviewed and hired. Thus, the only one of the five candidates who doesn't have to be interviewed is J, and choice B is correct.

11. **(B)** This question triggers the contrapositive of the sixth condition. If L were not interviewed, the contrapositives of the first and second conditions would also be triggered. This would result in four candidates not being interviewed: G, J, L, and O. However, the question dictates that exactly four candidates are hired. We can therefore infer that L is interviewed and M is not hired, and choice B must be false.

Questions 12-18

Setup:

- six of seven researchers will be selected
- three anthropologists (A): F J M
- four linguists (L): N O R S
- two three-person teams: 1 2
- no researcher will be on both teams
- each team ⟶ 1^+ A and 1^+ L

Conditions:

#1: 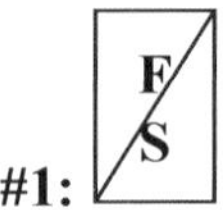

#2: N / R

#3: M / R   M / S

#4: $J_1 \longrightarrow R_2$; $\sim R_2 \longrightarrow \sim J_1$

Overview:
The fourth condition, if triggered, sets off a number of deductions. With J_1 and R_2, we must place one of F and M on team 2. Placing M on team 2 would violate the third condition, and we must therefore place F on team 2. The first and third conditions preclude M, N, and S from being on team 2, leaving only O to occupy that slot. Finally, since only one of M and S could be on team 1 (third condition), we must place N in the final open slot. Thus, there are only two viable solutions when the fourth condition is triggered.

	M|S	O
A	J	F
L	N	R
	1	2
		~M
		~N
		~S

12. (A) violates the second condition
    (B) violates the first condition
    (C) Correct
    (D) violates the setup condition that each team must include at least one anthropologist
    (E) violates the fourth condition

13. **(A)** Since this triggers the fourth condition, we can use our diagram to select the correct answer choice. O, F, and R must all be on team 2 under this scenario, and choice A is therefore correct.

14. **(D)** Since we have inferred two solutions with N on team 1, it makes sense to look for an answer choice which matches one of them. Choice D matches one of the solutions, and it is therefore correct.

15. **(C)** Since F and M are on the same team, we know that J must be on the other team, due to the last setup condition. According to our diagram, F and M cannot be on the same team when the fourth condition is triggered. We can therefore infer that F and M are on team 1, and J is on team 2. Since neither R nor S can be on team 1 (first and third conditions) N or O must be the third member. Choices A, B, D, and E all contradict this scenario, so we can eliminate them, leaving choice C as the correct answer. Under this scenario, one of N, O, and R would be the third member of team 2.

	M	___
A	F	J
L	N|O	S
	1	2
	~R	
	~S	

16. **(B)** Recycling our work from question 15, we know that if F and M are to be on the same team, they have to be on team 1. Thus, choice B is correct.

17. **(A)** From question 12, we know that choice A could be true.

18. **(B)** To satisfy the condition that each team has at least one anthropologist, we must place either F or J on team 1. Placing J on team 1 would trigger the fourth condition; our diagram for this scenario is incompatible with the question. We can therefore definitively place F on team 1. With F and M placed, we can deduce from the first and third conditions that S is not on either team. Since all six of the other researchers must be placed, we have to place J on team 2, and choice B is correct.

	O	N
A	F	J
L	R	M
	1	2
	~S	~S

Questions 19-24

Setup:

- five candidates: Q R S T U
- each will speak once at each meeting
- three meetings: 1 2 3
- five consecutive time slots for each meeting
- no two candidates will speak in the same time slot at any meeting

Conditions:

#1: each candidate ⟶ first or second at at least one of the meetings
#2: Q_5 ⟶ Q_1; R_5 ⟶ R_1; S_5 ⟶ S_1; T_5 ⟶ T_1; U_5 ⟶ U_1
#3: no candidate speaks fourth at more than one meeting

Overview:
To represent the first condition, we can box the first two slots of all three meetings. Since the boxed slots must contain all five candidates, we can infer that one of the candidates will occupy two of the six slots.

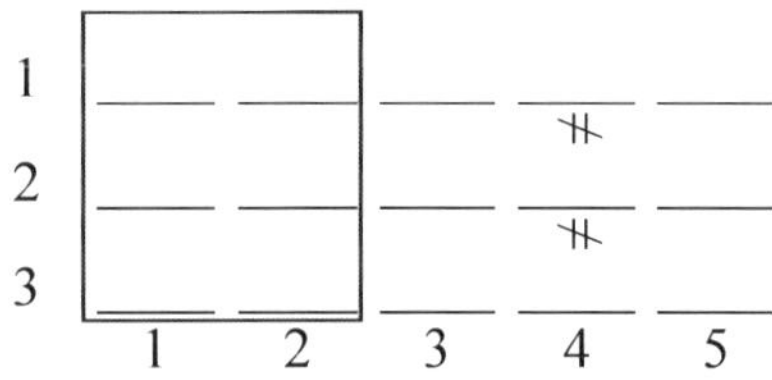

19. (A) violates the first condition
    (B) violates the second condition
    (C) violates the third condition
    (D) Correct
    (E) violates the second condition

20. **(D)** With R occupying two of the six boxed slots, we know that the remaining four candidates must occupy the open slots. Therefore, R can occupy any but the first two slots at the third meeting, and choice D is correct.

21. **(B)** Applying the second condition, we must place T in the first slot of meeting three. Due to the first condition, S must occupy the second slot of meeting three. Choice A, C, and D violate this scenario, and we can eliminate them. U cannot be fifth, since the second condition would be triggered, and the first slot of each meeting is already occupied. Thus, we can eliminate choice E, and B is left as the correct answer, as proven by the following diagram.

1	R	U	S	T	Q
2	Q	R	U	S	T
3	T	S	R	U	Q
	1	2	3	4	5

22. **(E)** With R and S collectively occupying the first slot of each meeting, the second condition dictates that they are the only candidates who can speak fifth at any of the meetings. We must therefore place S fifth for meetings 1 and 2, and R fifth for meeting 3. Choice E is thus correct.

1	R				S
2	R				S
3	S				R
	1	2	3	4	5

23. **(C)** This question tests our command of the first condition. We know that one particular candidate cannot occupy three of the boxed slots, so we can eliminate choices A and B. In addition, if one particular candidate followed at least two candidates at every meeting, the first condition would also be violated, allowing us to eliminate choices D and E. Choice C is left as the correct answer.

24. **(A)** Due to the first condition, two of the remaining boxed slots must be occupied by Q and R. Since one candidate cannot speak fifth at all three meetings (first condition), one of Q and R must speak fifth at at least one of the meetings. Therefore, choice A is correct.

1		S			
2		T			
3		U			
	1	2	3	4	5

Questions 1-5

Setup:

- o two recipes: A M
- o seven flavorings: F G L N P S T
- o no flavoring is included in more than one recipe

Conditions:

#1: $A = 3^-$

#2: 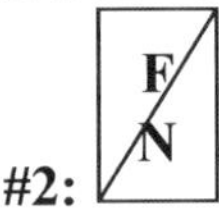

#3: 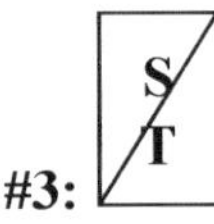

#4: 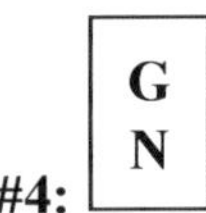

Overview:

In combination, the first and fourth conditions allow us to infer two basic molds.

#1

A	M
	L
S|T	P
G	T|S
N	F

#2

A	M
	- - - - - - -
	____
- - - - - - -	T|S
S|T	G
F	N

Mold #1: With the GN piece included in the appetizer recipe, the second condition stipulates that F must be included in the main-dish recipe. Since one of S and T must occupy the final slot above A (third condition), L and P must be placed above M.

Mold #2: With the GN piece included in the main-dish recipe, the second condition stipulates that F must be included in the appetizer recipe. Other than the S|T split, we cannot immediately infer anything else from this mold. Note that you could use this mold to create six possible solutions, but it would likely use up more time than it's worth.

1. (A) violates the first condition
   (B) violates the second condition
   (C) violates the third condition (S and T are both included in the appetizer recipe)
   (D) Correct
   (E) violates the third condition

2. **(A)** This question triggers the first mold. We know that the appetizer must include G and N, and choice A is therefore correct.

3. **(A) Correct – see mold #2**
   (B) violates the third condition
   (C) violates the second condition
   (D) violates the fourth condition
   (E) violates the first condition

4. **(B)** According to both molds, only the main-dish recipe can include both L and P. Thus, choice B is correct.

5. Since this question removes the fourth condition, we can use the other three conditions to eliminate the incorrect answers.

   (A) violates the third condition (S and T are both included in the appetizer recipe)
   (B) violates the second condition (N and F are both included in the appetizer recipe)
   (C) Correct
   (D) violates the third condition
   (E) violates the second condition

<u>Questions 6-10</u>

Setup:
- seven singers: J K L M N O P
- each singer will perform alone
- each singer will give exactly one performance

Conditions:

#1: | **KJ** |

#2: M – P
#3: $\mathbf{L_3 \longrightarrow N_5; \sim N_5 \longrightarrow \sim L_3}$ **(contrapositive)**
#4: $\mathbf{P_2}$ **or** $\mathbf{P_5}$

Overview:
Our basic sketch is the following:

P|			|P		
1	2	3	4	5	6	7
		L———→N				~M

The conditions interact in such a way that if the third condition is triggered, we can derive a complete solution.

L_3 ——→

M	P	L	O	N	K	J
1	2	3	4	5	6	7

With N occupying the fifth slot, the fourth condition dictates that P must occupy the second slot. The KJ piece (first condition) must occupy the sixth and the seventh slots. M must be first, due to the second condition, leaving O to occupy the fourth slot.

6. **(A) Correct**
   (B) violates the second condition
   (C) violates the fourth condition
   (D) violates the first condition
   (E) violates the third condition

7. **(B)** Since this question triggers the third condition, we know that K must be sixth, and choice B is correct.

8. **(C)** With N fifth, the fourth condition dictates that P must be second. Applying the second condition, we know that M must be first. The KJ piece can either be placed third and fourth or sixth and seventh. Accordingly, only choice C could be true.

M	P	K	J	N	L|O	O|L
M	P	L|O	O|L	N	K	J
1	2	3	4	5	6	7

9. **(E)** Applying the fourth condition, we know that P must be fifth. The KJ piece can either be placed third and fourth or sixth and seventh. Due to the contrapositive of the third condition, L cannot be third. Only choice E could be true (under the second scenario).

	M	K	J	P		
L|	M		|L	P	K	J
1	2	3	4	5	6	7
		~L				

10. **(A)** Combining this with the first condition, we have the following piece: [KJL]. Due to the possible placements of P, this piece also has limited placements. With P placed fifth, if we place the KJL piece in the first, second, and third slots, the third condition is triggered and violated. Thus, J cannot be second under this scenario, and choice A is correct.

1	2	3	4	5	6	7
~~K~~	~~J~~	~~L~~	~~ ~~	~~P~~		
M	K	J	L	P		
M	P	K	J	L		
M	P		K	J	L	
M	P			K	J	L

Questions 11-17

Setup:
- six textbooks
- three introductory: F G H
- three advanced: X Y Z
- each will be evaluated once by the editor and once by the publisher
- editor: J
- publisher: R

Conditions:
#1: $F_J - F_R$; $G_J - G_R$; $H_J - H_R$
#2: $X_R - X_J$; $Y_R - Y_J$; $Z_R - Z_J$
#3: $\sim II_R$
#4: X_{4J}

Overview:
We can infer that R cannot evaluate two advanced textbooks consecutively since this would lead to R evaluating two introductory textbooks consecutively, violating the third condition. Accordingly, R must evaluate at least one introductory textbook during the first three weeks. If R evaluated two introductory textbooks during the first three weeks, this would have to happen in the first and third weeks (third condition). However, this would violate the first condition. Therefore, we know that R must evaluate exactly one introductory textbook during the first three weeks, and it must be during the second week. With a sequence of A, I, and A for the first three weeks, we can infer that the second three weeks for R are sequenced I, A, and I respectively. To satisfy the first condition, J must review an introductory textbook during the first week. To satisfy the second condition, J must review an advanced textbook during the sixth week.

J	I			A X		A
R	A	I	A	I	A	I
	1	2	3	4	5	6

We can create three distinct molds which represent the textbook-type arrangements based on the possible placements of the other advanced textbook for J.

#1	J	I	A	I	A X	I	A
	R	A	I	A	I	A	I
		1	2	3	4	5	6

#2	J	I	I	A	A X	I	A
	R	A	I	A	I	A	I
		1	2	3	4	5	6

#3	J	I	I	I	A X	A	A
	R	A	I	A	I	A	I
		1	2	3	4	5	6

11. (A) violates the fourth condition
    (B) Correct
    (C) violates the third condition
    (D) violates the first condition
    (E) violates the second condition

12. **(A)** Since this could be true under either the first or the third mold, our best approach is to plug the information into our main diagram, and note what must follow. Since R must evaluate H after J, and R must evaluate an advanced textbook during the fourth week, we can place an H in R's fourth slot. This only leaves R's second slot to accommodate F. Due to the first condition, J must evaluate F during the first week. Hence, choice A is correct.

J	F	G|	H	X	|G	
R		F		H		G
	1	2	3	4	5	6

13. **(D)** This question triggers the first mold. Since J only has one slot left (the sixth) to accommodate an advanced textbook, we must place Y in that slot. The only arrangement of advanced textbooks for R which will satisfy the second condition is Z, X, and Y. Therefore, choice D is correct.

J		Z		X		Y
R	Z		X		Y	
	1	2	3	4	5	6

14. **(B)** This question directly tests our inference regarding the arrangement of textbook types. As we inferred, R must evaluate an advanced textbook during the third week, and choice B is correct.

15. Since R must evaluate an advanced textbook in during week 3 and week 5, they must be Y and Z, in either order. To satisfy the second condition, J must evaluate Y and Z during the fifth and sixth weeks, in either order. Thus, we are dealing with the third mold. G and H must occupy the two remaining open slots for both J and R.

J	F	G|H	H|G	X	Y|Z	Z|Y
R	X	F	Y|Z	G|H	Z|Y	H|G
	1	2	3	4	5	6

(A) X must be the first advanced textbook J evaluates
(B) X must be the first advanced textbook J evaluates
(C) J evaluates all three introductory textbooks in succession
(D) J must evaluate one of Y and Z during week 5
(E) Correct

16. **(A)** Glancing back at our molds reveals that week 1 is the only week during which J must evaluate an introductory textbook. Therefore, choice A is correct.

17. (A) J must evaluate an advanced textbook during week 6
(B) J must evaluate an introductory textbook during week 1
(C) R must evaluate an advanced textbook during week 3
(D) Correct – see the following acceptable diagram

J	H	Y	F	X	G	Z
R	Y	H	X	F	Z	G
	1	2	3	4	5	6

(E) violates the second condition

Questions 18-23

Setup:
- nine different treatments
- three antibiotics (A): F G H
- three dietary regimens (D): M N O
- three physical therapies (P): U V W

Conditions:
#1: all three antibiotics cannot be prescribed
#2: exactly one D
#3: ~O ⟶ ~F; F ⟶ O (contrapositive)
#4: W ⟶ ~F; F ⟶ ~W (contrapositive)
#5: G ⟶ ~N or ~U; N and U ⟶ ~G (contrapositive)
#6: V ⟶ H; ~H ⟶ ~V (contrapositive)
V ⟶ M; ~M ⟶ V (contrapositive)

Overview:
As a consequence of the first two rules, we can infer two possible allocations of prescriptions to types:

A	D	P
1	1	3
2	1	2

When all three Ps are prescribed, the sixth rule dictates that H and M be prescribed. For this scenario, we have:

#1

		U
		V
H	M	W
A	D	P

Under the second allocation, we must exclude F. Why? Due to the contrapositive of the third rule, if F were selected, O would be selected. The fourth rule would preclude W from being selected. However, the sixth rule would require M to be prescribed, but with O already occupying that slot, this isn't possible. Therefore, we know that G and H are both selected under this allocation, and we can create three additional molds by excluding a different one of U, V, and W.

#2

A	D	P
G		U
H	M	V

#3

A	D	P
G		U
H	M|O	W

#4

A	D	P
G		V
H	M	W

Mold #2: With V selected, the sixth condition dictates that M must also be selected.

Mold #3: Since U and W are selected, fifth condition precludes N from being selected.

Mold #4: With V selected, the sixth condition dictates that M must also be selected.

18. (A) violates the first condition
    (B) violates the second condition
    (C) violates the second condition
    (D) violates the fifth condition
    (E) Correct – see the third mold

19. (A) violates the first condition
    (B) violates the sixth condition
    (C) violates the fourth condition
    (D) violates the sixth condition
    (E) Correct – see the first mold

20. **(E)** This could only be true under the third mold, and we can infer a complete solution. Hence, choice E is correct.

A	D	P
G		U
H	O	W

21. **(E)** Since this is true of the second, third, and fourth molds, we can check the choices against the molds to eliminate those that are incorrect. Only choice E is possible (under the fourth mold), and it is therefore correct.

22. **(D)** Again, we can check the choices against the molds to eliminate those that are incorrect. Only choice D is possible (under the fourth mold), and it is thus correct.

23. **(C)** Our molds reveal that neither F nor N can be prescribed under any scenario. Since N is the only one of the two listed, choice C is correct.

Questions 1-5

Setup:
- two committees: P T
- seven volunteers: F G H J K L M

Conditions:
#1: each committee = 3^+ members

#2: 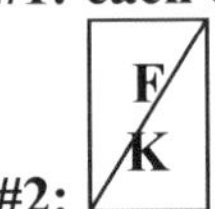

#3: K ⟶ [K J]; ~J ⟶ ~K (contrapositive)
#4: M ⟶ 1^+ committee
#5: 1^+ member in common

Overview:
Combining the conditions doesn't allow us to infer much, so it's best to create our sketch and head to the questions.

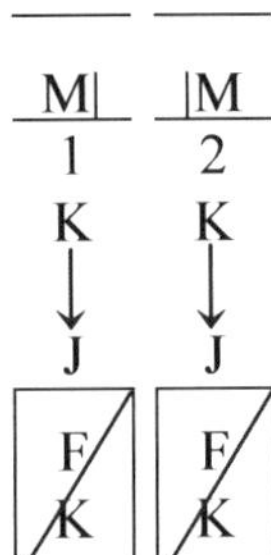

1. (A) violates the fourth condition
   (B) Correct
   (C) violates the third condition (T)
   (D) violates the first condition (T)
   (E) violates the second condition (P)

2. **(B)** This is a rare question type in which we're given an acceptable solution and asked to replace one of the variables with K. Replacing H, L, or M on the planting committee would violate the second condition. Replacing H on the trails committee would violate the fifth condition. Finally, replacing F on the planting committee would violate the third condition. Consequently, we can eliminate choices A, C, D, and E, leaving B as the correct answer.

P	T		P	T
F			F	
H	G	⟶	H	K
L	H		L	H
M	J		M	J

3. **(D)** None of the conditions preclude G, H, or L from being on both committees. To satisfy the fourth condition, we must place M on the trails committee. J and/or K could be on trails, but neither one must be on trails. Thus, choice D is correct.

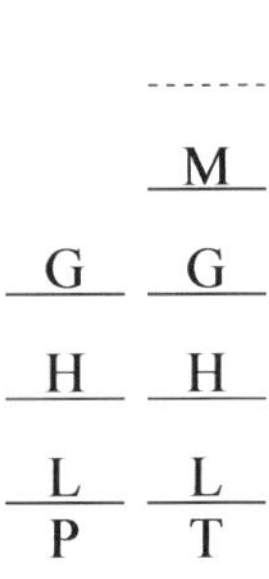

4. **(E)** Applying the third condition, we know that J is also on both committees. Since planting has exactly three members, we must place M on trails to satisfy the fourth condition. Thus, the only one of the choices that must be true is E.

P	T

	M
J	J
K	K
L	L

5. **(D)** The conditions don't specify a maximum number per committee, so we can place six people on each one. The second condition precludes us from placing seven people on each committee. We can place all five of the other people in addition to one of F and K on both committees. Thus, the correct answer is choice D.

P	T
F|K	K|F
G	G
H	H
J	J
L	L
M	M

Questions 6-12

Setup:

- six tourists: H I K L M N
- four guides: V X Y Z
- each tourist ⟶ 1 guide
- each guide ⟶ 1^+ tourist
- V: F
- X: T S
- Y: F T
- Z: S R

Conditions:

#1: H_Y and I_Y

#2: L_Z

#3: K_X ⟶ M_{French}; $\sim M_{French}$ ⟶ K_X (contrapositive)

Overview:
Incorporating the third condition, our diagram is as follows:

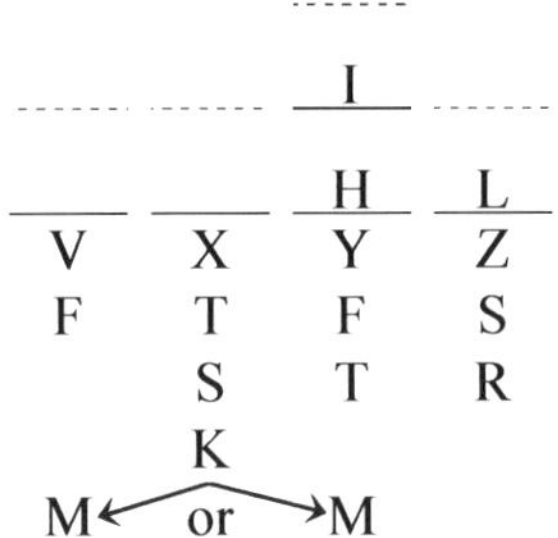

We can further draw out distinct molds based on the possible placements of K.

#1

|M

I

M|N	K	H	L
V	X	Y	Z

#2

I

K	M|N	H	L
V	X	Y	Z

#3

K|

I |K

M|N	N|M	H	L
V	X	Y	Z

Mold #1: With K assigned to X, the third condition is triggered, and consequently, M must be assigned to either V or Y.

Mold #2: With K assigned to V, one of M and N must be assigned to X.

Mold #3: With K assigned to either Y or Z, either one of M and N must be assigned to V, and the other must be assigned to X.

6. (A) see mold #1
   (B) this could be true under the second or the third mold
   (C) Correct – K and M cannot both be assigned to Z, as one of V and X would be lacking a tourist
   (D) this could be true under the second or the third mold
   (E) this could be true under the first or the third mold

7. **(A)** Choice A presents an immediate impossibility. If Z were assigned three tourists, only one tourist could be assigned to V and X, which violates the setup condition that each guide must be assigned at least one tourist.

8. (A) see mold #2
   (B) Correct – this would only leave one of V and X without a tourist
   (C) see mold #2
   (D) see mold #3
   (E) see mold #3

9. **(E)** Applying this information to our master sketch, we know that K must be assigned to either X or Z. We should therefore narrow our focus to the first and third molds. In both molds, one of M and N must be assigned to V. Since V only speaks French, we know that one of M and N must also speak French, and choice E is therefore correct.

10. **(B)** Applying this information to our master sketch, we know that N must be assigned to either X or Z. If N is assigned to Z, then one of K and M is assigned to X. If N is assigned to X, then one of K and M can be assigned to X. In either case, a maximum of three people can speak Turkish (I, H, and one of K and M), and choice B is correct.

V	X	Y	Z
		I_T	N
K|M	M|K	H_T	L

or

V	X	Y	Z
	M|K	I_T	
K|M	N_S	H_T	L_S

11. This could be true using either the first or the second mold. If K is assigned to X, then the third condition is triggered, and M must be assigned to V. Otherwise, V wouldn't have any assigned tourists.

V	X	Y	Z
	N	I	
M	K	H	L

or

V	X	Y	Z
	M	I	
K	N	H	L

   (A) N must speak either Spanish or Turkish
   (B) N must speak either Spanish or Turkish
   (C) N must speak either Spanish or Turkish
   (D) M and K cannot both be assigned to X
   (E) Correct – this could be true in the first scenario

12. There are two options for this scenario. All four must either speak French or Turkish. Therefore, we must assign M and N as a pair to either V or X.

V	X	Y	Z
M		I	
N	K	H	L

or

V	X	Y	Z
	M	I	
K	N	H	L

   (A) K cannot be assigned to Z
   (B) only L is assigned to Z
   (C) only K and L could both speak Spanish
   (D) either one or four tourists could speak Turkish
   (E) Correct – this must be true under the second option

Questions 13-18

Setup:
- six people: K L M O P S
- each plays exactly one of two sports
- sports: G T
- G and/or T = 1^{+} ⟶ they are ranked from lowest to highest (no ties)

Conditions:
#1: O_T
#2: L_G
#3: L_{G1}
#4: M_G ⟶ P_G (M – P – S); P_T ⟶ M_T (contrapositive)
M_G ⟶ S_G; S_T ⟶ M_T (contrapositive)
#5: M_T ⟶ S_T (O – S – M); S_G ⟶ M_G (contrapositive)
#6: P_T ⟶ K_T (K – O – P); K_G ⟶ P_G (contrapositive)

Overview:
We can use our diagram to make necessary inferences as we work through the questions. Note that we can combine the third and fourth conditions to infer a four-person order in the event that M plays golf.

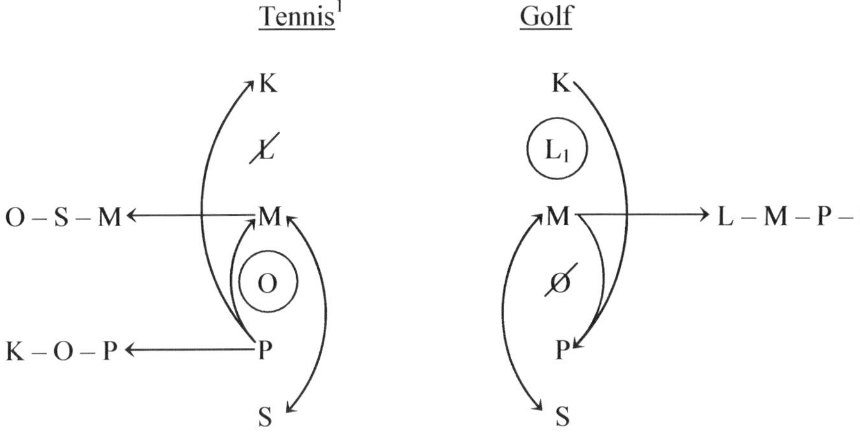

13. (A) M and S must play the same sport
(B) violates the sixth condition
(C) Correct
(D) violates the sixth condition
(E) violates the fifth condition

[1] Visit Manhattan LSAT (http://www.manhattanlsat.com) to learn more about using this diagram.

14. **(A)** Choice A presents an impossibility. Following the chain from S_T, we have M_T, and S precedes M. Thus, S cannot be the lowest-ranking tennis player.

15. (A) violates the contrapositive of the fourth condition (M should be included)
    (B) violates the sixth condition (should be K – O – P)
    (C) violates the fifth condition (should be O – S – M)
    (D) Correct
    (E) violates the sixth condition (O should be included, and the order should be K – O – P)

16. **(C)** Following the chain from S_G, we have M_G and P_G. The only uncertainty is which sport K plays, and choice C is therefore correct.

G	T
O	L
K|	S
	M
	P
	|K

17. **(B)** Since the ordering given by the sixth condition runs contrary to the question, we can conclude that P plays golf. Therefore, L and P play the same sport as each other, and choice B is correct.

18. This question adds an additional condition: $S_G \longleftrightarrow P_T$; $P_G \longleftrightarrow S_T$.
    (A) K, M, and S would all play the same sport
    (B) M and S would play the opposite sport as K and P
    (C) Correct – since M and S play the same sport, this would violate the new condition
    (D) K and S would play the same sport as each other
    (E) M and S would play the opposite sport as K

Questions 19-24

Setup:
- sequence of seven songs
- ballads (B): F G H
- dance tunes (D): R S V X

Conditions:

#1: 

#2: **H – V**

#3: **S|V __ V|S**

#4: **FS**

#5: ~RF ⟶ G – R; R – G ⟶ RF (contrapositive)

Overview:
Combining the first condition with the fact that there are seven songs, we can ascertain that the dance tunes occupy the first, third, fifth, and seventh slots. Therefore, the ballads must occupy the second, fourth, and sixth slots.

D	B	D	B	D	B	D	B B B D D D D
							F G H R S V X
1	2	3	4	5	6	7	
~V							

19. (A) violates the first condition
    (B) violates the fourth condition
    (C) violates the third condition
    (D) violates the second condition
    (E) Correct

20. **(D)** Since two songs of the same type cannot be played consecutively, choice D must be true.

21. **(A)** Because the fourth song must be a ballad, it must be one of F, G, and H. Only G is listed among the choices, and A is therefore correct.

22. **(A)** The first song must be a dance tune, so we can immediately eliminate choices D and E. Placing V first would violate the second condition. Thus, we can eliminate choice C. Placing S first would force V into the third slot (third condition). Due to the second condition, H would have to be second, which would violate the fourth condition. Choice A is therefore correct.

(A)	R	F	S	H	V	G	X
(B)	S	H	V				
	1	2	3	4	5	6	7

23. **(A)** We know that V cannot be first, due to the first condition. To satisfy the third condition, we must place V fifth. Due to the second condition, H must be either second or fourth. Applying the fourth condition, we know that F must also be second or fourth. Therefore, the only available slot left for G is the sixth, and choice A is correct.

R|X	F|H	S	H|F	V	G	X|R
1	2	3	4	5	6	7

24. **(D)** In question twenty-two, we ruled out either of S or V as the first song. With R placed last, the only song that could be first is X. The first song must be a dance tune, so we can eliminate choices A through C. Since X must be first, we can eliminate choice E, and D is left as the correct answer.

X		S|V		V|S		R
1	2	3	4	5	6	7

<u>Questions 1-7</u>

Setup:

- eight physics students
- four majors (M): F G H J
- four nonmajors (N): V W X Y
- four laboratory benches: 1 2 3 4
- each student is assigned to exactly one bench
- exactly two students to each bench

Conditions:

#1: each bench ⟶ 1 M

#2: 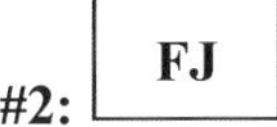

#3: 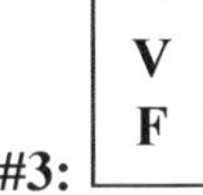

#4: 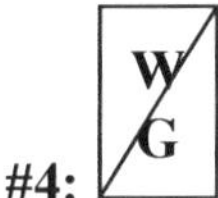

Overview:
Combining the first condition with the fact that there are four benches, we can infer that exactly one nonmajor will be assigned to each bench. We can combine the pieces given by the second and third conditions into a larger piece: V / F J

				~V	
N	____	____	____	____	V W X Y
M	____	____	____	____	F G H J
	1	2	3	4	
	~J			~F	

1. (A) violates the first condition (bench 4)
   (B) violates the third condition (bench 2)
   (C) Correct
   (D) violates the second condition (benches 3 and 4)
   (E) violates the fourth condition (bench 2)

2. **(B)** This question places the large piece into the second and third benches. Due to the fourth condition, G must be assigned to bench 1. Thus, choice B is correct.

X|Y	V	Y|X	W
G	F	J	H
1	2	3	4

3. **(A)** The only way to separate G and H is by assigning the large piece to the second and third benches. As such, choice A must be true.

	V		
G|H	F	J	H|G
1	2	3	4

4. **(D)** With this information, we can assign the large piece to either benches 2 and 3 or benches 3 and 4. The fourth condition dictates that W be assigned to bench 3 in the first case and bench 4 in the second case. Thus, only choice D could be true.

Y	V	W	X		Y	X	V	W
H	F	J	G	or	H	G	F	J
1	2	3	4		1	2	3	4

5. **(E)** Under this scenario, the large piece can be assigned to either benches 1 and 2 or benches 2 and 3. Due to the fourth condition, W must be assigned to the bench 2 in the first case, and bench 1 in the second case. In either case, J is not paired with Y, and choice E is therefore correct.

V	W	X	Y		W	V	X	Y
F	J	H	G	or	H	F	J	G
1	2	3	4		1	2	3	4

6. **(A)** Combining this with the large piece, we have: [— / H] – [V / F J]. Choice A is therefore correct.

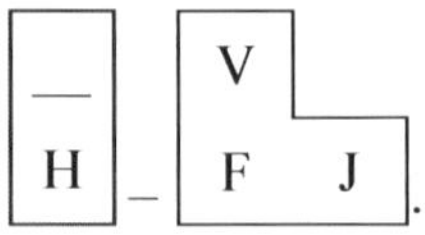

7. (A) this configuration doesn't allow room for the large piece

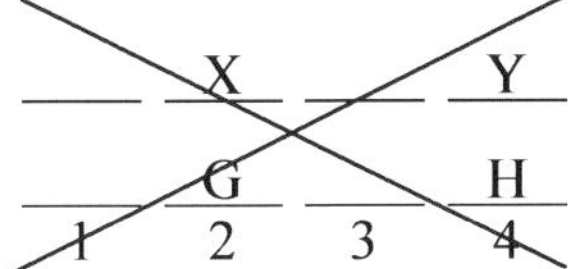

(B) with J assigned to the fourth bench, the large piece must be assigned to benches 3 and 4, forcing W and G to violate the fourth condition

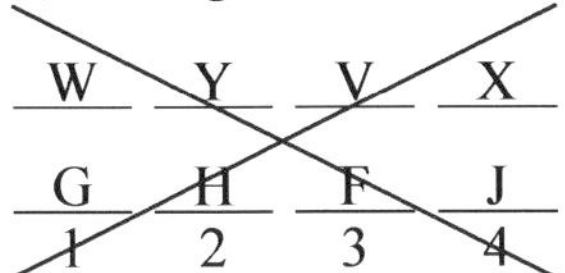

(C) violates the third condition (bench 2)

(D) Correct – see the following diagram

V	W	Y	X
F	J	H	G
1	2	3	4

(E) with J assigned to the second bench, the large piece must be assigned to benches 1 and 2, forcing W and G to violate the fourth condition

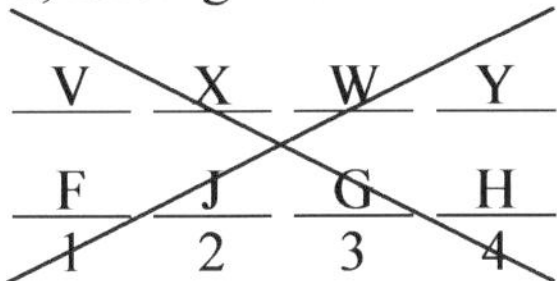

Questions 8-12

Setup:

- seven packages: L M N O P S T

Conditions:

#1: P_1 or P_7

#2: L – N

#3: M – T

#4: L|O __ O|L

#5: M|P __ P|M

Overview:
Combining the first and fifth conditions, we can create two molds

	1	2	3	4	5	6	7
#1	P		M				
#2					M	T	P
	~N ~T						~L

Mold #1: With P first, the fifth condition dictates that M be placed third.

Mold #2: With P seventh, the fifth condition dictates that M be placed fifth. Due to the third condition, T must be sixth.

8. (A) violates the fifth condition
   (B) violates the first condition
   (C) Correct
   (D) violates the second condition
   (E) violates the third condition

9. (A) violates the second condition
   (B) violates the third condition
   (C) since T must follow M (third condition), at the earliest, it could be fourth
   (D) our molds illustrate that M must be either third or fifth
   (E) Correct – see the following diagram

P	O	M	L	N	T	S
1	2	3	4	5	6	7

10. **(A)** Could this be true under the first mold? L would have to occupy the second slot (second condition), violating the fourth condition. Therefore, we must use the second mold. Applying the fourth condition, we know that L and O must occupy the first and third slots, in either order. S must occupy the second slot. With two possible solutions, only choice A could be true.

L|O	S	O|L	N	M	T	P
1	2	3	4	5	6	7

11. **(C)** This could only be true of the first mold. Applying the fourth condition, we must place L and O in the fifth and seventh slots. The second condition dictates that L precede O in this case. Placing N sixth leaves S to occupy the first slot, and choice C is correct.

P	S	M	T	L	N	O
1	2	3	4	5	6	7

12. **(A)** Using the first mold, the fourth condition dictates that we place O second and L fourth. Using the second mold, the first four slots are fairly wide open. In either case, L cannot be fourth, and choice A is therefore correct.

P	O	M	L	___	___	___
1	2	3	4	5	6	7

N, T, S

___	___	___	___	M	T	P
1	2	3	4	5	6	7

L|O _ O|L, N|S _ S|N

Questions 13-18

Setup:
- five persons: N O P T V
- three activities: M S R

Conditions:

#1: 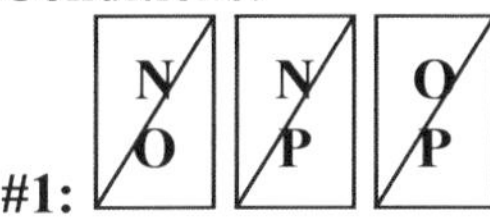

#2: S = 2 persons

#3: 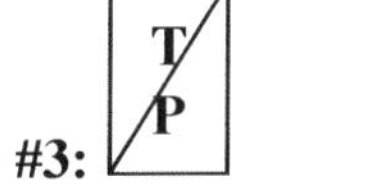

#4: $N_M \longleftrightarrow V_M$

Overview:

We can make a deduction about P. Since P cannot be grouped with N, O, or T, if P is paired with another, it must be V. We can also make some deductions about the number of people who participate in each activity. If either M or R had three participants, P and V would have to be paired with soccer (second condition). However, this would violate the first condition, since N and O would be grouped together. Therefore, we know that the allocation of people to activities is 2, 2, 1.

M	S	R
~N		
~V		

(slots: 1 M, 2 S, 2 R)

or

M	S	R
N ↕ V		

(slots: 2 M, 2 S, 1 R)

13. (A) violates the first condition
    (B) violates the third condition
    (C) violates the fourth condition
    (D) Correct
    (E) violates the second condition

14. **(D)** Applying the fourth condition, we know that N does not go to a movie. If P is paired with another, it must be with V going to a soccer game. Applying the first and fourth conditions leads to a complete solution. If P goes to a movie alone, the first condition prompts an NO split, leaving T to go to a restaurant. Finally, if P goes to a restaurant alone, we can apply the conditions to obtain a complete solution. Since T cannot attend a soccer game under any of these scenarios, choice D is correct.

	P	T
O	V	N
M	S	R
~N		

	N|O	T
P	V	O|N
M	S	R
~N		

	T	N
O	V	P
M	S	R
~N		

15. (A) since a maximum of two people can attend the movie, this violates the fourth condition
    (B) Correct – see the third diagram for question #14
    (C) since a maximum of two people can attend the movie, this violates the fourth condition
    (D) violates the first condition
    (E) violates the third condition

16. **(B)** Scanning the choices reveals that choice B matches with our third diagram for question #14. Therefore, it could be true. We can also invalidate the incorrect choices.
    (A) P and V would have to attend a soccer game together, violating the fourth condition
    (C) P and V would have to attend a soccer game together, violating the fourth condition
    (D) P would have to be paired with another, violating either the first or the fourth condition
    (E) P would have to go to a movie alone, leaving N and O to attend a soccer game together, violating the first condition

17. **(E)** Due to the fourth condition, we know that V cannot go to a movie. We can therefore eliminate choices B and D. Among choices A, C, and E, P is only listed with choice E. Since our second diagram for question #14 allows for P to go to a movie alone and fulfills this question's condition, P must be included in the list, and choice E is correct.

18. **(C)** This question changes the allocation of people to activities to 3, 1, 1, representing S, M, and R respectively. Since P can only be paired with V, P cannot be among those who attend a soccer game, and choice C is correct.

Questions 19-24

Setup:
- two of four lawmakers
- lawmakers (L): F G H I
- two of three scientists
- scientists (S): V Y Z
- one member is the chairperson each year
- chairperson1 ⟶ ~panel2
- chairperson2 ⟶ panel1

Conditions:

#1: 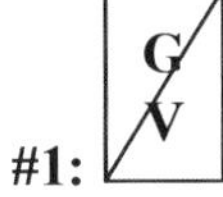

#2: 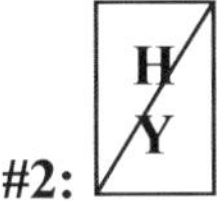

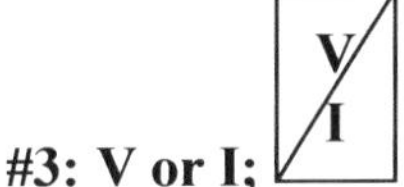

Overview:
The third condition gives two options that are mutually exclusive. We can set up molds to represent the panel when either condition is triggered.

#1			#2		
	S	V		S	Y
	S	Z		S	Z
	L	F		L	F|G
	L	H		L	I
		~G			~V
		~I			~H
		~Y			

Mold #1: With V on the panel, the first and third conditions dictate that neither G nor I are on the panel. Since H must be on the panel (we must have two Ls due to the setup conditions), the second condition precludes Y from being on the panel. Thus, Z must be on the panel.

Mold #2: With I on the panel, the third condition dictates that V cannot be on the panel. With V not on the panel, the setup conditions dictate that both Y and Z must be on the panel. The only uncertainty remaining is which of F and G is on the panel.

19. **(B)** Checking the choices against our molds reveals that only choice B could be true.

20. **(D)** This question prompts us to use the first mold for the first year. Since the chairperson (V) cannot be on the panel during the second year (setup condition), we must use the second mold for the second year. Only choice D presents a pair who must be on the panel in the second year, and it is therefore correct.

S	V	Y
S	Z	Z
L	F	F|G
L	H	I
	1	2

21. **(A)** Again, we must use the first mold for the first year, and the second mold for the second year. Due to the final setup condition, we must look for people who could be on the panel both years. Z is on the panel both years, and F could be on the panel both years. Only F is listed among the choices, and A is correct.

22. **(A)** Looking back at the molds, the only thing that we know for certain when F is on the panel is that G is not on the panel. Therefore, choice A is correct.

23. **(A)** This question is very similar to #21 except that we must use the second mold for the first year, and the first mold for the second year. F and Z are the only people who could be on the panel both years, and F is the only one of the two listed. Thus, choice A is correct.

24. **(E)** Since we know that Z is on the panel both years (mold #1 and mold #2), choice E must be true.

Questions 1-6

Setup:
- seven investors: F G H J K L M
- each view a building site exactly once
- each day exactly one investor will view the site

Conditions:
#1: F_3 or F_5
#2: ~L_4 and ~L_6
#3: $J_1 \longrightarrow H_2$; ~$H_2 \longrightarrow$ ~J_1 (contrapositive)
#4: $K_4 \longrightarrow L_5$; ~$L_5 \longrightarrow$ ~K_4 (contrapositive)
#5: [HG]

Overview:
From the conditions, we can create the following diagram.

1	2	3	4	5	6	7
		F|		|F		
~G			~L		~L	~H
J⟶H			K⟶L			

1. (A) violates the second condition
   (B) violates the first condition
   (C) violates the fifth condition
   (D) violates the fourth condition
   (E) Correct

2. **(E)** Combining this information with the third condition, we know that H occupies the second slot. Due to the fifth condition, G must occupy the third slot. The first condition dictates that we place F fifth. Since L cannot be fourth or sixth (second condition), it must be seventh. Finally, placing K fourth would trigger the fourth condition, but F already occupies the fifth slot. Therefore, we must place M fourth and K sixth respectively, and choice E is correct.

J	H	G	M	F	K	L
1	2	3	4	5	6	7

3. **(C)** Applying the fourth condition, we know that L is fifth. F must be third, due to the first condition. J cannot be first because this would trigger the third and fifth conditions, but F is already third. Could J be second? H and G would have to be sixth and seventh respectively, leaving M to occupy the first slot. However, since J must precede M, we must instead place J sixth and M seventh, leaving the HG piece to fill the first two slots.

H	G	F	K	L	J	M
1	2	3	4	5	6	7

4. **(C)** Combining this information with the fifth condition, we know that G occupies the third slot. Applying the first condition, we know that F is fifth. With F fifth, the fourth condition cannot be triggered. Therefore, we know that K cannot be fourth. We can eliminate choices A, D, and E because they contain K. In deciding between choices B and C, we only need to figure out whether J could be fourth. Other than the third condition, nothing constrains the placement of J, so it could be fourth. Thus, choice C is correct. The following diagram further proves the validity of choice C.

	H	G	J	F	K|M	
1	2	3	4	5	6	7

5. **(D)** Combining the new information with the fifth condition, we have the following two pieces: [KHG] [LF]. We cannot place F fifth since that would violate the second condition. Therefore, we must place the LF piece in the second and third slots. Spanning the KHG piece across the fourth through the sixth slots would trigger and violate the fourth condition. As a result, we must place it in the fifth through the seventh slots. Placing J first would trigger and violate the third condition, so we must place it fourth, leaving M to occupy the first slot. Thus, choice D is correct.

M	L	F	J	K	H	G
1	2	3	4	5	6	7

6. Applying the fifth condition, we have the following:

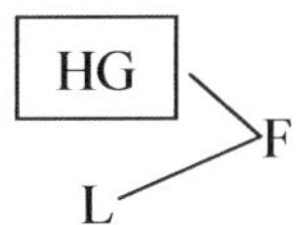

(A) F is preceded by at least three variables

(B) Correct – see the following diagram

L	H	G	M	F	K	J
1	2	3	4	5	6	7

Choices C through E all present the same problem. The first condition dictates that F be placed fifth, and since the HG piece precedes F, it must occupy the first two slots. L must precede F, but it cannot be fourth (second condition), making each of these choices an impossibility.

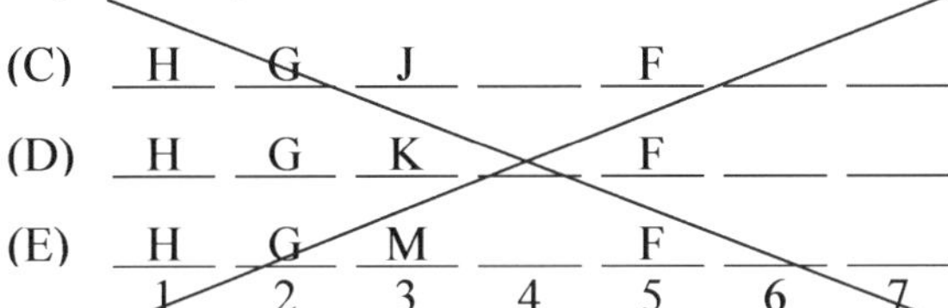

Questions 7-12

Setup:

- o five consecutive habitats: 1 2 3 4 5
- o seven reptiles: S S S S L L L
- o five females: F F F F F
- o two males: M M

Conditions:

#1: each habitat ≤ 2 reptiles

#2: 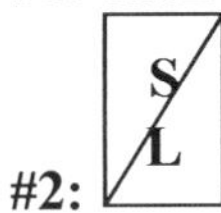

#3: 

Overview:
Since each reptile has two characteristics, it makes sense to determine what combinations of traits are possible. There are five females and only three lizards, which means that at least two snakes are female. We can further break down the allocations into two additional possibilities: one with three female snakes and one with four female snakes.

	S	S	S	S	L	L	L
1)	F	F	M	M	F	F	F
2)	F	F	F	M	F	F	M
3)	F	F	F	F	F	M	M

With ten slots and seven reptiles, we can add three Xs to balance the game.

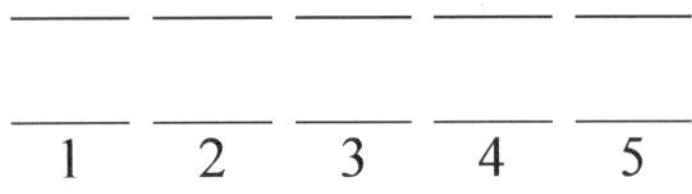

Combining the first and second conditions, we can infer that at least one of the lizards occupies a habitat by itself.

7. (A) violates the second condition (fourth habitat)
   (B) Correct
   (C) violates the third condition (second and third habitats)
   (D) violates the first condition (fifth habitat)
   (E) violates the third condition (second and third habitats)

8. **(E)** We're given that there are two male lizards which is only true of the third allocation. Therefore, all the other five reptiles are female. The third condition dictates that all four female snakes occupy the first two habitats. The only uncertainty is which one of habitat 3 and habitat 5 houses the female lizard. As such, only choice E could be true.

FS	FS	X	ML	X
FS	FS	FL|X	ML	X|FL
1	2	3	4	5

9. **(C)** This question directly tests our inference regarding the first and second conditions. We know that at least one lizard occupies a habitat by itself, and choice C is therefore correct.

10. This question is tough to tackle without testing the answer choices.

(A)

MS	X	FL	X	FS
FS	MS	FL	FL	FS
1	2	3	4	5

(B)

X	X	MS	X	FL
ML	MS	FS	FS	FL
1	2	3	4	5

(C)

FL	X	FS	X	X
FL	FS	FS	MS	ML
1	2	3	4	5

(D) Correct – this configuration would require us to place three lizards and three snakes into a total of three habitats (3, 4, and 5), a possibility which is precluded by the second condition.

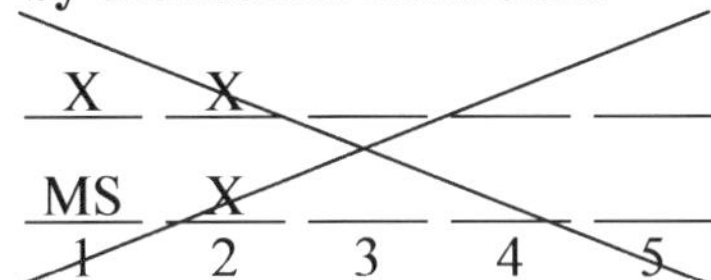

(E)

X	X	MS	FS	FL
X	FL	MS	FS	FL
1	2	3	4	5

11. **(A)** With this information, we can infer the following habitat occupations:

L	X	X	S	S
L	L	X	S	S

Since the snakes cannot be in habitats that are next to each other, and the third habitat is empty, each of the two snake habitats must be immediately next to one of the lizard habitats. We can make a further deduction about the allocation. Since the snakes are grouped in pairs, if one of the lizards were male, two snakes would also have to be male, due to the third condition. However, we're given that only two reptiles are male. Therefore, we must use the third allocation. We can use our deductions up to this point to eliminate choices B through E, leaving A as the correct answer. The following diagram also proves the validity of choice A.

FS	FL	X	MS	X
FS	FL	X	MS	FL
1	2	3	4	5

12. **(C)** This question triggers the third allocation. With two male lizards occupying habitats by themselves, the third condition dictates that their habitats be separated from the female snakes by at least one habitat. Thus, the female snakes must occupy either the first two or the last two habitats, and the female lizard must occupy the third habitat. Choice C is therefore correct.

FS	FS	X	X	X		X	X	X	FS	FS
FS	FS	FL	ML	ML	or	ML	ML	FL	FS	FS
1	2	3	4	5		1	2	3	4	5

Questions 13-19

Setup:
- seven film buffs: G I L M R V Y
- three films: F H K
- each film buff sees exactly one film
- the films are each shown once, one at a time

Conditions:
#1: # $\text{buffs}_H = 2(\#\text{buffs}_F)$

#2: 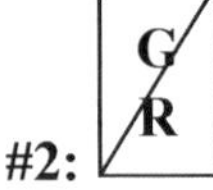

#3: 

#4: 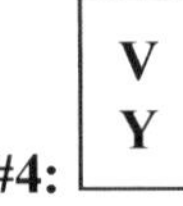

#5: L_H
#6: G_F or G_K

Overview:
Combining the fact that there are seven film buffs with the first condition, we can infer two possible allocations of buffs to films:

F	H	K
1	2	4
2	4	1

We can make some additional upfront deductions. The VY piece cannot occupy the slots for the film that is seen by two buffs. The reason for this is that the second and third conditions list two variable pairs which cannot be grouped together. Therefore, we know that the VY piece must always occupy two slots above whichever film is seen by four of the film buffs.

F	H	K
		____
		|G
	____	Y
G|	L	V

F	H	K
	____	
	L	
	Y	
G|	V	|G

We can set up molds to further flesh out the possible arrangements.

#1

F	H	K
		R
		M|I
	I|M	Y
G	L	V

#2

F	H	K
		I|M
		G
	____	Y
____	L	V

#3

F	H	K
	____	
	L	
I|M	Y	
G	V	____

#4

F	H	K
	M|I	
	L	
R	Y	
I|M	V	G

Mold #1: I and M must each occupy a slot over either H or K, leaving R to fill the final slot above K.

Mold #2: With G placed over K, the second condition dictates that R cannot be placed over K, leaving one of I and M to fill that slot.

Mold #3: With G placed over F, the second slot must be occupied by either I or M, due to the second condition.

Mold #4: I and M must each occupy a slot over either F and H, leaving R to fill the final slot above F.

13. (A) violates the sixth condition
    (B) V cannot see F under any of the molds
    (C) V cannot see F under any of the molds
    (D) Correct – this matches mold #1
    (E) M and R cannot both be grouped with H under any of the molds

14. **(A) Correct – this could be true under the second mold**
    (B) H must be seen by two or four film buffs
    (C) violates the fourth condition
    (D) K must be seen by either one or four film buffs
    (E) H must be seen by either two or four film buffs

15. **(C)** According to the possible allocations, H must be seen by either two or four film buffs. Therefore, a complete and accurate list of the buffs who don't see H must have either three or five members. On this basis, we can eliminate choices A and B. Since the other three choices each consist of three members, we can narrow our focus to the third and fourth molds. Since the VY piece must be grouped with H, we can eliminate choices D and E, leaving C as the correct answer. The following diagram proves the validity of choice C.

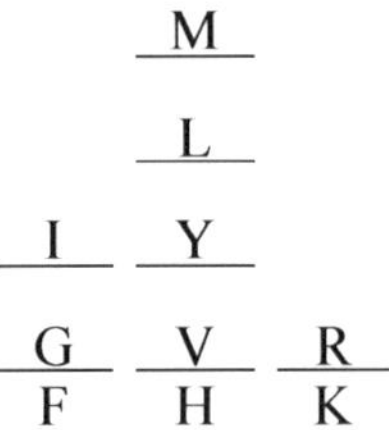

16. **(A)** This question narrows our focus to the third and fourth molds. According to both molds, V sees H, and choice A is therefore correct.

17. We can check the choices against our mold to eliminate those that are incorrect.
    (A) see molds #2 and #3
    (B) this could be true under any of the first three molds
    (C) this could be true under any of the molds
    (D) see molds #3 and #4
    (E) Correct – this is true of all the molds

18. **(B)** This question triggers the second mold. A quick scan of the answer choices reveals that only B could be true.

		M
		G
	I	Y
R	L	V
F	H	K

19. **(E)** Since each answer choice lists two film buffs, we can check them against the third and fourth molds. Each of choices A through D presents an acceptable pair. As we previously inferred, the VY piece must be grouped with the movie that is seen by four buffs, and choice E must be false.

Questions 20-24

Setup:
- six cars: 1 2 3 4 5 6
- arranged from front (1) to back (6)
- each car is exactly one color
- colors: G G O O P P

Conditions:

#1: 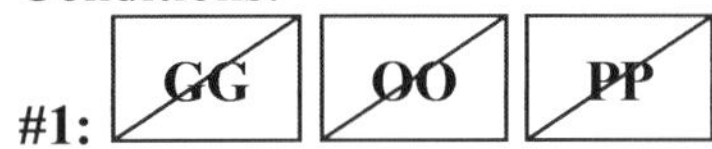

#2: P_5 or P_6
#3: $\sim O_1$
#4: $\sim G_4$

Overview:
The basic diagram is as follows.

G|P			O|P	P|	|P
1	2	3	4	5	6
~O			~G		

We can further break down the options into the following two molds:

	1	2	3	4	5	6
#1	G|P			O	P	
#2	G|P			P|O		P

Each of the molds yields three solutions, for a total of six.

	1	2	3	4	5	6
#1	G	O	P	O	P	G
#2	G	P	G	O	P	O
#3	P	O	G	O	P	G
#4	G	O	G	P	O	P
#5	G	O	P	O	G	P
#6	P	O	G	O	G	P

Solution #1: With G first (mold #1), the remaining P can be placed third. Since G cannot be fourth (fourth condition), we can place it sixth, leaving the two Os to fill the second and fourth slots.

Solution #2: With G first (mold #1), the remaining P can be placed second. Since G cannot be fourth, and the Os cannot be adjacent to each other (first condition), the two Os must fill the fourth and sixth slots, leaving G to occupy the third slot.

Solution #3: With P first (mold #1), an O must occupy the fourth slot (fourth condition). Since the two Gs cannot be adjacent to each other, we must place one sixth, leaving the remaining O to occupy the second slot, and the remaining G to occupy the third slot.

Solution #4: With G first and P fourth (mold #2), the remaining P must be placed sixth (first and second conditions). An O must be placed fifth, due to the first condition, leaving O and G to occupy the second and third slots, respectively.

Solution #5: With G first and O fourth (mold #2), we must place the remaining O second (first condition), leaving G to occupy the fifth slot, and P to occupy the third slot.

Solution #6: With P first and O fourth (mold #2), we must place a G fifth (first condition), and the remaining O must be placed second, leaving the remaining G to occupy the third slot.

20. **(A)** Checking the choices against the solutions reveals that only A presents an impossibility.

21. **(B)** This is true of solutions #3, #5, and #6. Accordingly, only choice B must be true.

22. **(E)** This is only true of solution #4. Thus, choice E is correct.

23. We can use our solutions to eliminate the incorrect choices.

    (A) Correct – the second slot must be occupied by either O or P
    (B) see solutions #1, #2, #3, #5, and #6
    (C) see solutions #1, #2, and #3
    (D) see solution #2
    (E) see solutions #1 and #2

24. **(D)** This question changes our variable selection: G G G O P P. Due to the first condition, we must spread out the Gs. Since we cannot place a G fourth (fourth condition), we must assign one G to each of the first and third slots. Thus, choice D is correct. If the third G is placed sixth, the second condition dictates that P must be fifth, and we must place the remaining P in the second slot, due to the first condition. If the third G is placed fifth, the second condition dictates that P must be sixth. An O and a P must occupy the second and fourth slots, in either order.

G	P	G	O	P	G
G	O|P	G	P|O	G	P
1	2	3	4	5	6

Questions 1-5

Setup:
- six racehorses: K L M N O P
- arranged in a straight line
- numbered consecutively 1 through 6

Conditions:

#1: **K|L __ L|K**

#2: 

#3: **M – N**

#4: **P_3**

Overview:
Due to the fourth condition, the piece given in the first condition can only occupy the second and third or the fourth and the sixth slots. We can set up molds to represent each possible placement and ordering of K and L.

	1	2	3	4	5	6
#1	M|O	L	P	K	O|M	N
#2	M|O	K	P	L	N|	|N
#3	M	N	P	L	O	K
#4	M	N	P	K	O	L

Mold #1: With L second and K fourth, the third condition dictates that N be placed either fifth or sixth. Due to the second condition, N must be placed sixth.

Mold #2: With K second and L fourth, the third condition dictates that N be placed either fifth or sixth. Therefore, the first slot must be occupied by either M or O.

Mold #3: With L fourth and K sixth, due to the second condition, N cannot occupy the fifth slot. Combining this with the third condition, we must place M and N first and second respectively, leaving O to fill the fifth slot.

Mold #4: With K fourth and L sixth, due to the second condition, N cannot occupy the fifth slot. Combining this with the third condition, we must place M and N first and second respectively, leaving O to fill the fifth slot.

1. (A) violates the first condition
   (B) Correct
   (C) violates the fourth condition
   (D) violates the third condition
   (E) violates the second condition

2. **(E)** Glancing at our molds, we know that K can occupy the second, fourth, or the sixth slot. Therefore, choice E is correct.

3. (A) see the second mold
   (B) see the first mold
   (C) this could happen under any of the molds
   (D) this could happen under the first or the second mold
   (E) Correct – this cannot be true under any of the molds

4. (A) see the third and fourth molds
   (B) Correct – this is true of all four molds
   (C) see the first and second molds
   (D) this doesn't have to be true under any of the molds
   (E) this doesn't have to be true under any of the molds

5. (A) this could be true under the second mold
   (B) this could be true under the first or the second mold
   (C) Correct – this cannot be true under the second mold since N must be either fifth or sixth
   (D) see the third mold
   (E) this could be true under the first two molds and is true of the third and fourth molds

Questions 6-12

Setup:
- four different researchers: G H L P
- each one will learn one, two, or three languages
- languages: R S T Y

Conditions:
#1: exactly one researcher ⟶ R
#2: exactly two researchers ⟶ S
#3: exactly two researchers ⟶ T
#4: exactly three researchers ⟶ Y

#5: 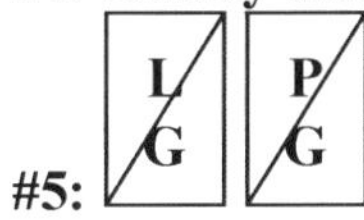

#6: G ⟶ [G H]

Overview:
Combining the fourth and the fifth conditions, we know that P, L, and H must all learn Yoruba. We also know that G cannot learn Rundi, due to the sixth condition. Since G must learn at least one language, we will have a GH piece over either the S or the T.

R	S	T	Y
			P
	G|	|G	L
___	H|	|H	H
~G			~G

6. (A) as we inferred, L must learn Yoruba
   (B) due to the fifth condition G would be forced into the R slot, violating the sixth condition
   (C) H would learn four languages, violating the setup conditions
   (D) Correct – see the following diagram

R	S	T	Y
			P
	G|	|G	L
L|P	H	H	H

   (E) as we inferred, P must learn Yoruba

7. **(B)** We have already placed an L over Y. Since G and L cannot be together (fifth condition), we must place an L over R. Finally, the third L must occupy a slot over whichever of S and T that G doesn't learn. Therefore, choice B must be true.

			P
	G|L	L|G	L
L	H|	|H	H
R	S	T	Y

8. **(C)** Since we know that G cannot learn Rundi (sixth condition), that slot must be occupied by L, H, or P. Each of these also learns Yoruba, and choice C therefore, cannot be true.

9. **(B)** There are two possibilities for such a list. The list could consist solely of H, in which case, G would be placed above S. It could also consist of two of H, L, and P, in which case the GH piece would be placed over T. If P were the only one of H, L, and P that learned Swahili, G would also have to be placed above S, violating the fifth condition. Therefore, choice B is correct.

10. **(A)** According to our master diagram, G would have to learn both Swahili and Tigrinya. Applying the sixth condition, H would also learn these two languages. Since H learns three languages, the setup conditions dictate that either L or P learn Rundi. Comparing the answer choices to the diagram reveals that only choice A could be true.

			P
	G	G	L
L|P	H	H	H
R	S	T	Y

11. For this question, we can use our previous work to eliminate incorrect answer choices.
    (A) see question #10
    (B) Correct – we have placed an H above the Y, and the sixth condition dictates that wherever we place a G, we must also place an H
    (C) see question #10
    (D) see question #10
    (E) see the following diagram

			P
	L	G	L
P	P	H	H
R	S	T	Y

12. **(D)** Since we have already placed one H (above Y), and we must have at least one GH piece, the GH piece must be placed over the S or the T. In either case, H cannot learn Rundi, and choice D is therefore correct.

			P					P
	G	P	L			P	G	L
L|P	H	L	H	or	L|P	L	H	H
R	S	T	Y		R	S	T	Y

Questions 13-18

Setup:
- three days: M T W
- health officer will inspect six buildings
- three hotels: G J L
- three restaurants: S V Z
- exactly two buildings inspected each day: one in the morning and one in the afternoon

Conditions:

#1: ~G_W; ~J_W; ~L_W

#2: **G – J or [J over G]**

#3: **[G over S, crossed out]**

#4: $Z_A \longrightarrow L_A$; $L_P \longrightarrow Z_P$ (contrapositive)

Overview:

Due to the first condition, we know that two of S, V, and Z will be inspected on Wednesday.

P	____	____	____	$L \longrightarrow Z$
A	____	____	____	$Z \longrightarrow L$
	M	T	W	
			~G	
			~J	
			~L	

13. (A) violates the third condition
    (B) violates the first condition
    (C) violates the second condition
    (D) Correct
    (E) violates the fourth condition

14. (A) violates the fourth condition
    (B) violates the second condition
    (C) Correct – see the following diagram

P	G	S|Z	Z|S
A	L	J	V
	M	T	W

    (D) to satisfy the second condition, G would have to be inspected Monday afternoon, which violates the third condition
    (E) since neither G nor J could occupy the Wednesday afternoon slot (first condition), V would be inspected then, forcing G and J into the Monday and Tuesday afternoon slots respectively (second condition), which violates the third condition

15. (A) see question #13
    (B) Correct – G cannot be inspected on Wednesday due to the first condition. Placing G and V together on Tuesday precludes satisfaction of the second condition since J cannot be inspected on Wednesday (first condition).

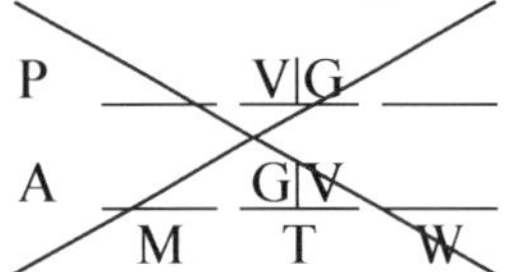

    (C) J and L cannot both be inspected on Monday since the second condition would be violated
    (D) L and S could be paired on Tuesday; G and J would be inspected on Monday and V and Z would be inspected on Wednesday

P	J	L	Z
A	G	S	V
	M	T	W

    (E) L and V could also be inspected on Tuesday – see question #18

16. **(B)** Since J cannot be inspected on Wednesday (first condition), it must be inspected on Tuesday afternoon. We can therefore eliminate choices C and D. Choice A can be eliminated because it violates the fourth condition. Choice E violates the first condition. The following diagram proves the validity of choice B.

P	S|V	J	V|S
A	L	G	Z
	M	T	W

17. **(D)** Due to the third condition, we must place G on Tuesday. To satisfy the second condition, we have to place J in the afternoon slot on Tuesday. Since L cannot be inspected on Wednesday (first condition), it must be inspected on Monday afternoon. Placing Z on Wednesday morning would trigger and violate the fourth condition, so we must instead place it in the afternoon slot. Hence, choice D is correct.

P	L	J	Z
A	S	G	V
	M	T	W

18. **(D)** This triggers the fourth condition, and we must place L in the Tuesday morning slot. Since G cannot be paired with S (third condition), the Monday afternoon slot must be filled by either J or V. In either case, it must be true that L precedes S, and choice D is therefore correct.

P	J	S|V	V|S		P	V	J|S	S|J
A	G	L	Z	or	A	G	L	Z
	M	T	W			M	T	W

Questions 19-23

Setup:
- three members: F G H
- three bills: R S T
- each member votes for against each bill

Conditions:
#1: each member votes for at least one bill and against at least one bill
#2: 2 members ⟶ + on R
#3: 1 member ⟶ + on S
#4: 1 member ⟶ + on T
#5: F ⟶ + on R and - on S
#6: G ⟶ - on R
#7: H ⟶ - on T

Overview:
Placing the known votes into the diagram along with the given numbers of votes for the three bills reveals that there are four possible solutions.

```
F   +    -    +|-
G   -    +|-  -|+
H   +    -|+  -
    R    S    T
    +    +    +
    +    -    -
    -    -    -
```

We can further draw out all the solutions before moving on to the questions.

```
#1  F   +  -  -        #2  F   +  -  +
    G   -  -  +            G   -  -  -
    H   +  +  -            H   +  +  -
        R  S  T                R  S  T

#3  F   +  -  -        #4  F   +  -  +
    G   -  +  +            G   -  +  -
    H   +  -  -            H   +  -  -
        R  S  T                R  S  T
```

19. **(D)** Checking the choices against our solutions reveals that only choice D could be true (solution #3).

20. **(E)** Glancing at the solutions reveals that this is only true of the third solution, and we know that H votes against the school bill.

21. **(A)** This is true of the first and third solutions. Only choice A could be true (solution #1), and it is therefore correct.

22. **(C)** This is only true of the third solution, and it must be true that G votes for the school bill. Hence, choice C is correct.

23. **(E)** This is only true of the third solution, and it must be true that H votes for exactly one bill. Therefore, choice E is correct.

Questions 1-6

Setup:

- seven bills: 1 2 3 4 5 6 7

Conditions:

#1: 3 or 4 bills must be paid on Wednesday; the rest on Thursday

#2: 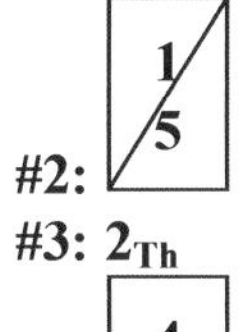

#3: 2_{Th}

#4: [4 / 7]

#5: $6_W \longrightarrow 7_{Th}$; $7_W \longrightarrow 6_{Th}$ (contrapositive)

Overview:

Since the piece given by the fourth condition occupies two slots, it makes sense to create molds depicting what must be true when it is placed on each day.

#1

W	Th
3|	|3
4	6
7	2
1|5	5|1

#2

W	Th
	4
6	7
3	2
1|5	5|1

Mold #1: Placing the 4-7 piece on Wednesday triggers the contrapositive of the fifth condition, and we know that bill 6 must be paid on Thursday.

Mold #2: Placing the 4-7 piece on Thursday fills up all its slots, and we know that bills 3 and 6 must be placed on Wednesday.

1. **(D)** This could only happen under the first mold. We know that the bills paid must be 3, 4, 7, and one of 1 and 5. Only choice D presents a matching combination.

2. **(C)** Our molds reveal that the only bill that cannot be paid on Wednesday is bill 2. Therefore, choice C is correct.

3. **(A)** This triggers the second mold. We know that exactly three bills are paid on Wednesday, and choice A is correct.

4. **(B)** This triggers the second mold. The only other bill that must be paid on Wednesday is bill 3, and choice B is therefore correct.

5. **(B)** This question prompts us to use the second mold. We know that bills 4, 7, 2, and one of 1 and 5 must be paid on Thursday. Only choice B presents a viable pair, and it is correct.

6. To complete this question, we can check the answer choices against our molds.
   (A) bill 2 must be paid on Thursday (fourth condition) – this doesn't lead to any inferences
   (B) bill 1 could still be paid on either day (second mold)
   (C) Correct – see the second mold
   (D) bill 3 could be paid on either day (first mold)
   (E) this cannot be true – see the first mold

Questions 7-13

Setup:
- two mannequins: 1 2
- ten articles of clothing
- three hats: NH RH YH
- three jackets: NJ RJ YJ
- three skirts: NS RS YS
- one red tie: RT
- each mannequin wears one hat, one jacket, and one skirt

Conditions:

#1: (N R Y, crossed out) in any combination
#2: for each mannequin, $H_{color} \neq J_{color}$
#3: NS_2
#4: RT_1

Overview:
Since each article can only be worn by one mannequin, we can infer that the mannequins must wear different colors of each article type. As a result, mannequin 1 must wear either the red or the yellow skirt. Combining the first two conditions, we know that each mannequin must wear exactly two colors. The second condition further dictates that mannequin 1 must wear an additional red item and that mannequin 2 must wear an additional navy item.

```
T  _R_
S  _R|Y_ ≠ _N_
J  _R|_ ≠ _N|_
     ⧣      ⧣
H  _|R_ ≠ _|N_
    1       2
```

7. (A) violates the first condition (mannequin 1)
   (B) violates the second condition (mannequin 1)
   (C) violates the third condition
   (D) Correct
   (E) violates the second condition (mannequin 1)

8. This could be true question offers no additional information.

   (A) violates the first condition
   (B) violates the second condition
   (C) due to the first and the second conditions, this cannot be true
   (D) since mannequin 1 must wear at least two red items, this cannot be true
   (E) Correct – see the following diagram

```
T  _R_
S  _R|Y_  _N_
J  _N|R_  _Y_
H  _R|Y_  _N_
    1      2
```

9. **(E)** Combining this with our setup, we know that mannequin 1 must wear the red hat, and that mannequin 2 must wear the navy hat. Thus, only choice E could be true.

```
T  _R_
S  _N|R_  _N_
J  _N_   _R|Y_
H  _R_   _N_
    1     2
```

10. **(E)** From this information, we can deduce that mannequin 1 must wear the red skirt. Either mannequin could wear the red jacket. The mannequin that does not wear the red jacket will wear the red hat. Since each mannequin must wear exactly two colors, mannequin two must wear navy and red. Therefore, choice E must be true.

T _R_

S _R_ _N_

J _R|_ _N|R_

H _|R_ _R|N_
   1 2

11. **(B)** We previously inferred that mannequin 1 must wear either the red jacket or the red hat. Since mannequin 2 wears the red jacket, mannequin 1 must wear the red hat. Hence, answer choice B is correct.

T _R_

S _R|Y_ _N_

J _N|Y_ _R_

H _R_ _N_
   1 2

12. Only mannequin 1 could wear the yellow skirt, and it must do so in this case. The question indirectly tells us that mannequin 1 wears red and yellow, and that mannequin 2 wears navy and yellow.

T _R_

S _Y_ _N_

J _R|Y_ _Y|N_

H _Y|R_ _N|Y_
   1 2

(A) mannequin 1 cannot wear any navy articles
(B) Correct
(C) mannequin 1 must wear the yellow skirt
(D) mannequin 2 cannot wear any red articles
(E) mannequin 2 cannot wear any red articles

13. **(C)** We previously inferred that mannequin 2 must wear either the navy jacket or the navy hat. Since mannequin 1 cannot wear the navy skirt (third condition), mannequin 2 must wear the navy hat. Hence, answer choice C is correct.

	1	2
T	R	
S	R|Y	N
J	R|	R|Y
H	|R	N

Questions 14-19

Setup:
- o seven awards: F G H J K L S
- o presented consecutively, one at a time

Conditions:
#1: $\sim G_1$
#2: H – K
#3: L – J
#4: 

#5: KL

Overview:
We can combine the second condition with the fourth condition and the third condition with the fifth condition to create the following chain:

14. **(A)** From our diagram, we know that F must precede J, and choice A is therefore correct.

15. **(E)** Since H must be followed by three variables (K, L, and J), we can place J seventh. F must be third, due to the fourth condition. The first condition dictates that we place S first and G second. Therefore, choice E must be true.

S	G	F	H	K|L	L|K	J
1	2	3	4	5	6	7

16. **(C)** Since our chain contains five variables, and G is only followed by four slots, we must place F and H in the first two slots, not necessarily in that order. We can further infer that J must be either sixth or seventh, since it is preceded by both K and L. Either K or L must occupy the fifth slot since they're adjacent (fifth condition), and they must precede J. Thus, only choice C could be true.

F|H	H|F	G		K|L	J|	|J
1	2	3	4	5	6	7

17. **(C)** Since J must be preceded by four variables (F, H, K, and L), the earliest slot it can occupy is the fifth. Therefore, choice C is correct.

18. We can redraw our sketch to incorporate this new information.

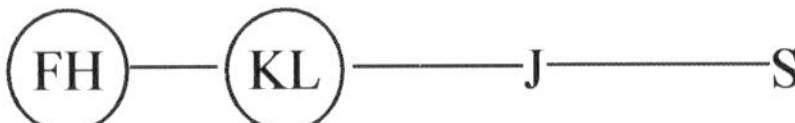

(A) Correct – this would force G into the first slot, violating the first condition
(B) G would be fifth
(C) H could be second and L could be third
(D) they could occupy the fourth and fifth or the fifth and sixth slots
(E) S could be sixth and G could be seventh

19. Since the order of the two variable pairs is undetermined, we're looking for the answer choice that locks down both pairs, and definitively places G and S.

(A) S could still occupy multiple slots
(B) S could still occupy multiple slots
(C) G and S each have multiple placement options
(D) Correct – G must be second due to the first condition, and S is the only variable that can precede it, so it is first

S	G	F	H	K	L	J
1	2	3	4	5	6	7

(E) S could still occupy multiple slots

<u>Questions 20-24</u>

Setup:
- six piano classes given sequentially
- two with more than one student; four with exactly one student
- four females: G H I K
- five males: L N O P S
- each student attends exactly one class

Conditions:

#1: 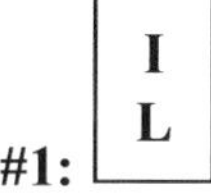

#2: 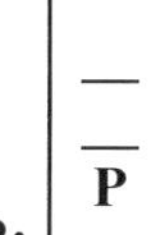

#3: K ⟶ first female; male – K
#4: I – G – P
#5: G – O

Overview:
The first, second, and fourth conditions allow us to string together multiple pieces. From the third condition, we know that K must precede both H and I. Either N or S must precede K, due to the third condition. Since only two of the classes have multiple students, we can deduce that K and G are both alone. Finally, since only one of N and S could be grouped with P, we know that at least one of H and O must be grouped with P.

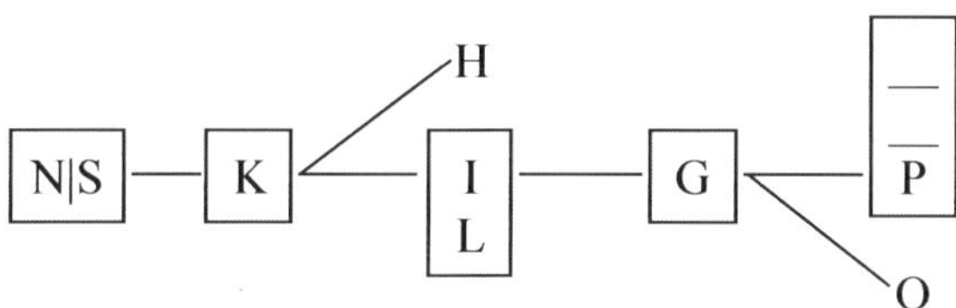

20. **(E)** From our diagram, we know that only N or S could attend the first class. S is the only one of the two listed, and choice E is therefore correct.

21. **(A)** G's class must be preceded by at least three other classes. Therefore, at the earliest, it could be fourth. Since it is followed by at least one class, at the latest, it could be fifth. Thus, choice A is correct.

22. We can eliminate the choices that aren't compatible with our diagram.
    (A) G precedes P
    (B) Correct – N would attend the first class
    (C) K precedes P
    (D) L precedes P
    (E) violates our inference that one of H and O must be grouped with P

23. Applying this information to our inference regarding H, O, and P, we know that H must be grouped with P. One of N and S will also attend a class with P.

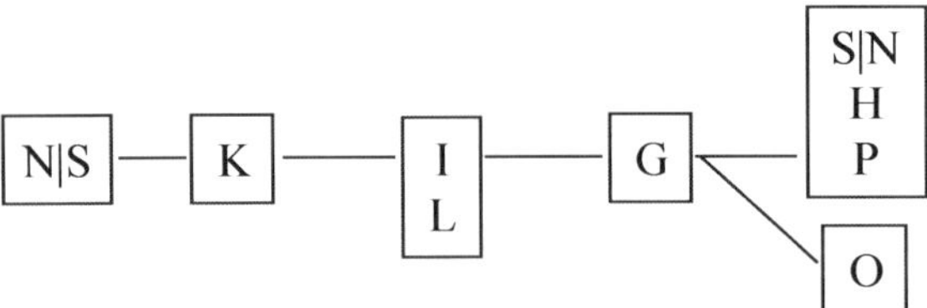

(A) G must attend the fourth class
(B) at the earliest, H can attend the fifth class
(C) I must attend the third class
(D) Correct – O would attend the sixth class
(E) S could attend the first, fifth, or sixth class

24. **(E)** Since O cannot attend a class with P, we know that H must be grouped with P. Since H attends the last class, choice E is correct.

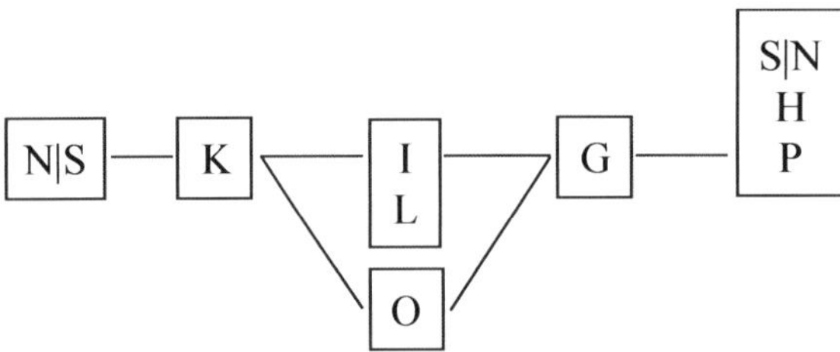

Questions 1-5

Setup:

- one delivery
- six loaves of bread
- each of the loaves is exactly one of three kinds: O R W
- each is either sliced (S) or unsliced (U)

Conditions:

#1: 2^+ kinds
#2: $\leq 3R$
#3: $\sim W_U$
#4: $O_U{}^{1+}$
#5: $2^+ U \longrightarrow R_U{}^{1+}$; $\sim R_U \longrightarrow \sim 2^+ U$ (contrapositive)

Overview:
Since there are exactly six loaves, and at least one is unsliced, the maximum number of loaves that can be sliced is five. All six loaves could be unsliced, since there is no restriction on the number of oatmeal loaves. As a consequence of the second condition, in addition to the unsliced oatmeal loaf, we must have at least two more non-rye loaves.

------	------
------	------
------	------
------	------
------	O
S	U
O	O
R	R
W	$2^+ \downarrow$ R

1. (A) violates the first condition
   (B) violates the fifth condition
   (C) violates the third condition
   (D) Correct
   (E) violates the fifth condition

2. **(A)** Checking the choices against the conditions reveals that choice A violates the fifth condition. Given three unsliced loaves, at least one of them would have to be rye.

3. (A) five loaves would be sliced
   (B) this could be true
   (C) Correct – this violates the fourth condition
   (D) one sliced loaf would be either rye or wheat
   (E) there would be exactly one unsliced rye loaf

4. (A) each of the six loaves could be oatmeal or wheat
   (B) see question #1
   (C) as we inferred, all six loaves could be unsliced
   (D) Correct – if there were five sliced oatmeal loaves, all six loaves would be oatmeal, which violates the first condition
   (E) five sliced wheat loaves and one unsliced oatmeal loaf is a viable solution

5. **(B)** This question locks down the possible allocations to either four sliced and two unsliced or five sliced and one unsliced. If there are two unsliced loaves, we know the second one must be rye. If there is only one unsliced loaf, the fifth sliced loaf could be either oatmeal or rye. Thus, only choice B could be true.

S	U
W	
W	
W	R
W	O

S	U
O|R	
W	
W	
W	
W	O

Questions 6-10

Setup:
- six messages: 1 2 3 4 5 6
- each message was left by one of: F G H L P T

Conditions:
#1: ≤ 1 person left more than one message
#2: no person left more than three messages
#3: H_1 ⟶ P_6; ~P_6 ⟶ ~H_1 (contrapositive)
#4: G ⟶ F and P; ~F or ~P ⟶ G (contrapositive)
#5: F ⟶ P (all) – T (all); ~P or ~T ⟶ ~F (contrapositive)
#6: P ⟶ H (all) – L (all); ~H or ~L ⟶ ~P (contrapositive)

Overview:
Combining the first and the second conditions, we can deduce three possible allocations of messages to individuals:
3, 1, 1, 1
2, 1, 1, 1, 1
1, 1, 1, 1, 1, 1
Thus, at most two of the variables can be unselected. The fourth, fifth, and sixth conditions can be linked into chains.

```
   ↗F ⟶ P – T; ~P or ~T ⟶ ~F↘
G<                              >~G (contrapositive)
   ↘P ⟶ H – L; ~H or ~L ⟶ ~P↗
```

The contrapositive chains tell us that if any one of P, T, H, and L is not selected, two other variables will also not be selected. Since the possible allocations only allow for two variables to be unselected, we can infer that H, L, P, and T must each leave at least one message. Plugging this back into the sixth condition, we know that we cannot place an H last or an L first. We can further infer which variables will be selected under the different allocations. Since G triggers F (fourth condition), and the second allocation only allows one of F and G to be selected, it must be F.
3, 1, 1, 1: H, L, P, T
2, 1, 1, 1, 1: F, H, L, P, T
1, 1, 1, 1, 1, 1: F, G, H, L, P, T

```
____ ____ ____ ____ ____ ____
 1    2    3    4    5    6
 H ─────────────────────→ L
~L                        ~H
```

6. (A) violates the fifth condition
   (B) violates the fourth condition
   (C) violates the third condition
   (D) Correct
   (E) violates the first condition

7. **(A)** Since the question specifies that one person leaves exactly two messages, we know to look at the second allocation. F is selected, so we know that all Ps must precede all Ts (fifth condition). As a result, we can eliminate choices D and E. We can also eliminate choices B and C since we already inferred that H cannot be last and L cannot be first. Therefore, only choice A could be true, and it is correct.

8. **(A)** With G selected, we must look to the third allocation. F is also selected, meaning that all Ps must precede all Ts (fifth condition). Therefore, T cannot leave the first message, and choice A is correct.

9. **(D)** Choices A through C directly test our inference regarding H, L, P, and T being selected. Choices D and E directly test our grasp of the possible allocations. Since our third allocation allows for all six people to leave one message each, choice D doesn't have to be true, and it is therefore correct.

10. Combining this with the contrapositive of the third condition, we know that H cannot be first.

    (A) as noted above, H cannot be first
    (B) according to the second allocation, F would be selected, meaning that the placed P would have to precede two Ts (fifth condition)
    (C) Correct – see the following diagram

F	H	L	L	P	T
1	2	3	4	5	6

    (D) H must precede L, due to the sixth condition, but H cannot be first as noted above
    (E) T would have to be sixth (fifth condition), and H and L would have to occupy the first two slots, which violates the third condition

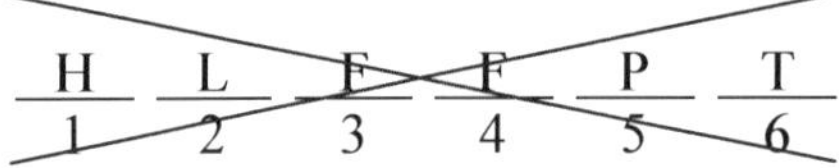

Questions 11-16

Setup:
- five cars: F M O T V
- cars are washed once each, one at a time
- each car receives one of three kinds of wash: R S P

Conditions:
#1: $\sim S_1$; 1^+ car ⟶ S
#2: exactly 1 car ⟶ P
#3: 2nd wash = 3rd wash
#4:

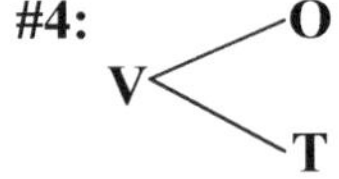

#5: O – M – F

#6:

R	R
	M

Overview:
We can combine the fourth and the fifth conditions to relate all the cars to one another.

From this, we know that V must be first, either O or T must be second, and either F or T must be last. Since M could be placed either third or fourth, the sixth condition tells us that the third wash must be regular in either case. In combination with the third condition, we know that the second wash is also regular.

R|P	R	R			R S P
V	O|T	M|	|M	F|T	F M O T
1	2	3	4	5	

11. (A) V must be first
    (B) Correct
    (C) violates the second condition
    (D) violates the first condition
    (E) violates the first condition

12. **(A)** Since all of the first three cars receive regular washes, the first and the second conditions dictate that the fourth and the fifth cars receive a super and a premium wash, although not necessarily in that order. Due to the sixth condition, we must place M third, and the fifth condition dictates that we place O second. Thus, choice A must be true.

R	R	R	P|S	S|P
V	O	M	F|T	T|F
1	2	3	4	5

13. **(B)** Combining this condition with the second condition and our diagram, we know that the fourth and fifth cars must receive super washes. The second condition dictates that we place a P above the first car. Applying the sixth and fifth conditions, we can place O second and M third. The only uncertainty remaining is the relative ordering of F and T, and thus, choice B could be true.

P	R	R	S	S
V	O	M	F|T	T|F
1	2	3	4	5

14. **(E)** This question directly tests our inference regarding the second and third washes.

15. **(B)** Since we know the second and third cars must both receive regular washes, we should check to see which car has to occupy one of those slots. O can be preceded by a maximum of two cars (V and T), so it has to be either second or third. Thus O must receive a regular wash. Due to the sixth condition, M must also receive a regular wash, and choice B is therefore correct.

16. This question prompts us to redraw our original sketch. The second and third conditions dictate that neither the second nor the third car receives a premium wash. Since V could be preceded by J, either J or V could be first.

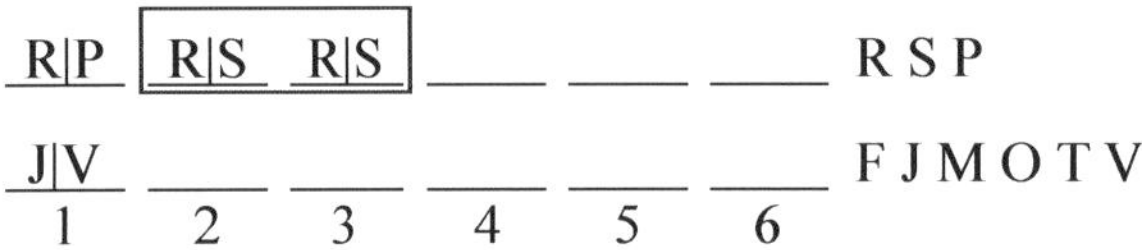

(A) Correct – since O is followed by at least two variables (F and M), it could only receive a premium wash if it occupied the fourth slot. However, M and F would have to occupy the fifth and sixth slots, violating the sixth condition

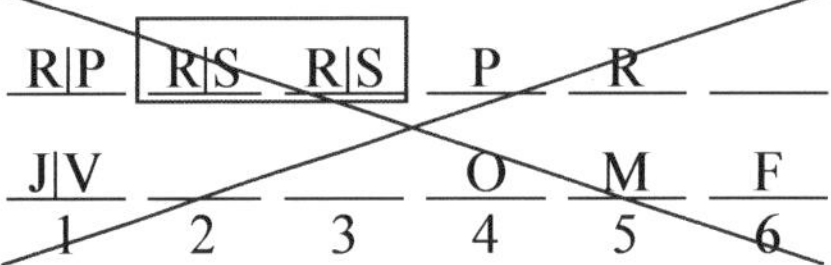

(B) V could occupy the second slot
(C) that would still leave two cars to be paired with a P and an S
(D) M would be third, and three cars would receive super washes
(E) J is unrestricted and can occupy any one of the six slots

Questions 17-23

Setup:
- seven toy-truck models: F G H J K M S
- each truck is assembled on one of seven assembly lines: 1 2 3 4 5 6 7

Conditions:
#1: F – J
#2: MG (boxed)
#3: H_1 or H_7
#4: S_4

Overview:
The first and second conditions tell us where four of the variables cannot be placed. Although there's not much else in the way of inferences, we can anticipate that the MG piece will play a large role in the questions since it will occupy two slots on either side of S.

H|			S			|H
1	2	3	4	5	6	7
~J		~M		~G		~F
~G						~M

17. (A) violates the third condition
    (B) Correct
    (C) violates the second condition
    (D) violates the fourth condition
    (E) violates the first condition

18. **(C)** Since J must be preceded by F (first condition), the lowest-numbered line on which it could be assembled is 2, and choice C is therefore correct.

19. With K placed on line 5, the MG piece is fairly restricted. It could occupy slots 1 and 2, slots 2 and 3, or slots 6 and 7.

H|			S	K		|H
1	2	3	4	5	6	7

(A) G cannot flank H since M immediately precedes G
(B) the MG piece would have to occupy the first two slots, but J must be preceded by F (first condition)
(C) Correct – see the following diagram

M	G	F	S	K	J	H
1	2	3	4	5	6	7

(D) J would have to be first, but this violates the first condition
(E) M cannot occupy the third slot, since it is immediately followed by G

20. **(D)** The simplest approach to this question is to work our way down from five. For F and J to be separated by five lines, they would have to occupy the first and seventh slots, which violates the third condition. If we place F second and J seventh, or F first and J seventh, we can create diagrams which don't violate the conditions. Thus, there can be at most four lines between the two and choice D is correct.

H	F	K	S	M	G	J
F	M	G	S	K	J	H
1	2	3	4	5	6	7

21. **(A)** With K second, the MG piece can either begin on the fifth line or the sixth line. Since F must precede J (first condition) F cannot occupy the last open slot, and it therefore must precede S. Hence, choice A is correct.

F|	K	|F	S	M	G	
F|	K	|F	S		M	G
1	2	3	4	5	6	7

22. **(A)** Combining this with the second condition, we have MGF. Since F must precede J (first condition), we must place the three-variable piece in the first, second and third slots. Hence, it must be true that F is assembled on the third line, and choice A is correct.

M	G	F	S	J|K	K|J	H
1	2	3	4	5	6	7

23. According to the second condition, G must be placed in the second slot. The third condition dictates that H must be placed in the seventh slot. As a consequence of the first condition, J cannot be third, and F cannot be sixth.

M	G		S			H
1	2	3	4	5	6	7
		~J			~F	

(A) violates the first condition
(B) if F occupied the fifth slot, J would have to be sixth (first condition)
(C) violates the first condition
(D) Correct – with K third, F and J must occupy the fifth and sixth slots

M	G	K	S	F	J	H
1	2	3	4	5	6	7

(E) violates the second condition

Part 4: PrepTests 31-40

Questions 1-6

Setup:
- four boys: F J M P
- three girls: N R T
- assigned to adjacent lockers: 1 2 3 4 5

Conditions:
#1: each locker assigned to one or two; each child assigned to one locker
#2: each shared locker is assigned to one boy and one girl

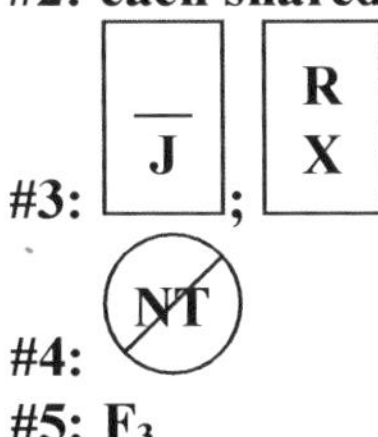

#5: F_3

Overview:
We are placing seven people into ten slots, and we can mark off any vacant slots with Xs. There are five lockers and four boys. This means that only one of the three girls can be assigned a locker to herself. Since we know that R doesn't share a locker (third condition), we can infer that the two other girls do. We can also infer that R cannot be placed in the third locker, since F is already assigned to it.

G	___	___	___	___	___	N R T
B	___	___	F	___	___	F J M P
	1	2	3	4	5	
			~R			

1. **(E)** This question draws upon our inference about how many of the girls must share lockers. We already know that N and T must share lockers and the third condition tells us that J shares a locker. Thus, choice E is correct.

2. **(B)** Due to the fourth condition, N must be assigned to either the first or the fifth locker. However, since the question tells us that M is assigned to the first locker alone, we can confidently place N in the fifth locker. Since T is paired with F, and R cannot be paired with anyone, the only girl that J can be paired with is N. Therefore, J must be assigned to the fifth locker. R can be assigned to either the second or fourth locker, and we have two possible outcomes.

G	X	R	T	X	N		G	X	X	T	R	N
B	M	X	F	P	J	or	B	M	P	F	X	J
	1	2	3	4	5			1	2	3	4	5

3. **(D)** With the four boys assigned to consecutive lockers and J placed in the fifth locker, we know that the boys must be assigned to lockers numbered two through five. We can therefore place M|P dual options above the second and fourth lockers. Since we know J must share a locker with one of the girls (third condition), we can place a N|T dual option above his slot. As a consequence of the fourth condition, the other girl has to be assigned to either the second or third locker. Thus, the first and fourth lockers will not be shared, and choice D is correct.

```
G   R     ___   ___    X    N|T
B   X     M|P    F    P|M    J
    1      2     3     4     5
```

4. **(C)** Once R is placed, the remaining four lockers must have boys assigned to them. Since F is already placed in the third locker, there are three lockers to which J could be assigned.

5. **(A)** As a consequence of the fourth condition and the stimulus, we have to separate N and T by R. With F assigned to the third locker, the third condition dictates that J must be assigned to the first locker with either N or T. Thus, choice A must be true.

```
G  N|T    R    T|N    X     X
B   J     X     F    M|P   P|M
    1     2     3     4     5
```

6. **(C)** Since the first two lockers are not shared, the last three must be, as there are three girls to place. Due to the fourth condition, we have to separate N and T by R. Therefore R is assigned to locker 4 and, since J has to be paired with a girl, J is assigned to locker 5.

```
G   X     X    N|T    R    T|N
B  M|P   P|M    F     X     J
    1     2     3     4     5
```

Questions 7-13

Setup:

- ten types of CDs: NJ UJ NO UO NP UP NR UR NS US
- some of the items are on sale

Conditions:
#1: UP; ~NO
#2: NP and UP ⟶ NS and US; ~NS or ~US ⟶ ~NP or ~UP (contrapositive)
#3: NJ and UJ ⟶ ~NR and ~UR; NR or UR ⟶ ~NJ or ~UJ (contrapositive)
#4: ~NJ and ~UJ ⟶ NP; ~NP ⟶ NJ or UJ (contrapositive)
#5: NR ⟶ ~NS and ~US; NS or US ⟶ ~NR (contrapositive)
UR ⟶ ~NS and ~US; NS or US ⟶ ~UR (contrapositive)

Overview:
Since we know that used pop is on sale, we can infer that if the contrapositive of the second condition is triggered, new pop will not be on sale. Combining the first two conditions, we know that if new pop is on sale, then both new soul and used soul are on sale. We can also link the fourth condition into the equation: ~NJ and ~UJ ⟶ NP ⟶ NS and US. The contrapositive of this chain can be broken into two pieces:

~NS ⟶ ~NP ⟶ NJ or UJ
~US ⟶ ~NP ⟶ NJ or UJ

For a more visual representation of the conditions, we can use the following diagram.

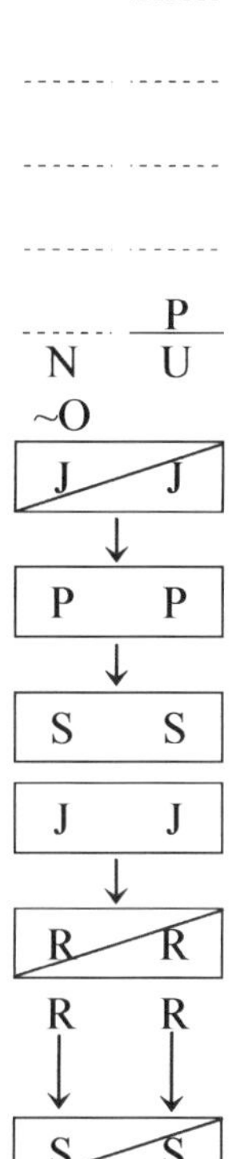

7. For this acceptable-list question, we can check the individual conditions against the choices.
   (A) violates the third condition
   (B) violates the fifth condition
   (C) violates the fourth condition
   (D) violates the second condition
   (E) Correct

8. **(E)** This triggers the contrapositive of the second condition, and, as we inferred, new pop is not on sale. Therefore, choice E is correct.

9. **(A)** Since both types of jazz are on sale, we know that neither type of rap is on sale. The only condition requiring that at least one type of CD is on sale is the fourth condition, which is satisfied by the condition given in the stimulus. Therefore, other than new jazz, none of the other new types must be on sale, and choice A is correct.

10. This cannot-be-true question offers no new information.
    (A) none of the conditions stipulates that either type of opera or rap must be on sale
    (B) all we can infer from this scenario is that new pop would also be on sale (fourth condition)
    (C) none of the conditions stipulates that either type of opera or soul must be on sale
    (D) Correct – due to the fourth condition, new pop must be on sale. Since both types of pop are on sale, both types of soul must be on sale (second condition), which contradicts the second condition given in the answer choice.
    (E) all we can infer from this situation is that new pop would also be on sale (fourth condition)

11. **(A)** From the fourth condition, we know that new pop is on sale. Since used pop is on sale (first condition), the second condition is triggered, and both types of soul must be on sale. Since rap and soul cannot both be on sale (fifth condition), we know that rap is not on sale. Thus, we can eliminate choices B, C, D, and E, and choice A is the correct answer. We cannot infer anything about used opera.

12. **(A)** From the fourth condition, we know that either one of the jazz types or new pop must be on sale. Since the question implicitly states that new pop is not on sale, we know that one of the jazz types must be on sale. The question precludes new jazz from being on sale, and we can therefore infer that used jazz must be on sale.

13. **(C)** Due to the first condition, used pop is one of the four types on sale. Of the four additional used types, used rap and used soul cannot both be on sale (fifth condition). We can therefore infer that used jazz, used opera, and one of used rap and used soul will be on sale, and choice C is correct.

R|S

O

J

P

U

Questions 14-18

Setup:
- one week: M T W Th F
- tours of three divisions: O P S
- one tour conducted each day

Conditions:
#1: each division is toured at least once
#2: ~O_M
#3: ~P_W
#4: [SS] and no others
#5: O_{Th} ⟶ P_F; ~P_F ⟶ ~O_{Th} (contrapositive)

Overview:
Since we know what cannot go in the first and third slots and there are only three divisions, we can create dual options for those two slots. Combining the double-S piece with the condition that each division must be toured at least once, we can deduce that either O or P will be toured twice, as illustrated by the following allocation table.

O	P	S
2	1	2
1	2	2

The basic diagram follows:

P|S		O|S		
M	T	W	Th	F
~O		~P		
			O⟶P	

We can establish four distinct molds based on the placement of the double-S piece.

	M	T	W	Th	F
#1	S	S	O	O|P	O|P
#2	P	S	S	O|P	P|O
#3	P	O|P	S	S	O|P
#4	P	O|P	O|P	S	S

Mold #1: With the double-S piece spanning Monday and Tuesday, the third and fourth conditions dictate that O must be placed in the Wednesday slot.

Mold #2: With the double-S piece spanning Tuesday and Wednesday, the second and fourth conditions dictate that P must be placed in the Monday slot. Since O cannot be placed in both the Thursday and Friday slots (fifth condition), we must use the second acceptable allocation.

Mold #3: With the double-S piece spanning Wednesday and Thursday, the second and fourth conditions dictate that P must be placed in the Monday slot.

Mold #4: With the double-S piece spanning Thursday and Friday, the second and fourth conditions dictate that P must be placed in the Monday slot.

14. This cannot-be-true question offers no new information.
    - (A) see molds #1, #3, and #4
    - (B) see molds #2 and #3
    - **(C) Correct – this violates the fourth condition**
    - (D) see mold #1
    - (E) see molds #1 and #4

15. **(B)** This could only be true of molds #1, #3, and #4. From the various options, we can create five acceptable solutions. Only choice B matches one of these solutions (the third one), and it is therefore correct.

M	T	W	Th	F
S	S	O	P	P
S	S	O	O	P
P	P	S	S	O
P	P	O	S	S
P	O	O	S	S

16. **(A)** This could only be true of mold #3. Since O must be toured at least once (first condition), we must place Os in both the Tuesday and Friday slots. Thus, choice A is correct.

P	O	S	S	O
M	T	W	Th	F

17. This could be true of molds #2, #3, and #4. Applying the information to the three molds yields the following three diagrams.

P	S	S	O|P	P|O
P	O	S	S	O|P
P	O	O|P	S	S
M	T	W	Th	F

(A) P must be on Monday
(B) P must be on Monday
(C) P must be on Monday
(D) either O or S must be on Tuesday
(E) Correct – this could be true of the third diagram

P	O	O	S	S
M	T	W	Th	F

18. **(A)** This could only be true of mold #2 or mold #4. Therefore, we know that P occupies the Monday slot, and choice A is correct.

Questions 19-23

Setup:
- crew of up to five workers
- at most three days
- five tasks in this order: F W T S P
- G: T
- H: S, T
- I: F, P
- K: F, S
- L: W, T
- M: S
- O: W, P

Conditions:
#1: 1^{+} task each day
#2: T and P on different days
#3: each crew member: 1^{+} task, only 1 per day
#4: each task: done by one worker, completed in one day

Overview:
Since we're given the order of the tasks, and we need to determine which person completes each task, it makes sense to group the people in terms of the individual tasks. Due to the second condition, there must be a day division between either taping and sanding or sanding and priming.

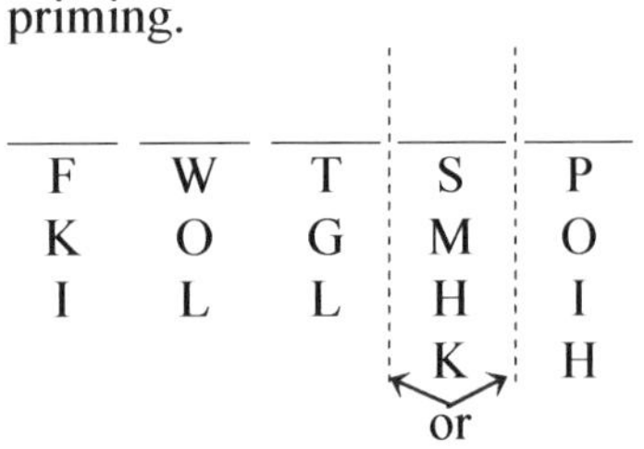

F	W	T	S	P
K	O	G	M	O
I	L	L	H	I
			K	H

or

19. (A) either L or O must be selected (wallboarding)
    (B) Correct
    (C) either G or L must be selected (taping)
    (D) either G or L must be selected (taping)
    (E) either I or K must be selected (framing)

20. **(D)** Since we're asked to find two workers who could complete tasks on the first and the third days, we know that the number of tasks per day is two, one, and two, respectively. The simplest way to complete the problem is to check each of the four possible framing/wallboarding combinations in terms of which two variables could be duplicated for the last two tasks. Of KO, KL, IO, and IL, only KO could be duplicated for sanding and priming, and choice D is therefore correct.

21. **(A)** Fortunately, the first choice contains a clear violation of the conditions. Since neither G nor L is listed, taping could not be completed, and therefore, choice A is correct.

22. **(E)** From this information, we can deduce that either taping alone or wallboarding and taping are completed on the second day. Since taping is definitely completed on the second day, either G or L must be included for the answer to be correct. We can eliminate choices A, B, and C since they contain neither G nor L. Since H can complete neither wallboarding nor taping, it cannot be among the listed variables, and we can eliminate choice D as well. Therefore, choice E is the correct answer.

F	W	T	S	P
K	O	G	M	O
I	L	L	H	I
	or		K	H

23. Since we haven't made any inferences regarding this information, we'll have to check the answer choices individually.

(A) G can only complete one task (taping)
(B) K would complete sanding and H would complete priming, but H cannot complete any of the first three tasks
(C) I would have to complete priming, but L cannot complete sanding
(D) Correct – see the following diagram

K	L	L	K	
F	W	T	S	P

(E) O would have to complete priming, but L cannot complete sanding

Questions 1-6

Setup:
- eight students: G H I K L N O R
- six will give reports
- three consecutive days: M T W
- exactly two reports each day: A P

Conditions:
#1: G ⟶ G_T
#2: O ⟶ O_A
R ⟶ R_A

#3: N_M or N_T ⟶ (H I) on the following day

Overview:
We can infer that if neither O nor R occupies one of the morning slots, they are out, and all the other variables will be selected.

P ____ ____ ____ ~O ~R

A ____ ____ ____
M T W
~G ~G

1. (A) violates the second condition
   (B) violates the second condition
   (C) Correct
   (D) violates the third condition
   (E) violates the first condition

2. **(D)** From this condition, we can deduce that G, H, I, N, O, and R all give reports. Since neither O nor R can give afternoon reports (second condition), they must both give morning reports. Only answer choice D contains both O and R, and it is therefore correct.

3. **(B)** This question tests our grasp of the third condition. If N gives a report on Monday or Tuesday, then H gives one on the following day. For N and H to give reports on the same day, it would have to be on Wednesday. Choice B is therefore correct.

4. G must give a report on Tuesday, due to the first condition. Since all three give reports on different days, N and R must occupy slots on Monday and Wednesday. N cannot give a report on Monday, since this would trigger and violate the third condition (G occupies one of the Tuesday slots). Therefore, we know that R occupies the morning slot on Monday, and N occupies a slot on Wednesday.

```
P  ____  ____  ____

A  _R__  ____  ____
    M     T     W
          G     N
```

(A) Correct – as we deduced in #3, N and H can both be on Wednesday
(B) N must be on Wednesday
(C) N must be on Wednesday
(D) O would have to occupy the morning slot (second condition), but R is already there
(E) R must occupy the Monday morning slot

5. **(D)** Placing the variables into their respective slots, we shift our focus to the answer choices. Choices A through C exclude both O and R. In combination with the first condition, G would have to occupy the Tuesday morning slot. Since choices A and C do not meet violate this deduction, we can eliminate them. Revisiting choice B, N would have to be placed in the Monday afternoon slot, violating the third condition. In choice E, neither O nor G gives a report. This forces N into the Monday afternoon slot, which violates the third condition. Only choice D could be true; see the following diagram.

```
P  _L__  _K__  _H__

A  _R__  _G__  _I__
    M     T     W
```

6. **(B)** Combining this with the second condition, we know that neither O nor R give reports. As a result, the afternoon slots must be filled by I, G, and N. G has to give the Tuesday afternoon report, due to the first condition. If N were placed in the Monday afternoon slot, the third condition would be triggered and broken. Therefore, the order of the afternoon reports must be I, G, and N. Hence, choice B is correct.

```
P  _I__  _G__  _N__

A  ____  ____  ____  H K L
    M     T     W
```

<u>Questions 7-11</u>

Setup:

- between 5 and 6 of 9 works will be selected
- FN FN FN RN RN RN FP FP

Conditions:
#1: ≤ 4 F
#2: 3 ≤ #N ≤ 4
#3: #FN ≥ #RN
#4: FP and FP ⟶ ~RP; RP ⟶ ~FP^{1+} (contrapositive)

Overview:
The fourth condition tells us that a maximum of two plays are selected (could be FP and FP, or FP and RP). Combining the second and third conditions, we can deduce that at least two French novels are selected. If not, the third condition would be violated. Since the number of novels cannot exceed four (second condition) at least one Russian novel must not be selected. We can infer the following possible allocations of French novels and Russian novels.

FN	RN
2	1
2	2
3	0
3	1

We can set up three distinct molds to represent the possible allocations of French works and Russian works.

	#1 N	#1 P	#2 N	#2 P	#3 N	#3 P
			R		R	
	F|R		F|R		F|R	
	F	F|R	F		R	F|R
	F	F	F	F|R	F	F

Mold #1: If three novels are selected, at least two of them must be French, due to the third condition. Since there's only one Russian play, at least one of the plays selected must be French.

Mold #2: If four novels are selected, at least one of them must be Russian, since there are only three French novels. If only one play is selected, it could be either French or Russian.

Mold #3: If four novels and two plays are selected, at least one of the plays must be French, since there is only one Russian play.

7. (A) violates the third condition
   (B) violates the fourth condition
   (C) Correct
   (D) violates the first condition
   (E) violates the second condition

8. **(A)** Since no new information is given, we must check the answer choices against the molds. Only choice A could be true (under mold #1), and it is correct.

9. This could be true of all three molds. With three French novels selected, we know that at least two Russian novels are not selected.

   (A) at least five works must be selected
   (B) violates the first condition
   (C) Correct
   (D) violates the first condition
   (E) as we inferred, at least two Russian novels are not selected

10. **(D)** This question directly tests our inference regarding French novels. To satisfy both the second and the third conditions, at least two French novels must be selected. Thus, choice D is correct.

11. **(A)** Fortunately, scanning the answer choices reveals an immediate violation in choice A. To satisfy the second condition, all three French novels would have to be selected. However, if only one play were selected, only four works in total would be selected. Therefore, choice A must be false.

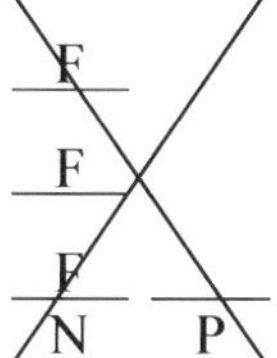

Questions 12-18

Setup:
- eight compositions: F H L O P R S T
- performed consecutively (once each and one at a time)

Conditions:

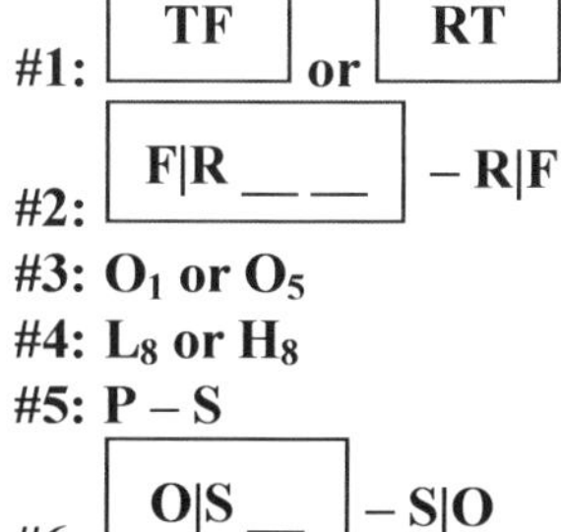

Overview:
Due to the fifth condition, we know that S cannot occupy the first slot. Combining the fourth and the fifth conditions, we also know that P cannot be seventh.

O|				|O			L|H
1	2	3	4	5	6	7	8
~S						~P	

12. **(A) Correct**
    (B) violates the first condition
    (C) violates the third condition
    (D) violates the sixth condition
    (E) violates the second condition

13. **(E)** As we previously inferred, P cannot be seventh, and choice E is correct.

14. **(A)** Applying this information to the third condition, we must place O first. Since F and R must be separated by at least two variables (second condition), R must be either second or third. When it is second, the fifth condition dictates that S cannot be third. When R is third, the fifth condition dictates that S cannot be second. Therefore, S must be either fourth or seventh, and choice A is correct.

O	R			T	F		L|H
1	2	3	4	5	6	7	8
		~S				~P	

O		R		T	F		L|H
1	2	3	4	5	6	7	8
	~S					~P	

15. **(E)** Combining this information with the first condition, we have the following piece:

[RTO]. In this case, O cannot be first, so we must place it fifth, due to the third condition. To satisfy the second condition, S must be either sixth or seventh, and choice E is correct.

		R	T	O	S|	|S	L|H
1	2	3	4	5	6	7	8

16. **(C)** The third and the sixth conditions dictate that we place O in the first slot. Since P must precede S (fifth condition), P must be either second or third. R and F must be separated by at least two variables (second condition), so in either case, we must place one of them in the open slot adjacent to P. Only choices C and D have O in the first slot, and only choice C has one of F and R adjacent to P. Hence, choice C is correct.

O   F|R   P   S   ___   ___   ___   L|H

O   P   F|R   S   ___   ___   ___   L|H
1   2   3   4   5   6   7   8

17. **(C)** Applying the third and the sixth conditions, we know that O must occupy the first slot. The first condition requires two open adjacent slots into which we can place T and F or R and T. Thus, we must place them into the fourth and fifth slots. As a result, the fifth composition could be F or T, and choice C is correct.

O   ___   P   T   F   S   ___   L|H

O   ___   P   R   T   S   ___   L|H
1   2   3   4   5   6   7   8

18. **(D)** Since F precedes O, O cannot be first. The third condition dictates that we place it fifth. With O fifth, the question stipulates that F be placed second. To satisfy the second condition, R must be either sixth or seventh. If R were seventh, T would have to be first, due to the first condition. S would have to be third, but with no open slots for P, the sixth condition would be violated. Hence, R must be sixth, and choice D is correct.

T| F   ___   ___   O   R |T   L|H

~~T   F   S   ___   O   ___   R   L|H~~
1   2   3   4   5   6   7   8

Questions 19-24

Setup:

- seven consecutive days: 1 2 3 4 5 6 7
- features one of three breeds of kitten (K): H M S
- features one of three breeds of puppy (P): G N R

Conditions:

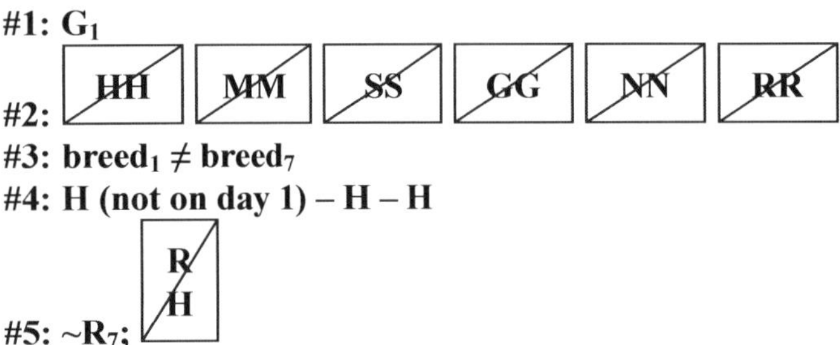

Overview:
Combining the first two conditions reveals that the second puppy must be either N or R. Since the seventh puppy is neither G (third condition) nor R (fifth condition), we can infer that it must be N. Applying the second condition, we know that the sixth puppy is either G or R. From the fourth condition, we know that the first kitten is either M or S.

	1	2	3	4	5	6	7	
P	G	N|R				G|R	N	G N R
K	M|S							H M S
	~H	~G				~N	~G ~R	

19. (A) violates the fourth condition
    (B) violates the third condition
    (C) violates the fourth condition
    (D) violates the second condition
    (E) Correct

20. Since we must place three Hs (fourth condition), and they cannot be consecutive (second condition), we must place them third, fifth, and seventh. Combining this information with the fifth condition, we know that R cannot occupy the third or fifth puppy slots.

	1	2	3	4	5	6	7
P	G	N|R	G|N		G|N	G|R	N
K	M|S		H		H		H
			~R		~R		

    (A) H must be featured on day 3
    (B) Correct – day 4 doesn't have any restrictions
    (C) violates the fifth condition
    (D) violates the second condition
    (E) violates the third condition

21. (A) violates the second condition
 (B) violates the third condition
 (C) violates the fifth condition
 (D) Correct – the fifth slots are unrestricted by the conditions
 (E) since N is the seventh puppy, this violates the second condition

22. In combination with the second and the fourth conditions, this tells us that we must place Hs in the second, fourth, and sixth kitten slots. Applying the fifth condition, we know that the respective puppy slots cannot be occupied by Rs. Consequently, we must place an N in the second puppy slot and a G in the sixth kitty slot.

P	G	N	G|R	G|N	N|R	G	N
K	M|S	H		H		H	S|M
	1	2	3	4	5	6	7
		~R		~R		~R	

 (A) could be G and M or S
 (B) Correct – the puppies must be N and G respectively
 (C) could be R and M or S
 (D) could be G and H
 (E) could be N and M or S

23. We can check the answer choices against our master diagram and the conditions.

 (A) Correct – see the following diagram

P	G	R	N	G	N	G	N
K	M	S	H	M	H	M	H
	1	2	3	4	5	6	7

 (B) this could only happen if the three Gs were spread from the third through the sixth slots, but the second condition would be broken
 (C) H cannot be first (fourth condition)
 (D) H cannot be first (fourth condition)
 (E) R cannot be first (first condition)

24. Since this condition is identical to the one applied in number twenty-two, we can reuse that diagram.

 (A) G cannot be fifth and sixth (second condition)
 (B) N cannot be second and third (second condition)
 (C) violates the fifth condition
 (D) Correct – we need not have more than one R
 (E) at most, Rs could be placed in the third and fifth puppy slots

Questions 1-5

Setup:
- seven television programs: H J L P Q S V
- programs are ranked from first through seventh (most to least popular)

Conditions:

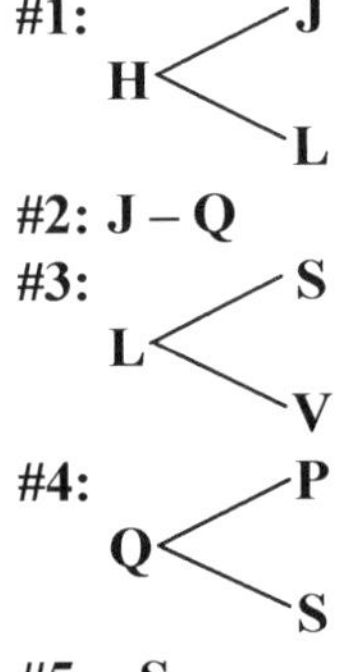

#5: ~S_7

Overview:
We can combine the conditions into the following master sketch.

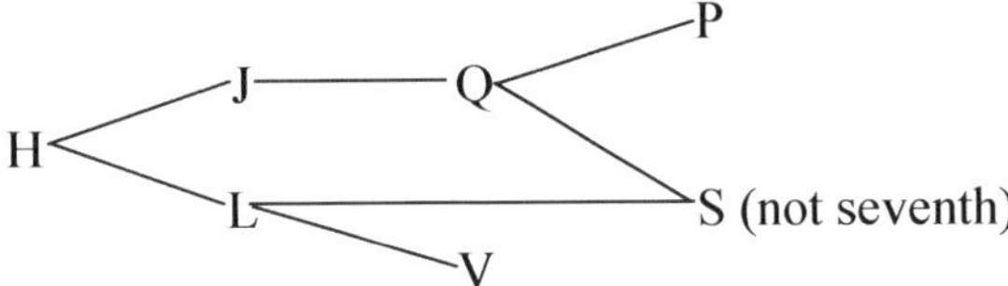

From the fifth condition, we can deduce that either P or V must be seventh.

1. (A) violates the first condition
   (B) violates the second condition
   (C) Correct
   (D) violates the third condition
   (E) violates the fifth condition

2. **(A)** Since J and L are the only two variables that could immediately follow H, we know that J must be second in this case.

H	J	L				P|V
1	2	3	4	5	6	7

3. **(E)** We're looking for the variable which either cannot be preceded by two others or cannot be followed by four others. P cannot be third, since the only variables that can follow it are L, S, and V.

4. **(D)** For this question, we can redraw our sketch. S must precede P due to the fifth condition. Since the relationship between J and V is uncertain, it could be true that J precedes V.

5. **(B)** We can redraw our sketch to include this condition. L does not have to be fourth. It could also be ranked fifth (followed by V and one of P and S) or sixth (followed by only V).

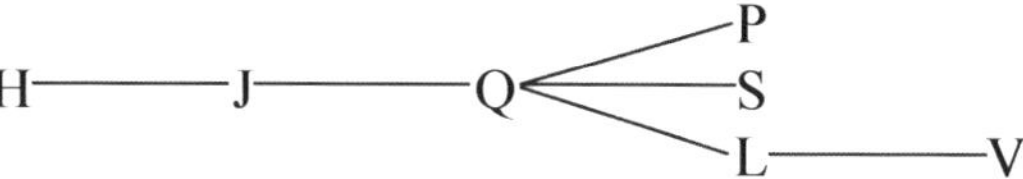

Questions 6-12

Setup:
- six kinds of birds: G H J M S W

Conditions:
#1: H ⟶ ~G; G ⟶ ~H (contrapositive)
#2: J ⟶ H; ~H ⟶ ~J (contrapositive)
M ⟶ H; ~H ⟶ ~M (contrapositive)
#3: W ⟶ G; ~G ⟶ ~W (contrapositive)
#4: ~J ⟶ S; ~S ⟶ J (contrapositive)

Overview:
We can use our diagram to make any necessary inferences.

In[1] Out

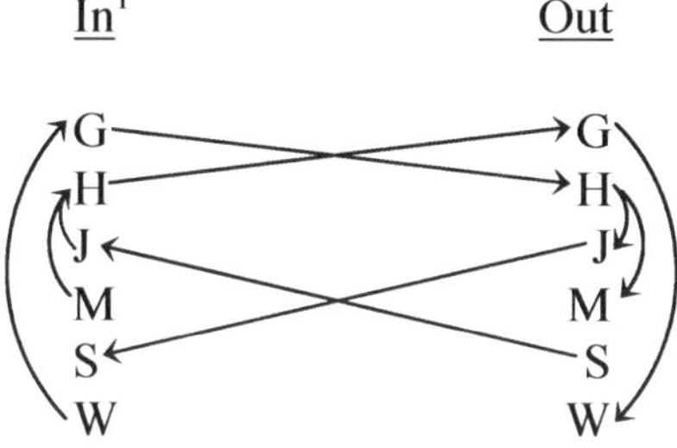

6. (A) violates the fourth condition
   (B) violates the contrapositive of the second condition
   (C) violates the contrapositive of the third condition
   (D) Correct
   (E) violates the first condition

[1] Visit Manhattan LSAT (http://www.manhattanlsat.com) to learn more about using this diagram.

7. **(E)** Following the chain from M and H selected, we know that G and W are both out. Since J and S are the only remaining variables, it must be true that a maximum of two others could be selected. Therefore, answer choice E is correct.

In	Out
M	G
H	W
J	
S	

8. **(D)** Following the chain from J not selected, we know that S must be selected. Therefore, choice D must be false.

9. **(C)** According to the first condition, we can only select one of G and H. If we exclude G, we must also exclude W (contrapositive of condition #3). If we exclude H, we must also exclude J and M (contrapositive of condition #3). Therefore, the maximum is four, and choice C is correct.

In	Out
H	G
J	W
M	
S	

10. To tackle this question, we can follow the chain from the first of each pair being selected. If it leads to the second variable being out, the answer choice is correct.

    (A) Correct – J ⟶ H ⟶ ~G ⟶ ~W
    (B) J in doesn't lead to S out
    (C) S in doesn't lead to W out
    (D) J in doesn't lead to M out
    (E) S in doesn't lead to M out

11. **(A)** Following the chain from G in, we have H, J, and M out, and S in. Therefore, choice A must be true.

In	Out
G	H
S	J
W|	M
	|W

12. Since this is the last question of the game, we can modify our diagram to include the additional constraint.

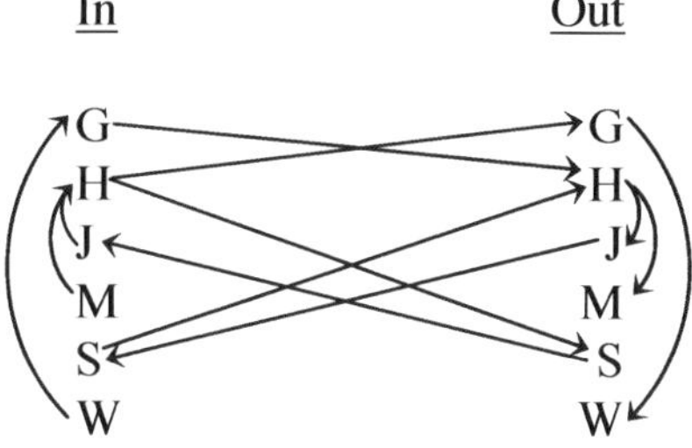

(A) from J in, we have H in and S out
(B) Correct
(C) from M in, we have H in and S out
(D) from J out, we have S in, H out, and M out
(E) G and H both lead to three others being out: H, J, and M; and S, G, and W respectively. If we exclude G and H, we must exclude J, M, and W as well. Therefore, we know that more than two variables must be out.

Questions 13-18

Setup:
- six of ten stones to be selected
- rubies (R): F G H
- sapphires (S): J K M
- topazes (T): W X Y Z

Conditions:
#1: T=2⁺
#2: 2S ⟶ 1R; ~1R ⟶ ~2S (contrapositive)
#3: W ⟶ ~H; H ⟶ ~W
W ⟶ ~Z; Z ⟶ ~W
#4: **M ⟶ W; ~W ⟶ ~M (contrapositive)**

Overview:
We can make some immediate inferences about numbers. The first condition, in combination with the third condition, tells us that two or three topazes must be selected. If two are selected, then we need to select four of rubies and sapphires. If three topazes are selected, then we need to select three of rubies and sapphires. We can make an allocation table to track the numbers in the game.

R	S	T
1	3	2
3	1	2
3	0	3
0	3	3
1	2	3
2	1	3

Note that we cannot have a 2, 2, 2 allocation due to the second condition.

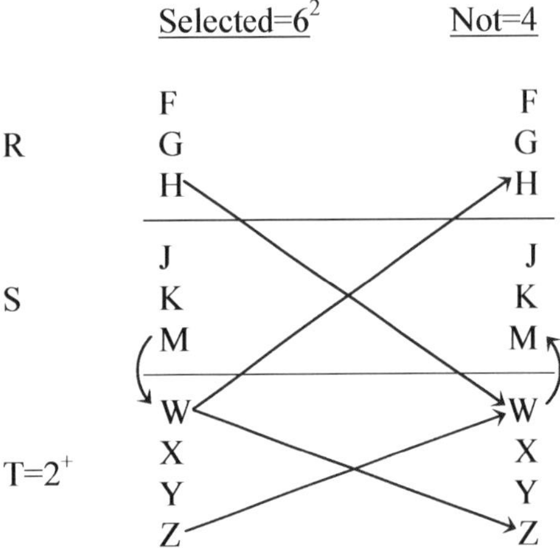

13. (A) violates the fourth condition
    (B) violates the first condition
    (C) violates the second condition
    (D) Correct
    (E) violates the third condition

14. (A) see the allocation table
    (B) see the allocation table
    (C) since we only need two topazes (first condition), we need not select X
    (D) see the allocation table
    (E) Correct – every possible allocation has three of one type represented

[2] Visit Manhattan LSAT (http://www.manhattanlsat.com) to learn more about using this diagram.

15. Following the chain from Z being selected, we know that neither W nor M is selected.
    (A) M is out
    (B) M is out
    (C) M is out
    (D) with a maximum of three topazes, only five stones could be selected (M is out)
    (E) Correct – all three rubies would be selected

In	Out
F	W
G	M
H	J
X	K
Y	
Z	

16. **(D)** Referring back to our allocation table, we know that one sapphire and three topazes are selected. Therefore, choice D must be true.

17. (A) see the allocation table
    (B) see the allocation table
    (C) see the diagram for question #18
    (D) Correct – since we can only select one of W and Z (third condition), in order to satisfy the first condition, we must select at least one of X and Y
    (E) we can satisfy the first condition by selecting W and Y

18. **(B)** This condition triggers the second condition, and we can infer that one ruby and three topazes will be selected. Following the chain from M being selected, we know that W is selected, and that neither H nor Z is selected. Choice B is the only one of the choices that could be true.

		Y
	M	W
F|G	J	X
R	S	T
~H		~Z

Questions 19-23

Setup:
- ten stores on Oak Street
- N: 1 3 5 7 9 (west to east)
- S: 2 4 6 8 10 (west to east)
- directly across pairs: 1 and 2; 3 and 4; 5 and 6; 7 and 8; 9 and 10
- each store is decorated with lights in exactly one of three colors: G R Y

Conditions:

#1: 

#2: 

#3: exactly 1 Y on each side of the street
#4: R_4
#5: Y_5

Overview:
The fourth and fifth conditions allow us to place two variables directly into our diagram. In conjunction with the first two conditions, we can place Gs in the third and sixth slots. Since we already have one Y placed on the north side, and we can't have two Gs next to each other (first condition), we can place an R in the first slot. The first condition creates dual options for the second, seventh, and eighth slots. We can also place a dual G|R option in the ninth slot due to the third condition.

	1	3	5	7	9
N	R	G	Y	G|R	G|R
S	G|Y	R	G	R|Y	
	2	4	6	8	10

19. (A) violates the third condition
    (B) Correct
    (C) G occupies the sixth slot
    (D) the placement of G and R (fourth and sixth) is reversed
    (E) violates the third condition

20. **(D)** Combining this information with our diagram and the first condition, we must place a R in the ninth slot. Therefore, choice D must be true.

	1	3	5	7	9
N	R	G	Y	G	R
S	G|Y	R	G	R|Y	G|Y
	2	4	6	8	10

21. **(B)** This question directly tests our inference regarding store 1. We know that choice B must be true.

22. **(E)** This condition essentially tells us that we need to place one G in each column. The first and the second conditions dictate that we place them in a zigzag pattern. Since we have definitively placed Gs in the third and sixth slots, we must place the other three in the second, seventh, and tenth slots. Therefore, answer choice E must be true.

	1	3	5	7	9
N	R	G	Y	G	R
S	G	R	G	Y	G
	2	4	6	8	10

23. **(D)** We have already inferred that a Y could be placed in either the second or the eighth slot. Combining the new condition with the first condition, we know that Ys cannot occupy both the eighth and the tenth slots. Therefore, we must place a Y in the second slot; the other one will occupy either the eighth or the tenth slot. Hence, choice D is correct.

	1	3	5	7	9
N	R	G	Y	G/R	G/R
S	Y	R	G	R/Y	
	2	4	6	8	10

Questions 1-7

Setup:

- o supermarket clerks: J K L M O
- o nine parallel aisles: 1 2 3 4 5 6 7 8 9
- o each aisle is stocked by one clerk
- o no clerk stocks more than two aisles

Conditions:

#1: O ⟶ 1 aisle

#2: K_2

#3: $\sim M_1$

#4: ~~JJ~~

#5: MKM

#6: L_1 or L_9 (not both)

#7: K – K – O – L

L or L

Overview:

Since we know that O only stocks one aisle, and no clerk can stock more than two aisles, it follows that J, K, L, and M each stock two aisles. The conditions also allude to this fact. J is the least restricted of all the variables; we only know that we can't have two consecutive Js (fourth condition). Our master sketch includes all but the two Js.

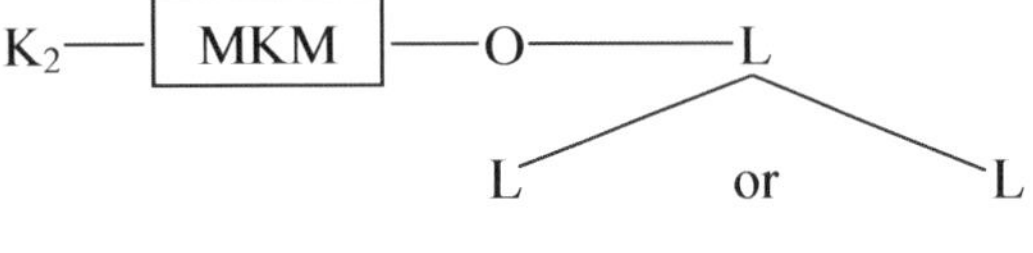

L|	K							|L
1	2	3	4	5	6	7	8	9
~M								

1. (A) violates the fourth condition
   (B) violates the fifth condition
   (C) Correct
   (D) violates the fifth condition
   (E) violates the first condition

2. **(E)** Since the MKM piece is followed by at least two variables, the latest position at which it can begin is the fifth slot. Its placement options are third through fifth, fourth through sixth, and fifth through seventh. No matter where it is placed, the fifth slot must be occupied by either K or M. Since choices A through D contain one of the two, we can eliminate them, and choice E is therefore correct.

3. **(B)** We know that K cannot stock the third aisle, due to the fifth. We also know that O cannot be placed third, since it must follow the MKM piece. Therefore, each of J, L, and M could be placed third, and choice B is correct.

4. **(D)** Due to the MKM piece's potential placements (third through fifth, fourth through sixth, and fifth through seventh), M could stock any of the aisles from 3 through 7, and choice D is correct.

5. **(A)** We can't place L in the first and ninth slots, due to the sixth condition, but we can place Ls in the first and eighth slots. If the MKM piece spans the third through the fifth slots, we must place a J ninth (fourth condition), which creates J|O dual options for the sixth and seventh slots. If the MKM piece spans the fourth through the sixth slots, we must place an O seventh (seventh condition), leaving the two Js to fill the third and ninth slots. The MKM piece cannot span the fifth through the seventh slots, since this would violate the seventh condition. As J could be sixth in the first scenario, choice A is correct.

L	K	M	K	M	J|O	O|J	L	J
L	K	J	M	K	M	O	L	J
1	2	3	4	5	6	7	8	9

6. **(E)** With the third slot occupied, the MKM piece can span the fourth through the sixth slots or the fifth through the seventh slots. Since the sixth slot must be occupied by either K or M, choice E must be false.

7. **(B)** When the MKM piece spans the third through the fifth slots, we must place Js in the sixth and eighth slots (fourth condition), leaving O to occupy the seventh slot. When the MKM piece spans the fourth through the sixth slots, we must place a J third (fourth condition), which creates dual J|O options for the seventh and eighth slots. The MKM piece cannot span the fifth through the seventh slots in this case, since O would have to be placed eighth, leaving two Js to occupy the third and fourth slots, which would violate the fourth condition. In neither acceptable scenario can O stock the sixth aisle, and choice B is therefore correct.

L	K	M	K	M	J	O	J	L
L	K	J	M	K	M	J|O	O|J	L
1	2	3	4	5	6	7	8	9

Questions 8-12

Setup:

- five different lectures given during a five-week course
- no lecture is given more than once
- each lecture is delivered by a different speaker

Conditions:
#1: each speaker specializes in whichever philosopher he or she lectures on
#2: each philosopher can be lectured on no more than once
#3: first week's speaker: K, L, and M
#4: second week's speaker: K, L, M, and N
#5: third and fourth weeks' speakers: M and N
#6: fifth week's speaker: N, O, and P

Overview:
Combining the fifth condition with the condition that no lecture is given more than once, we know that the third and fourth lectures must be on M and N, not necessarily in that order. Since M and N cannot occur outside of the third and fourth weeks, we can infer that the first and second weeks will consist of K and L (third and fourth conditions), not necessarily in that order. We can also infer that the fifth week's lecture will be on either O or P, due to the sixth condition.

K|L	L|K	M|N	N|M	O|P
1	2	3	4	5
K	K	M	M	~N
L	L	N	N	O
~M	~M			P
	~N			

8. **(E)** We can eliminate choices A through D based on our inference regarding M and N. We know that the fifth lecture could be on O, and choice E is therefore correct.

9. **(A)** To put the lectures in alphabetical order, the first four in order must be K, L, M, and N. Since the fifth lecture could be on O or P, there are two solutions, and choice A is correct.

K	L	M	N	O
K	L	M	N	P
1	2	3	4	5

10. For this question, we need to see how the answer choices affect our diagram.

    (A) this wouldn't lock down the fifth lecture
    (B) this wouldn't lock down the fifth lecture
    (C) Correct – this would lock down all three dual options: K|L, M|N, and O|P
    (D) the first two lectures wouldn't be determined
    (E) the first two lectures wouldn't be determined

11. **(D)** Due to the dual options in the first four slots, we know that we must have one British and one German philosopher represented in each of the two pairs (one/two and three/four). We can break this down further into four scenarios. All the answer choices are possible with the exception of D, and it is therefore correct.

B|G	G|B	B|G	G|B	___
1	2	3	4	5

B	G	B	G	___
B	G	G	B	___
G	B	B	G	___
G	B	G	B	___
1	2	3	4	5

12. **(B)** On the surface, this replacement opens things up considerably. We can no longer count M and N out for the lectures outside the third and the fourth. However, since the fourth lecture is still limited to one of M and N, if the third lecture is on S, only one of the first, second, and fifth lectures could be on either M or N. Choice B presents an impossibility, since placing M and N second and third respectively eliminates both options for the fourth lecture.

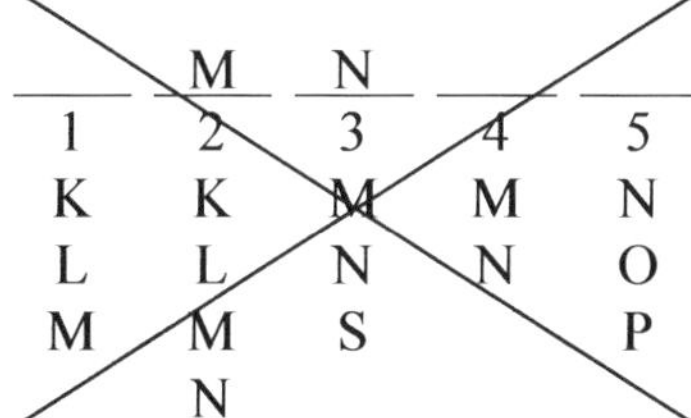

Questions 13-18

Setup:
- seven trains: Q R S T V W Y

Conditions:
#1: the trains arrive one at a time
#2: Y_4 or W_4
#3: W – S – Y
#4:
T
R
V

#5: 

Overview:
Combining the second and third conditions, we know that if W occupies the fourth slot, S and Y must occupy two of the last three slots, and if Y occupies the fourth slot, W and S must occupy two of the first three slots. We can use the fourth and fifth conditions to create two molds based on which of W and Y is fourth.

#1				W			
	1	2	3	4	5	6	7

Q, R – T|V   S – Y, V|T

#2				Y	T|V	Q	V|T
	1	2	3	4	5	6	7

W – S, R

Mold #1: Could Q occupy one of the last three slots? This would force T and V to be next to each other in the second and third slots, which would violate the fifth condition. Therefore, Q must occupy one of the first three slots, and one of T and V must occupy one of the last three slots.

Mold #2: Could Q occupy one of the first three slots? This would force T and V to be next to each other in the sixth and seventh slots, which would violate the fifth condition. Therefore, Q must occupy one of the last three slots. Since T and V must follow R (fourth condition), they must occupy two of the last three slots. To satisfy the fifth condition, we must separate T and V with Q.

13. (A) violates the fifth condition
    (B) violates the third condition
    (C) Correct
    (D) violates the second condition
    (E) violates the fourth condition

14. **(A)** This could only happen under the second mold. W must be first, but it is uncertain which of R and S follows it. Since there are two sets of dual options, there are a total of four solutions, and choice A is correct.

W	R|S	S|R	Y	T|V	Q	V|T
1	2	3	4	5	6	7

15. **(E)** This question directly tests our interpretation of the third condition. From the chain, we know that W must precede Y, and choice E is correct.

16. **(B)** To quickly tackle this question, we can check the answer choices against our molds. Only choice B is possible. For further verification that this could be true, see our diagram for number fourteen.

17. Combining this with the third condition gives the following piece: | WSY |. We can plug this into the two molds to see what could be true.

___	___	___	W	S	Y	V|T
1	2	3	4	5	6	7

Q, R – T|V

R	W	S	Y	T|V	Q	V|T
1	2	3	4	5	6	7

(A) the sixth train must be either Q or Y
(B) the sixth train must be either Q or Y
(C) in the first scenario, R cannot be third since one of T and V also occupies one of the first three slots
(D) S must be either third or fifth
(E) Correct – this could be true under the first mold

18. **(C)** Since this could only happen under the first mold, we know that W is fourth, and choice C is correct.

Questions 19-24

Setup:
- six doctors: J K L N O P
- two clinics: R S

Conditions:
#1: $J_S \longrightarrow K_R$; $K_S \longrightarrow J_R$ (contrapositive)
#2: $J_R \longrightarrow O_S$; $O_R \longrightarrow J_S$ (contrapositive)
#3: $L_S \longrightarrow N_R$; $N_S \longrightarrow L_R$ (contrapositive)
$L_S \longrightarrow P_R$; $P_S \longrightarrow L_R$ (contrapositive)
#4: $N_R \longrightarrow O_R$; $O_S \longrightarrow N_S$ (contrapositive)
#5: $P_R \longrightarrow K_S$; $K_R \longrightarrow P_S$ (contrapositive)
$P_R \longrightarrow O_S$; $O_R \longrightarrow P_S$ (contrapositive)

Overview:
We can use our diagram to make the necessary inferences.

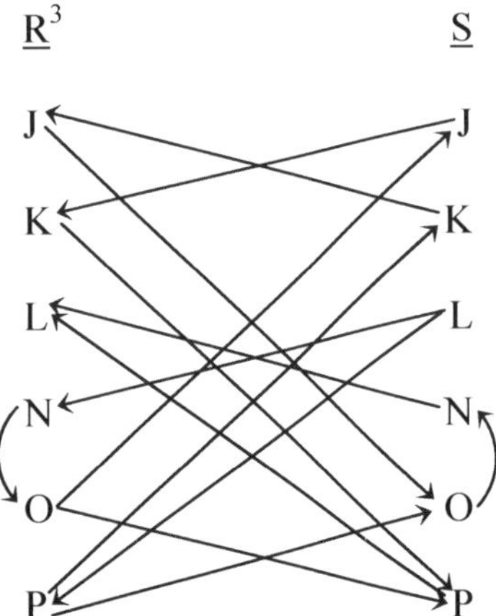

Since this diagram is fairly cluttered, alternatively, we could chain together the conditions in a more straightforward way. Starting from the first condition, we can scan the rest of the conditions and contrapositives for connections. Adding connections to the front and back, we have:

$(L_S) \longrightarrow N_R \longrightarrow O_R \longrightarrow J_S \longrightarrow K_R \longrightarrow P_S \longrightarrow (L_R)$

Note that L_S leads to L_R, which is not possible. Therefore, we can infer that L must be at Randsborough.

To form the contrapositive chain, we only need to reverse the order of the terms and their respective subscripts. Since we know that L cannot be at Souderton, we can start from P at Randsborough.

$P_R \longrightarrow K_S \longrightarrow J_R \longrightarrow O_S \longrightarrow N_S \longrightarrow L_R$

19. (A) from our first chain, we know that J_S leads to P_S
    (B) Correct
    (C) from our second chain, we know that K_S leads to N_S
    (D) the fifth condition tells us that K or P (or both) must be at Randsborough
    (E) violates the contrapositive of the fourth condition

20. **(A)** This question ties in perfectly with our second chain. As such, we know that J is at Randsborough.

[3] Visit Manhattan LSAT (http://www.manhattanlsat.com) to learn more about using this diagram.

21. **(C)** Since P_R leads to both K_S and O_S, and we're trying to minimize the number of doctors assigned to Souderton, we must assign P to Souderton. The second condition dictates that at least one of J and O must be assigned to Souderton. If it were O, N would also be assigned to Souderton (fourth condition). Thus, by assigning J to Souderton, we achieve the minimum number, which is two. Choice C is therefore correct.

22. **(A)** The fourth condition and its contrapositive tell us that N and O must be together if N is at Randsborough or if O is at Souderton. They could only be at separate clinics if N is at Souderton. From this, we can isolate pieces of our original chains.

    $O_R \longrightarrow J_S \longrightarrow K_R$
    $N_S \longrightarrow L_R$

    Since J is at Souderton, choice A must be true.

23. We can check the choices one at a time by starting with the first doctor in each choice at Randsborough and seeing if that leads to the second doctor at Souderton. To do so, we can use relevant pieces of our original chains.

    (A) $J_R \longrightarrow O_S \longrightarrow N_S \longrightarrow L_R$
    (B) $J_R \longrightarrow O_S \longrightarrow N_S \longrightarrow L_R$
    (C) $K_R \longrightarrow P_S \longrightarrow L_R$
    (D) the fourth condition confirms this as a possibility
    (E) Correct – $\mathbf{N_R \longrightarrow O_R \longrightarrow J_S \longrightarrow K_R \longrightarrow P_S}$

24. **(B)** This condition triggers our second chain, and we know that N must be at Souderton. Therefore, choice B is correct.

Questions 1-5

Setup:

- o four of eight candidates will be selected
- o experienced astronauts (E): F J K L
- o inexperienced astronauts (I): M N P T
- o geologists (G): F M P T
- o radiobiologists (R): J K L N

Conditions:

#1: exactly two Es and two Is will be selected
#2: exactly two Gs and two Rs will be selected
#3: P or L or both are selected

Overview:

Since each person has two characteristics, it makes sense to group them accordingly.

EG	ER	IG	IR
F	J	M	N
	K	P	
	L	T	

Combining the first and the second conditions, we know that at least one of J, K, and L must be selected, and that at least one of M, P, and T must be selected. Therefore, any acceptable scenario will have both an experienced radiobiologist and an inexperienced geologist. We can set up two molds based on the profession of the second experienced astronaut.

#1

____	F	N	____
ER	EG	IR	IG
J			M
K			P
L			T

#2 ____ ____

____	____
ER	IG
J	M
K	P
L	T

Mold #1: If the second experienced astronaut is a geologist, to satisfy the first and second conditions, we must have an inexperienced radiobiologist. Since F and N are the only members of their respective categories, they must be selected under this scenario.

Mold #2: If the second experienced astronaut is also a radiobiologist, to satisfy the first and second conditions, we must have another inexperienced radiobiologist.

1. (A) violates the third condition
   (B) violates the second condition (3 Gs are selected: F, M, and P)
   (C) violates the first condition (only 1 E is selected: F)
   (D) Correct
   (E) violates the second condition (only 1 G is selected: T)

2. **(A)** Since an EG and an IG are selected, we must use mold #1, and choice A is therefore correct.

3. **(D)** This triggers mold #1. To satisfy the third condition, we must select P. We already inferred that N is selected under this scenario, and choice D is therefore correct.

J	F	N	P
ER	EG	IR	IG

4. **(B)** This triggers mold #2. Due to the third condition, L must be selected. Therefore, either J or K could fill the second ER slot, and choice B is correct.

J|K	M
L	T
ER	IG

5. **(A)** We must use mold #1 for this question. As we already inferred, F must be selected under this scenario, and choice A is therefore correct.

Questions 6-12

Setup:
- six new cars: T V W X Y Z
- each is equipped with at least one of the three options: P L S
- no car has any other options

Conditions:
#1: V ⟶ P and S
#2: W ⟶ P and L
#3: W and Y do not share any options
#4: $X_{\#options} > W_{\#options}$
#5: V and Z have exactly one option in common
#6: $T_{\#options} < Z_{\#options}$

Overview:
Since many of the conditions are based on the number of options for the various cars, it makes sense to use the cars as the base of our diagram. Combining the second and fourth conditions, we know that X has all three options. Combining the second and third conditions, we know that Y must have a sunroof and no other options. We also know that W has exactly two options (a leather interior and power windows). Combining the fifth and sixth conditions, we know that Z has two options and T has one. If Z had all three options, the fifth condition would be broken. Since Z has exactly one of P and S, it must also have L. T could have any of the three options.

T	V	W	X	Y	Z
			S		
	S	L	L		L
	P	P	P	S	P|S

6. **(C)** The options for V, W, X, and Y are determined. Therefore, choice C is correct.

7. **(A) Correct – since V and Y don't have leather interiors, this must be false**
   (B) could be all but W
   (C) could be T, W, X, and Z
   (D) could be V, W, X, and one of T and Z
   (E) could be V, X, Y, and one of T and Z

8. **(E)** Combining this with our diagram, we know that Z has power windows. Since T only has one option, it cannot have a leather interior. Therefore, choice E must be false.

T	V	W	X	Y	Z
			S		
	S	L	L		L
P|S	P	P	P	S	P

9. **(D)** Combining this with our diagram, we know that T doesn't have a leather interior. If Z had power windows, it wouldn't have any options in common with Y. Therefore, Z must have a sunroof, and T must have power windows. Since only three of the cars have leather interiors, choice D must be false.

T	V	W	X	Y	Z
			S		
	S	L	L		L
P	P	P	P	S	S

10. Combining this with our diagram, we know that Z must have a sunroof (due to W), and T must have either a leather interior or power windows (due to Y).

<table>
<tr><td></td><td></td><td></td><td>S</td><td></td><td></td></tr>
<tr><td></td><td>S</td><td>L</td><td>L</td><td></td><td>L</td></tr>
<tr><td>L|P</td><td>P</td><td>P</td><td>P</td><td>S</td><td>S</td></tr>
<tr><td>T</td><td>V</td><td>W</td><td>X</td><td>Y</td><td>Z</td></tr>
</table>

(A) could be V, W, and X
(B) could be T, V, W, and X
(C) Correct – V, X, Y, and Z all have sunroofs
(D) could be V, X, Y, and Z
(E) could be T, W, X, and Z

11. **(D)** Combining this with our diagram, we know that T has a leather interior. Choice D doesn't have to be true, since Z could have a leather interior and power windows.

<table>
<tr><td></td><td></td><td></td><td>S</td><td></td><td></td></tr>
<tr><td></td><td>S</td><td>L</td><td>L</td><td></td><td>L</td></tr>
<tr><td>L</td><td>P</td><td>P</td><td>P</td><td>S</td><td>P|S</td></tr>
<tr><td>T</td><td>V</td><td>W</td><td>X</td><td>Y</td><td>Z</td></tr>
</table>

12. **(D)** Since the condition being replaced is the only one regarding X, this change only affects X's options. It must still have a leather interior and power windows, but it is uncertain whether or not it has a sunroof. As X and Z both have leather interiors, choice D must be false.

<table>
<tr><td></td><td></td><td></td><td>-------</td><td></td><td></td></tr>
<tr><td></td><td>S</td><td>L</td><td>L</td><td></td><td>L</td></tr>
<tr><td></td><td>P</td><td>P</td><td>P</td><td>S</td><td>P|S</td></tr>
<tr><td>T</td><td>V</td><td>W</td><td>X</td><td>Y</td><td>Z</td></tr>
</table>

<u>Questions 13-17</u>

Setup:
- Kim family members: Q R S T U
- each sits in a separate seat
- two rows: G H
- each row has three seats: 1 2 3

Conditions:
#1: each family member sits next to at least one other family member
#2: T_H and U_H

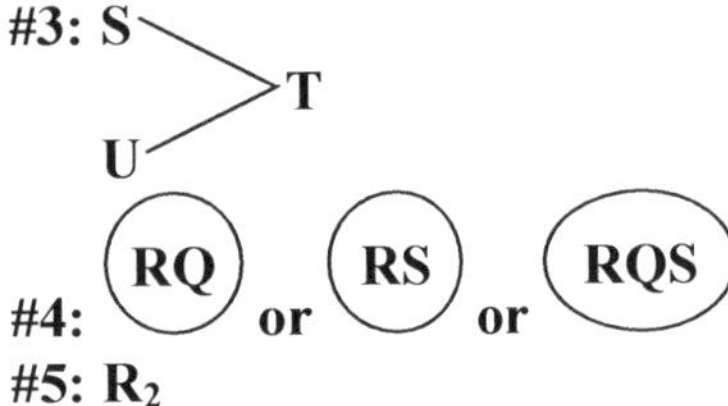

#5: R_2

Overview:
As we have five variables and six slots, we can use an X to represent the unfilled seat. Due to the first condition, X must be placed on the end of either row G or row H. Since R is next to either Q or S, and the second condition places both T and U in row H, we can definitively place R in row G. T can only be in H2 or H3, due to the third condition. We can create molds which represent these possibilities.

#1

G	S	R	Q|X
H	U	T	X|Q
	1	2	3

#2

G	S|	R	
H	U	|S	T
	1	2	3

#3

G	S|	R	
H	|S	U	T
	1	2	3

Mold #1: With T in H2, U must be in H1 (second and third conditions) and S must be in G1 (third condition).

Mold #2: With T in H3 and U in H1, S could occupy either G1 or H2 (third condition).

Mold #3: With T in H3 and U in H2, S could occupy either G1 or H1 (third condition).

13. **(A) Correct – this could be true under any of the molds**
    (B) R is in H2
    (C) S can only be in seat 1 or seat 2
    (D) T can only be in seat 2 or seat 3
    (E) U can only be in seat 1 or seat 2

14. (A) R must occupy G2
    (B) Correct – this could be true under either the second or the third molds
    (C) Q and S could only occupy the same row under the first or the third molds; in either case, they would be separated by R
    (D) R must occupy G2, and T is in row H (second condition)
    (E) R must occupy G2, and U is in row H (second condition)

15. **(C)** This triggers mold #1. Since we have Q|X dual options for G3 and H3, R could be flanked by X. Therefore, choice C doesn't have to be true, and it is correct.

16. **(E)** X could fill either G3 or H3 in mold #1. It could fill either G1 or H1 in mold #3. Therefore, choice E is correct.

17. **(E)** Scanning our molds, we know that S, T, and U could all occupy H2. Since choices A, B, and C do not contain T, we can eliminate them. The only difference between choices D and E is the exclusion/inclusion of Q, so we must check to see if Q could occupy that slot. Under the second mold, we could place Q in H2. This forces S into G1, and X into H3. Therefore, Q could occupy H2, and choice E is therefore correct.

	1	2	3
G	S	R	X
H	U	Q	T

Questions 18-23

Setup:

- seven professors: M N O P R S T
- hired during seven years: 9 0 1 2 3 4 5
- each professor has one or more specialty
- professors hired in adjacent years or in the same year do not share any specialties

Conditions:

#1: M_3 and R_1
#2: M, O, and T share at least one specialty
#3: N and R share a specialty
#4: N – P – M and N – S – M
#5: O and S share a specialty; O_0

Overview:
The first and fifth conditions allow us to place M, R, and O directly into the diagram. Since we aren't given any specific information about the specialties, we need not represent them in the diagram. We will use the conditions in combination with the setup condition about the specialties to place the other variables. Due to the second condition and the placements of O and M, T cannot be placed in any year other than 1995. We know that N precedes M (fourth condition); since N and R share a specialty (third condition) N must have been hired in 1989. Combining the fourth and the fifth conditions, we know that S must have been hired in 1992. Although we don't know with which (if any) variables P shares a specialty, the fourth condition allows us to infer that P was hired after 1989 and before 1993. Since none of the professors were hired in 1994, we can fill that slot with an X.

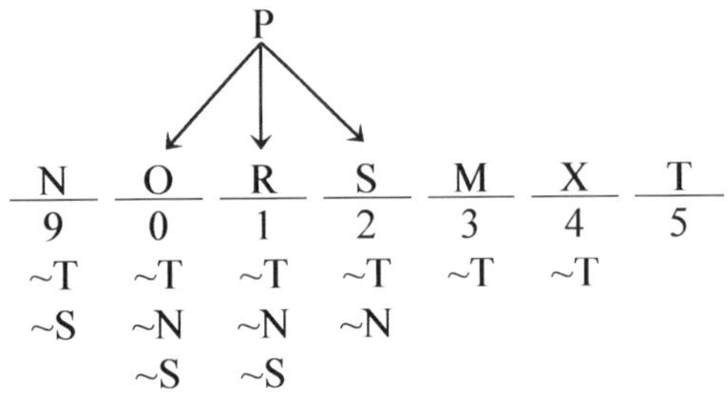

18. **(C)** We have already inferred that N, O, and R were hired during these years. Since P could have been hired in either 1990 or 1991, P must also be included in the list. Therefore, choice C is correct.

19. This question limits P's potential years to 1990 and 1992.
   (A) Correct – P would have been hired in 1992
   (B) R and S are next to each other
   (C) this violates the condition given in the question
   (D) we have already inferred that none of the professors were hired during 1994
   (E) as our diagram shows, this is not possible

20. (A) this must be true
   (B) could be true
   (C) could be true
   (D) this must be true
   (E) Correct – T must have been hired in 1995

21. (A) P could also have been hired in 1990
   (B) P has three possible hiring years
   (C) this must be false
   (D) Correct
   (E) this must be false

22. Since P is the only floating variable, it must be placed along with S in 1992.

			P			
N	O	R	S	M	X	T
9	0	1	2	3	4	5

(A) Correct – O, P, and T have at least one year between each other
(B) since P and M are in adjacent years, this couldn't happen
(C) only R was hired in 1991
(D) only M was hired in 1993
(E) P was hired in 1992

23. This question restricts P's year to either 1990 or 1991.

(A) P could have been hired in 1991
(B) P could have been hired in 1990
(C) P could have been hired in 1991
(D) this cannot be true
(E) Correct – since S was hired in 1992, P must precede S

Questions 1-6

Setup:

- o stand carries at least on kind of fruit
- o fruit: F K O P T W

Conditions:

#1: K ⟶ ~P; P ⟶ ~K (contrapositive)
#2: ~T ⟶ K; ~K ⟶ T (contrapositive)
#3: O ⟶ P; ~P ⟶ ~O (contrapositive)
O ⟶ W; ~W ⟶ ~O (contrapositive)
#4: W ⟶ F or T; ~F and ~T ⟶ ~W (contrapositive)

Overview:
Since at least one kind of fruit must be selected (setup condition), and one of K and T must be selected (second condition), K alone and T alone are both acceptable solutions. We also know that at least one of K and P must not be selected.

In	Out
K|T	K|P

We can use the following diagram to make any necessary inferences.

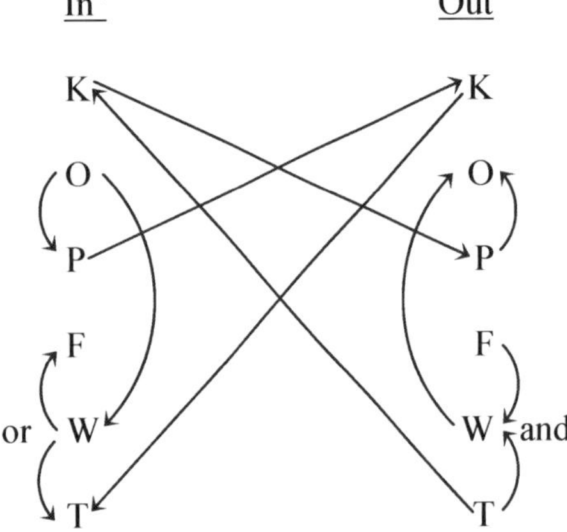

1. (A) violates the second condition
   (B) Correct
   (C) violates the second condition
   (D) violates the third condition
   (E) violates the first condition

[4] Visit Manhattan LSAT (http://www.manhattanlsat.com) to learn more about using this diagram.

2. **(D)** This question directly tests our interpretation of the second condition. Taking its contrapositive, we have ~K ⟶ T. Thus, one of K and T must be selected. Choice D is the only choice with one of the two, and it is therefore correct.

3. For this question, we must make sure that the second condition is satisfied, and that none of the other conditions is broken. To verify choices A and B against the conditions, we only need to make sure that selecting the first kind listed doesn't preclude the second kind from being selected.
   (A) K ⟶ ~P ⟶ ~O; no inferences from T in
   (B) T in doesn't allow us to make any inferences regarding W
   (C) no inferences from F in; K ⟶ ~P ⟶ ~O; W ⟶ F or T
   (D) O ⟶ P and W; no inferences from T
   (E) Correct – this violates the first condition; K and P cannot both be selected.

4. **(C)** Combining this with the contrapositive of the third condition, we know that O is not selected. Due to the first condition, only one of K and P can be selected. Therefore, with O, W, and one of K and P not selected, a maximum of three variables can be selected, and choice C is therefore correct.

In	Out
K|P	K|P
F	O
T	W

5. The only thing we can infer from this information is that either F or T is selected (fourth condition). Therefore, we have to check the choices against the conditions to invalidate them.
   (A) T would be selected (fourth condition)
   (B) K would be selected (second condition)
   (C) P doesn't have to be selected
   (D) this could be true – see the following scenario

In	Out
W	O
P	K
T	|F
F|	

   (E) Correct – if P is selected, K must not be selected (first condition); if K is not selected, T must be selected (second condition).

6. **(C)** The only thing this condition suspension does is lift the requirement that we must have K or T. Therefore, we need to check the choices against the remaining three conditions for violations. Choice C violates the fourth condition. With W selected, F or T must also be selected.

Questions 7-13

Setup:

- five telephone calls: F G H I M
- each call: L T
- cities: V V S S K

Conditions:

#1: I_1M_2 or M_1I_2

#2:

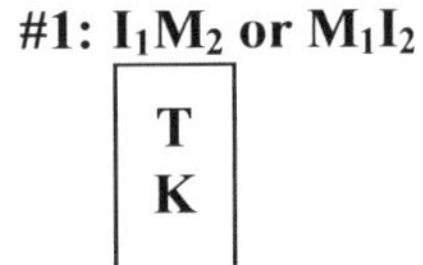

#3:

#4:

#5:

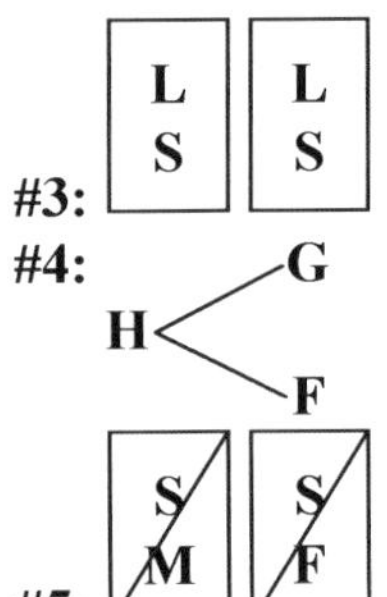

Overview:

Combining the first and the fourth conditions, we must place H third, which creates dual F|G options for the fourth and fifth slots. We can build the second condition directly into the diagram. Since neither M nor F can be paired with an S, we know that I and G must both be paired with Ss. Combining this with the third condition creates the following:

L	L
S	S
I	G

___	___	T	___	___	L T
___	___	K	___	___	K S S V V
I|M	M|I	H	F|G	G|F	F G H I M
1	2	3	4	5	

7. **(E)** Since this question asks solely about the ordering of the calls, we can check them against our main diagram. Only choice E is possible.

8. **(A)** This question is essentially a repeat of the previous question. The only difference is that it references individual variables and positions. Checking the choices against our diagram reveals that only choice A could be true.

9. **(C)** Combining this information with the fifth condition and our diagram, we know that the first call has to be I. Therefore, choice C not only could be true, but must be true.

L		T		
S		K		
I	M	H	F|G	G|F
1	2	3	4	5

10. **(C)** Since we inferred that I is paired with an L, M's call must be first. Therefore, the second call (I), must be live, and choice C must be false.

T	L	T		
	S	K		
M	I	H	F|G	G|F
1	2	3	4	5

11. **(A)** This question directly tests our inference that G must be paired with an L.

12. **(A)** To meet this condition, we must flank the T (in third position) with an L on each side. Since we cannot have two consecutive Ls, we must place Ts in the first and fifth slots. Combining this with our previous inferences, we must place I second and G fourth. As such, there is only one possible ordering of calls in this scenario.

T	L	T	L	T
K|V	S	K	S	V|K
M	I	H	G	F
1	2	3	4	5

13. **(B)** From our initial diagram and inferences, we know that I must be first, and M must be second. Consequently, the first city slot must be occupied by an S, and choice B cannot be true.

L	T	T		
S	V	K	S|V	V|S
I	M	H	G|F	F|G
1	2	3	4	5

Questions 14-18

Setup:

- passengers: G H I K L M
- seats are in consecutive rows numbered: 1 2 3
- each row: W A

Conditions:

#1: [H / G] boxed vertically, in aisle (A)

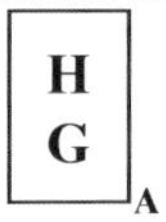

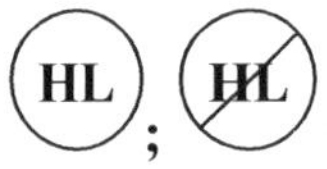

#2: M_A ⟶ (HL); (~~HL~~) ⟶ M_W (contrapositive)

#3: (GK) ⟶ [M / I]; [~~M / I~~] ⟶ (~~GK~~) (contrapositive)

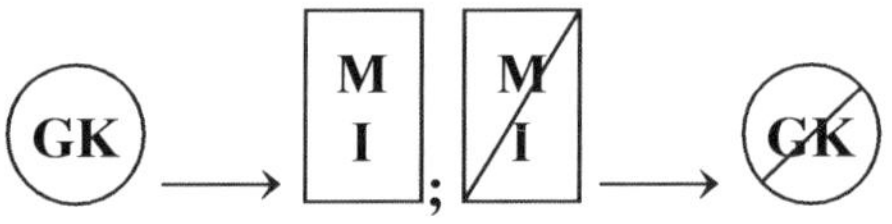

#4: K_W ⟶ M_3; $\sim M_3$ ⟶ K_A (contrapositive)

#5: K_3 ⟶ I_1; $\sim I_1$ ⟶ $\sim K_3$ (contrapositive)

Overview:

We can infer two placement options for the GH piece: A1 and A2 or A2 and A3.

	W	A	
3	___	___	K ↓
2	___	H	
1	___	G	I

or

	W	A	
3	___	H	~K
2	___	G	
1	___	___	

If the GH piece occupies the second and third aisle seats, K cannot occupy the third window seat, due to the fourth condition. Although four of the five conditions are phrased as conditional statements, they are still very restrictive. Each of the second and third conditions, if triggered, yields exactly one acceptable solution.

M_A ⟶

	W	A
3	K	M
2	L	H
1	I	G

KG ⟶

	W	A
3	M	L
2	I	H
1	K	G

When the second condition is triggered, K must occupy a window seat. This triggers the fourth condition, and M must occupy the third aisle seat. Since L and H occupy the same row, L must be in the second row. With only the first and third window seats remaining, we must place K in the third one, since doing otherwise would trigger and violate the third condition.

When the third condition is triggered, we know that K occupies a window seat. The KG piece cannot be placed in the second row, since we also need to accommodate the MI piece. Therefore, the KG piece must occupy the first row, and the MI piece must occupy the second and third window seats, leaving L to occupy the third aisle seat.

14. (A) violates the contrapositive of the fifth condition
    (B) combining this with the first condition, there would be four passengers in aisle seats
    (C) G cannot occupy a window seat (first condition)
    (D) this triggers and violates the second condition
    (E) Correct – see the M_A diagram above

15. **(A)** Applying the fourth condition, we know that M occupies a seat in the third row. If M occupies the third window seat, I must occupy either the third or the first aisle seat. In either case, to avoid violating the third condition, we cannot place K in the same row as G. If M occupies the third aisle seat, the M_A solution above is triggered. Only choice A could be true (see the M_A solution above), and it is therefore correct.

3	M	I
2	K	H
1	L	G
	W	A

3	M	H
2	L	G
1	K	I
	W	A

16. **(D)** Applying the contrapositives of the third and fourth conditions, we know that G and K are not in the same row, and that K occupies an aisle seat. K cannot occupy the third aisle seat, since the fifth condition would be triggered, and I would have to occupy the window seat in row 1. Therefore, K must occupy the aisle seat in row 1. Hence, choice D is correct.

3	L|I	H
2	I|L	G
1	M	K
	W	A

17. **(B)** This triggers the fifth condition, and I must occupy the window seat in row 1. This creates dual L|M options for the second and third window seats. Comparing the choices to our diagram reveals that only choice B could be true.

3	M|L	K
2	L|M	H
1	I	G
	W	A

18. **(C)** From this, we can infer that the GH piece occupies the second and third aisle slots. The contrapositive of the fifth condition is triggered, and K cannot be in the third row. K cannot occupy the second window seat, since this would trigger and violate the third condition. If K is in the first window seat, M must occupy the third window seat (fourth condition). Since we're given that I doesn't occupy a seat in the first row, I must occupy the second window seat, and L must occupy the first aisle seat. If K occupies the first aisle seat, we know that I, L, and M occupy window seats. Thus, only choice C could be true (under the second scenario).

	W	A			W	A
3	M	H		3	___	H
2	I	G		2	___	G
1	K	L	or	1	___	K

Questions 19-23

Setup:
- o four flights: 1 2 3 4
- o each flight has exactly one pilot and exactly one co-pilot
- o pilots: F G K L
- o co-pilots: R S T U

Conditions:
#1: flights are in numerical order

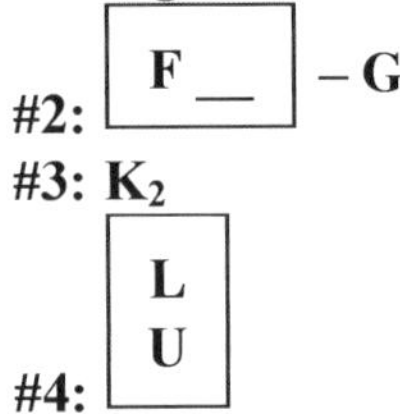

Overview:
Combining the second and third conditions allows us to definitively place F on the first flight. This, in turn, creates G|L dual options for the third and fourth flights. Applying the fourth condition, we also know that U is on either the third or the fourth flight.

	1	2	3	4	
P	F	K	L|G	G|L	F G K L
C	___	___	U|	|U	R S T U

19. **(A)** We know that F is assigned to the first flight, so we can eliminate choices C, D, and E. Since U must be assigned to either the third or the fourth flight, we can eliminate choice B, and A is correct.

20. **(C)** Combining this with our initial diagram, we must assign U to the third flight and R to the fourth flight. This allows us to definitively place L and G third and fourth, respectively. With dual S|T options for the first two flights, K's flight cannot be earlier than T's, and choice C is therefore correct.

	1	2	3	4
P	F	K	L	G
C	S|T	T|S	U	R

21. **(D)** From this condition, we can place L and G on the third and fourth flights respectively. Only choice D could be false; S could be assigned to the fourth flight.

	1	2	3	4
P	F	K	L	G
C			U	

22. **(C)** Due to the fourth condition, if L is assigned to the fourth flight, U is also assigned to that flight. If G is assigned to the fourth flight, R, S, and T could all co-pilot that flight. Thus, there are four possible pairings for the fourth flight, and choice C is correct.

L	G	G	G
U	R	S	T

23. **(D)** Combining this condition with our initial diagram, we must assign L and S to the third and fourth flights, respectively. We're left with dual R|T options for the first and second slots, and it could, therefore, be false that R's flight precedes T's.

	1	2	3	4
P	F	K	L	G
C	R|T	T|R	U	S

Questions 1-5

Setup:
- four dormitories: R T V W
- each has a North wing and a South wing

Conditions:
#1: each wing is assigned either M or F
#2: M M M
#3: F_{RN} and F_{TN}
#4: M ⟶ (M / F)
#5: M_{VS} ⟶ M_{WN}; F_{WN} ⟶ F_{VS} (contrapositive)

Overview:
Since there are exactly three Ms, and there are eight slots, there must be five Fs. As a consequence of the second and fourth conditions, we know that at least one of Richards South and Tuscarora South must have an M. We can also infer that if both wings of any one dormitory have Fs, each of the other dormitories must have exactly one M. Although it appears from the fifth condition that Veblen South and Wisteria North must be the same, if we're given that Veblen South has an F, we can't infer anything about Wisteria North.

N	F	F		
S				
	R	T	V	W

1. **(D)** Since we must place three Ms (second condition), and each M must be paired with an F (fourth condition), we must distribute Ms evenly across R, T, and W. Since neither the fifth condition nor its contrapositive is triggered, dual F|M options are created for Wisteria North and Wisteria South. Only choice D contains two wings that could house females.

N	F	F	F	F|M
S	M	M	F	M|F
	R	T	V	W

2. (A) we could have M_{TS}, M_{VS}, and M_{WN}
   (B) Correct – the fourth condition would preclude us from distributing all three Ms
   (C) we could have M_{TS}, M_{VS}, and M_{WN}
   (D) we could have M_{RS}, M_{VS}, and M_{WN}
   (E) we could have M_{RS}, M_{VS}, and M_{WN}

3. **(D)** This triggers the contrapositive of the fifth condition, and we know that Veblen South must also have an F.

N	F	F		F
S			F	
	R	T	V	W

4. **(D)** This triggers the fifth condition. Richards South and Tuscarora South are still uncertain, so we can place F|M dual options in those slots. Therefore, the complete and accurate list must include all the slots into which we have definitively placed Fs, and choice D is correct.

N	F	F	F	M
S	M|F	F|M	M	F
	R	T	V	W

5. **(D)** With females in both wings of Tuscarora, we must distribute one M to each of R, V, and W. Depending on whether Veblen South houses males or females, we can set up two solutions. If Veblen South houses males, the fifth condition is triggered, and Wisteria North must also house males. If not, either wing of Wisteria could house males. Thus, only choice D could be true.

N	F	F	F	M
S	M	F	M	F
	R	T	V	W

N	F	F	M	M|F
S	M	F	F	F|M
	R	T	V	W

Questions 6-11

Setup:
- seven trucks: S T U W X Y Z
- arrive one at a time
- each truck is either green or red: G R

Conditions:

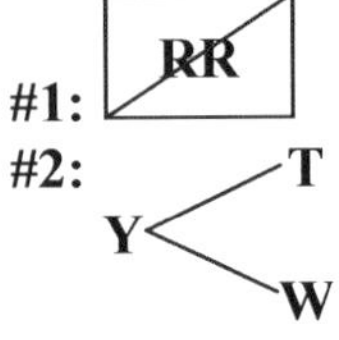

#3: $R_1 - R_2 - Y$
#4: S_6
#5: Z – U

Overview:
The fourth condition allows us to place S directly into the diagram. Combining the first and third conditions, we know that there must be at least three trucks in front of Y. Since Y is followed by T and W (second condition), and S is sixth (fourth condition), we can place Y fourth. This creates T|W dual options for the fifth and seventh slots. Because two of the first three trucks are red, the first condition dictates that the second truck must be green, and the first and third trucks must be red. Since the third truck is red, we know that the fourth truck must be green, due to the first condition.

R	G	R	G				R G
			Y	T|W	S	W|T	S T U W X Y Z
1	2	3	4	5	6	7	

Z – U, X

6. **(A) Correct**
   (B) Y must be fourth
   (C) Y must be fourth
   (D) X cannot be sixth
   (E) violates the fourth condition

7. **(B)** Since S and T are next to each other, they cannot both be red, due to the first condition.

8. **(C)** Combining this information with the fifth condition allows us to place Z and U in the first and second slots respectively. Therefore, we know that U must be green, and choice C is correct.

R	G	R	G			
Z	U	X	Y	T|W	S	W|T
1	2	3	4	5	6	7

9. **(A)** Combining this with our initial diagram, we know that one of the last three trucks is green. Since two of the last three trucks are red, they must be the fifth and the seventh, due to the first condition. Therefore, S must be green, and choice A is correct.

R	G	R	G	R	G	R
			Y	T|W	S	W|T
1	2	3	4	5	6	7

Z – U, X

10. **(B)** The only variables that meet this criteria are those which we have definitively placed in particular slots. As S and Y must occupy the sixth and fourth slots respectively, the correct answer is two.

11. To tackle this question, we can check the answer choices against our diagram.
    (A) U could be third
    (B) X could be third
    (C) T could be fifth
    (D) W could be fifth
    (E) Correct – Z cannot be third, due to the fifth condition

<u>Questions 12-18</u>

Setup:
- six books occupy three shelves
- shelf 1: 1 book; shelf 2: 2 books; shelf 3: 3 books
- two grammar books (G): F H
- two linguistic monographs (M): P S
- two novels (N): V W

Conditions:

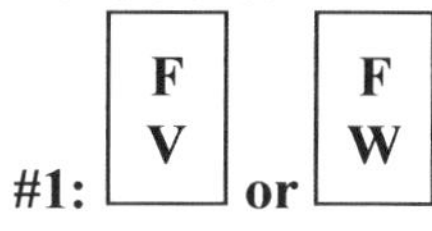

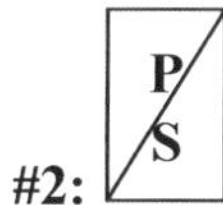

Overview:
Since the piece created by the second condition can only be on the second or third shelves, we can set up molds for each situation. Placing it on the second shelf, we must split the two monographs between the first and third shelves. Placing it on the third shelf, we have three options for the two monographs: first and third, first and second (molds #3 and #4), or second and third. The only condition regarding the monographs is that they cannot be on the same shelf, so they are interchangeable in all scenarios. Thus, there are a total of ten acceptable solutions.

#1

		WN
	FG	HG
M	VN	M
1	2	3

#2

		M
	HG	FG
M	VN	WN
1	2	3

#3

		WN
	HG	FG
M	M	VN
1	2	3

#4

		HG
	WN	FG
M	M	VN
1	2	3

#5

		M
	HG	FG
VN	M	WN
1	2	3

Mold #1: Due to the third condition, we have to place V on the second shelf. We can place W and H into the remaining two slots on the third shelf.

Mold #2: Due to the third condition, we have to place V on the second shelf. We must place W on the third shelf, and H on the second shelf.

Mold #3: The placement of the monographs, combined with the third condition dictate that we place V on the third shelf. When H is on the second shelf, W fills the remaining slot on the third shelf.

Mold #4: The placement of the monographs, combined with the third condition dictate that we place V on the third shelf. When W is on the second shelf, H fills the remaining slot on the third shelf.

Mold #5: Because the monographs occupy slots on the second and third shelves, we must place V on the first shelf (third condition). W must occupy the novel slot on the third shelf, and we can place H into the remaining slot on the second shelf.

12. (A) violates the third condition
    (B) Correct
    (C) violates the first condition
    (D) violates the second condition
    (E) violates the second condition

13. **(A)** We can check the choices against our molds. Choice A cannot be true, since the first shelf book must be either a novel or a monograph.

14. We can eliminate the answer choices that could be false by checking them against the molds.

    (A) see molds #3 and #5
    (B) see molds #1 and #2
    (C) see molds #3 and #4
    (D) Correct – this is true of all five molds
    (E) see molds #3 and #4

15. **(E)** We can narrow our focus to the fourth mold for this question. Since the monographs are split between the first and second shelves, either one could be on the first shelf, and choice E is therefore correct.

16. (A) see mold #5
    (B) see mold #3
    (C) see mold #4
    (D) see molds #1, #2, and #5
    (E) Correct – the only novel that could be on the first shelf is V (mold #5)

17. **(C)** This could only be true under the first mold. Checking the answer choices against this mold reveals that only choice C could be true.

18. This could be true under the first, third, and fifth molds. We can eliminate choices that aren't true for all three molds.

    (A) this doesn't have to be true under any of the three molds
    (B) see molds #3 and #5
    (C) this doesn't have to be true under any of the three molds
    (D) this doesn't have to be true under any of the three molds
    (E) Correct – this is true of all three molds in question

<u>Questions 19-24</u>

Setup:

- five swim team members: J K L M O
- one swims laps 1 and 6
- one swims laps 2 and 7
- one swims laps 3 and 8
- one swims laps 4 and 9
- one swims laps 5 and 10

Conditions:

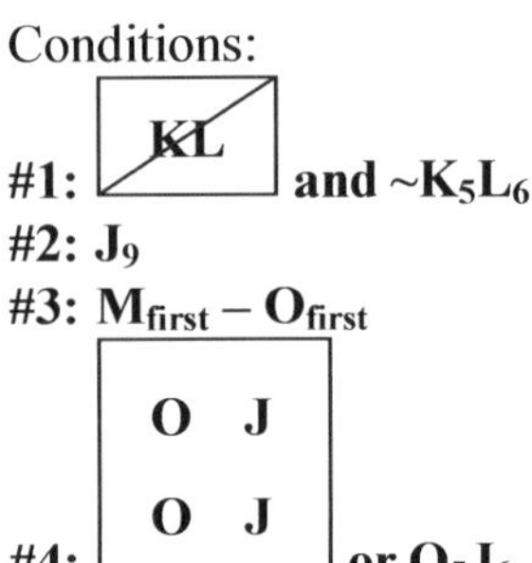

Overview:
Combining the setup conditions with the second condition, we know that J cannot swim the fourt lap. As a consequence of the third condition, M cannot swim the fifth lap, and O cannot swim the first lap. Combining this with the setup conditions, we also know that M cannot swim the tenth lap, and O cannot swim the sixth lap. To efficiently represent the setup condition that one person swims each of the two-lap pairs, we can set up two rows of slots.

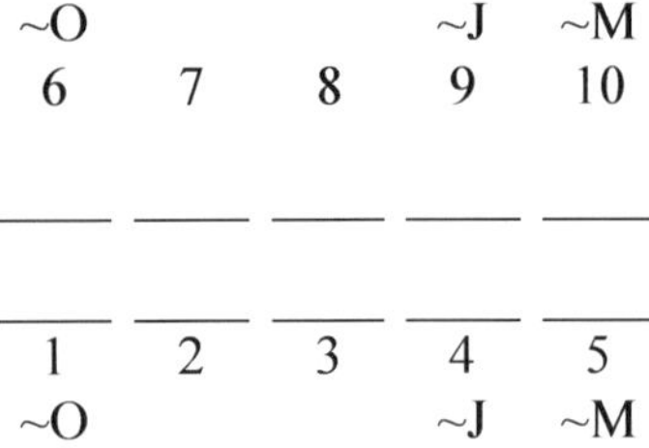

19. **(A) Correct**
    (B) violates the second condition
    (C) violates the fourth condition
    (D) violates the third condition
    (E) violates the first condition

20. **(A)** Combining this with the fourth condition, we know that O must swim the second and seventh laps. The third condition dictates that M must swim the first and sixth laps. Applying the first condition, we know that L swims the fourth and ninth laps and K swims the fifth and tenth laps. Thus, we know who swims every lap, and choice A is correct.

6	7	8	9	10
M	O	J	L	K
M	O	J	L	K
1	2	3	4	5

21. Combining this with the fourth condition, we can definitively place J in the fifth and tenth slots. We can either place M between L and K, or place L and K next to each other. If L and K are next to each other, the first condition dictates that L must precede K. Before mapping out the possible scenarios, it proves useful in this case to eliminate the incorrect choices.

6 7 8 9 10

___ ___ ___ O J

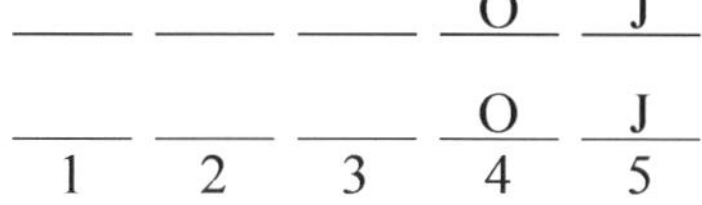

___ ___ ___ O J

1 2 3 4 5

(A) J swims the fifth lap
(B) J swims the fifth lap
(C) J swims the fifth lap
(D) Correct – this would create K|M dual options for laps 1 and 2 and 6 and 7
(E) J swims the fifth lap

22. (A) we already inferred that this cannot happen
(B) Correct – see the following diagram

6 7 8 9 10

M O J L K

M O J L K

1 2 3 4 5

(C) since J can't swim the fourth lap (second condition), and M's first lap must precede O's first lap, the first three slots would have to be M, O, and J respectively, leaving K to fill the fourth slot, which violates the first condition
(D) violates the third condition
(E) violates the third condition

23. **(B)** Due to the setup conditions, if two of the answer choices represent both laps in one of the pairs, both choices are incorrect. Since 1 and 6 will be occupied by the same swimmer, we can eliminate choices A and D. Questions 19, 20, and 21 allow us to eliminate choice C. Finally, question 21 allows us to eliminate choice E. Why can't J swim the second lap (choice B)? To satisfy the fourth condition, O would have to swim the first lap. However, that violates the third condition, and choice B is therefore correct.

24. Due to the symmetrical nature of the game, this question is essentially identical to number 19, albeit with different answer choices.

(A) violates the fourth condition
(B) violates the first condition
(C) Correct
(D) violates the second condition
(E) violates the third condition

Questions 1-7

Setup:
- eight clowns: Q R S T V W Y Z
- clowns get out of the car one at a time

Conditions:

#1:

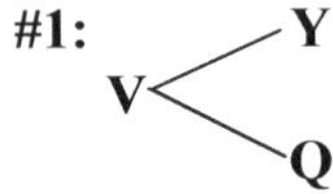

#2: Z – Q
#3: R – T – V
#4: V – S
#5: R – W

Overview:
Combining all the conditions yields the following sketch:

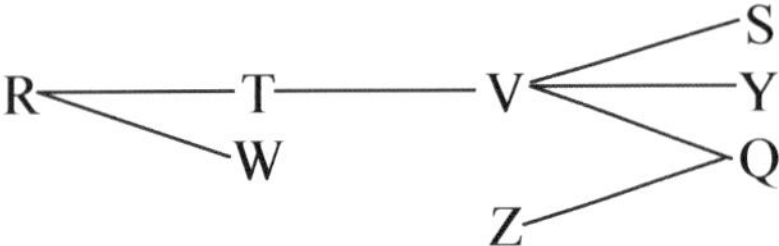

1. (A) violates the third condition
   (B) violates the first condition
   (C) violates the second condition
   (D) violates the fifth condition
   (E) Correct

2. (A) Y is preceded by at least three others
   (B) R can only be preceded by Z
   (C) Q is preceded by at least four others
   (D) Correct
   (E) V can be preceded by a maximum of four others

3. We know that Z must be followed by Q due to the second condition. Therefore, Q must be last. Since none of the others can precede R, R must be first.

R						Z	Q
1	2	3	4	5	6	7	8

(A) R must be first
(B) since T must be followed by S, V, and Y, this cannot be true
(C) Correct – see the following diagram

R	T	V	S|Y	W	Y|S	Z	Q
1	2	3	4	5	6	7	8

(D) V must be followed by S and Y
(E) as noted above, Q must be eighth

4. With T fourth, V, S, Y, and Q must occupy the fifth, sixth, seventh, and eighth slots, not necessarily in that order. Referring back to our original sketch, we know that V must precede S, Y, and Q, and we can definitively place it fifth. Since Z could still be first, we have a dual R|Z option for the first slot.

R|Z			T	V			
1	2	3	4	5	6	7	8

S, Y, Q

(A) Z could be first
(B) Z could be first
(C) V could be second
(D) Correct
(E) Y could be sixth, seventh, or eighth

5. **(D)** With Q fifth, we know that it is followed by three variables. The only ones that can follow Q are S, Y, and W. Therefore, W cannot precede Q, and choice D must be false.

R|Z				Q			
1	2	3	4	5	6	7	8

S, W, Y

6. **(E)** Since R and Z are the only ones that can be first, placing R second means that Z must be first. As a result, we know that Z precedes all of the remaining variables, and choice E must be true.

Z	R						
1	2	3	4	5	6	7	8

7. From this condition, we can deduce that R must be first. We can also redraw our sketch to reflect the relationship between V and Z.

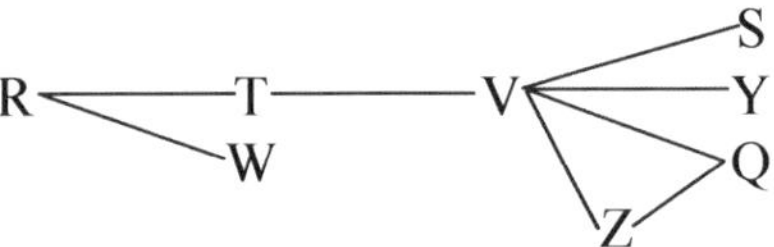

(A) R must be first
(B) T must be followed by at least five variables
(C) Q must be preceded be at least four variables
(D) V must be followed by at least four variables
(E) Correct – see the following diagram

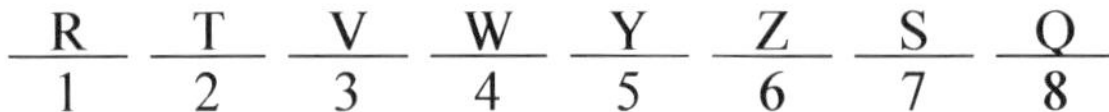

Questions 8-13

Setup:
- six tasks: H M P S T W
- each exhibited one at a time
- three volunteers: F G L
- each volunteer will demonstrate exactly two tasks

Conditions:

#1:

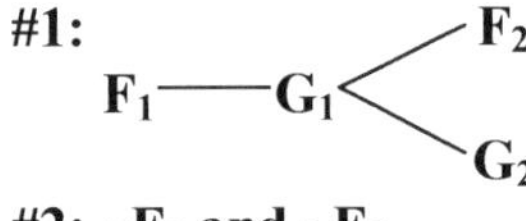

#2: $\sim F_1$ and $\sim F_6$

#3:

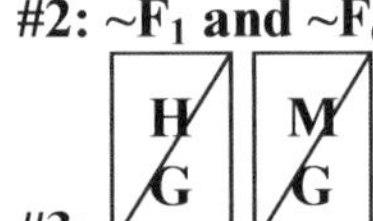

#4:

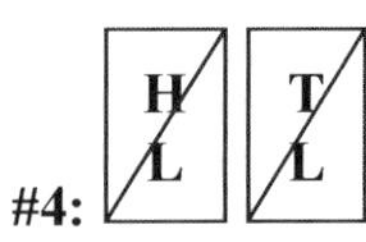

#5: **TM**

Overview:
Since F is neither first nor last, and F_1 precedes G_1, we know that only L can be first. Also, since neither G nor L can demonstrate harvesting, F must demonstrate it.

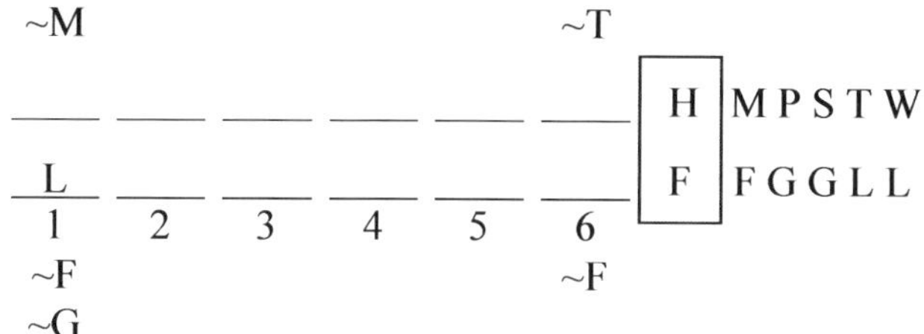

8. (A) violates the second condition
   (B) violates the first condition
   (C) Correct
   (D) violates the third condition
   (E) violates the fifth condition

9. **(A)** This question directly tests the inference that F must demonstrate harvesting.

10. **(B)** With the second L placed fourth, we can definitively place F and G second and third, respectively. Since F cannot be sixth (second condition), F must be fifth, and G must be sixth. Harvesting can be placed with either one of F's slots, and since second is the only one listed in the answer choices, choice B is correct.

	H|			|H	
L	F	G	L	F	G
1	2	3	4	5	6

11. **(A)** We're given [PT / GF]. Due to the first condition, we can place an M immediately after the T. Since F must also demonstrate harvesting (initial inference), and the third condition precludes G from demonstrating milling, L must demonstrate milling. Combining this work with the sequencing provided by the first condition, we can fill out our diagram with dual S|W options for the first and sixth slots. Hence, choice A must be true.

S|W	H	P	T	M	W|S
L	F	G	F	L	G
1	2	3	4	5	6

12. **(D)** This question directly tests the deduction that L must be first.

13. Since this question provides no new information, we must check the answer choices against the conditions and our inferences.
    (A) since F demonstrates harvesting and F cannot be first, this isn't possible
    (B) applying the fifth condition, threshing would be first, but L can't demonstrate threshing (fourth condition)
    (C) since L cannot demonstrate threshing, this isn't possible
    (D) violates the fifth condition
    (E) Correct – our diagram for #11 proves the validity of this choice

Questions 14-19

Setup:
- seven job applicants: F G H I W X Y
- seven new positions
- M: 1 position
- P: 3 positions
- S: 3 positions

Conditions:

#1: 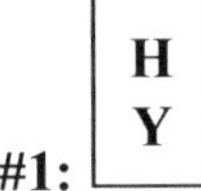

#2: 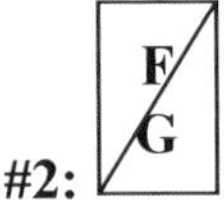

#3: $X_S \longrightarrow W_P$; $\sim W_P \longrightarrow \sim X_S$ **(contrapositive)**
#4: F_P

Overview:
Since H and Y are together, and management only has one position, neither can be hired for that department. Combining the second and fourth conditions, we know that G cannot be hired for a production position.

M	P	S
	____	____
	____	____
____	F	____
~H	W←	—X
~Y	~G	

14. (A) violates the third condition
    (B) violates the fourth condition
    (C) violates the first condition
    (D) violates the first condition
    (E) Correct

15. **(D)** We already inferred that G cannot be hired for a production position. The conditions and opening conditions don't preclude any of the others from being hired for production positions. For further verification, choice E on #14 disproves choices A and E, and the completed diagram for choice C on #16 disproves choices B and C. Choice C is also incorrect because it doesn't include G.

16. (A) this only tells us that H and Y must be hired for sales positions
    (B) any of F, I, W, and X could be hired for the management position
    (C) Correct – H and Y must be hired for production positions. This also triggers the contrapositive of the third condition, and X must be hired for the management position. With one slot left, G must be hired for the sales department.

	Y	G
	H	I
X	F	W
M	P	S

    (D) this only tells us that H and Y must be hired for sales positions
    (E) this only tells us that H and Y must be hired for sales positions

17. **(B)** To answer this question, we need to find the answer choice that violates one or more of the conditions. Scanning the choices reveals that choice B triggers the third condition, and then violates the first condition. There would be no place for the HY piece.

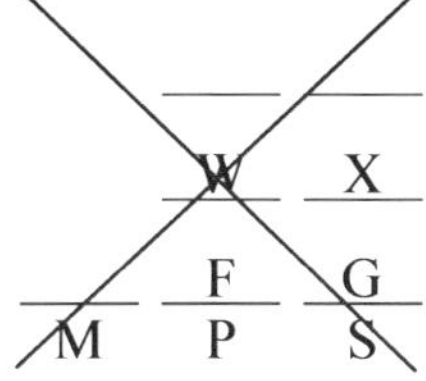

18. **(B)** Combining this information with the fourth condition, we know that X is also hired for a production position. Since we need at least two slots for the HY piece, it must be placed above the sales department, and G could still be hired for the management position or a sales position. Choice B is a direct violation of our deductions, and it is therefore the credited response.

	___	|G
	X	H
G|	F	Y
M	P	S

19. **(C)** We can diagram what happens when X is hired for a management position and what happens when X is hired for a sales position. When X is hired for a management position, the HY piece can be placed over either production or sales, and G must be hired for a sales position (second condition). When X is hired for a sales position, the third condition is triggered, and the HY piece must be placed over sales. Scanning the choices reveals that only choice C could be true.

	H	W
	Y	I
X	F	G
M	P	S

	W	G
	I	H
X	F	Y
M	P	S

	I	H
	W	Y
G	F	X
M	P	S

Questions 20-24

Setup:

- five pieces: N O S T V
- pieces are performed one at a time in succession
- each piece is performed with two instruments
- 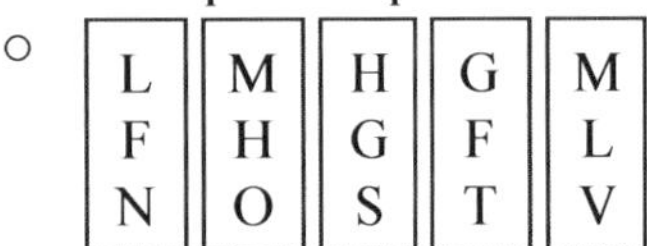

L	M	H	G	M
F	H	G	F	L
N	O	S	T	V

Conditions:

#1: each piece shares an instrument with the piece before or after it (or both)

#2: N_2 or T_2

Overview:
What differentiates this from the average game is that the pairings of instruments to pieces is given. Although the questions mostly ask about the ordering of the pieces, the instruments completely control which orderings are possible. To better visualize how the first condition works, it's helpful to note how this condition can be satisfied. First, note which pieces share instruments.

Instrument:	F	H	G	L	M
Piece:	NT	OS	ST	NV	OV

We know that the first and second pieces must share an instrument, and that the fourth and fifth pieces must share an instrument. There are three different ways this can happen.

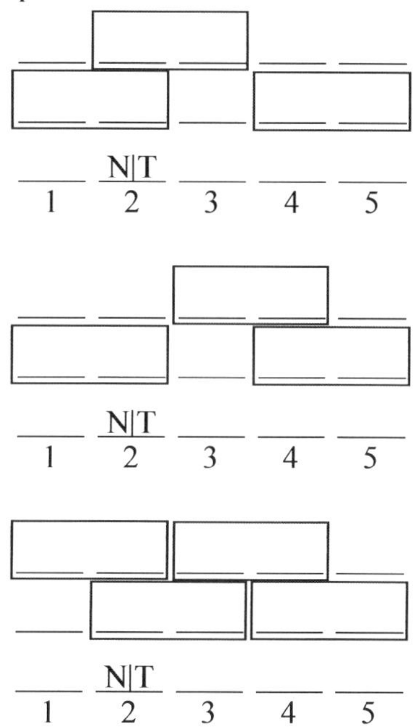

As a consequence of the two conditions, there are only four possible combinations of first and second pieces.

1	2	3	4	5
T	N			
V	N			
N	T			
S	T			

20. (A) violates the second condition (S_2)
    (B) violates the first condition (O in TON)
    (C) violates the first condition (VS)
    (D) Correct
    (E) violates the first condition (OT)

21. **(A)** Since both N and T are both performed with the fiddle, we know that the fiddle must be used for either the first or the second piece (or both). Therefore, it cannot be used for both the third and the fourth pieces, and choice A is correct.

22. **(A)** For this question, we can start with the four possible arrangements of the first two slots and create solutions. Since each piece except the first shares an instrument with the piece after it, we can chain them together using our circled pairs above. Checking the answer choices against the solutions reveals that only choice A could be true.

T	N	V	O	S
V	N	T	S	O
N	T	S	O	V
S	T	N	V	O
1	2	3	4	5

23. **(B)** This question directly tests our inference regarding the first two slots. Since O doesn't share any instruments with N or T, it cannot be first.

24. **(D)** With S fifth, to satisfy the first condition, we must place either O or T fourth. If T were fourth, N would have to be second. V would have to be first to satisfy the first condition, but O doesn't share any instruments with N or T, which violates the first condition.

V	N	~~O~~	T	S
1	2	3	4	5

Therefore, O must be fourth, and we can create three solutions based on the first two slots. Choice D is the only one that could be true as evidenced by the second solution.

T	N	V	O	S
V	N	T	O	S
N	T	V	O	S
1	2	3	4	5

Questions 1-6

Setup:
- eight files ordered from first to eighth
- red files: H M O
- green files: P V X
- yellow files: T Z

Conditions:

#1: [H __] – O
#2: X – V
#3: X and V separated by the same number of files as H and O
#4: [ZM]
#5: ~R_1

Overview:
Due to the fifth condition, the first file will be either green or yellow. The third condition stipulates that the variables in the first two conditions span the same number of slots as each other. Thus, we know that H, O, X, and V must be at least two slots from the respective ends. The fourth condition tells us that M can't be first and Z can't be last.

~R								
G|Y	____	____	____	____	____	____	____	R R R G G G Y Y
____	____	____	____	____	____	____	____	H M O P V X T Z
1	2	3	4	5	6	7	8	
~H	~O					~H	~Z	
~M	~V					~X	~H	
~O							~X	
~V								

1. (A) violates the fifth condition
   (B) violates the fourth condition
   (C) violates the first condition
   (D) Correct
   (E) violates the third condition

2. **(C)** Since none of the conditions specify a relationship between Z and H, we can try to maximize the number of files between them with each one preceding the other. With Z first, the highest-numbered slot H can occupy is six (first condition). Since H is a red file, the lowest-numbered slot it can occupy is two. The highest-numbered slot Z can occupy is seven. In either case, the number of slots between Z and H is four.

Z	M				H		O
	H		O			Z	M
1	2	3	4	5	6	7	8

3. **(A)** This question stem tells us to create three RG pieces: [RG] [RG] [RG]

   Since each green file is immediately preceded by a red file, the first file cannot be green. Due to the fifth condition, it cannot be red, and it therefore has to be yellow.

4. **(C)** Pairing this information with the third condition, we know that the two spans have to be interlocked. Since H cannot be first (fifth condition), we can place X first and V seventh. H is second and O is eighth. Thus, the greatest number of files that can separate X from V is five.

X	H					V	O
1	2	3	4	5	6	7	8

5. Although this question provides new information, we can eliminate three of the choices using the conditions alone. To choose between C and D, we must figure out whether or not H can be sixth under this scenario. Combining the new information with the fourth condition reveals that M must be sixth, and H therefore cannot be sixth.

   (A) violates the fifth condition
   (B) violates the fifth condition
   (C) Correct
   (D) M is sixth
   (E) violates the first condition (H cannot be seventh)

Questions 6-11

Setup:
- three employees: M S T
- three-day conference
- three sessions per day: H I R

Conditions:

#1: each conference participant ⟶ exactly two sessions, on different topics and different days

#2: ~M_I and ~S_I

#3: ~T_3

#4: at most two employees attend a given session together

Overview:

Since M and S do not attend any sessions on investing (second condition), each one will attend both a session on regulations and a session on hiring. The third condition tells us that if anyone attends a session on investing, it will be T. At most, T could attend one session on investing, due to the first condition. From the third condition and the first condition, we can infer that T attends one session on Monday, and another session on Tuesday. To keep all this information in mind, we can expand the variable set: M_R M_H S_R S_H T_1 T_2[6]. Due to the fourth condition, we cannot have all three people attend the same session. The interaction of the second and third conditions allows us to place an X as a placeholder on the third day's investing session. Alternatively, you could remove the slot from the diagram altogether.

R	____	____	____	
I	____	____	X	~M ~S
H	____	____	____	
	1	2	3	
			~T	

6. **(D)** To maximize the number of sessions the employees attend, we have to ensure that every session the employees attend is attended by only one employee. We can place M and S (separately) on the third day and either the first or the second day. T will attend a session on investing on the same day as M and S attend regulations and hiring, and he will attend a session on either regulations or hiring on the day M and S have off. Thus, six is the correct answer.

R	M|S	T|	S|M		R	T|	M|S	S|M
I	T	X	X		I	X	T	X
H	S|M	|T	M|S	or	H	|T	S|M	M|S
	1	2	3			1	2	3

7. This must be false question offers no new information.
   (A) one would be regulations and the other would be hiring
   (B) one would be regulations and the other would be hiring
   (C) could be M and S together or one of M and S together with T
   (D) this would have to be T (see question number six)
   (E) Correct – the second and third conditions dictate that only two of the sessions on the third day can be attended

8. **(C)** Since T doesn't attend any sessions on the third day, the sessions must be attended by M and S. From the first condition, we can conclude that whichever of M and S attends the regulations session on the third day will attend the hiring session on one of the first two days, and whichever of M and S attends the hiring session on the third day will attend the regulations session on one of the first two days. Therefore, M and S do not attend any sessions together.

	1	2	3
R			M|S
I			X
H			S|M

9. (A) see question #6
   (B) Correct – since we have six variables to place, this would mean three sessions were attended by two people each; T would have to attend with each of M and S during the first two days, but M and S would have to attend the same session on the third day, thus violating the first condition
   (C) their sessions could be on any of the three days
   (D) T can attend any of the sessions on the first two days
   (E) T would attend both regulations and hiring during the first two days

10. **(A)** Combining this information with the second condition, we know that T attends the investing session on the first day. Since M and S attend separate sessions on the first day, they must not attend the same session on either the second or the third day (first condition). Hence, A is correct.

	1	2	3
R	M|S		
I	T		X
H	S|M		

11. **(A)** From the question, we know that M attends one of regulations and hiring while T attends investing, or that M and T attend one of regulations and investing together. Since M has already attended one session after the first day, and S hasn't yet attended a session, M and S cannot attend two additional sessions together (M would have to attend three sessions, which violates the first condition).

Questions 12-18

Setup:
- five children: S T U W Z
- three are left-handed: L L L
- two are right-handed: R R
- each of the five children was born in a different year
- seven years: 0 1 2 3 4 5 6

Conditions:

#1: 

#2: 

#3: #4: 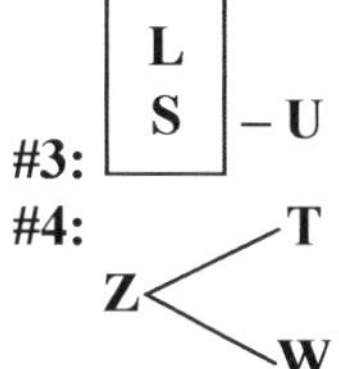

#5: left-handed child in 1991

#6: 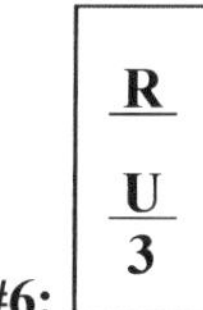

Overview:
The large number of conditions is a big clue that we can make some immediate inferences. The fifth and the sixth conditions, combined with the first and the second conditions, tell us that neither a right-handed nor a left-handed child could have been born in 1992, and we can therefore place Xs in the corresponding slots. From those conditions, we also know that if a child was born in 1990, he or she could not be left-handed, and if a child was born in 1994, he or she could not be right-handed. With only two Ls left to place, the non-consecutive conditions allow us to place them in the fourth and sixth slots. Because S is left-handed and precedes U, she must have been born in 1991. Due to the fourth condition, Z can be placed in either 1990 or 1994. Since there's only one R left to place, it will be in either 1990 or 1995. Therefore, children could not have been born in both years. We can place two Xs in each row to balance the game.

~L	~R ~L		~R				
R|X	L	X	R	L	X|R	L	L L L R R X X
Z|	S	X	U	|Z			S T U W Z X X
0	1	2	3	4	5	6	

12. (A) S must have been born in 1990
    (B) violates the fourth condition
    (C) violates the sixth condition
    (D) children cannot have been born in both 1990 and 1995
    (E) Correct

13. **(D)** From this information, we can pair Z with 1994. Combining this with the fourth condition creates dual T|W options for 1995 and 1996. Since we have established that U precedes Z, choice D cannot be true.

X	L	X	R	L	R	L
X	S	X	U	Z	T|W	W|T
0	1	2	3	4	5	6

14. This must be false question offers no additional information, but rather tests us on one of the initial inferences.
    (A) a child would have been born in 1995
    (B) a child would have been born in 1990
    (C) Correct – since a child must have been born in 1996, this cannot be true
    (D) Z could be born in 1990
    (E) either T or W could be born in 1995

15. **(B)** This question firms up the sequence given in the fourth condition: Z – W – T. It also tests our inference that children cannot have been born in both 1990 and 1995. When Z is paired with 1990, W is paired with 1994 and T is paired with 1996. When Z is paired with 1994, W is paired with 1995 and T is paired with 1996. Thus, there are two possible orderings.

Z	S	X	U	W	X	T
X	S	X	U	Z	W	T
0	1	2	3	4	5	6

16. **(D)** Given our inference about 1990 and 1995, we know that one of the children must have been born in 1990. Since Z must precede T and W, Z must be paired with 1990. Dual T|W options are created for 1994 and 1996. Thus, choice D must be true.

X	S	X	U	T|W	X	W|T
0	1	2	3	4	5	6

17. **(D)** For T to be right-handed, he must have been born in 1995, since both 1994 and 1996 were years in which left-handed children were born. Our inference about 1990 and 1995 allows us to place Z in 1994. The only open slot is 1996, and we can place W there. D must, therefore, be true.

X	L	X	R	L	R	L
X	S	X	U	Z	T	W
0	1	2	3	4	5	6

18. **(D)** With this information, we can place Z in the 1990 slot. Therefore, she must be right-handed. From our 1990 and 1995 inference, we know that the 1995 slot is unoccupied. T|W dual options are created for the 1994 and 1996 slots. Thus, choice D must be false.

R	L	X	R	L	X	L
Z	S	X	U	T|W	X	W|T
0	1	2	3	4	5	6

Questions 19-23

Setup:
- o fish species: J K L M N O P
- o for each species, the store has several fish available

Conditions:
#1: K ⟶ ~O; O ⟶ ~K (contrapositive)
#2: M ⟶ ~N; N ⟶ ~M (contrapositive)
#3: M ⟶ O; ~O ⟶ ~M (contrapositive)
#4: N ⟶ O; ~O ⟶ ~N (contrapositive)
#5: O ⟶ P } **P⟷O**
#6: P ⟶ O }
#7: O ⟶ 2^+

Overview:
From the fifth and the sixth conditions, we can infer that she either purchases fish of types O and P, or of neither O nor P.

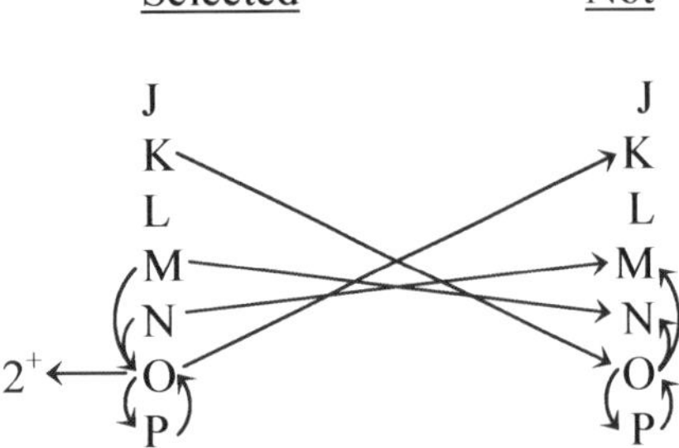

19. (A) violates the third condition
    (B) violates the first condition
    (C) Correct
    (D) violates the seventh condition
    (E) violates the second condition

20. **(A)** Following the chain from P not being selected, we know that O, N, and M must also not be selected. Each one of choices B, C, D, and E contains one of these variables, and A is therefore correct.

21. **(A)** Looking at our diagram, it becomes apparent that when K is selected, O, N, M, and P are not selected. K is the only variable such that, when it is selected, four other variables are not selected. Therefore, to maximize the number of species, we must not select K, and A is correct.

22. This must be false question offers no new information.
    (A) OOPJ
    (B) OOPL
    (C) Correct – following the chain from M, we know O and P must also be selected. Since the seventh condition dictates that if she selects O, she must purchase two or more O, the number of fish selected would have to be four (MOOP)
    (D) OOP
    (E) OOP

23. **(B)** Since we know that she selects at least one fish, she can select J, K, or L without selecting fish of other species. Therefore, the minimum must be one and we can eliminate D and E. From question number twenty-one, we know that if we're trying to maximize the number of species, we must exclude K. The second condition dictates that we can only select one of M and N. Therefore, the maximum is five, and choice B is correct.

[5] Visit Manhattan LSAT (http://www.manhattanlsat.com) to learn more about using this diagram.

Questions 1-6

Setup:

- six kinds of food: K L M O T Z
- one food at a time
- no food is added more than once

Conditions:

#1: M_3 ⟶ L_6; ~L_6 ⟶ ~M_3 (contrapositive)
#2: Z_1 ⟶ L – O; O – L ⟶ ~Z_1 (contrapositive)
#3: ~T_5 and ~K_5
#4: T – M – K or K – M – T

Overview:
We can't have a situation in which the first two conditions are triggered, since L being sixth precludes it from preceding O. Also, from the fourth condition, we can conclude that M is neither first nor sixth. We also know that if the second condition is triggered, L cannot be last.

1	2	3	4	5	6
~M				~T ~K	~M

M ⟶ L (M in 3 ⟶ L in 6)

Z ⟶ ~L (Z in 1 ⟶ ~L in 6)

1. (A) violates the third condition
   (B) violates the first condition
   (C) violates the fourth condition
   (D) Correct
   (E) violates the second condition

2. **(C)** As a consequence of the fourth condition, M cannot be first, and C is therefore correct.

3. **(A)** The contrapositive of the second condition tells us that when O precedes L (which it does in this case), Z cannot be first. Therefore, choice A must be true.

4. (A) violates the first condition
   (B) due to the third and fourth conditions, either K or T would have to be sixth
   (C) Correct – see the following diagram

L	O	K|T	Z	M	T|K
1	2	3	4	5	6

   (D) violates the second condition
   (E) with Z first, there would be no room for either K or T to precede M, thus violating the fourth condition

5. **(D)** This question triggers the second condition, and we know that L must precede O. Since two of the choices present L, it's best to check those first. Placing L third, we can avoid violating the fourth condition:

Z	K|T	L	M	O	T|K
1	2	3	4	5	6

However, placing L fourth presents a problem, in that O must be either fifth or sixth. Since either K or T must also follow L, due to the fourth condition, one of them must go sixth. Therefore, we have to place O fifth. The fourth condition dictates that M has to be third, but this violates the first condition.

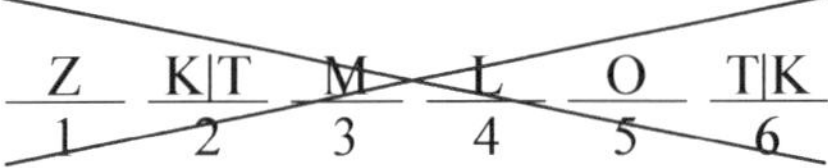

Questions 6-10

Setup:

- five of seven cold medications
- medications: F G I K L M
- the tested medications are to be ranked from first (best) to fifth (worst)

Conditions:

#1: L_2
#2: F_1 or G_1
#3: I is tested
#4: H and G ⟶ H – G
#5: K and F ⟶ K – F
#6: M ⟶ F; ~F ⟶ ~M (contrapositive)
M ⟶ H; ~H ⟶ ~M (contrapositive)

Overview:
We have a number of conditionals with which to contend. Since I must be third, fourth, or fifth, it's a good idea to include it in the diagram as a reminder.

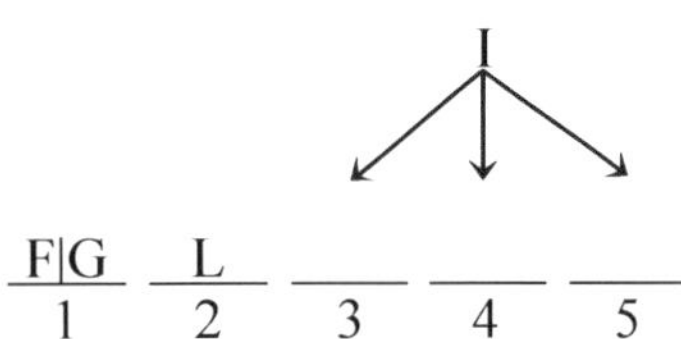

6. (A) violates the first condition
   (B) violates the third condition
   (C) violates the sixth condition
   (D) Correct
   (E) violates the fifth condition

7. This could be true question offers no additional information.

   (A) if F were first, we would only have three slots for G, H, I, and M; if G were first, we would only have three slots for F, H, I, and M
   (B) since F couldn't be first, G would be, but H and G would trigger the fourth condition
   (C) Correct – see the following diagram

G	L	I	K	F
1	2	3	4	5

   (D) F would have to be first, triggering and violating the fifth condition
   (E) with F first, and M being tested, we only have three slots for M, I, G, and H (sixth condition)

8. **(A)** To tackle this must be true question, we can try to disprove the answer choices. If F were not tested, M would not be tested (contrapositive of the sixth condition). With two variables out, G, H, and K would all be tested. With F out, G would have to be first, which violates the fourth condition.

9. **(E)** The answer to question six and the diagram from question seven allow us to eliminate choices B, C, and D immediately. All we need to do at this point is figure out whether or not I can be fifth. Drawing up a quick diagram reveals that I can be fifth, and E is therefore correct.

F	L	M	H	I
1	2	3	4	5

10. This question prompts us to draw two scenarios: one with F first, and one with G first.

F	L	I		
G	L	I		
1	2	3	4	5

   (A) could be true under the first scenario
   (B) Correct – this could only happen under the first scenario, which would trigger and violate the fifth condition
   (C) could be true under the second scenario
   (D) could be true under the first scenario
   (E) could be true under the second scenario

Questions 11-17

Setup:
- each flight departs from one and arrives at another city
- five cities: H M P T V
- cities are connected if there are nonstop flights between them
- each city is connected with at least one other city

Conditions:
#1: M is connected with exactly one other city
#2: ~HT
#3: _H ⟶ _T; ~_T ⟶ ~_H (contrapositive)
#4: PT ⟶ ~PV; PV ⟶ ~PT (contrapositive)

Overview:
We can infer that H is not connected to M. If they were connected, the third condition would be triggered, thus violating the first condition. Due to the fourth condition, P can be connected with a maximum of three other cities. Since there are five cities, there are ten possible connections, without taking into consideration the conditions. The first condition eliminates three of the connections, the second condition eliminates one connection, and the fourth condition eliminates one connection. Thus, at a maximum, there can be five different connections. Since there are five cities, and each one must be connected to at least one other (final setup condition), there must be, at a minimum, three connections. We can note the possible connections before application of the conditions along with the possible connections with the conditions.

Possible Connections	With Conditions	
MH	~~MH~~	
MP	MP	exactly 1 (MP, MT, MV)
MT	MT	
MV	MV	
HP	HP	
HT	~~HT~~	
HV	HV	
TV	TV	
TP	TP	not both (TP, PV)
PV	PV	

Redrawing our diagram for a more visual representation of the possibilities, we have the following:

```
  ------
  ------
_____ _____ ------
 MP   HP⟶TP
 MT   HV   PV
 MV   ↓
      TV
```

11. (A) Correct
    (B) violates the first condition
    (C) violates the third condition
    (D) violates the fourth condition
    (E) violates the second condition

12. **(B)** Since P cannot be connected to both T and V (fourth condition), it must be connected to both M and H under this scenario. Combining this information with the third condition reveals that P must also be connected to T. Only choice B presents a pair of cities that could be connected, and it is therefore correct. Note that V must be connected to at least one of H and T, due to the last setup condition.

```
      -------
      _____
 MP    HP    TP
 ___  ___   ___
 MP    HP    TP
~MT    HV   ~PV
~MV    TV
```

13. **(A)** This question directly tests the inference that M and H cannot be connected.

14. Each answer choice presents a restricted scenario in which two cities are connected only with each other.

    (A) Correct – see the following diagram

	HV	
MP	TV	
MP	~HP	~TP
~MT	HV	~PV
~MV	TV	

    (B) since at least one of HP and HV must be selected, T must be connected to at least one of P and V (third condition)
    (C) since H must be connected to at least one of P and V (last setup condition), at least one of the HP and TV pairs will be selected
    (D) at least one of the HP, HV, and TV pairs must be selected
    (E) at least one of the HP and HV pairs must be selected, and if HP is selected, the third condition is triggered

15. **(D)** This question prompts us to eliminate the PV, HP, and MP pairs. Therefore, the HV pair must be selected. This triggers the third condition, and we know that the TV pair is also selected. Only choice D could be true, and it is therefore correct. The two cities connected to T would be P and V.

	HV	
	TV	TP
~MP	~HP	TP
MT	HV	~PV
MV	TV	

16. **(B)** As we initially inferred, the maximum number of connections is five. The only uncertainty in this scenario is which of P, T, and V M is paired with.

	HP	
	HV	
	TV	TP
MP	HP	TP
MT	HV	~PV
MV	TV	

17. **(C)** Since V is the only city that can be connected to four other cities, it must be connected to H, T, M, and P under this scenario. Therefore, choice C is correct.

Questions 18-23

Setup:

- six individual animals selected
- three monkeys: F G H
- three pandas: K L N
- three raccoons: T V Z

Conditions:

#1: F ⟶ ~H; H ⟶ ~F (contrapositive)
#2: N ⟶ ~T; T ⟶ ~N (contrapositive)
#3: H ⟶ K; ~K ⟶ ~N (contrapositive)
#4: K ⟶ N; ~N ⟶ ~K (contrapositive)

Overview:
We can use our diagram to make any necessary inferences.

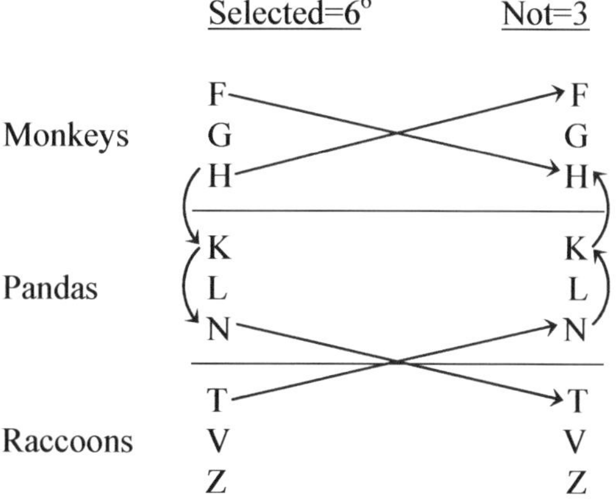

Note that if T is selected, three other animals (N, K, and H) are not selected. Since six animals must be selected, this results in a complete solution.

T ⟶

In	Out
F	G
G	K
L	N
T	
V	
Z	

[6] Visit Manhattan LSAT (http://www.manhattanlsat.com) to learn more about using this diagram.

18. (A) violates the second condition
    (B) violates the first condition
    (C) violates the fourth condition
    (D) Correct
    (E) violates the third condition

19. **(C)** Following the chain from H, we know that K and N must be selected, and F and T cannot be selected. From this, we can eliminate choices A and B. Since all three pandas are selected, we can also eliminate D and E. Therefore, C is the only choice that could be true.

20. **(C)** Following the chains from each of the first variables presented, C is the only choice that violates a condition. If K is selected, N must also be selected, and T must not be selected.

21. **(B)** We have previously noted that selecting T results in a complete solution. Accordingly, choice A is correct.

22. **(A)** This question triggers our T solution, and choice A is therefore correct.

23. (A) see question #21
    (B) Correct – excluding any particular kind of animal would limit the selection to five animals
    (C) we could select L or N alone
    (D) we could select F or G alone
    (E) we could select V or Z alone

Part 5: PrepTests 41-50

Questions 1-7

Setup:
- six hangers: 1 2 3 4 5 6
- six dresses: G L P O R S
- a different dress is on each hanger

Conditions:
#1: G – P
#2: R_1 or R_6
#3: W_3 or S_3
#4: SL (boxed)

Overview:
From the conditions, we can create this diagram:

R|		W|S			|R
1	2	3	4	5	6
~P					~G
~L					~S

1. **(A) Correct**
   (B) violates the third condition
   (C) violates the first condition
   (D) violates the fourth condition
   (E) violates the second condition

2. **(B)** This question presents two new conditions. If S were first, W would be third and G would be fifth. However, due to the first condition, P would be sixth, thereby violating the second condition. If S were fifth, the fourth condition would dictate that L be sixth, and R would have to be first. However, since G can't be third (third condition), this cannot happen. Therefore, S must be third, and G can be either first or fifth. Out of the answer choices, B is the only one that could be true.

G	P|W	S	L	W|P	R
R	W	S	L	G	P
1	2	3	4	5	6

3. **(E)** Since S isn't third, W must be third. S can't be second or sixth, due to the fourth condition. Therefore, it must be fourth. With R first, G and P will be second and sixth, respectively. With R sixth, G and P will be first and second, respectively. In either case, W is third, and is the only item that can immediately precede S.

R	G	W	S	L	P
G	P	W	S	L	R
1	2	3	4	5	6

4. **(E)** With P on the second hanger, G must be first (first condition). With G first, R must be sixth (second condition). Finally, we can place the SL piece either third and fourth or fourth and fifth. In either case, R must be sixth.

G	P	S	L	W	R
G	P	W	S	L	R
1	2	3	4	5	6

5. This cannot be true question offers no new information.
   (A) L could be fourth and G could be fifth
   (B) Correct – if R is first P cannot be second (first condition), and if R is sixth, there is nothing immediately to its right
   (C) see question #2
   (D) see question #2
   (E) this is true whenever R is first

6. In order for an item to be placed immediately to the right of R, it must be placed first, due to the second condition.
   (A) see question #3
   (B) L could be fifth and R could be sixth
   (C) P would be fifth and R could be sixth
   (D) Correct – S would have to be second, but due to the third and fourth conditions, this isn't possible

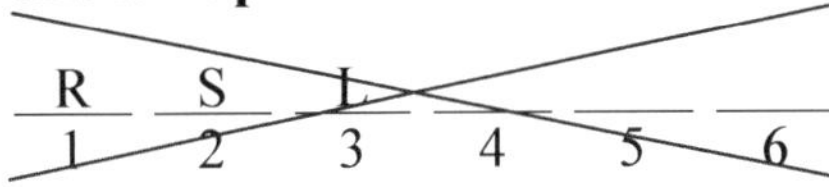

   (E) this could happen if R were first and W were second, or if W were fifth and R were sixth

7. **(D)** This question temporarily replaces the SL piece with [SW]. Since either S or W must occupy the third slot (third condition), this piece could either be second and third or third and fourth. Since choice D places S fifth, it must be false.

1	2	3	4	5	6
	S	W			
		S	W		

Questions 8-12

Setup:
- four songs: N Q R S
- each song is performed on a different instrument
- instruments: F G H K

Conditions:
#1: ~F_1

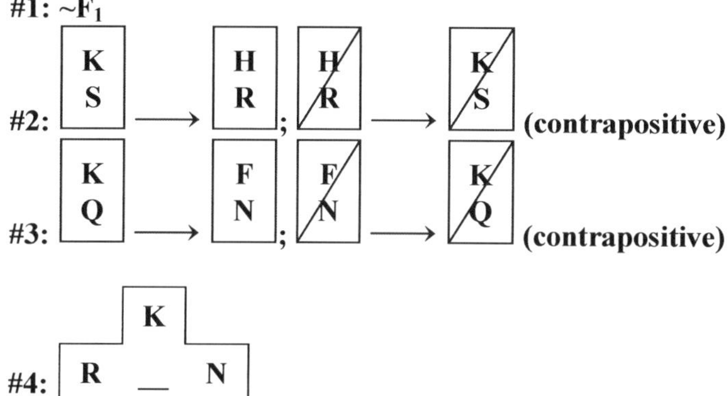

#4: [R _ N] with K above the blank

Overview:
Since the fourth condition precludes the keyboard from being paired with R or N, it must be paired with either S or Q. This means that either the second or the third condition must be triggered. Also, due to the size of the piece created by the fourth condition, it must span either the first through the third slots or the second through the fourth slots. As a result, we can trigger the second and third conditions (separately) with these two placements of the piece to create four molds, which encapsulate every viable solution. Due to the first condition, we can definitively place the F and the G in the third mold, thus creating a complete solution.

#1 H K F|G G|F
R S N Q
1 2 3 4

#2 G|H K F H|G
R Q N S
1 2 3 4

#3 G H K F
Q R S N
1 2 3 4

#4 G|H H|G K F
S R Q N
1 2 3 4

8. (A) unacceptable song sequence
   (B) Correct – it is a direct match with the third mold
   (C) violates the first condition
   (D) unacceptable song sequence
   (E) matches with the fourth mold, but F and K are switched

9. **(E)** Checking the answer choices against the molds reveals that E could occur under either the first or the fourth mold.

10. **(C)** Checking the choices against the molds, we can see that irrespective of the mold, the song performed on the flute cannot immediately precede R.

11. **(E)** The question tells us to look at the third and fourth molds. Only E could be true, under the fourth mold.

12. **(A)** Since Q is third, we need to use the fourth mold. Since Q must be played on the keyboard, A must be false.

Questions 13-17

Setup:
- seven members or the board of directors: G H L M U W Z
- two committees: F I
- only board members serve on these committees

Conditions:
#1: $G_F \longrightarrow H_I$; $H_F \longrightarrow G_I$ (contrapositive)
#2: $L_F \longrightarrow M_I$; $M_F \longrightarrow L_I$ (contrapositive)
$L_F \longrightarrow U_I$; $U_F \longrightarrow L_I$ (contrapositive)
#3: $W_F \longleftrightarrow Z_I$; $W_I \longleftrightarrow Z_F$
#4: $U_F \longleftrightarrow G_I$; $U_I \longleftrightarrow G_F$
#5: $Z_F \longrightarrow H_F$; $H_I \longrightarrow Z_I$ (contrapositive)

Overview:
We can use our diagram to make any necessary inferences.

Finance[1] Incentives

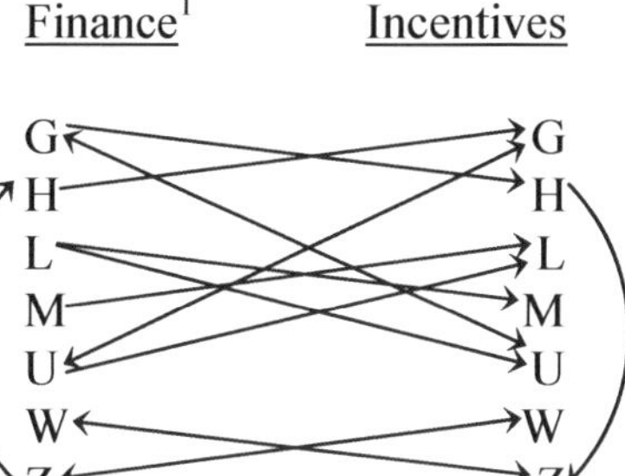

13. (A) violates the first condition
    (B) violates the fifth condition
    (C) following the chain from H_F, we must also have U_F
    (D) violates the third condition
    (E) Correct

14. **(C)** Following the chain from H_I, we must have Z_I, and therefore we cannot have W_I, as this would violate the third condition.

15. **(C)** The first, third, and fourth conditions dictate that only one of each of the following pairs can serve on the finance committee: G|H, W|Z, and U|G. We can therefore eliminate D and E. If we select H, Z, and U from these pairs, we can also select M to serve on finance without violating any conditions. Thus, the maximum number who can be on the finance committee is four, and our hypothetical selection is H, Z, U, and M.

16. Following the chain from M_F and W_F, we must have L_I and Z_I.
    (A) L cannot serve on finance
    (B) violates the fourth condition
    (C) Z cannot serve on finance
    (D) Correct – we already deduced that L must serve on incentives, and the chain from U_I leads us to G_F
    (E) Z cannot serve on finance

17. **(B)** Following the chain from G_I, we are led to U_F and L_I, and thus, choice B is correct.

[1] Visit Manhattan LSAT (http://www.manhattanlsat.com) to learn more about using this diagram.

Questions 18-24

Setup:
- eight people: F G H I K M O P
- sitting evenly spaced around a circular picnic table
- two are sitting across from each other if and only if they are separated by three people

Conditions:

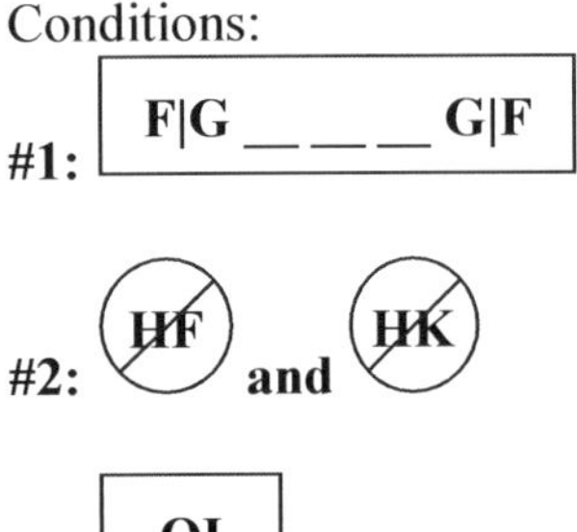

Overview:
A flat linear diagram takes up the least amount of space, and is therefore the preferred diagram. Alternatively, you could draw wheel spokes or a circle to represent the table. Since there is only one condition regarding O, we can place it in the leftmost slot without concern for which variable is placed last. Since there are limited placements for the piece given in the first condition, we can set up two distinct molds. It is important to remember that left to right is clockwise, and right to left is counterclockwise. We will refer to the slots by number, only for the sake of clarity. The actual seat numbers are never mentioned, and are irrelevant to the questions.

18. (A) violates the first condition
    (B) if K were in the third slot, either F or G would have to be in the eighth slot (see the first mold)
    (C) Correct – see the first mold
    (D) violates the third condition
    (E) violates the second condition

19. Since G and O are next to each other, we know to use the first mold. Due to the second condition, K cannot be in the fifth slot. It therefore must be occupied by either M or P.

O I G H M|P K| F |K
~K

(A) F cannot be separated from K by one slot
(B) F and O are separated by two slots
(C) H and I do not have P between them
(D) Correct – this would place M immediately to the right of F

O I G H P K F M

(E) the placement of F precludes this outcome

20. **(A)** We can create two viable scenarios that fulfill this condition: one for each of the molds. Using the first mold, H must be fifth, since it cannot be next to G or F (second condition). Since K cannot be next to H (second condition), it must be eighth, and dual M|P options are created for the fourth and sixth slots. Similarly, using the second mold, H must have one variable separating it from both F and G. This creates M|P dual options for the fifth and seventh slots. F and H can both be next to M in either case, and choice A is therefore correct.

O I F M|P H P|M G K

O I K F|G M|P H P|M G|F

21. **(C)** We can narrow our focus to the first mold with this question. Since we must separate H and K (second condition), we have to place P in the fifth slot. Due to the second condition, whether F is third or seventh, it must be next to K, and choice C is therefore correct.

O I F|G K|H P H|K G|F M

22. **(A)** The first mold allows us to place M in the third slot, which is immediately clockwise and adjacent to I. Therefore, I and M do not have to be separated by any variables.

O I M F|G K|H P H|K G|F

23. **(B)** Using the first mold, the second condition dictates that we place F third and G seventh. Under the second mold, it appears that we still have F|G dual options in the fourth and eighth slots. However, if G were placed in the eighth slot, the second condition would leave no slots open for H. In both cases, G cannot be next to O, and choice B is therefore correct.

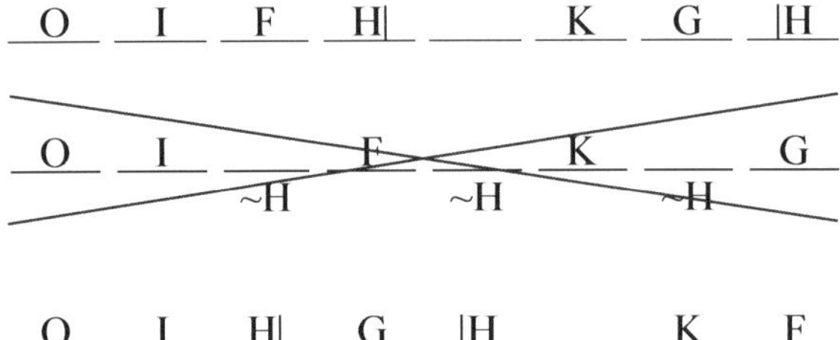

24. **(C)** Applying this information to the molds, we see that G and K are separated by two people (counting clockwise from G to K) in the fourth scenario, and choice C is therefore correct.

#1 O I F|G K|H M|P P|M G|F H|K

From this, we can generate two diagrams:

O I F K M|P P|M G H

O I G H M|P P|M F K

#2 O I K|H F|G M|P P|M H|K F|G

From this, we can generate two diagrams:

O I K F M|P P|M H G

O I H G M|P P|M K F

Questions 1-5

Setup:

- a panel of five scientists
- three botanists: F G H
- three chemists: K L M
- three zoologists: P Q R

Conditions:

#1: 1^+ scientist of each type
#2: 2^+ botanists ⟶ ≤ 1 zoologist; 2^+ zoologists ⟶ ≤ 1 botanist (contrapositive)
#3: F ⟶ ~K; K ⟶ ~F (contrapositive)
#4: K ⟶ ~M; M ⟶ ~K (contrapositive)
#5: M ⟶ P; ~P ⟶ ~M (contrapositive)
M ⟶ R; ~R ⟶ ~M (contrapositive)

Overview:
From the first and second conditions, we can infer that if either the conditional or its contrapositive (second condition) is triggered, we would have to select 1 zoologist or 1 botanist. From the first condition, we can infer two possible allocations of scientists to specialties: 3, 1, 1 and 2, 2, 1. The fourth condition tells us that the maximum number of chemists that can be selected is two. If a question indicates the first allocation, the number of chemists selected will be one. Since we can only select more than one of either the botanists or the zoologists, if a question indicates the second allocation, there will be two chemists selected.

```
            ____

            ____

3, 1, 1 ⟶  ____   ____   ____
            B|Z     C     Z|B

            ____   K|M

2, 2, 1 ⟶  ____    L     ____
            B|Z     C     Z|B
```

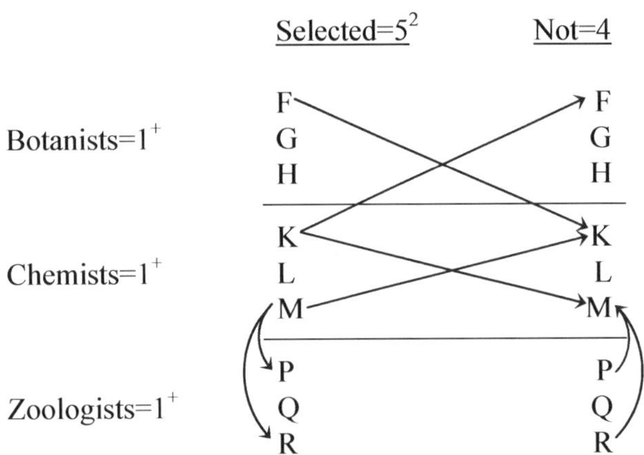

1. (A) violates the second condition
   (B) violates the first condition (no zoologists are selected)
   (C) Correct
   (D) violates the fourth condition
   (E) violates the fifth condition

2. **(E)** Since M is the only chemist selected, the allocation is 3, 1, 1. The fifth condition dictates that both P and R are selected. This, combined with the allocation, tells us that all three zoologists must be selected. Any one of the three botanists could be selected.

   R

   Q

   P   M   F|G|H
   Z   C   B

3. **(E)** Combining this information with the contrapositive of the second condition, we know that there is only one botanist selected (F). Following the chain from F, we know that K is not selected. M cannot be the fifth scientist selected since P would also be selected, thereby making a six-person panel. With K, M, and the other botanists not selected, the fifth member has to be P, and E is therefore correct.

   R

   Q

   P   L   F
   Z   C   B

[2] Visit Manhattan LSAT (http://www.manhattanlsat.com) to learn more about using this diagram.

4. **(D)** Since R is not selected, M is also not selected. If the allocation is 3, 1, 1, all three botanists will be selected, and if it is 2, 2, 1, then both K and L will be selected. Due to the third condition, under the second allocation, F will not be selected, and choice D is correct.

```
F

G                            G    K

H    L    P        or        H    L    P
B    C    Z                  B    C    Z
```

5. **(A)** Since at least two botanists are selected, we know that only one zoologist is selected (second condition). Selecting M would trigger the fifth condition, which can't happen under this scenario. We can therefore eliminate choices B, C, and D. Under the 3, 1, 1 allocation, F would be selected, and K would not be selected. Under the 2, 2, 1 allocation, both K and L would be selected, and F would not. Therefore, choice A is correct.

```
F

G                              G    K

H    L    P|Q|R      or        H    L    P|Q|R
B    C    Z                    B    C    Z
```

Questions 6-12

Setup:
- six bays: 1 2 3 4 5 6
- each one is holding a different type of cargo
- six cargo types: F G L M P T

Conditions:
#1: L – G
#2: T – L
#3: F – P
#4: (PT)

Overview:
Combining the conditions, we can create the following sketch:

6. **(A) Correct**
   (B) G must follow F
   (C) L must follow F
   (D) F must precede T
   (E) F must precede T

7. **(A)** Since G is at the end of the chain, it can either be fifth or sixth. Therefore, it can't be fourth, and choice A is correct.

8. **(C)** If M followed G, seven slots would be required. Therefore, M must immediately precede L, and the only uncertainty is which of P and T comes first.

F	P|T	T|P	M	L	G
1	2	3	4	5	6

9. **(D)** L must be preceded by at least three bays and it must be followed by at least one bay, so it can be either fourth or fifth. Since bay 4 isn't given, choice D is correct.

10. (A) no conditions govern the placement of M
    (B) no conditions govern the placement of M
    (C) Correct – F and L must be separated by at least two bays
    (D) this could happen – the sequence would be TPL
    (E) this could happen – the sequence would be FTP

11. From this question stem, we can deduce the following sequence:
    F——[TP]——L——G

    (A) bay 1 would hold M
    (B) M would be first or second
    (C) Correct – T must be followed by at least three bays and cannot be fourth
    (D) M would be sixth
    (E) no conditions govern the placement of M

12. **(C)** Since P is followed by L and G, they must be fifth and sixth respectively. Due to the fourth condition, T has to be third. The only uncertainty is which of F and M is first. and C is therefore correct.

F|M	M|F	T	P	L	G
1	2	3	4	5	6

Questions 13-18

Setup:

- three kinds of cookie: O P S
- exactly three batches of each kind are made each week: O O O P P P S S S
- each batch is made on a single day

Conditions:

#1: $O_1 - O_2 - O_3$; $P_1 - P_2 - P_3$; $S_1 - S_2 - S_3$

#2: at least one batch on Monday

#3: 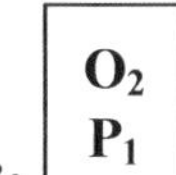

#4: $\frac{S_2}{Th}$

Overview:

The third condition allows us to make some inferences about the O_2P_1 piece's placement. Since it must be preceded by one O and followed by two Ps, it can either be placed on Tuesday or Wednesday. Combining this information with the fourth condition, we know that S_2 follows the O_2P_1 piece. Combining the first condition with the fourth condition, we know that S_3 is placed on Friday. From the second condition, we know that either O_1, S_1, or both are baked on Monday. Since only O_1 and S_1 could be on Monday, Monday has a maximum of two batches.

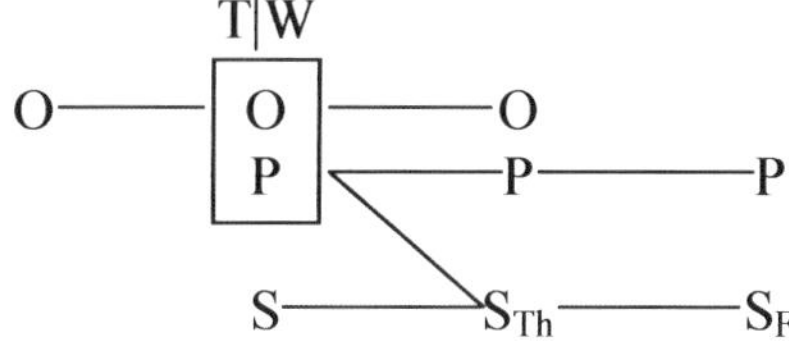

We can create two distinct molds based on the placement options for the OP piece.

#1

M	T	W	Th	F
O	O			
X	P			
			S	S

#2

M	T	W	Th	F
		O_2		
X	X	P	P	P
			S	S

Mold #1: When the OP piece is placed on Tuesday, O_1 must be placed on Monday.

Mold #2: When the OP piece is placed on Wednesday, P_2 and P_3 must be placed on Thursday and Friday, respectively.

13. **(A) Correct**
    (B) violates the fourth condition
    (C) violates the second condition
    (D) O_1 has to precede P_1
    (E) violates the third condition

14. **(A)** This question indirectly asks which of the five days could be days on which all three types are baked. We'll go through them one by one.

    M: at most O_1 and S_1
    T: could have O_2, P_1, and S_1
    W: could have O_2, P_1, and S_1
    Th: could have O_3, P_2, and S_2
    F: could have O_3, P_3, and P_3

    Therefore, Monday is the only day on which no more than two batches could be baked and A is correct.

15. This question triggers mold #1. Checking each of the choices against the mold reveals that C cannot be true.

    (A) could be O_1 and S_1
    (B) could be O_2 and P_1
    (C) Correct – only P could have its second batch made on Wednesday
    (D) could be P_2 and S_2
    (E) could be any two of O_3, P_3, and S_3

16. **(D)** This could only be true of mold #1. We must place P2 and P3 in the Thursday and Friday slots, respectively. Since P and S must both be baked on Thursday, choice D is correct.

M	T	W	Th	F
O	O	X		
X	P	X	P	P
		X	S	S

17. **(A)** This could only be true of mold #1. We must place P2 and P3 in the Wednesday and Thursday slots, respectively. Scanning the choices reveals that only A could be true, and it is therefore correct.

M	T	W	Th	F
O	O			X
X	P	P	P	X
			S	S

18. **(E)** This could only be true of mold #1. We must place O3 and S1 in the Wednesday slots. Only choice E need not be true, and it is therefore correct

M	T	W	Th	F
O	O	O	X	X
X	P			
X	X	S	S	S

Questions 19-23

Setup:
- five students: J K L M O
- each reviews one or more of exactly three plays
- plays: S T U
- the students do not review any other plays

Conditions:

#1: $K_{\#reviews} < M_{\#reviews}$; $L_{\#reviews} < M_{\#reviews}$

#2: 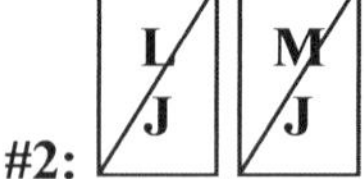

#3: 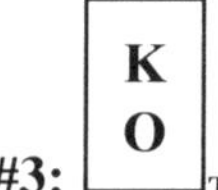

#4: exactly two of the students review exactly the same play(s) as each other

Overview:

The first condition tells us that M could review two or three plays, and K and L could each review either one or two plays. Since each student must review at least one play, we know that M must review two plays. If M reviewed three plays, the second condition would dictate that J couldn't review any of the plays. Since M reviews two plays, the first condition stipulates that K and L must each review one play. Revisiting the second condition, we know that J reviews one play. We're not given any information about how many plays O can review, so we'll leave it as one, two or three. So far, the allocation is:

J: 1
K: 1
L: 1
M: 2
O: 1, 2, or 3

Taking the second condition into consideration, the highest number of reviewers for any of the three plays is four. Also, since K only reviews one play, and has already been assigned to T, S and U can be assigned no more than three reviewers.

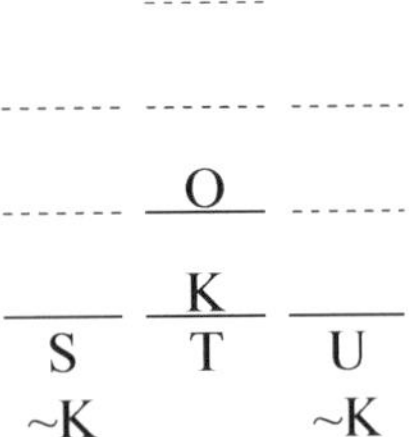

Using the second condition, we can create three distinct molds based on the placement of J.

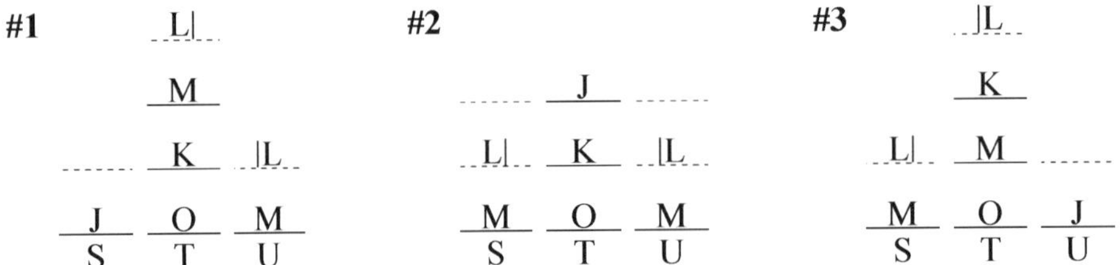

Mold #1: With J assigned to S, M must be assigned to both T and U. L must be assigned to either T or U. The fourth condition allows for two acceptable scenarios. If L is assigned to T, O must be assigned to at least one of S and U. If L is assigned to U, O cannot be assigned to either of S and U.

Mold #2: With J assigned to T, M must be assigned to both S and U. L must be assigned to either T or U. The fourth condition dictates that O must be assigned to at least one of S and U.

Mold #3: With J assigned to U, M must be assigned to both S and T. L must be assigned to either S or T. The fourth condition allows for two acceptable scenarios. If L is assigned to S, O cannot be assigned to either of S and U. If L is assigned to T, O must be assigned to at least one of S and U.

19. **(A) Correct – this could be true of mold #2 or mold #3**
    (B) violates the third condition
    (C) violates the second condition
    (D) violates the third condition
    (E) M must review two plays (see above)

20. **(B)** This question tests our command of the allocation of plays to each reviewer. Comparing the choices to our allocation, it must be true that M reviews more plays (two) than J (one).

21. **(E)** This could only be true of mold #2. L, M, and O must all be assigned to U. The only remaining uncertainty is whether or not O is also assigned to S. Only choice E is possible under this scenario, and it is therefore correct.

......	J	O
......	K	L
M	O	M
S	T	U

22. **(D)** Since T must be assigned at least three reviewers, we can eliminate choices A and B. For T to be assigned three reviewers, it would have to be assigned K, M, and O, or J, K, and O. Only choice D matches one of these scenarios, and it is therefore correct.

23. **(D)** Since M reviews two plays and J reviews one, and they cannot review any of the same plays (second condition), M must review every play that J does not. Therefore, choice D must be true.

Questions 1-5

Setup:

- o six groups: F G J M P V
- o each group marches as a unit
- o ordered from first (front) to sixth (back)

Conditions:

#1: | **P __ __** | **– M**

#2: | **F __ V** |

#3: G_1, G_3, or G_5

Overview:
Since the first and second conditions specify pieces that are four or more slots and three slots respectively, and there are only six slots total, the pieces cannot be disconnected. The three-slot piece beginning with F must either straddle the other piece or be inside of it.

1. (A) violates the first condition
   (B) violates the first condition
   (C) violates the second condition
   (D) Correct
   (E) violates the first condition

2. **(E)** This information, combined with the second condition, creates | FGV |. Since this piece cannot straddle the other one, it has to be inside of it. Accordingly, it could either occupy the second through the fourth slots, or the third through the fifth slots. However, placing it in the third through fifth slots would violate the third condition, since G would be fourth. Therefore, it has to occupy the second through the fourth slots, and V must be fourth.

P	F	G	V	J|M	M|J
1	2	3	4	5	6

3. **(A)** This information, combined with the second condition, creates | FPV_ | – M. Since this super piece takes up at least five slots, we can place F either first or second. When F is first, G has to be fifth (third condition), and M has to be sixth (first condition). When F is second, G could be either first or fifth, thus creating G|J dual options for those slots. In both cases, M is sixth.

F	P	V	J	G	M
G|J	F	P	V	J|G	M
1	2	3	4	5	6

4. **(E)** With J fifth, the first four slots are not enough to accommodate the F _ V piece surrounded by P and M. Therefore, the only acceptable place for M is sixth. If the three-slot piece started at the first slot, P would be second (first condition). G would be fourth, which would violate the third condition. Consequently, the three-slot piece must start at the second slot with G|P dual options in the first and third slots.

F	P	V	G	J	M
G|P	F	P|G	V	J	M
1	2	3	4	5	6

5. Since this question asks what cannot be true, we can use our previous work to disprove some of the answer choices.

   (A) see question #1

   (B) Correct – as the following diagrams show, there is no way to create a scenario that does not violate either the first condition or the second condition

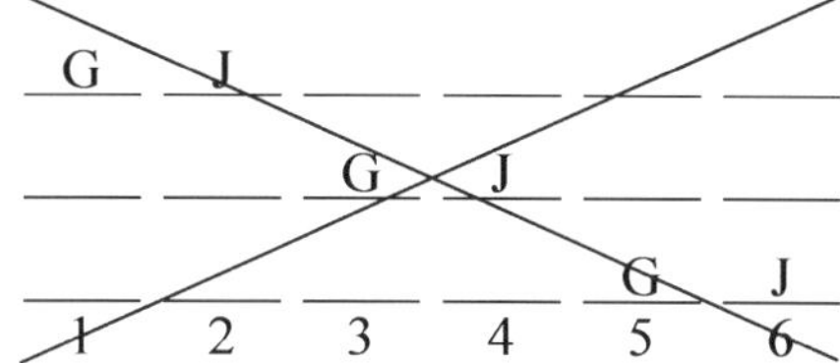

   (C) could happen – see the following diagram

F	P	V	J	G	M
1	2	3	4	5	6

   (D) could happen – see the following diagram

G	P	F	J	V	M
1	2	3	4	5	6

   (E) see question #4

Questions 6-12

Setup:

- six seats: 1 2 3 4 5 6
- six athletes: L M O S V Z
- each athlete rows at exactly one of the seats

Conditions:

#1: M – S

#2:

#3: V

O

Z

Overview:

Combining all three conditions gives the following sketch:

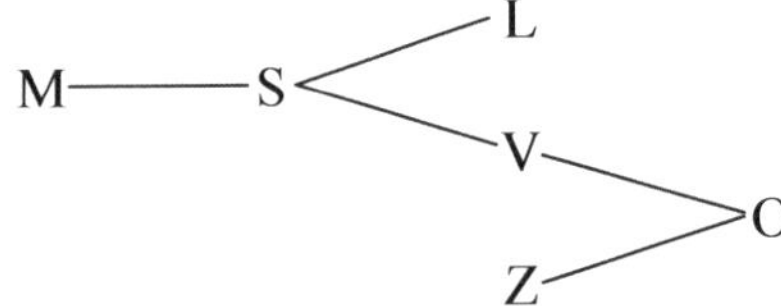

6. (A) violates the third condition (O must follow V)
   (B) if S is third, Z must be first or second
   (C) Correct
   (D) L is preceded by M and S; therefore O would have to be last
   (E) V is preceded by M, S, L, and Z, so it can't be fourth

7. **(E)** Since there are six seats, V has to be followed by exactly one athlete. Since V must be followed by O, O must be sixth.

				V	O
1	2	3	4	5	6

M – S – L, Z

8. **(E)** L must be preceded by M and S (in that order). Since the last three slots are occupied by V, O, and Z, O has to be last, creating V|Z dual options for the fourth and fifth slots.

M	S	L	V|Z	Z|V	O
1	2	3	4	5	6

9. **(A)** As our master sketch shows, S must precede O.

10. **(D)** The only thing concrete we know about Z is that it precedes O. Therefore, it could occupy any one of the slots except for the sixth, and five is the correct answer.

11. **(A)** With this information, we can redraw our sketch. Since none of the other variables precede S, it must immediately follow M.

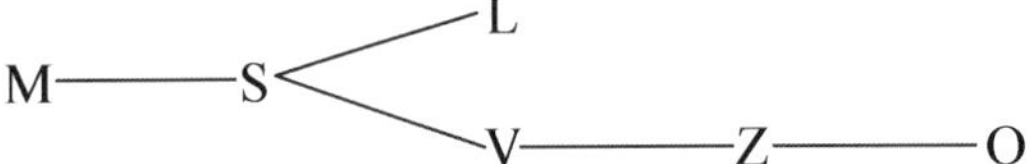

12. **(C)** This condition suspension prompts us to redraw our sketch with S preceding M. Since Z is the only variable that can precede S, S cannot be third, and choice C is therefore correct.

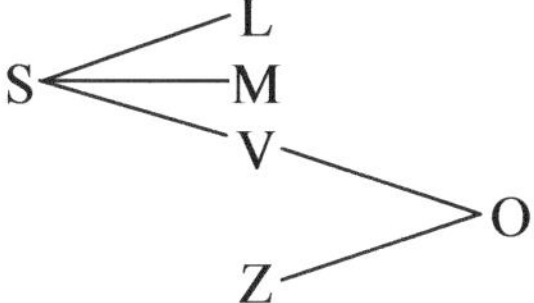

<u>Questions 13-17</u>

Setup:
- six paintings: Q R S T V Z
- three are sold to a museum and three are sold to a private collector
- two are from each of three periods: 1 2 3
- the private collector and museum each buy one painting from each period

Conditions:
#1: S_P – Z_M

#2: T – Q or (T Q)
#3: V_2

Overview:
The periods provide a logical base for the diagram. An important consequence of the second condition is that if T is from the third period, Q is also from the third period.

M ____ |V ____ Z

P ____ V| ____ S

1 2 3

~Z V ~S

13. (A) violates the second condition
(B) Correct
(C) violates the first condition (S needs to be sold to the private collector)
(D) violates the third condition
(E) violates the first condition (S must precede Z)

14. **(B)** Combining this information with the first condition, we can place S in the second slot next to the private collector and Z in the third slot next to the museum. The third condition stipulates that V go in the top slot over the second period. As we're left with Q, R, and T, the answer choice must include two of these, or one of these paired with S. Since B includes R and T, it is correct.

M	___	V	Z
P	___	S	___
	1	2	3

15. **(D)** The first condition precludes Z from being from the first period and the third condition precludes V from being from the first period. Since Z is in choice E, we can immediately eliminate it. Placing any of the other four variables as the first period painting that the private collector buys does not violate any of the conditions, and thus, choice D is correct.

Q: T would be placed as the first period painting the museum purchases
R: we don't have any conditions about R
S: Z would be either the second or third period painting the museum purchases
T: Q would be from the first, second, or third period

16. **(B)** This question revisits the scenario from question number fourteen. If Q were placed in the first period, it wouldn't have any paintings preceding it. Therefore, we have to place Q as the third period painting purchased by the private collector. S is the only variable that matches the criteria in the question stem, and B is correct.

M	T|R	V	Z
P	R|T	S	Q
	1	2	3

17. **(B)** The question stem creates this piece: [ZT]. Due to the first condition, we can place S with the first period paintings and Z and T as the second and third period paintings purchased by the museum. The second condition dictates that Q be placed as a third period painting, leaving R to fill the remaining first period slot. Hence, B must be true.

M	R	Z	T
P	S	V	Q
	1	2	3

Questions 18-22

Setup:
- six lunch trucks
- each sells one of six kinds of food: F H I P S T
- each truck serves one or more of three buildings: X Y Z

Conditions:
#1: F_Y, H_Y, and $\_{}_Y$
#2: exactly 2 Fs
#3: $I_{\#buildings} > S_{\#buildings}$
#4: ~T_Y
#5: 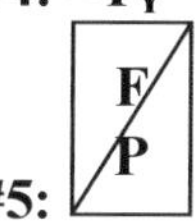

#6: 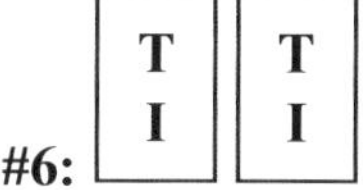

Overview:
Since we're given the exact number of trucks that serve building Y, it makes sense to use the buildings as our base. The first condition tells us to place an F and an H above Y. The fourth condition tells us that the taco truck doesn't serve Y. The fifth condition, combined with our diagram, tells us that the falafel truck doesn't serve Y. Therefore, the third truck to serve Y must be either the ice cream truck or the salad truck. Since we know that the falafel truck serves one of either X and Z (second condition), and the pita truck must serve at least one building (setup conditions), we can place F|P dual options above buildings X and Z. Finally, since the taco truck doesn't serve Y, the sixth condition allows us to place an I and a T above buildings X and Z.

X	Y	Z
------		------
------		------
I	I|S	I
T	F	T
F|P	H	P|F
	~T	
	~P	

18. **(D)** Because of the first condition, we can eliminate A, B and E (they're missing Y). The second condition rules out the possibility of all three buildings being served by the falafel truck, and choice D is therefore correct.

19. **(C)** Since the ice cream truck serves both X and Z, and the pita truck serves either X or Z, it must be true that at least one of X and Z is served by both trucks.

20. **(E)** Since we already know that the ice cream truck serves two of the buildings, the hot dog truck must serve all three. We can also definitively place an S in the final slot for building Y. As a result, the ice cream truck and the taco truck must serve buildings X and Y.

X	Y	Z
H		H
I	S	I
T	F	T
F|P	H	P|F

21. **(A)** Neither the falafel nor the pita truck can serve all three buildings, since they cannot both serve any particular building. Due to the third condition, the salad truck cannot serve all three buildings. Finally, the fourth condition precludes the taco truck from serving all three buildings. Thus, we're left with the hot dog truck and the ice cream truck as the only two that can serve all the buildings

22. **(C)** Since the falafel truck has to serve one of X and Z (second condition), the pita truck cannot serve both of these buildings. Hence, choice C is correct.

Questions 1-6

Setup:
- seven different meetings
- each meeting is with exactly one of five dignitaries
- dignitaries: F M R S T

Conditions:
#1: F – F – F; one with each of the other dignitaries

#2: 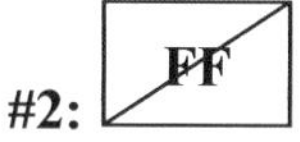

#3: **TS**

#4: ~M_1 and ~M_7

Overview:
Although we cannot infer much from the conditions, it is clear that the first and third conditions will play a large role in the questions since collectively they represent five of the seven slots.

1	2	3	4	5	6	7
~M						~M
~S						~T

1. (A) violates the first condition (only two meetings with F)
   (B) violates the second condition
   (C) Correct
   (D) violates the third condition
   (E) violates the fourth condition

2. **(D)** This new information leaves us with six slots for the three F meetings and the TS piece. Since the F meetings can't be back to back, they have to be first and sixth, and either third or fourth. If the second meeting with F is placed fourth, the meeting with M is fifth, and choice D is therefore correct.

F	T	S	F	M	F	R
F	M	F	T	S	F	R
1	2	3	4	5	6	7

3. **(E)** Due to the second condition and the TS piece, Garibaldi must also meet with F seventh. We can place the final F either fourth or fifth. According to these two placement options, Garibaldi could either meet with F or S fourth.

M|R	F	T	S	F	R|M	F
M|R	F	R|M	F	T	S	F
1	2	3	4	5	6	7

4. **(E)** This new information creates an even larger piece: [TSR]. Combining this with the second condition, we need to place Fs first and seventh. The final F will be either third or fifth. Therefore, choice E must be true.

F	M	F	T	S	R	F
F	T	S	R	F	M	F
1	2	3	4	5	6	7

5. **(D)** Due to the third condition, S must be second. The second condition dictates that we place Fs in the third, fifth, and seventh slots. This creates M|R dual options in the fourth and sixth slots. Hence, D could be true.

T	S	F	M|R	F	R|M	F
1	2	3	4	5	6	7

6. **(A)** With this information, we have an extra piece with which to contend: [RM]. The only way to accommodate this piece along with the TS piece without violating the second condition is to place the Fs first, fourth, and seventh. The placements of these two pieces create two possible solutions for this scenario.

F	T	S	F	R	M	F
F	R	M	F	T	S	F
1	2	3	4	5	6	7

Questions 7-12

Setup:
- six dogs: G H K L P S
- two placed each of three days: M T W

Conditions:

#1: 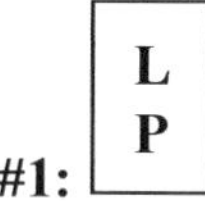

#2: 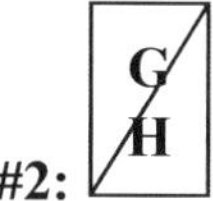

#3: $K_M \longrightarrow G_T$; $\sim G_T \longrightarrow \sim K_M$ (contrapositive)
#4: $S_W \longrightarrow H_T$; $\sim H_T \longrightarrow \sim S_W$ (contrapositive)

Overview:
Combining the first two conditions, we can create two acceptable pairings of dogs. G can either be paired with K or S.

#1 _L_ _K_ _S_ **#2** _L_ _S_ _K_

_P_ _G_ _H_ _P_ _G_ _H_

Including the conditionals, our diagram with the days is:

____ ____ ____

____ ____ ____
M T W
K⟶G
S⟵H

7. (A) violates the first condition
   (B) violates the third condition
   (C) violates the second condition
   (D) violates the fourth condition
   (E) Correct

8. Since the answer choices only specify pairings, we can check them against our molds. Another way to approach this question would be to do it after completing all the questions that present new information.
   (A) the first mold disproves this choice
   (B) Correct
   (C) the first mold disproves this choice
   (D) the first mold disproves this choice
   (E) the first mold disproves this choice

9. **(A)** Due to the first condition, we know that the L must also be placed on Tuesday. With both Tuesday slots filled, we cannot trigger the third or fourth conditions, as triggering either would require an additional slot, which we don't have. Therefore, we must place K on Wednesday and H on Monday. This creates G|H dual options for Monday and Wednesday, and thus, choice A could be true.

G|H	L	H|G
S	P	K
M	T	W

10. **(E)** This new information tells us that the pairings are consistent with the first mold. It's a safe bet that some of the later answer choices will present information that will separate one of the pairs. We can try to disprove E by placing S on Wednesday. However, this triggers the fourth condition, which would split up S and H. Therefore, choice E is correct.

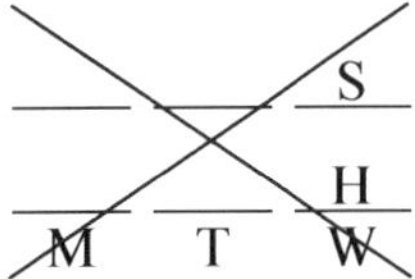

11. **(D)** Since H and S are not paired, the pairings will be consistent with the second mold. We can place the HS piece on either Monday and Tuesday or Tuesday and Wednesday. This creates two possible solutions. Due to the pairing of L and P, P cannot be placed on Tuesday under either scenario.

K	G	L		L	K	G
H	S	P	or	P	H	S
M	T	W		M	T	W

12. **(A)** As in the previous question, this can happen on either Monday and Tuesday, or Tuesday and Wednesday. With the piece occupying slots on Monday and Tuesday, H must be placed on Wednesday (second condition). Since neither conditional can be triggered, K must be placed on Wednesday. With the piece occupying slots on Tuesday and Wednesday, the second condition dictates that H is placed on Monday. We can create K|S dual options for the open slots on Monday and Tuesday. Under either scenario, H cannot be placed on Tuesday, and choice A is correct.

S	L	K		K|S	S|K	L
G	P	H	or	H	G	P
M	T	W		M	T	W

Questions 13-17

Setup:
- five archaeological sites
- each site discovered by one of three archaeologists: F G O
- each dates from one of three centuries (A.D.) : 8 9 10

Conditions:
#1: second site is from the 9th century
#2: ~O_4 and ~O_5
#3: exactly one G; [10 / G]
#4: 8 ⟶ [8 / O]; ~O ⟶ ~8 (contrapositive)
#5: third site is from a more recent century than the first and the fourth

Overview:
With five conditions, we can be sure there are immediate inferences to be made. Combining the second condition with the contrapositive of the fourth condition, we can infer that the fourth and fifth sites are from either the 9th or the 10th century. Due to the fifth condition, the fourth site has to be from the 9th century, and the first site has to be from the 8th or 9th century. We can also definitively place a 10 over the third site visited. Combining the inference about the fourth site with the second and third conditions, we can place an F on the fourth site. Finally, since neither of the first two sites are from the 10th century, they cannot have been discovered by G (third condition), and we can place F|O dual options in both slots.

8|9	9	10	9	9|10
F|O	F|O		F	F|G
1	2	3	4	5
~G	~G		~O	~O
			~G	

13. (A) violates the first condition
    (B) violates the inference that G didn't discover either of the first two sites
    (C) violates the inference that G didn't discover either of the first two sites
    (D) violates the third condition (there can only be one G)
    (E) Correct

14. **(C)** Combining this new information with the third condition allows us to place a G in the third slot. With only one of the sites from the 10th century, the fifth site must have been discovered in the 9th century. Due to the third condition, we can place an F in the fifth slot.

8|9	9	10	9	9
F|O	F|O	G	F	F
1	2	3	4	5
~G	~G		~O	~O
			~G	

15. **(A)** As our master diagram shows, the first site visited is the only one that can date from the 8th century.

16. **(E)** Our master diagram shows that the first, second, and fourth sites cannot have been discovered by G.

17. **(D)** This question tests our command of the possible allocations. Since there's exactly one G, and neither the setup nor the conditions specify that O must have discovered any of the sites, the maximum number of sites that F could have discovered is four.

Questions 18-22

Setup:
- five-day workweek: M T W Th F
- three parking lots: X Y Z
- each lot has a different price
- three prices: 10 12 15
- she visits each of the lots at least once during the workweek

Conditions:
#1: 15_{Th}
#2: $X_{price} > Z_{price}$
#3: W: 12|15; F: 10|12
#4: #Z > #X

Overview:
Combining the first two conditions, we know that Z cannot be placed on Thursday, and we can place an X|Y dual option there. We can also figure out the possible allocations. Combining the condition that she must visit each of the lots during the week with the fourth condition, she can either visit Z twice or three times. The following table summarizes the possible allocations of days to lots.

X	Y	Z
1	2	2
1	1	3

The second condition limits the lot pricing, and we can note the possibilities.

X	Y	Z
~10	10	10
12	12	12
15	15	~15

___	___	12|15	15	10|12	10 12 15
___	___	___	___	___	X Y Z
M	T	W	Th	F	
			~Z		

18. **(A) Correct**
    (B) violates the combination of the second and third conditions
    (C) she can only park once in lot X
    (D) she didn't park in lot Y
    (E) Z can't be fourth due to the second condition

19. **(E)** Due to the third condition, choice E is correct.

20. **(E)** Combining this new information with the second condition, we can group each of the lots with its respective price: X: \$15; Y: \$10; Z: \$12. Since both acceptable allocations include only one X, we can place an X on the Thursday slot. Since we already have an X, the Wednesday lot has to be \$12, and it is therefore Z. Finally, due to the third condition, the Friday lot has to be \$10, which means that it is lot Y. Hence, E is correct.

___	___	12	15	10
___	___	Z	X	Y
M	T	W	Th	F

21. **(D)** The first and second conditions dictate that she cannot park in lot Z on Thursday.

22. **(C)** Since Wednesday and Thursday cannot be the days she parks in the $10 lot (see our original diagram), we can eliminate choices D and E immediately. None of the answer choices has Friday, so we can place a 15 above the Wednesday lot and a 12 above the Friday lot. Could either Monday or Tuesday be the only day she parks in the $10 lot? Our two tables indicate that if she parks in exactly one $10 lot during the week., it must be lot Y. Thus, the allocation would be X, Y, Z, Z, Z. However, since Z can be either $10 or $12, and we have a maximum of two slots that could be $12 under this scenario (Friday along with one of Monday and Tuesday), we can rule out this possibility. Therefore, we can eliminate choices A and B, leaving C as the correct answer. The following diagram proves the validity of choice C.

10	10	15	15	12
Z	Z	Y	Y	X
M	T	W	Th	F

Questions 1-6

Setup:
- five clients + workout: R S T U W Y
- 6 hours: 1:00 2:00 3:00 4:00 5:00 6:00

Conditions:
#1: S – W
#2: W – T
#3: 

#4: U – R

Overview:
We can combine the first three conditions into the following chain:

1. (A) violates the first condition
   (B) violates the second condition
   (C) violates the third condition
   (D) violates the fourth condition
   (E) Correct

2. **(B)** S and U are the only two who can be first, and hence, B is correct.

3. **(C)** If we place U third, it must be followed by the YW|WY piece, T, and R. However, we only have six slots, making this an unacceptable scenario.

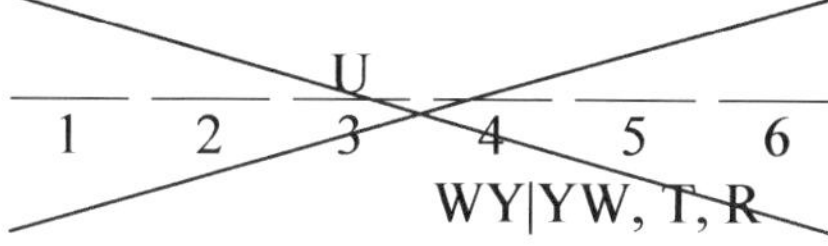

4. **(D)** Combining this information with the third condition creates the following piece:

   SYW. Under this scenario, the meeting with Y will require at least two slots after it, in order to accommodate W and T. Placing this meeting fifth violates this condition, and D is therefore correct.

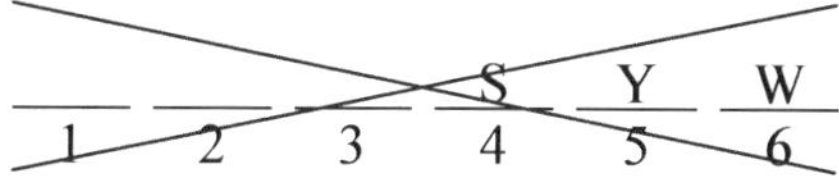

5. **(B)** Combining this new information with our initial sketch, we know that S must be first with W|Y dual options in the second and third slots. Due to the fourth condition, we can place U fifth and R sixth. Choice B is therefore correct.

S	W|Y	Y|W	T	U	R
1	2	3	4	5	6

6. This question tests our understanding of the WY connection. Although W has been removed from the answer choices, it has to be next to Y.

    (A) W precedes S, which violates the first condition
    (B) T precedes W, which violates the second condition
    (C) violates the fourth condition
    (D) T precedes W, which violates the second condition
    (E) Correct - see the following diagram

S	U	R	W|Y	Y|W	T
1	2	3	4	5	6

Questions 7-11

Setup:

- six people: L N O P S T
- four games in a row: 1 2 3 4
- two people play in each game
- each person plays in at least one game

Conditions:

#1: ~T_1 and ~T_2
#2: L_4

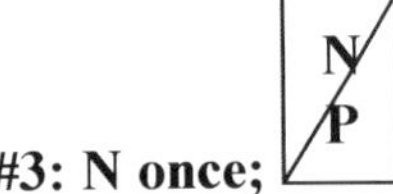

#3: N once;

#4: S twice; SOS **; O once**

Overview:
Because the SOS piece occupies slots in three consecutive games, we can create two molds: one with it occupying slots in the first, second, and third games, and another with it occupying slots in the second, third, and fourth games.

#1

	T|		|T
S	O	S	L
1	2	3	4
~T		~T	

#2

	T		L
	S	O	S
1	2	3	4
~T		~T	

Mold #1: When the SOS piece starts at the first game, T can be placed either second or fourth.

Mold #2: When the SOS piece starts at the second game, T must be placed in the second game.

Because of T's restricted nature, he can only play against O, L, and S. The fourth condition tells us that S plays in exactly two games. This condition, coupled with eight slots and six players, tells us that one of the other players plays in two games. That player cannot be N, due to the third condition. It cannot be O either, due to the fourth condition. Therefore, the other player who plays in two games is either L, P, or T.

7. **(A) Correct**
   (B) violates the first condition
   (C) violates the third condition (N cannot play in two games)
   (D) violates the third condition (N cannot play in two games)
   (E) violates the second condition

8. **(A) Correct – see the following diagram**

P	T	L	N
S	O	S	L
1	2	3	4

   (B) violates the third condition (N must play in exactly one game)
   (C) violates the fourth condition
   (D) violates the fourth condition
   (E) violates the first condition

9. This condition tells us to use the first mold.

   (A) Correct – see the following diagram

P	N	L	T
S	O	S	L
1	2	3	4

   (B) O only plays in the second game
   (C) S plays in the first and third games
   (D) N can only play against O or S
   (E) P can only play against O and/or S

10. **(A) Correct – see the following diagram**

P	T	N	L
L	S	O	S
1	2	3	4

   (B) violates the third condition
   (C) violates the fourth condition
   (D) stands in the way of the SOS piece
   (E) violates the second condition

11. **(C)** As we originally inferred, T can only play against O, L, or S. Therefore, he cannot play against N and P, and C is correct.

12. **(E)** The question tells us to use the second mold. T has to play in the second game, and E is therefore correct.

Questions 13-17

Setup:
- seven friends: R S T U W Y Z
- friends will appear alone or in group photographs with one another

Conditions:
#1: S ⟶ W; ~W ⟶ ~S (contrapositive)
#2: U ⟶ S; ~S ⟶ ~U (contrapositive)
#3: ~Y ⟶ R; ~R ⟶ Y (contrapositive)
#4: W ⟶ ~T; T ⟶ ~W (contrapositive)
W ⟶ ~R; R ⟶ ~W (contrapositive)

Overview:
Using our diagram, we can make the necessary inferences as we work through the questions.

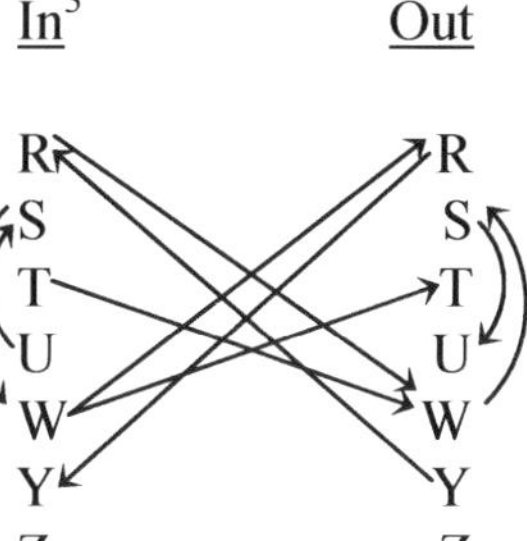

13. (A) violates the fourth condition
    (B) Correct
    (C) violates the fourth condition
    (D) violates the first condition
    (E) violates the first condition

14. **(E)** Following the chain from T, we know that W, S, and U are not in the photograph. E, therefore, must be true.

15. **(D)** Following the chain from Y being out, we know that R is in, and W, S, and U are all out. To maximize the remaining variables, we can add in T and Z, neither of which violates any conditions. Therefore, D is correct.

16. **(B)** When Z is in, no conditions are triggered. Following the chain from U, we know that S and W are in, and that R and T are out. Since R is out, Y must be in. Since S, W, and Y are in with U and Z, the correct answer is B.

17. **(A)** Following the chain from S, W has to be in, R and T are out, and Y is in. However, this places four friends (S, Z, W, and Y) in the photograph, thus violating the question stem.

Questions 18-22

Setup:
- three nations: X Y Z
- each nation exports two crops
- five crops: O R S T W
- each crop is exported by at least one of the nations

[3] Visit Manhattan LSAT (http://www.manhattanlsat.com) to learn more about using this diagram.

Conditions:

#1: W/O (not together)

#2: $X_S \longleftrightarrow Y_S$

#3: $Y_R \longrightarrow X_T$ **and** Z_T; $\sim X_T$ **or** $\sim Z_T \longrightarrow \sim Y_R$ **(contrapositive)**

#4: $Y \neq Z$

Overview:

Since we have six slots and five crops, the allocation of slots to crops is 2, 1, 1, 1, 1, and one crop must be exported by two nations. Due to the second condition, whenever soybeans are exported by either X or Y, soybeans will represent the 2 in the allocation. We can also infer that the second and third conditions cannot both be triggered in any acceptable solution, since this would create a situation in which soybeans and tea are both exported by two nations. Therefore, when Y exports rice, Z must export soybeans. Conversely, when either X or Y exports soybeans, either X or Z must export rice. Consequently, Y cannot export both rice and soybeans. Including the conditional conditions along with this inference, our diagram looks like this:

```
____  ____≠____

____  ____≠____
  X     Y     Z
  S⟷S
  T⟵R⟶T
     R/S (not together)
```

18. **(A) Correct**
    (B) violates the third condition
    (C) violates the first condition
    (D) violates the fourth condition
    (E) violates the second condition

19. Combining this information with the second condition, we know that Y also exports soybeans. Since we only have three slots left, oranges, rice, and wheat must occupy them.

(A) Correct - see the following diagram

S	S ≠	R
T	O ≠	W
X	Y	Z

(B) Z would have to export O and W, which violates the first condition
(C) none of the three slots can contain T
(D) none of the three slots can contain S
(E) none of the three slots can contain T

20. **(E)** Since Z doesn't export soybeans, one of X and Y must export soybeans. Due to the second condition, we know that both X and Y export soybeans. With two open slots, we need to place oranges and rice. Pairing rice with Y would place oranges with X. However, it would also trigger the third condition, placing tea with X when there is not a slot to accommodate it. Therefore, we must place rice with X and oranges with Y. Hence, E must be true, and the other choices cannot be true.

S	S ≠	T
R	O ≠	W
X	Y	Z

21. **(C)** Due to the second condition, if X exported soybeans, Y would also export soybeans. However, since Z exports soybeans, this condition violates the fourth condition. Choice C also presents an allocation impossibility, since we know that none of the crops are exported by all three countries.

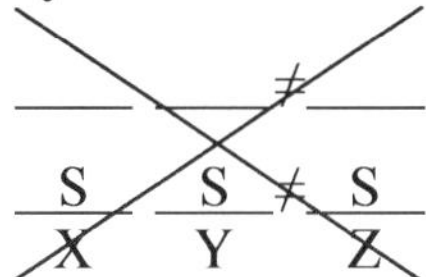

22. **(C)** Choice C presents a scenario which triggers the third condition, and then violates the fourth condition. Since Y exports rice, both X and Z export tea. However, Y already exports tea, thereby violating the fourth condition. Choice C also presents an allocation impossibility, since we know that a single crop cannot be exported by all three countries.

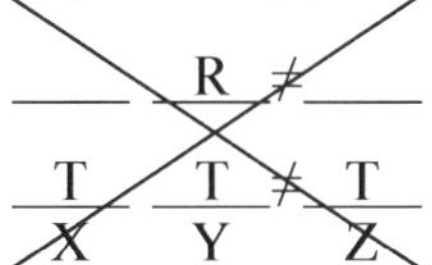

Questions 1-6

Setup:
- six guideposts: 1 2 3 4 5 6
- six animals: F G H L M P

Conditions:
#1: G_3 or G_4
#2: M – H
#3: F – L – M

Overview:
We can combine the second and third conditions into the following chain: F – L – M – H. Displaying the two possible placements of G, our diagram looks like this:

		G|	|G		
1	2	3	4	5	6

1. **(A) Correct**
   (B) violates the first condition
   (C) violates the third condition
   (D) violates the third condition
   (E) violates the second condition

2. **(A)** Since F must be followed by at least three variables and G is either third or fourth (first condition), the latest F can be is second.

3. **(D)** Combining this information with the third condition reveals that F must be first and L must be second. Due to the first condition, G must be fourth. With dual H|P options for the fifth and sixth slots, the lowest numbered post P can occupy is the fifth one.

F	L	M	G	H|P	P|H
1	2	3	4	5	6

4. **(A)** M cannot be last, since it is followed by H. It cannot be first or second, since it is preceded by both F and L. Combining this with the new information creates G|M dual options in the second and third slots, which forces F into the first slot and L into the second slot.

F	L	G|M	M|G	H|P	P|H
1	2	3	4	5	6
~M	~M			~M	~M

5. **(E)** The only variable that is not restricted by any of the conditions is P, and E is therefore correct.

6. **(A)** Combining this information with the other conditions reveals that the LM piece can be placed either second and third or fourth and fifth. A is the only one of the choices that could be true.

F	L	M	G	H|P	P|H
F|P	P|F	G	L	M	H
1	2	3	4	5	6

Questions 7-11

Setup:
- four cassette tapes: 1 2 3 4
- two sides each
- each side contains exactly one of four genres
- genres: F H J R

Conditions:
#1: F F H H J J R R
#2: Tape 1 has J on one side, but neither H nor R
#3: Tape 2 has no J
#4: F not one higher than R

Overview:
The second condition dictates that the second side of Tape 1 must be either folk or jazz.

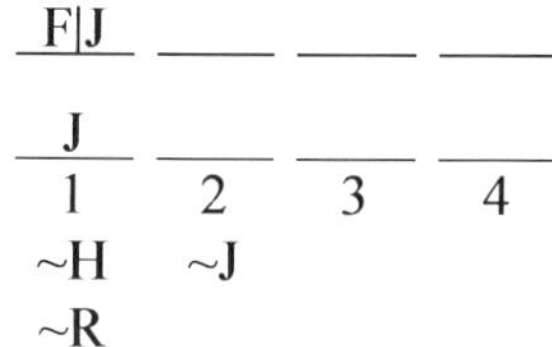

7. (A) violates the third condition
   (B) Correct
   (C) Tapes 1 and 2 violate the fourth condition
   (D) violates the second condition
   (E) Tapes 3 and 4 violate the fourth condition

8. (A) R could be presented on either Tape 2 or Tape 3, as long as that tape didn't precede a tape with F
   (B) H could be featured solely on Tape 4

J	F	R	H
J	F	R	H
1	2	3	4

   (C) Correct – if Tape 2 has two sides of R, Tape 3 cannot feature F, due to the fourth condition. Since we have two Fs to place, at least one of them must be on Tape 4.

F|J	R		
J	R		F
1	2	3 ~F	4

   (D) violates the third condition
   (E) our diagram for choice B proves this answer incorrect

9. (A) this would force either Tapes 2 and 3 or Tapes 3 and 4 to violate the fourth condition
   (B) Correct – the second side of Tape 1 would have to be F, and one of the remaining slots would be F and the other two Rs

F	F|R	J	F|R
J	R	H	F|R
1	2	3	4

   (C) with both Fs accounted for, the second side of Tape 1 would be J, leaving no available J for Tape 4
   (D) if Tape 3 has one side of J, the second side of Tape 1 has to be F, which means that Tape 4 could not have two sides of F
   (E) violates the third condition

10. (A) violates the second condition
    (B) violates the third condition
    (C) Correct – see the following diagram

F	H	J	R
J	R	H	F
1	2	3	4

    (D) violates the second condition
    (E) this would violate the fourth condition, since one side of R would have to be on either Tape 2 or Tape 3

11. **(B)** This cannot be true question poses a number of scenarios. Since the fourth condition has played a big role thus far, keep a close eye on any situation that triggers it. In choice B, with both Rs placed and both Hs placed, we're left with two Fs and one J. Since at least one F has to go on Tape 4, the fourth condition is broken.

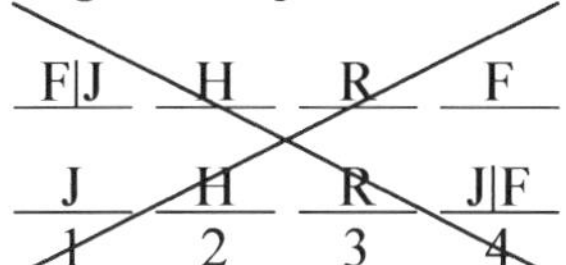

Questions 12-16

Setup:
- five towns: J L N O P
- storm is the only form of precipitation
- two types of precipitation: H R
- the storm passes over each town once and doesn't pass two towns at the same time

Conditions:

#1: P_3

#2: H_2

#3: 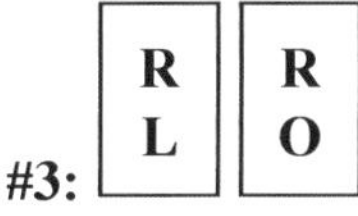

#4: L, N > J

Overview:
Combining the second and third conditions, we know that neither L nor O can be second. Due to the fourth condition, J cannot be second. As a result, N must occupy the second slot. Since L must precede J (fourth condition), we can set up three molds: two with L first and one with L fourth. These represent all the acceptable orderings of towns.

#1

R	H			R
L	N	P	J	O
1	2	3	4	5

#2

R	H		R	
L	N	P	O	J
1	2	3	4	5

#3

R	H		R	
O	N	P	L	J
1	2	3	4	5

Molds #1 and #2: With L first, dual J|O options are created for the fourth and fifth slots, giving us two orderings of towns.

Mold #3: With L occupying the fourth slot, the fourth condition stipulates that J be placed fifth, and O must occupy the first slot.

12. **(A) Correct**
    (B) N must to be second
    (C) N must to be second
    (D) N must to be second
    (E) N must to be second

13. This could happen under either the second or the third mold. We only need to check the choices against them.
    (A) see mold #3
    (B) see mold #3
    (C) Correct – in both molds, the fourth town receives only rain
    (D) see mold #3
    (E) could happen under either mold

14. **(E)** This could only happen under the third mold. Due to the condition imposed by the question, we know that J must receive only rain. Only choice E could be false.

R	H	H|R	R	R
O	N	P	L	J
1	2	3	4	5

15. **(D)** This could only happen under the first mold. Since the fourth town can receive both hail and rain, or rain only, choice D could be false.

16. **(B)** This question triggers the third mold, and therefore, choice B must be true.

<u>Questions 17-23</u>

Setup:

- secret committee
- six members: F G H I M P
- each member serves on at least one subcommittee
- three subcommittees, each with three members

Conditions:
#1: one member serves on all three subcommittees

#2: 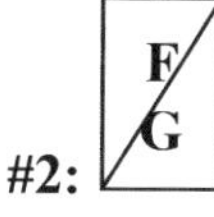

#3: 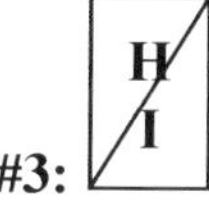

Overview:
Although the committee names and/or numbers don't play a role, it's helpful to include numbers in the master diagram for clarity. Boxing the bottom three slots helps in visualizing the first condition. Since there are five additional members and six remaining slots, one of those five has to be on two subcommittees. The allocation of subcommittees to members is therefore 3, 2, 1, 1, 1, 1. Due to the second and third conditions, F, G, H, and I cannot be the member who is on three subcommittees. That member has to be either M or P, and we can represent this on our diagram with M|P dual options.

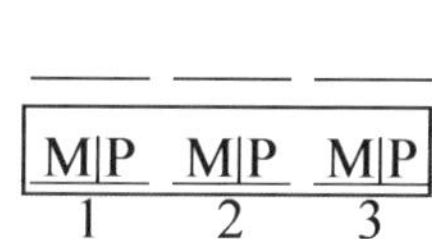

17. **(C)** Combining this information with our inference regarding the first condition, we know that M is not the member who is on three subcommittees. Since P is on three subcommittees, every other member must be on at least one subcommittee with him or her. Therefore, choice C must be true.

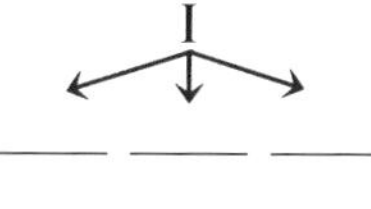

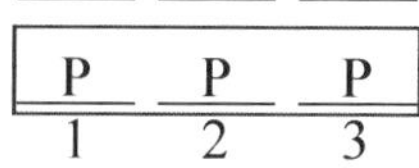

18. Combining this new information with the second condition, we know that P has to either serve on two or three subcommittees. If P serves on two subcommittees, then M would serve on three subcommittees. Plugging this and the new information into our diagram, we run into a situation in which H is paired with I, which violates the third condition. Therefore, we can confidently deduce that P serves on all three subcommittees. Since only one member is on all three subcommittees, we can eliminate choices D and E.

    (A) this would fill four slots, causing H and I to be paired together
    (B) this would fill four slots, causing F and G to be paired together
    (C) Correct – see the following diagram

1	2	3
H	H	M
F	G	I
P	P	P

    (D) see above
    (E) see above

19. Since only one member is on all three subcommittees, we can deduce that in this scenario, it is not M, but is P. Could M be on two subcommittees? No, because we can't have both I and M on two subcommittees each. Therefore, M must be on one subcommittee.

    (A) see above
    (B) Correct – see the following diagram

1	2	3
F	G	M
H	I	I
P	P	P

    (C) since P serves on all three subcommittees, this is not possible
    (D) with four slots left, one of F, G, H, or I would have to fill two slots, thereby violating the second or third condition
    (E) with four slots left, one of F, G, H, or I would have to fill two slots, thereby violating the second or third condition

20. **(D)** If P were on all three subcommittees, he or she would be on every subcommittee on which I and M served, validating that choice D could be true.

21. **(E)** Since either M or P is on all three subcommittees, it follows that they are on a subcommittee together.

22. **(D)** This question tests us on the allocation inference that we made at the beginning of the game. It follows that there is one member who serves on exactly two subcommittees.

Questions 1-5

Setup:

- seven products: P Q R S T W X
- each advertised exactly once

Conditions:

#1: Q – W

#2: [RX]

#3: 

#4: S_1 or S_7

#5: Q_4 or T_4

Overview:
The sequencing conditions allow us to place a few not laws under the first and seventh slots. Incorporating the fourth and fifth conditions, our diagram looks like this:

S|			Q|T			|S
1	2	3	4	5	6	7
~W						~Q
~X						~R

1. **(E)** As we have already noted, neither W nor X can be placed first and X is the only one of the two listed in the choices. Choice E is therefore correct.

2. Combining this new information with the first and second conditions creates the following: [RXQ] – W.

    (A) Correct – see the following diagram

T	R	X	Q	P|W	W|P	S
1	2	3	4	5	6	7

    (B) R must be followed by at least three variables
    (C) Q is before W
    (D) the earliest Q can be is third
    (E) the RXQ piece must begin at the first or second slot, thereby filling the second slot

3. (A) this would force X into the fourth slot, violating the fifth condition
   (B) this violates the fifth condition
   (C) Correct – see the following diagram

S	P	T	Q	W	R	X
1	2	3	4	5	6	7

   (D) this would force Q into the first slot (first condition) and S into the seventh slot (fourth condition), but T can't be fourth (third condition), thus violating the fifth condition
   (E) X has follow directly after R (second condition)

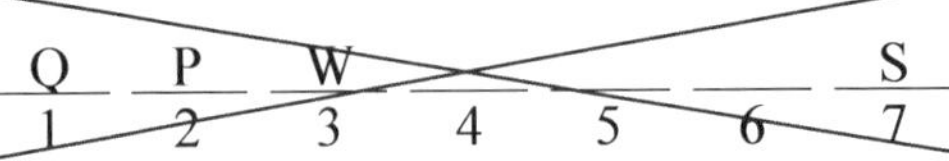

4. **(A) Correct – see the following diagram**

S	R	X	T	Q	P	W
1	2	3	4	5	6	7

   (B) violates the first condition
   (C) would place X fourth, which violates the fifth condition
   (D) Q would have to be first or second, placing T fourth, thus violating the third condition
   (E) R would have to be fourth, which violates the fifth condition

5. **(D)** Combining this information with the second condition, we can place X seventh. The fourth condition tells us that, since S isn't seventh, it is first. Our diagram from question number three provides a shortcut to the answer. If T were fourth, W would have to be second due to the third condition. However, the first condition tells us that Q must precede W, so this can't happen. Conversely, with Q in the fourth position, W must be fifth, due to the first condition.

S	P|T	T|P	Q	W	R	X
1	2	3	4	5	6	7

<u>Questions 6-11</u>

Setup:
- seven switches: 1 2 3 4 5 6 7
- each switch is either on or off
- the circuit load is the total number of switches that are on

Conditions:
#1: 1 ⟶ ~3; 3 ⟶ ~1 (contrapositive)
1 ⟶ ~5; 5 ⟶ ~1 (contrapositive)
#2: 4 ⟶ ~2; 2 ⟶ ~4 (contrapositive)
4 ⟶ ~5; 5 ⟶ ~4 (contrapositive)
#3: switch with the number that equals the circuit load is on

Overview:
Our diagram will allow us to make the necessary inferences as we work through the questions.

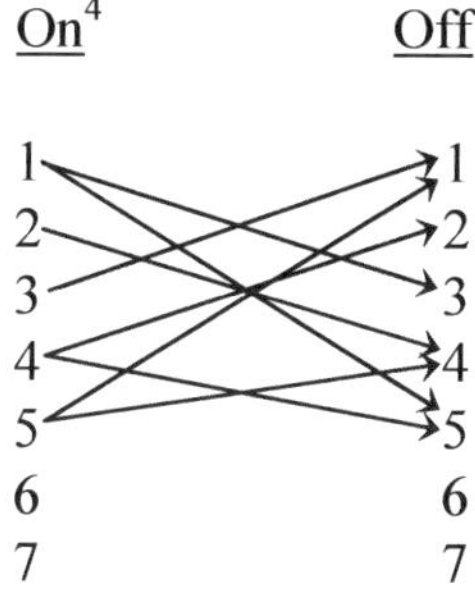

6. (A) violates the second condition
   (B) Correct
   (C) violates the third condition (3 isn't on)
   (D) violates the first condition
   (E) violates the first condition

7. Tackling this question quickly involves a key deduction. Out of the remaining switches, which ones can act as the circuit load indicator? Switch 2 can, if it is paired with one other switch. Switch 4 cannot act as the circuit load indicator since, if it's on, 2 and 5 are off, leaving a maximum of three on. Switch 5 similarly cannot act as the circuit load indicator since this would require all five remaining switches to be on, which can't happen. Therefore, the circuit load indicator has to be switch 2.
   (A) Correct – they would be the only two switches on
   (B) 2 and 5 would be off, leaving a maximum of three switches, but 1, 2, and 3 are all off, leaving no switch to act as the circuit load indicator
   (C) this creates the same problem as choice B
   (D) missing switch 2
   (E) missing switch 2

8. **(B)** Due to the third condition, switch 2 has to be on. However, if switch 4 is on, switch 2 has to be off, thus violating the condition in the question stem.

9. **(C)** If either switch 1 or switch 4 is on, two other switches must be off. Therefore, to maximize the circuit load, we should leave both 1 and 4 off. We're left with the solution 2, 3, and 5, which abides by all the conditions, and three is therefore the maximum circuit load under this scenario.

[4] Visit Manhattan LSAT (http://www.manhattanlsat.com) to learn more about using this diagram.

10. **(C)** Due to the first and second conditions, switches 1 and 4 must be off, eliminating choices A and D. We're left with 2, 3, and 7. 2 can't be the circuit load indicator (since if it were on, three switches would be on). 7 can't be the circuit load indicator (since we only have five available switches). Therefore, 3 must be the circuit load indicator, and choice C is correct.

11. **(C)** Since switches 1 and 2, when engaged, both cause two other switches to be off, we should leave them off for this question. With all the other switches turned on, 5 acts as the circuit load indicator, and we've reached the maximum of five switches.

Questions 12-17

Setup:
- five record stores: S T V X Z
- each store carries at least one of four types
- music types: F J O R
- none of the stores carries any other kind of music

Conditions:
#1: J ⟶ exactly 2 stores
#2: T ⟶ R and O only
#3: $S_{\text{\# of types}} > T_{\text{\# of types}}$
#4: X carries the most types
#5: S ⟶ J
#6: V and Z carry different types

Overview:
From the large number of conditions, we know that there are some immediate inferences to be made. Combining the third and the fourth conditions sets up this hierarchy of music types: $X_{\text{\# of types}} > S_{\text{\# of types}} > T_{\text{\# of types}}$. Since T carries two types, we can infer that S carries three types and X carries four types. This inference fills X's slots with all four types. Combining this inference with the first condition and the fifth condition, we can infer that neither V nor Z carries jazz. Since the greatest number of types that V and Z can carry combined is three, and they can't carry any of the same types, the greatest number of types that either one can carry is two. Pairing up V and Z to visually represent the sixth condition, our diagram looks like this:

S	T	X	V		Z
		R			
___		O			
___	O	J	......	≠	......
J	R	F	___	≠	___
S	T	X	V		Z
			~J		~J

12. (A) violates the fifth condition
    (B) violates the second condition
    (C) V can't carry three types
    (D) X must carry all four types
    (E) Correct – V would carry rock

13. (A) violates the sixth condition
    (B) violates our inference about V and Z not carrying jazz
    (C) X has to carry jazz
    (D) Correct – see the following diagram

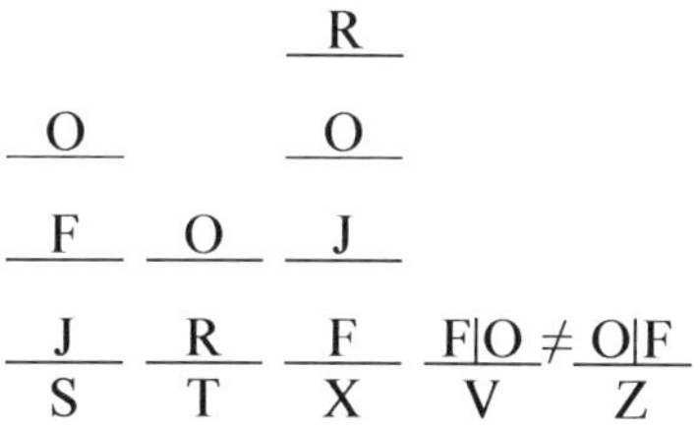

```
                R
   O            O
   F      O     J
   J      R     F     F|O ≠ O|F
   S      T     X      V     Z
```

    (E) X has to carry opera

14. We know that X carries folk, which means that none of the other stores carries folk in this case. This means that S must carry all three of the other types. With neither V nor Z carrying folk and jazz, one must carry opera while the other carries rock.

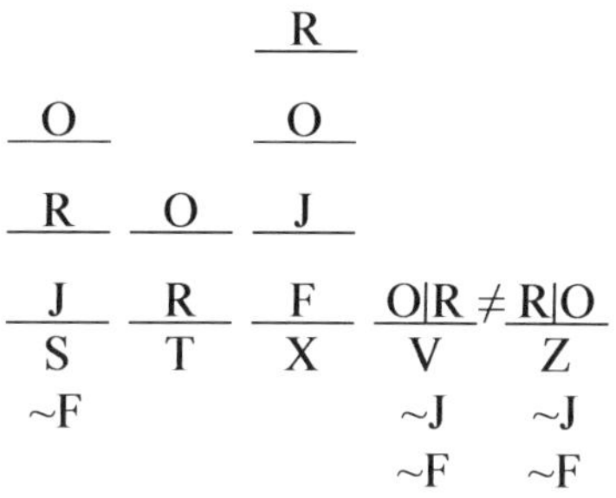

```
                R
   O            O
   R      O     J
   J      R     F     O|R ≠ R|O
   S      T     X      V     Z
  ~F                  ~J    ~J
                      ~F    ~F
```

    (A) V only carries one type
    (B) Correct - this must be true
    (C) V only carries one type
    (D) V only carries one type
    (E) Z only carries one type

15. (A) V can carry only one type
    (B) V could carry two types while Z carries one type or vice versa
    (C) Correct – the master diagram shows that Z can carry a maximum of two types
    (D) this cannot be true, since Z can carry a maximum of two types
    (E) this cannot be true, since X carries four types and S carries three types

16. Combining the new information with the diagram reveals that neither S nor Z can carry rock. This means that S has to carry the other three types. Z must carry either folk or opera, or both.

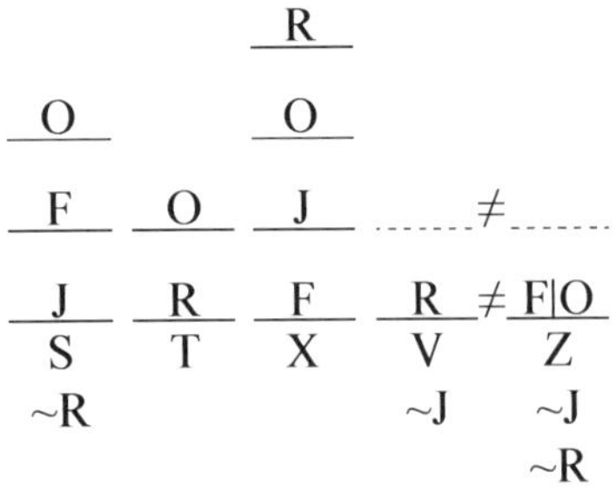

```
                 R
               ____

  O              O
 ____          ____

  F      O       J      .......≠.......
 ____   ____   ____

  J      R       F      R  ≠  F|O
 ____   ____   ____   ____   ____
  S      T       X      V      Z
 ~R                    ~J     ~J
                              ~R
```

(A) this isn't possible under the current scenario
(B) this could be true, but doesn't have to be
(C) Correct – since Z must carry either folk or opera, this must be true
(D) this would only be true if Z carries opera
(E) since V might only carry one type, this doesn't have to be true

17. Combining the new information with our master diagram creates an O|R dual option for S's third slot, and an O|R dual option for Z's first slot.

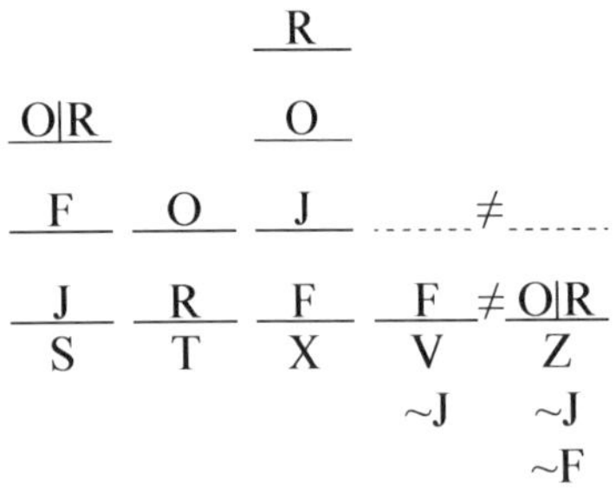

```
                 R
               ____

 O|R             O
 ____          ____

  F      O       J      .......≠.......
 ____   ____   ____

  J      R       F      F  ≠  O|R
 ____   ____   ____   ____   ____
  S      T       X      V      Z
                       ~J     ~J
                              ~F
```

(A) S and T must have either opera or rock in common
(B) Correct – one could carry opera while the other carries rock
(C) T and Z must have either opera or rock in common
(D) S and Z can only have either opera or rock in common
(E) V only has one open slot, so it could only have either opera or rock in common with T

Questions 18-22

Setup:

- five days of the week: M T W Th F
- each staff member works at least one day during the week
- six staff members: J K N O P S
- three supervisors: J N P

Conditions:
#1: exactly two people per day, at least one of whom is a supervisor
#2: O_T and O_W
#3: [NN]
#4: P – S or [S / P]
#5: K ⟶ other staff member's first day; ~other staff member's first day ⟶ ~K (contrapositive)

Overview:
We can set up two rows for each day, one for a supervisor and one for either a non-supervisor or a supervisor. The fourth condition allows us to infer that if S is on Monday, P must be on Monday, and if P's first day is Friday, S must also be on Friday.

	___	O	O	___	___	J K N O P S
Sup	___	___	___	___	___	J N P
	M	T	W	Th	F	
	S ↓ P				P_{first} ↓ S	

18. (A) violates the second condition
    (B) violates the fifth condition
    (C) Correct
    (D) violates the fourth condition
    (E) violates the third condition

19. **(E)** Combining this information with the fifth condition reveals that Thursday is P's first day. Since Thursday's slots are completely filled, the fourth condition stipulates that S must work on Friday, and E is therefore correct.

___	O	O	K	S
___	___	___	P	___
M	T	W	Th	F

20. **(B)** Scanning through the answer choices, B presents an obvious violation. Due to the fifth condition, Friday would have to be P's first day. However, that would not leave a slot for S's first day, thus violating the fourth condition.

21. **(A)** As noted in our diagram, the fourth condition dictates that if we fill both Monday slots, one of which being S, the other would have to be P.

22. (A) violates the third condition
    (B) Correct – see the following diagram

S	O	O	K	J
P	P	J	N	N
M	T	W	Th	F

    (C) since Wednesday is at least O's second day, this violates the fifth condition
    (D) this violates the fifth condition, since Thursday is at least N's second day
    (E) violates the first condition

Questions 1-6

Setup:
- five appliances: H M R T V

Conditions:
#1: H ⟶ ~R; R ⟶ ~H (contrapositive)
#2: H ⟶ ~T; T ⟶ ~H (contrapositive)
#3: V ⟶ ~H; H ⟶ ~V (contrapositive)
V ⟶ ~R; R ⟶ ~V (contrapositive)
V ⟶ ~T; T ⟶ ~V (contrapositive)

Overview:
A key point to notice is that when he uses the vacuum, there are three other appliances that he cannot use. He can therefore use a maximum of two appliances when he uses the vacuum.

1. (A) violates the first condition
   (B) violates the second condition
   (C) Correct
   (D) violates the third condition
   (E) violates the third condition

2. **(E)** If he used the vacuum, he wouldn't be able to use the hairdryer, the razor, or the television. He would only be using the vacuum, thus violating the question stem. If he used the hairdryer, he wouldn't be able to use the razor or the television. This would create a situation in which he would have to use the vacuum, but he can't use the vacuum and the hairdryer (third condition). Therefore, he can't be using the hairdryer or the vacuum.

In	Out
R	M
T	H
	V

V ⟶ ~H, ~R, ~T
H ⟶ ~R, ~T

3. **(E)** This question becomes easy when you look for the most restricted element. If Henri uses the vacuum, he can't use three other appliances. Therefore, the greatest number of appliances he can use along with the vacuum is one and E is proven correct.

4. **(A)** From the second question, we know that he can't use the vacuum, as that would prevent him from using three other appliances. If he used the hairdryer, that would prevent him from using two other appliances and force him to use the vacuum which violates the third condition. Following this line of reasoning, since he can't use the hairdryer or the vacuum, he must use the microwave, razor, and television.

In	Out
M	H
R	V
T	

5. **(A)** The simplest way to tackle this question is to look for the most restricted element. Recalling from the conditions that H ⟶ ~R, ~T it becomes clear that if he is using the hairdryer, it is the only one of the three listed in the question stem that he is using.

6. **(A)** In order for Henri to use 4 appliances simultaneously, he would have to use either the hairdryer or the vacuum. However, using the hairdryer prevents him from using two other appliances and using the vacuum prevents him from using three other appliances. Both of these scenarios leave him using fewer than three appliances, and A is therefore correct.

<u>Questions 7-11</u>

Setup:
- eight separate fields: G H J K L M P T
- each field is harvested once
- no two fields are harvested simultaneously
- harvesting of one field must be complete before harvesting another field

Conditions:

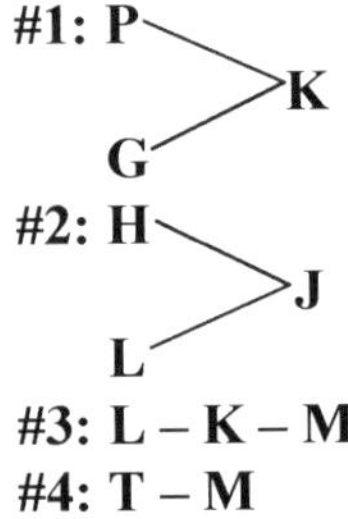

#3: L – K – M
#4: T – M

Overview:
Combining all four conditions, we can create the following master sketch:

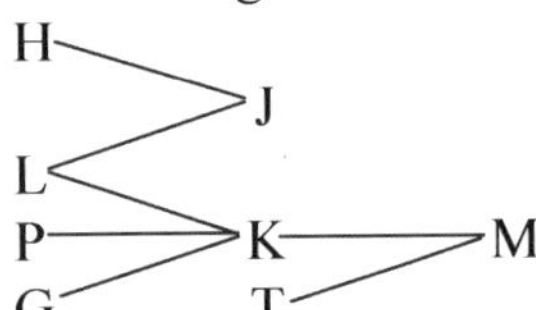

7. (A) violates the second condition
   (B) K must follow at least three others
   (C) Correct – H and J would follow M
   (D) G must come in front of K and M
   (E) T is in front of M

8. **(B)** If M is seventh, only one field follows it. Since the only field that can follow M is J, J has to be eighth. Therefore, J can't be fifth and B is correct.

						M	J
1	2	3	4	5	6	7	8

9. **(C)** Looking at our sketch, M has five fields preceding it. Therefore, it can't be fifth and C is correct.

10. **(E)** With J third, we can create the following diagram:

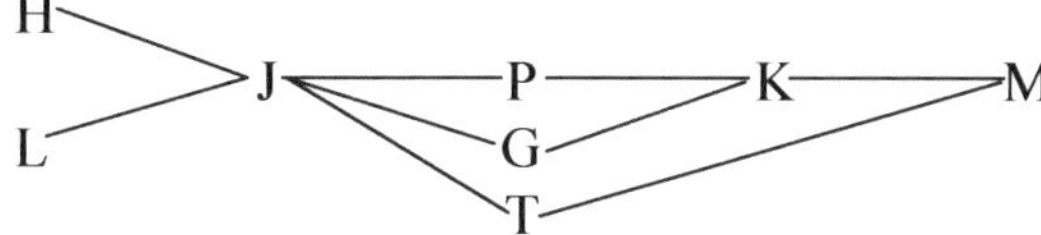

It is important to draw the additional lines as a visual reminder that G and T must both come after J. The only thing that must be true is that M is last, and E is therefore correct.

11. **(D)** The question stem tells us that two fields follow H. Since J must follow H and M follows all the other fields, J|M dual options are created in the seventh and eighth slots, and D must be true.

					H	J|M	M|J
1	2	3	4	5	6	7	8

12. **(E)** If L is fifth, it must be preceded by H, P, G, and T, and followed by J, K, and M. It could be true that M comes before J since we can't infer a direct relationship between the two fields.

				L			
1	2	3	4	5	6	7	8
H, P, G, T					J, K – M		

Questions 13-17

Setup:
- six technicians: S U W X Y Z
- each technician repairs at least one of these three types: R T V

Conditions:
#1: X and exactly three others ⟶ R
#2: Y ⟶ R, V
#3: 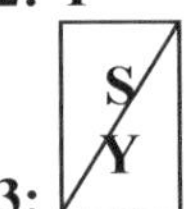
#4: Z more types than Y
#5: 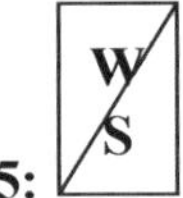
#6: U ⟶ exactly two types

Overview:
The large number of conditions is a big clue that we can make some immediate inferences. Combining the second and third conditions yields the inference that Stacy must repair radios. Since Yolanda repairs two types of machines, the fourth condition tells us that Zane repairs all three types. The only other person who can repair radios is Urma since Wim can't repair the same type as Stacy. According to the sixth condition, Urma must also repair either TVs or VCRs.

U		
S	U|	|U
Z	Z	Z
X	Y	Y
R	T	V
~W	~S	~S
~Y		

13. **(C)** From our initial diagram, we know which types S, Y, and Z repair. U can repair either TVs or VCRs. W can repair TVs or VCRs, or both. X can repair either of the other two types of machines.

14. **(A) Correct – S and U both repair radios and S doesn't repair any of the other types**
    (B) X and Y don't repair any of the same types
    (C) W doesn't have to repair radios
    (D) W only has to repair one type that Y repairs
    (E) this isn't possible, since U repairs only one other type than radios

15. (A) this could be true if W and X both repair more than one type
    (B) this could be true if either W or X repairs one type
    (C) this could be true if both W and X repair one type
    (D) Correct – U and Y both repair two types of machines
    (E) this could be true if either W or X repairs two types

16. (A) since U repairs two types and S repairs one type, this can't happen
    (B) Y doesn't repair radios and U only repairs one of either TVs and VCRs
    (C) Correct – U and X already both repair radios. If X repairs TVs or VCRs along with U, they would repair all and only the same types of machines.
    (D) W doesn't repair radios
    (E) Y doesn't repair radios

17. (A) U could repair TVs and W could repair VCRs or vice versa
    (B) X could also repair both TVs or VCRs along with U
    (C) Correct – U and Y must both repair either TVs or VCRs
    (D) W could repair both TVs and VCRs
    (E) X doesn't have to repair TVs or VCRs

<u>Questions 18-22</u>

Setup:
- three folk groups: G H L
- three rock groups: P Q T
- two stages: N S
- each stage has three two-hour performances
- N: 6 8 10
- S: 8 10 12

Conditions:
#1: P_6 or P_{12}
#2: G – H

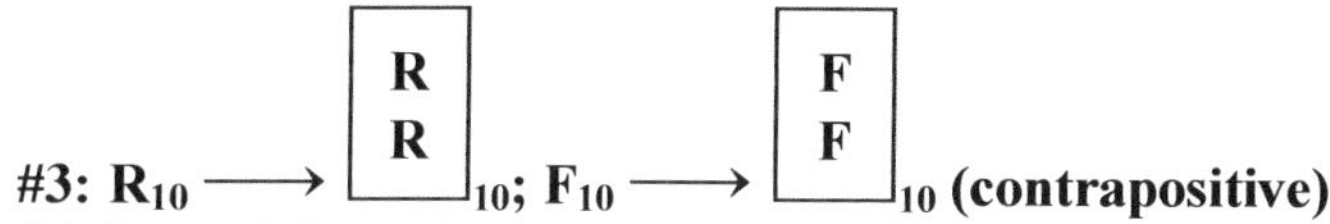

#3: R_{10} ⟶ [R R]$_{10}$; F_{10} ⟶ [F F]$_{10}$ (contrapositive)
#4: L_N and T_S or L_S and T_N
#5: FQ (not necessarily on the same stage)

Overview:
The second condition tells us that H can't be first and G can't be last. Combining the third condition with the fact that there are only two types of groups, we can infer that the bands that perform at 10 are either both folk or both rock.

	6	8	10	12
N	P|	___	F|R	
S		___	F|R	|P
	~H			~G

Since the placement of P and the type of group that can fill the 10 slots each have two options, we can draw up four distinct molds that encompass all the possibilities of the game:

#1

	6	8	10	12
N	P	___	F	
S		___	F	___

#2

	6	8	10	12
N	___	___	F	
S		___	F	P

#3

	6	8	10	12
N	P	___	R	
S		___	R	___

#4

	6	8	10	12
N	___	___	R	
S		___	R	P

Now, let's fill them out, so they'll be useful for the questions:

#1

	6	8	10	12
N	P	G|T	H|L	
S		T|G	L|H	Q

#2

	6	8	10	12
N	G	Q|T	H|L	
S		T|Q	L|H	P

#3

	6	8	10	12
N	P	G|L	Q|T	
S		L|G	T|Q	H

#4

	6	8	10	12
N	G	H|L	Q|T	
S		L|H	T|Q	P

Mold #1: To satisfy the fifth condition, Q must be placed at 12. Due to the second condition, G must occupy one of the 8 slots. This creates H|L dual options for the 10 slots. T must fill the other 8 slot.

Mold #2: With two folk groups at 10, G must be at 6 (second condition). This creates dual options for the 8 slots with our remaining two variables (Q and T).

Mold #3: We know that Q and T must occupy the 10 slots, since they're the only rock groups remaining to be placed. H must occupy the 12 slot, due to the second condition. This creates G|L dual options for the 8 slots.

Mold #4: Q and T must occupy the 10 slots, since they're the remaining rock bands. Due to the second condition, G must occupy the 6 slot.

A final note on the molds: the fourth condition dictates that each mold represents exactly two solutions.

18. **(A) Correct**
    (B) violates the fourth condition (L and T would both be on the south stage)
    (C) violates the first condition
    (D) violates the fourth condition
    (E) violates the fifth condition

19. **(A)** Fortunately, we don't need to check past the first choice. A glance at the molds reveals that in every case, G performs before 10.

20. **(A)** A quick glance at the molds reveals that G performs at 6 under the second and fourth molds, and A is thus correct.

21. **(D)** This could only occur under the first mold. Hence, there are two possible orderings for the north stage: P – G – L and P – T – H. Choice D features the second possibility and is therefore correct.

22. **(B)** This triggers the third and fourth molds. Since folk groups occupy both 8 slots in each mold, choice B must be true.

Questions 1-7

Setup:
- o six day film retrospective
- o one film shown per day
- o F F H H I I N N T T

Conditions:
#1: ~N_2 and ~N_4

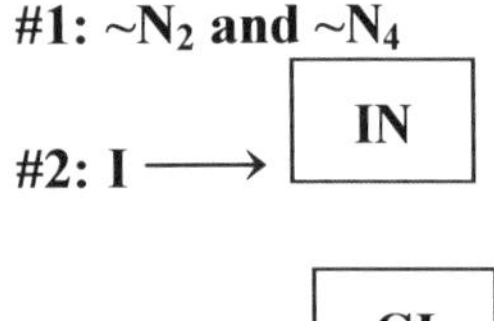

#3: **G** ⟶ **GI**

Overview:
Combining the first two conditions reveals that I cannot be first or third. We can also infer that I cannot go last since there would be no slots left for N. Combining this inference with the third condition reveals that G cannot be second. G also cannot be last, since there would be no slots left for I. Finally, we can chain together the second and third conditions to create a three-slot piece. If we place a G, it must be followed by both I and N, in that order. Consequently, G cannot be fifth. We can represent this inference as G ⟶ GIN.

1	2	3	4	5	6
~I	~N	~I	~N	~G	~I
	~G				~G

1. (A) violates the second condition
   (B) violates the first condition
   (C) violates the second condition
   (D) violates the third condition
   (E) Correct

2. **(D)** Combining this information with the second condition, we also know that N is placed in the third and sixth slots. Since we have used both Is and both Ns, we can't place either one in the first slot. Choice D places N in the first slot and therefore cannot be true.

	I	N		I	N
1	2	3	4	5	6
~I	~N	~I	~N	~G	~I
~N	~G		~I		~G

3. **(A)** With two Is, we also need to place two Ns. One of the Ns can't be first, since there would not be any slots in front of it for an I. The only other slots that an N could go are three, five, and six. As a result, we have to place an IN piece in the second and third slots and either the fourth and fifth or fifth and sixth. As a result, the third slot is filled, and we cannot place an F there.

<table>
<tr><td></td><td>I</td><td>N</td><td>I|</td><td>N|I</td><td></td></tr>
<tr><td>1</td><td>2</td><td>3</td><td>4</td><td>5</td><td>6</td></tr>
<tr><td>~I</td><td>~N</td><td>~I</td><td>~N</td><td>~G</td><td>~I</td></tr>
<tr><td></td><td>~G</td><td></td><td></td><td></td><td>~G</td></tr>
</table>

4. **(B)** A quick glance at our master diagram reveals that I could fill the second, fourth, or fifth slots.

5. **(D)** Placing F third and fifth means that G cannot be first, as that would trigger the GIN inference. Using both Fs further restricts all the remaining slots. Also, we know that Is cannot be placed to the left of any placed non-N variables. After distributing all the not conditions, slots one and six are limited to H, N, and T. Choice D is the only one that meets both criteria.

<table>
<tr><td>H|N|T</td><td>H|T</td><td>F</td><td>H|T</td><td>F</td><td>H|N|T</td></tr>
<tr><td>1</td><td>2</td><td>3</td><td>4</td><td>5</td><td>6</td></tr>
<tr><td>~I</td><td>~N</td><td>~I</td><td>~N</td><td>~G</td><td>~I</td></tr>
<tr><td>~G</td><td>~G</td><td></td><td>~I</td><td></td><td>~G</td></tr>
<tr><td>~F</td><td>~F</td><td></td><td>~G</td><td></td><td>~F</td></tr>
<tr><td></td><td>~I</td><td></td><td>~F</td><td></td><td></td></tr>
</table>

6. **(E)** This question eliminates the two Fs and the two Is. Due to the third condition, we can eliminate the two Gs, since a G must be followed by an I. We're left with two Hs, two Ns and two Ts. Since N cannot be second or fourth, we can create H|T dual options for both slots, and E is therefore correct.

<table>
<tr><td></td><td>H|T</td><td></td><td>H|T</td><td></td><td></td></tr>
<tr><td>1</td><td>2</td><td>3</td><td>4</td><td>5</td><td>6</td></tr>
<tr><td></td><td>~N</td><td></td><td>~N</td><td></td><td></td></tr>
</table>

7. **(D)** From this information, we can create the following chain: N – GIN. The GIN piece has to start at either the third or fourth slot. Consequently, the only options for the first N are the first slot or the third slot, and choice D is therefore correct.

<table>
<tr><td>N|</td><td></td><td>|N</td><td>G</td><td>I</td><td>N</td></tr>
<tr><td>N</td><td></td><td>G</td><td>I</td><td>N</td><td></td></tr>
<tr><td>1</td><td>2</td><td>3</td><td>4</td><td>5</td><td>6</td></tr>
<tr><td></td><td>~N</td><td></td><td>~N</td><td></td><td></td></tr>
</table>

Questions 8-12

Setup:
- five pieces of mail: F L M P S
- each piece is addressed to exactly one person
- three housemates: G J R
- each housemate has at least one piece addressed to her

Conditions:

#1: 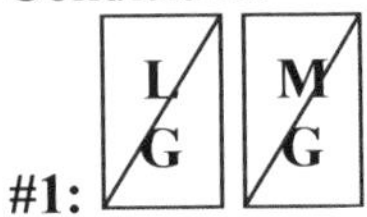

#2: 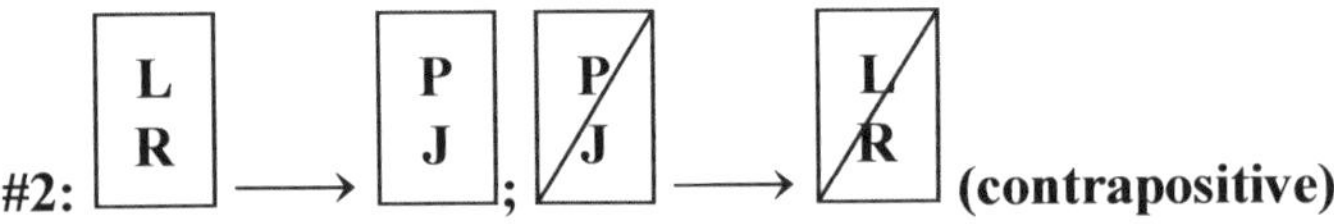 (contrapositive)

#3: housemate who receives the flyer receives at least one other piece

Overview:
Although there aren't any big initial inferences to be made, we can anticipate that G will play a significant role in the questions since the only pieces she can receive are the flyer, the postcard, and the survey. Including the conditional and its contrapositive, the master diagram looks like this:

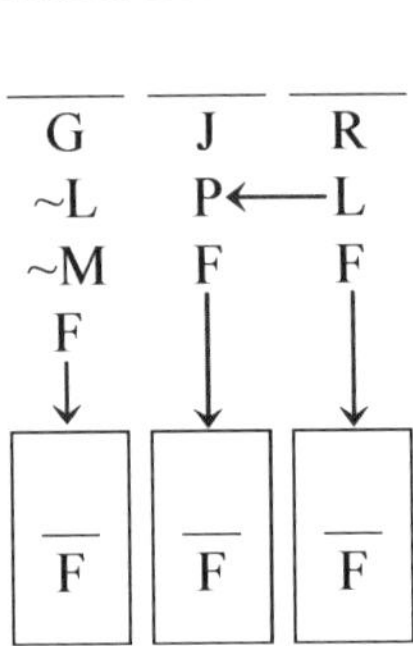

8. (A) this choice is missing the postcard
   (B) Correct
   (C) violates the first condition
   (D) violates the second condition
   (E) violates the third condition

9. **(B)** The key to this question is recognizing that when J doesn't receive the letter or the magazine, R has to receive either or both (due to the first condition). If J receives only the survey, R must receive the letter. However, this means that J receives the postcard. This scenario violates the question stem, and we can therefore eliminate C and D. The same problem occurs if J only receives the magazine. Since R receives the letter, J receives the postcard, thus violating the question stem. Eliminating E and looking at A and B, B is correct since J receiving only the letter or only the postcard does not violate any conditions.

10. **(E)** Since all the choices have three pieces of mail, we know the allocation is 3, 1, 1. The two slots left by J will be filled by G and R, and as such we need to make sure that none of the conditions are broken. In choice E, R must receive the letter since G cannot (first condition). However, this condition triggers the second condition, and J is already paired with three of the items.

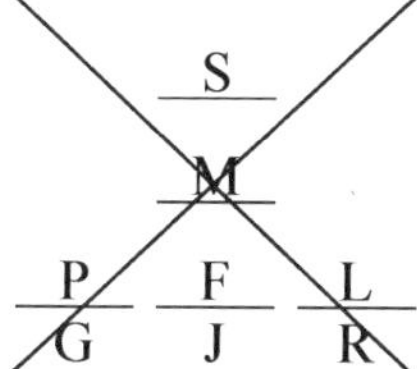

11. **(B)** The question stem tells us that the allocation is 2, 2, 1. It's a safe bet that G is probably only paired with one item since she is very restricted. Choice B triggers the second condition. Since G cannot receive the magazine, she must receive the flyer. This condition violates the third condition, since G only receives one piece of mail.

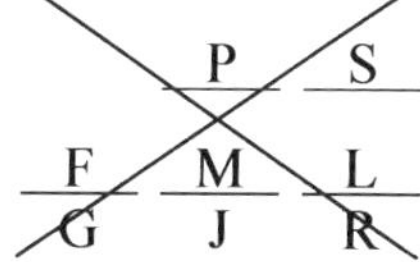

12. **(E)** Since G can't receive the magazine, either J or R must receive both the magazine and the survey. If J received the magazine and the survey, she would also have to receive the postcard. This is due to the fact that R would receive the letter, thus triggering the second condition. This, in turn, would violate the third condition. Noting that R must receive the magazine and the survey, we can draw two diagrams, the second of which proves choice E correct.

P		S			L	S
F	L	M	or	P	F	M
G	J	R		G	J	R

Questions 13-17

Setup:

o seven courses: G H L M P S Z

Conditions:
#1: M ⟶ L or S (not both); ~L and ~S ⟶ ~M (contrapositive)
#2: L ⟶ G; ~G ⟶ ~L (contrapositive)
L ⟶ ~P; P ⟶ ~L (contrapositive)
#3: S ⟶ P; ~P ⟶ ~S (contrapositive)
S ⟶ ~Z; Z ⟶ ~S (contrapositive)
#4: G ⟶ H; ~H ⟶ ~G (contrapositive)
G ⟶ Z; ~Z ⟶ ~G (contrapositive)

Overview:
The diagram will allow us to make necessary inferences as we work through the questions.

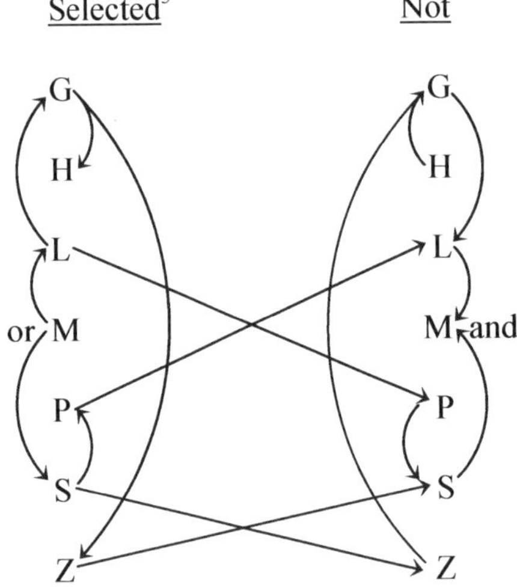

13. **(A) Correct**
    (B) violates the fourth condition
    (C) violates the first condition
    (D) violates the second condition
    (E) violates the first condition

14. **(C)** Following the chain in both directions, we know that P is out, G, H, and Z are selected, and S is out. Choice C is the only things that could be true.

15. **(A)** When H is not offered, G and L must not be offered. Although M might not be offered, that hinges on whether or not S is offered. Since we're not given that information, M is the only class among the choices that cannot be offered.

16. **(D)** Since M is offered, either L or S must also be offered. Offering L or S means that G would be offered, and it must be true that at least three courses are offered.

[5] Visit Manhattan LSAT (http://www.manhattanlsat.com) to learn more about using this diagram.

17. **(E)** Comparing the choices against the diagram reveals that if G is offered, Z is offered, and S is not offered.

Questions 18-22

Setup:
- eight computer processor chips: F G H J K L M O
- ranked from first (fastest) to eighth (slowest)

Conditions:
#1: there are no ties
#2: F_1 or G_1
#3: ~M_8
#4: H __ J

#5: K __ __ L

#6:
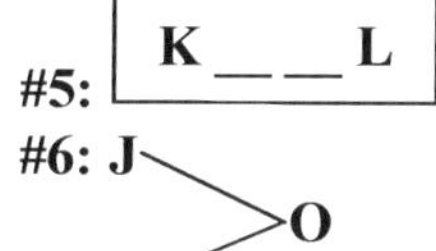

Overview:
The large number of conditions means that we can make some immediate inferences. If the pieces created by the fourth and fifth conditions were not overlapping, we would need additional slots, since neither H nor K is first and O follows both pieces. Armed with the information that the two pieces must overlap, we can create two molds with which to attack the questions:

#1 | HKJ __ L | – O

#2 | K __ HLJ | – O

18. (A) violates the third condition
 (B) Correct
 (C) J is in front of L in the first mold, but they are only separated by one slot
 (D) when K precedes H, they must be separated by one slot (second mold)
 (E) violates the sixth condition

19. **(E)** Looking at the second mold, the latest that H can be ranked is fifth, and hence, choice E is correct.

20. **(B)** O must be preceded by one of the pieces and either F or G (second condition). Therefore the earliest O can be is seventh. F has to be ranked eighth. The second chip has to be either H or K. Since H is the only one of the two given, B is correct.

G	H	K	J	M	L	O	F
1	2	3	4	5	6	7	8

21. **(D)** Since the first mold shows a higher potential ranking for J, we'll use it for this question. M would have to precede H and follow F or G. Hence, the highest J can be ranked is fifth.

F|G	M	K	J		L	O|	|O
1	2	3	4	5	6	7	8

22. (A) J could be fourth (first mold)
    (B) K could be second (second mold)
    (C) Correct
    (D) M could be second (see question number twenty-one)
    (E) O could be seventh (see question number twenty)

Questions 1-5

Setup:

- six consecutive stops
- four airlines: L M N O

Conditions:

#1: 

#2: 1=6

#3: 2=4

#4: 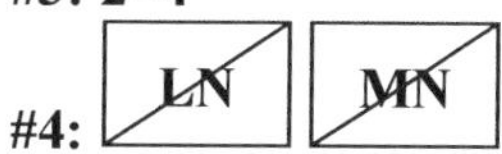

#5: N_5 or O_5

Overview:
From the first three conditions, we can deduce that the fourth and sixth destinations must be different. The basic diagram is:

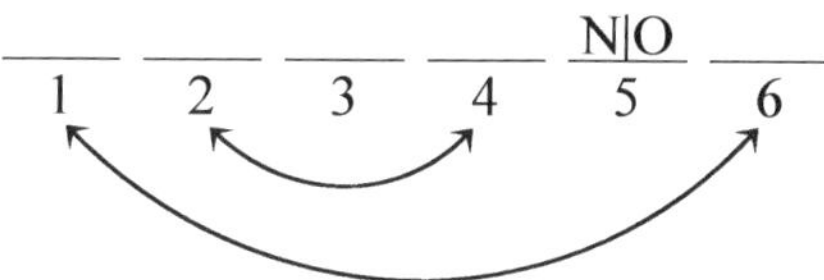

1. (A) violates the first condition
   (B) violates the third condition
   (C) violates the fourth condition
   (D) Correct
   (E) violates the second condition

2. **(B)** Combining this information with the fourth and fifth conditions, we know that O is fourth. The third condition tells us that O is also second. Since a variable cannot be placed twice in a row, N cannot occupy the sixth slot. Since the first and sixth are the same, N cannot occupy the first slot. The first condition and our diagram in progress tell us that O cannot be first. B is the only choice with L or M first and O second.

L|M	O	L|M|N	O	N	L|M
1	2	3	4	5	6

3. **(C)** Placing O fifth and limiting the variables to three has the effect of creating M|N dual options for slots one, two, four, and six. Due to the first three conditions, slots one and two must be filled with different destinations, and slots four and six must be filled with different destinations. Since the fourth condition stipulates that we can't have MN, the ordering of the first two slots has to be N and M respectively. The fourth condition also requires that we place O third.

N	M	O	M	O	N
1	2	3	4	5	6

4. **(E)** Since slots one and two are matched with four and six respectively, whatever is placed in those two slots will surround the fifth slot. As the fifth slot can only be N or O, choice E presents an impossibility, since the first condition precludes a variable from appearing twice in a row.

5. **(B)** Combining this condition with the third condition, O is also placed fourth. Combining the first condition and the fifth condition, we know that N has to be fifth. Since N can't be sixth (first condition) and O can't be first (first condition), L|M dual options are created for the first and sixth slots. Choice B represents one acceptable outcome for the fifth and sixth slots under this scenario.

L|M	O	L|M|N	O	N	L|M
1	2	3	4	5	6

Questions 6-11

Setup:

- five person committee to be selected
- three parents (P): F G H
- three students (S): K L M
- four teachers (T): U W X Z

Conditions:

#1: exactly one student
#2: F ⟶ ~H; H ⟶ ~F (contrapositive)
#3: M ⟶ ~Z; Z ⟶ ~M (contrapositive)
#4: U ⟶ ~W; W ⟶ ~U (contrapositive)
#5: F ⟶ Z; ~Z ⟶ ~F (contrapositive)
#6: W ⟶ H; ~H ⟶ ~W (contrapositive)

Overview:
The committee is to be selected from among ten variables. Since the number of students is fixed at one, the allocation of people selected to subgroups will be either 3, 1, 1 or 2, 2, 1.

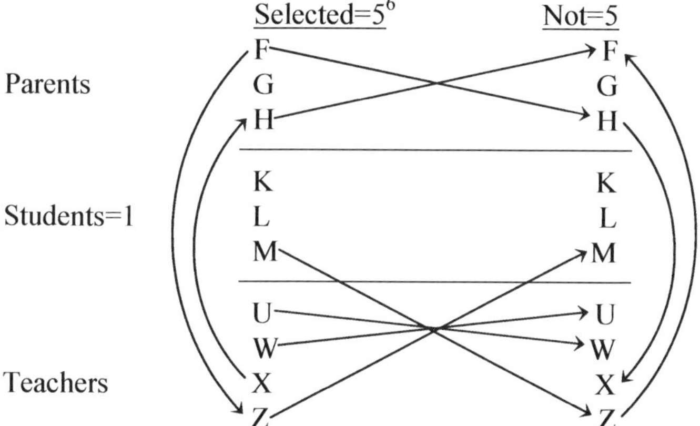

Due to the second and fourth conditions, the maximum number of parents selected is two and the maximum number of teachers selected is three. From this information, we can create two distinct molds, one in which the number of parents is maximized, and one in which the number of teachers is maximized.

#1

P	S	T
F|H		___
G	K|L|M	___

#2

P	S	T
		U|W
		Z
F|G|H	K|L	X

6. (A) violates the first condition
   (B) violates the fifth condition
   (C) violates the sixth condition
   (D) violates the fourth condition
   (E) Correct

7. **(D)** From the sixth condition, we know that H is also selected. From the second, third, and fourth conditions, we know that F, M, and U are not selected. Choices A, C, and E violate this scenario. Choice B violates the first condition and D is proven correct.

8. **(B)** If F is selected, Z is selected (fifth condition) and H is not selected (second condition). By the third condition, if M is selected, Z is not selected. Therefore, choice B represents an impossibility under the given conditions.

[6] Visit Manhattan LSAT (http://www.manhattanlsat.com) to learn more about using this diagram.

9. **(A)** By the fourth and sixth conditions, we know that H is selected and U is not selected. By the second condition, we know that F is not selected. Hence, A is the credited response.

10. **(E)** Combining this information with the first condition, we know that the committee must include three teachers. Since U and W cannot both be selected (fourth condition), X and Z must be selected. This scenario perfectly matches the second mold.

11. **(B)** With M selected, we know that the other two students are not selected due to the first condition. By the third condition, we know that Z is not selected. Finally, by the contrapositive of the fifth condition, we also know that F is not selected. We're left with five variables to fill four slots and since U and W cannot both be selected, a dual option is created. G, H, and X all must be selected.

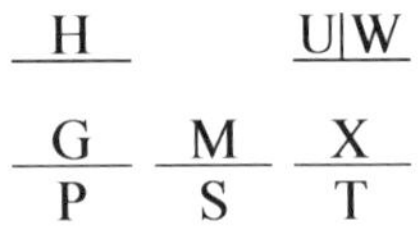

H		U|W
G	M	X
P	S	T

Questions 12-17

Setup:
- five years: 1991, 1992, 1993, 1994, 1995
- three friends: R S T
- each graduated during that period
- each bought his or her first car during that period

Conditions:
#1: R_G - T_G
#2: T_G - T_C
#3: S_C - S_G
#4: [R S]$_G$
#5: at least one of the friends graduated in 1993

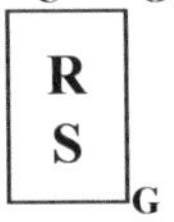

Overview:
You may be tempted to draw two rows of slots: one for the graduation years and one for the car purchase years. However, since the conditions are predominantly relative, and more than one person can graduate and/or buy a car in the same year, the game is easier to attack with sequencing lines to show the relationships. Combining the conditions gives the following sketch:

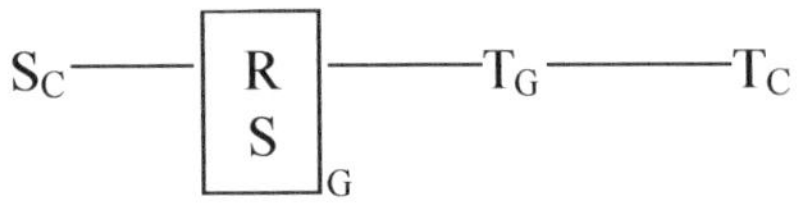

S_C —— [R S]$_G$ —— T_G —— T_C

12. (A) since R and S graduate in 1991, there's no room for S_C
    (B) Correct
    (C) violates the fourth condition
    (D) violates the first condition
    (E) since T_G is last, there's no room for T_C

13. **(B)** This question is asking what can be last. It can either be T_C or R_C, about which we weren't given any conditions. R_C is the only one that shows up in the answer choices, and it is therefore correct.

14. (A) could be R and S
    (B) could be R and S
    (C) Correct – this would have to be R and either S or T, but if it were S, there would be too few years to the right to accommodate the other variables, and if it were T, there would be too few years to the left to accommodate the other variables
    (D) could be R and T
    (E) could be R and T

15. **(A)** Since only R_C and S_C can be first (1991), choice A must be true.

16. **(E)** This question gives the following diagram:

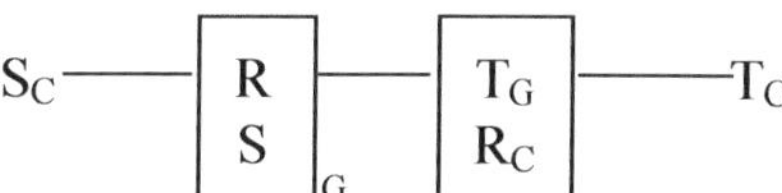

Since T_C is the only variable that can be last, choice E must be false.

17. **(E)** This question effectively locks down four of the variables. Other than the placed variables, S_C could be either first or second. As the diagram shows, T_C must be in 1995.

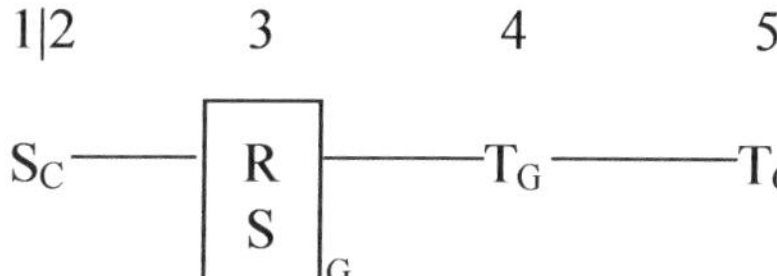

Questions 18-22

Setup:
- six letters: T U W X Y Z
- three spoonfuls: 1 2 3
- each of the letters must be in exactly one of the spoonfuls
- each spoonful must have between one and three letters

Conditions:

#1: T – U

#2: U – X or **U X** (boxed)

#3: W – Y

#4: 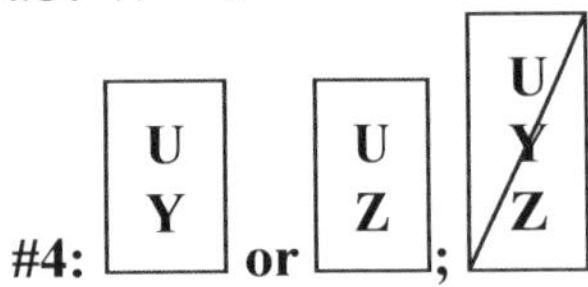

Overview:

The two possible allocations of letters to spoonfuls are 3, 2, 1 and 2, 2, 2.

1	2	3
~U		~T
~Y		~W

18. (A) violates the third condition
    (B) Correct
    (C) violates the third condition
    (D) violates the first condition
    (E) violates the second condition

19. **(D)** Since Y is alone in either the second or the third spoonful, and T has to be in an earlier spoonful than U, T has to be in the first spoonful. Because Y is unavailable to be paired with U, Z has to be paired with U. Due to the second condition, X has to be with both U and Z. Finally, since one of the spoonfuls already has three letters and Y is alone, W must be paired with T. Accordingly, D is the only choice that could be true.

1	2	3
		X
W		U
T	Y	Z

or

1	2	3
	X	
W	U	
T	Z	Y

20. **(E)** Since U can't be in the first spoonful with Z (first condition), it has to be paired with Y. When U and Y are in the second spoonful, X is the only letter that can be in the third spoonful, since T and W cannot be in the third spoonful. Putting U and Y in the third spoonful also ensures that X is in the third spoonful, since U cannot be in a later spoonful than X.

```
------- -------                  X
------- U          ------- ------- U
Z   Y   X      or   Z   T|W   Y
1   2   3           1    2    3
```

21. **(D)** A quick way to attack this problem is to notice that the first three choices do not contain Z. Looking at the second option for number twenty reveals that Z could be alone in the first spoonful if both T and W were in the second spoonful. We can therefore eliminate choices A, B, and C. The next variable to look at is X. If X were alone in the first spoonful, this would violate the second condition, since U would have to be in a later spoonful than X. Hence, choice D is correct.

22. **(A)** With T in the second spoonful, U has to be in the third spoonful (first condition). Due to the second condition, X also has to be in the third spoonful. The fourth condition tells us that either Y or Z must be in the third spoonful with U. Having accounted for four variables, there are two left, and either the first spoonful or the second spoonful can contain two letters.

```
                Y|Z
------- ------- X
W|Y|Z   T       U
  1     2       3
```

Part 6: Bonus Solutions

Questions 1-5

Setup:

- five digit product code

Conditions:

#1: 0 1 2 3 4

#2: each digit occurs exactly once

#3: $2^{nd} = 2 \times (1^{st})$

#4: $3^{rd} < 5^{th}$

Overview:

The third condition tells us that the first and second digits are either 1 and 2 or 2 and 4, respectively. Combining this information with the fourth condition, we can create two acceptable molds:

1st	2nd	3rd	4th	5th
1	2	0|3		3|4
2	4	0|1		1|3

We can further draw out all the possible solutions from these two molds.

	1st	2nd	3rd	4th	5th
#1	1	2	0	3	4
#2	1	2	0	4	3
#3	1	2	3	0	4
#4	2	4	0	1	3
#5	2	4	0	3	1
#6	2	4	1	0	3

1. **(A)** This is a direct match with the fifth solution, and choice A is therefore correct.

2. (A) see solutions #4, #5, and #6
   (B) this is only true of solution #3
   (C) Correct – 2 is either first or second
   (D) this is only true of the solutions #1 and #5
   (E) this is only true of solution #4

3. **(C)** According to the solutions, 0 can occupy either the third or the fourth slots. Since it's not third, it must be fourth, and choice C is therefore correct.

4. **(E)** Checking the choices against the solutions reveals that only choice E presents an impossibility, and it is thus correct.

5. (A) see solutions #3, #4, and #6
   (B) see solutions #4 and #5
   (C) see solution #2
   (D) see solutions #4 and #6
   (E) Correct – with 2 second (solutions #1, #2, and #3), the latest 4 can be is fifth; with 2 first (solutions #4, #5, and #6), 4 is second

<u>Questions 6-10</u>

Setup:
- 3 films: G H L
- 3 days: Th F S
- each film once during the festival, but not more than once a day
- at least one film per day
- films are shown one at a time

Conditions:
#1: H is last on Thursday
#2: G or L but not both on Friday, none after
#3: G or H but not both on Saturday, none after

Overview:
The second and third conditions limit the number of films for Friday and Saturday to two, but Thursday is unrestricted, in that all three films can be shown on that day. From the second condition, we can deduce that if two films are shown on Friday, the first will be Harvest. From the third condition, we can deduce that if two films are shown on Saturday, the first will be Limelight.

Th	F	S
H		
------	G|L	G|H
-------	-------	-------

6. (A) Greed is not shown
   (B) violates the second condition
   (C) Correct
   (D) violates the first condition
   (E) violates the second condition

7. **(A)** The second condition states that only Greed or Limelight can be last on Friday, and choice A, therefore, cannot be true.

8. **(D)** This question requires that Greed be shown as late as possible, so that Limelight can be shown as many times as possible. Putting Greed second on Saturday and filling in the rest of the slots with Harvest and Limelight reveals that at most, the festival can feature six showings.

H L G

L H L
Th F S

Assigning all three films to be shown on Thursday and filling in the rest of the slots with Greed and Harvest reveals the same maximum of six films shown during the festival.

H

L G

G H G|H
Th F S

9. **(E)** Since Greed is shown three times, it has to be last on both Friday and Saturday. Harvest can't also be shown on Saturday (due to the third condition). Therefore, it has to be shown on Thursday and Friday. Since Limelight can't be shown on Friday (all the slots are full), it has to be shown on either Thursday or Saturday. Scanning the answer choices shows that E matches up with the new diagram.

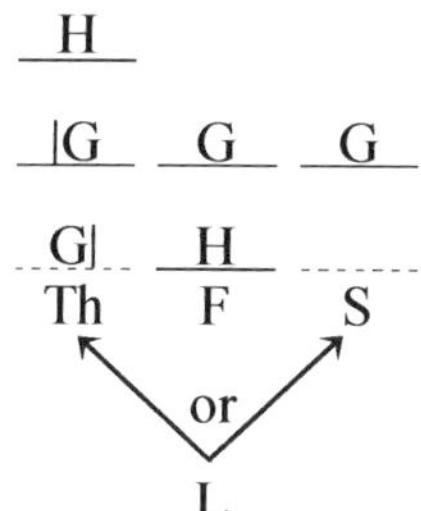

10. **(D)** For Limelight to be shown three times, it must be featured last on Friday and not last on both Thursday and Saturday. Greed could be featured on Thursday, Friday, or Saturday. Harvest will be featured last on Thursday and either first on Friday or last on Saturday. Since Greed or Limelight can be first on Thursday, D is the correct answer.

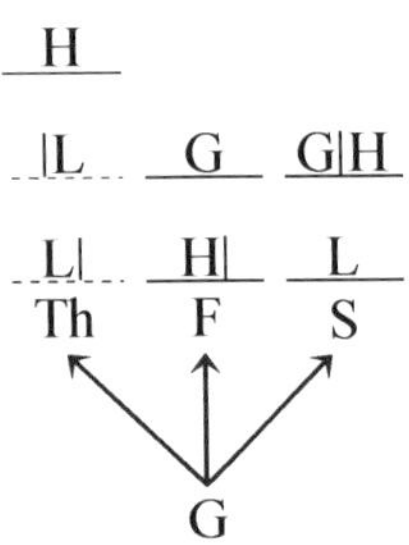

Questions 11-17

Setup:
- seven weeks
- four destinations: G J M T
- each destination at least once

Conditions:
#1: ~J_4
#2: T_7
#3: exactly two Ms, at least one G in between (M – G – M)

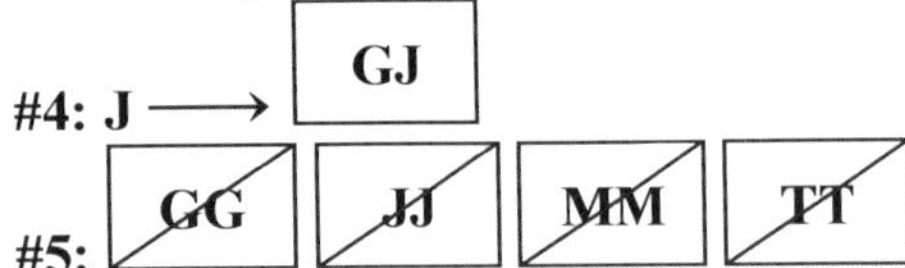

Overview:
We know for certain that M will be featured exactly twice. Therefore, we can't have a scenario in which one destination is featured four times and the other three are each featured once. The possible allocations of weeks to destinations are:

3, 2, 1, 1 (M represents the 2)
2, 2, 2, 1 (M and two other destinations are featured twice)

If Jamaica is featured twice, Guadeloupe must also be featured twice (due to the fourth condition), and our list of variables will be G G J J M M T. We can also deduce that Jamaica can't be first or immediately to the right of any placed destinations due to the fourth condition. The second condition and the fifth condition tell us that Trinidad cannot be sixth since it is already seventh. Since each destination must be featured at least once, there will be a GJ piece.

1	2	3	4	5	6	7
						T
~J			~J		~T	

11. **(A) Correct**
    (B) violates the third condition
    (C) violates the fourth condition
    (D) violates the first condition
    (E) violates the second condition

12. **(A)** The fifth condition states that a destination cannot be scheduled for two consecutive weeks, which would be the case if Trinidad were sixth.

13. **(D)** This new information, coupled with the fifth condition tells us that Trinidad can't be scheduled fourth. Also, since the GJ piece requires two spaces, it can only occupy either the first and second or the second and the third spaces.

1	2	3	4	5	6	7
			G|M	T	G|M	T
~J			~J		~T	
			~T		~J	

Two possible scenarios can be created with this new information:

1	2	3	4	5	6	7
G	J	M	G	T	M	T
M	G	J	G|M	T	G|M	T

(A) Trinidad can't be first
(B) Martinique can't be second
(C) Guadeloupe can't be third
(D) Correct – see the second scenario
(E) Jamaica can't be sixth

14. **(E)** We know that Guadeloupe is the destination for week four (due to the fourth condition). Since Martinique has to surround Guadeloupe on both sides, it becomes clear that Martinique has to be the destination during the sixth week. With slots 2, 3, and 6 open, we know that Martinique must be sixth (third condition) and that Martinique and Trinidad will each occupy one of the second and third slots.

1	2	3	4	5	6	7
G	M|T	T|M	G	J	M	T

15. **(A)** With Guadeloupe first and Trinidad second, we only have four slots for M – GJ – M, thus filling out the entire diagram. Therefore, it must be true that Martinique is scheduled for week 3.

G	T	M	G	J	M	T
1	2	3	4	5	6	7

16. **(A)** The fifth condition combined with the new information tells us that Martinique cannot be second or fourth. Therefore, the fourth slot has to be occupied by either Guadeloupe or Trinidad, eliminating B and C.

		M	G|T			T
1	2	3	4	5	6	7
~J	~M		~J		~T	
			~M			

Let's examine the other choices:

(A) Correct – see the following diagram

G	J	M	G	T	M	T
1	2	3	4	5	6	7

(D) violates the third condition

(E) under this scenario, the GJ piece would have to be placed in the first and second positions, leaving no open spaces for the M – G – M condition

17. **(D)** This question asks the test taker to re-examine the setup and conditions. Since any week featuring Jamaica must be preceded by a week featuring Guadeloupe, it's a good idea to look at any choices with Jamaica. If Jamaica were to be featured for three weeks, Guadalupe would also be featured for three weeks, thus occupying the remaining six slots on the diagram. This scenario would leave no space for the two voyages to Martinique and choice D is therefore correct.

Questions 18-23

Setup:

- three recycling centers: 1 2 3
- exactly five materials recycled: G N P T W
- each center recycles two to three materials

Conditions:

#1: W ⟶ [W N]

#2: 2 ⟶ 1; ~1 ⟶ ~2 (contrapositive)

#3: only one center recycles P; [P/G]

Overview:
We can deduce that Center 2 does not recycle plastic since Center 1 would also recycle plastic, violating the third condition.

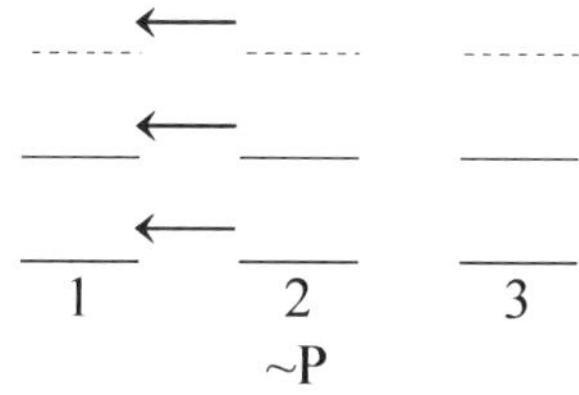

18. (A) Center 3 violates the first condition
    (B) Correct
    (C) violates the second condition
    (D) violates the third condition
    (E) violates the third condition

19. **(D)** Because Center 1 recycles every type of material that Center 2 does, Center 2 cannot recycle plastic. If it did, this would violate the second condition. Thus C and E are eliminated. Nothing prevents either Center 1 or Center 3 from recycling plastic, and thus choice D is correct.

20. **(C)** Since Center 2 recycles three types of materials, Center 1 must also recycle those same three types. As three is the maximum number of materials that can be recycled at any one center, and Center 2 cannot recycle plastic, the only center that can recycle plastic is Center 3. Thus, choice C is the correct answer.

21. **(D)** This question maximizes the number of materials that each center can recycle. Due to the second condition, Center 1 and Center 2 must recycle the same three materials. Logically, choices A, C, and E are all incorrect. Center 3 recycles plastic along with two other materials. In choice B, if Center 3 were the only center to recycle newsprint, no other center could recycle wood (due to the first condition). This would only leave tin and glass for the first two centers to recycle, violating the condition of the question stem. Thus, D is the only choice that could be true.

22. **(B)** We know that Center 3 can't recycle plastic due to the third condition. Center 2 can't recycle plastic because Center 1 would also recycle it, violating the third condition. Therefore, Center 1 must recycle plastic and recycle two other materials along with Center 2. Out of newsprint, tin, and wood, Center 1 must recycle two materials. Looking at the contrapositive of the first condition, if Center 1 didn't recycle newsprint, then it wouldn't recycle wood. Center 1 would therefore recycle plastic and tin. Following this line of reasoning, Center 2 would only recycle tin, which violates the condition that each center must recycle at least two types of materials. Therefore, Center 1 and Center 2 must recycle newsprint and B is correct.

1		2	3
P			-------
T|W	←	T|W	W|T
N	←	N	G

23. **(A)** Center 1 must also recycle newsprint due to the first condition. Since Center 1 is the only center to recycle wood, it must share two other types of material with Center 2, one of which has to be newsprint. Center 3 is the only center that can recycle plastic and it cannot recycle glass. Therefore, Center 1 and Center 2 must both recycle glass.

1		2	3
W			-------
G	←	G	T
N	←	N	P
~P		~P	~W
		~W	~G

(A) Correct – could be Center 3
(B) is incomplete because Center 1 recycles three types of material
(C) only Center 1 could recycle these two, but newsprint is missing from the list
(D) is incomplete because Center 1 recycles newsprint
(E) none of the three centers can recycle both glass and tin

APPENDIX

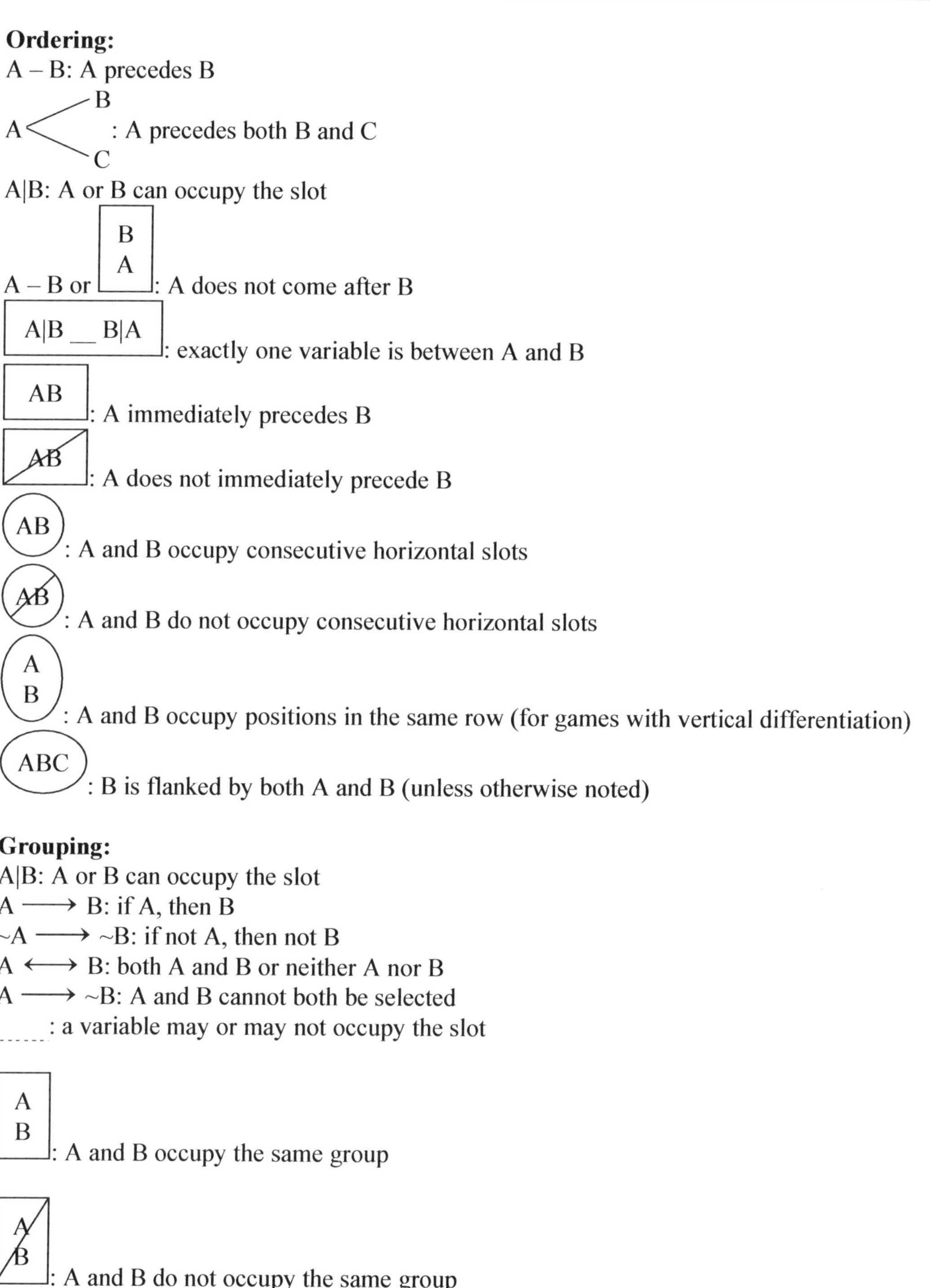
Ordering:
A – B: A precedes B
A B C : A precedes both B and C
A|B: A or B can occupy the slot
A – B or B A : A does not come after B
A|B __ B|A : exactly one variable is between A and B
AB : A immediately precedes B
AB : A does not immediately precede B
AB : A and B occupy consecutive horizontal slots
AB : A and B do not occupy consecutive horizontal slots
A B : A and B occupy positions in the same row (for games with vertical differentiation)
ABC : B is flanked by both A and B (unless otherwise noted)
Grouping:
A|B: A or B can occupy the slot
A ⟶ B: if A, then B
~A ⟶ ~B: if not A, then not B
A ⟷ B: both A and B or neither A nor B
A ⟶ ~B: A and B cannot both be selected
: a variable may or may not occupy the slot
A B : A and B occupy the same group
A B : A and B do not occupy the same group

Categorization systems are, by their nature, somewhat limited in their usefulness. Logic Games are full of patterns, and categorizing them by type can illuminate some of the patterns LSAC draws upon in creating them. On the other hand, some people become too preoccupied with placing each game into a well-defined box, and lose sight of the ends to which the categorization is supposed to lead. This is especially problematic with games that are typically referred to as "hybrid." Ideally, categorizing games should help you visualize how each individual game should be diagrammed and approached. It can also help you isolate particular types of games which give you the most trouble so that you can drill those types. Since some games have features which are consistent with more than one game type ("hybrid" games), for simplicity, each game is categorized according to its overarching feature. The following classification list excludes the additional limited designations. While these global limitations can often be used to work through a game more efficiently, it is not always essential to deduce them upfront.

Ordering

- **Relative:** ordering a set of variables relative to each other
- **Simple:** ordering a set of variables relative to fixed positions
- **Complex:** ordering two or more sets of variables relative to fixed positions

Grouping

- **In/Out:** assigning each entity to exactly one of two groups primarily through the application of conditional statements
- **Distribution:** assigning each entity to exactly one of a given number of groups

Assignment: assigning variables to positions in a structure

- **Determined:** the exact number of each variable to be placed in the diagram can be deduced from the setup and conditions
- **Undetermined:** the exact number of each variable to be placed in the diagram is left open by the setup and conditions and can vary from question to question

Miscellaneous: game types which are either rare or obsolete

Limited

- **Allocations:** limited slot structures or limited variable allocations can be deduced from the setup and conditions
- **Scenarios:** limited partially-completed diagrams can be deduced from the setup and conditions
- **Solutions:** limited completed diagrams can be deduced from the setup and conditions

Active Variables: the variables which are to be placed into a particular structure

PrepTest	Game	Type	Subtype
1	1	Miscellaneous	
	2	Assignment	Undetermined
	3	Ordering	Relative
	4	Assignment	Undetermined
2	1	Ordering	Relative
	2	Assignment	Determined
	3	Miscellaneous	
	4	Ordering	Complex
3	1	Assignment	Undetermined
	2	Ordering	Simple
	3	Assignment	Undetermined
	4	Assignment	Determined
4	1	Ordering	Relative
	2	Assignment	Undetermined
	3	Assignment	Determined
	4	Miscellaneous	
5	1	Assignment	Determined
	2	Assignment	Undetermined
	3	Grouping	In/Out
	4	Ordering	Complex
6	1	Grouping	Distribution
	2	Ordering	Relative
	3	Miscellaneous	
	4	Miscellaneous	
7	1	Ordering	Simple
	2	Assignment	Determined
	3	Grouping	Distribution
	4	Ordering	Complex
8	1	Assignment	Determined
	2	Miscellaneous	
	3	Ordering	Complex
	4	Assignment	Undetermined
9	1	Assignment	Undetermined
	2	Grouping	In/Out
	3	Assignment	Determined
	4	Miscellaneous	

10	1	Ordering	Relative
	2	Grouping	Distribution
	3	Miscellaneous	
	4	Grouping	In/Out
11	1	Grouping	Distribution
	2	Ordering	Simple
	3	Grouping	In/Out
	4	Miscellaneous	
12	1	Ordering	Simple
	2	Grouping	Distribution
	3	Assignment	Undetermined
	4	Miscellaneous	
13	1	Grouping	Distribution
	2	Ordering	Simple
	3	Assignment	Undetermined
	4	Miscellaneous	
14	1	Assignment	Determined
	2	Ordering	Complex
	3	Grouping	Distribution
	4	Assignment	Undetermined
15	1	Ordering	Simple
	2	Miscellaneous	
	3	Ordering	Simple
	4	Assignment	Undetermined
16	1	Grouping	Distribution
	2	Assignment	Determined
	3	Assignment	Undetermined
	4	Miscellaneous	
17	1	Ordering	Simple
	2	Assignment	Undetermined
	3	Assignment	Undetermined
	4	Assignment	Determined
18	1	Grouping	Distribution
	2	Ordering	Simple
	3	Miscellaneous	
	4	Miscellaneous	

19	1	Ordering	Simple
	2	Assignment	Determined
	3	Grouping	Distribution
	4	Grouping	Distribution
20	1	Assignment	Determined
	2	Grouping	In/Out
	3	Miscellaneous	
	4	Ordering	Complex
21	1	Assignment	Determined
	2	Miscellaneous	
	3	Assignment	Determined
	4	Assignment	Undetermined
22	1	Grouping	Distribution
	2	Ordering	Complex
	3	Assignment	Undetermined
	4	Assignment	Undetermined
23	1	Ordering	Simple
	2	Grouping	In/Out
	3	Grouping	Distribution
	4	Ordering	Complex
24	1	Grouping	Distribution
	2	Ordering	Simple
	3	Ordering	Complex
	4	Grouping	In/Out
25	1	Assignment	Undetermined
	2	Assignment	Determined
	3	Grouping	In/Out
	4	Ordering	Complex
26	1	Ordering	Complex
	2	Ordering	Simple
	3	Grouping	Distribution
	4	Assignment	Undetermined
27	1	Ordering	Simple
	2	Assignment	Determined
	3	Grouping	Distribution
	4	Ordering	Simple

28	1	Ordering	Simple
	2	Assignment	Undetermined
	3	Assignment	Determined
	4	Assignment	Determined
29	1	Grouping	Distribution
	2	Assignment	Undetermined
	3	Ordering	Simple
	4	Assignment	Determined
30	1	Miscellaneous	
	2	Ordering	Simple
	3	Ordering	Complex
	4	Ordering	Simple
31	1	Ordering	Complex
	2	Grouping	In/Out
	3	Ordering	Simple
	4	Assignment	Undetermined
32	1	Assignment	Undetermined
	2	Assignment	Undetermined
	3	Ordering	Simple
	4	Ordering	Complex
33	1	Ordering	Relative
	2	Grouping	In/Out
	3	Grouping	In/Out
	4	Assignment	Undetermined
34	1	Ordering	Simple
	2	Ordering	Simple
	3	Ordering	Simple
	4	Grouping	In/Out
35	1	Assignment	Undetermined
	2	Assignment	Undetermined
	3	Assignment	Determined
	4	Assignment	Determined
36	1	Grouping	In/Out
	2	Ordering	Complex
	3	Assignment	Determined
	4	Ordering	Complex

37	1	Assignment	Determined
	2	Ordering	Complex
	3	Grouping	Distribution
	4	Ordering	Complex
38	1	Ordering	Relative
	2	Ordering	Complex
	3	Grouping	Distribution
	4	Ordering	Complex
39	1	Ordering	Complex
	2	Assignment	Determined
	3	Ordering	Complex
	4	Grouping	In/Out
40	1	Ordering	Simple
	2	Ordering	Simple
	3	Miscellaneous	
	4	Grouping	In/Out
41	1	Ordering	Simple
	2	Ordering	Complex
	3	Grouping	In/Out
	4	Miscellaneous	
42	1	Grouping	In/Out
	2	Ordering	Relative
	3	Assignment	Determined
	4	Assignment	Undetermined
43	1	Ordering	Simple
	2	Ordering	Relative
	3	Assignment	Determined
	4	Assignment	Undetermined
44	1	Ordering	Simple
	2	Grouping	Distribution
	3	Ordering	Complex
	4	Ordering	Complex
45	1	Ordering	Simple
	2	Assignment	Undetermined
	3	Grouping	In/Out
	4	Assignment	Undetermined

46	1	Ordering	Simple
	2	Assignment	Determined
	3	Ordering	Complex
	4	Assignment	Undetermined
47	1	Ordering	Simple
	2	Grouping	In/Out
	3	Assignment	Undetermined
	4	Assignment	Undetermined
48	1	Grouping	In/Out
	2	Ordering	Relative
	3	Assignment	Undetermined
	4	Assignment	Determined
49	1	Ordering	Simple
	2	Grouping	Distribution
	3	Grouping	In/Out
	4	Ordering	Simple
50	1	Ordering	Simple
	2	Grouping	In/Out
	3	Assignment	Determined
	4	Assignment	Determined

PT 1, Game 1
1. B
2. A
3. B
4. E
5. E
6. C
7. E

PT 1, Game 2
8. B
9. D
10. A
11. B
12. D
13. C

PT 1, Game 3
14. C
15. E
16. D
17. B
18. D

PT 1, Game 4
19. E
20. A
21. A
22. B
23. E
24. C

PT 2, Game 1
1. D
2. A
3. A
4. E
5. D

PT 2, Game 2
6. D
7. E
8. A
9. E
10. C
11. B
12. C

PT 2, Game 3
13. A
14. D
15. D
16. B
17. C

PT 2, Game 4
18. E
19. B
20. E
21. A
22. E
23. B
24. D

PT 3, Game 1
1. D
2. B
3. A
4. E
5. C
6. A
7. D

PT 3, Game 2
8. C
9. A
10. C
11. A
12. A
13. D

PT 3, Game 3
14. A
15. D
16. D
17. E
18. D
19. A

PT 3, Game 4
20. B
21. C
22. D
23. B
24. C

PT 4, Game 1
1. D
2. C
3. D
4. D
5. C
6. D

PT 4, Game 2
7. E
8. C
9. A
10. E
11. E

PT 4, Game 3
12. B
13. C
14. E
15. A
16. D
17. B

PT 4, Game 4
18. E
19. C
20. D
21. A
22. A
23. C
24. B

PT 5, Game 1
1. C
2. D
3. E
4. E
5. C
6. E

PT 5, Game 2
7. A
8. B
9. B
10. B
11. D

PT 5, Game 3
12. B
13. B
14. C
15. C
16. D
17. B

PT 5, Game 4
18. B
19. C
20. C
21. D
22. A
23. E
24. E

PT 6, Game 1
1. A
2. D
3. C
4. D
5. E
6. D

PT 6, Game 2
7. C
8. E
9. C
10. A
11. B
12. B

PT 6, Game 3
13. E
14. A
15. D
16. A
17. D
18. B
19. C

PT 6, Game 4
20. D
21. C
22. B
23. B
24. A

PT 7, Game 1
1. C
2. A
3. C
4. C
5. E
6. C
7. D

PT 7, Game 2
8. B
9. C
10. E
11. E
12. E

PT 7, Game 3
13. B
14. C
15. E
16. A
17. E
18. B

PT 7, Game 4
19. E
20. D
21. B
22. D
23. B
24. A

PT 8, Game 1
1. D
2. B
3. D
4. D
5. A

PT 8, Game 2
6. C
7. B
8. B
9. D
10. A
11. B
12. E

PT 8, Game 3
13. C
14. C
15. E
16. B
17. D

PT 8, Game 4
18. D
19. B
20. E
21. D
22. B
23. E
24. C

PT 9, Game 1
1. C
2. D
3. B
4. A
5. C
6. D
7. A

PT 9, Game 2
8. D
9. B
10. B
11. B
12. C
13. E

PT 9, Game 3
14. D
15. B
16. B
17. C
18. D

PT 9, Game 4
19. E
20. A
21. D
22. D
23. B
24. A

PT 10, Game 1
1. B
2. C
3. C
4. C
5. E

PT 10, Game 2
6. A
7. E
8. E
9. E
10. B
11. C
12. B

PT 10, Game 3
13. B
14. D
15. C
16. D
17. E
18. C

PT 10, Game 4
19. B
20. C
21. E
22. B
23. D
24. A

PT 11, Game 1
1. A
2. E
3. B
4. D
5. C
6. B

PT 11, Game 2
7. B
8. D
9. B
10. B
11. D

PT 11, Game 3
12. D
13. C
14. E
15. B
16. A
17. C
18. A
19. C

PT 11, Game 4
20. E
21. E
22. A
23. B
24. A

PT 12, Game 1
1. E
2. B
3. C
4. B
5. C
6. D

PT 12, Game 2
7. E
8. A
9. E
10. D
11. B

PT 12, Game 3
12. D
13. B
14. B
15. A
16. C
17. C

PT 12, Game 4
18. D
19. C
20. B
21. A
22. E
23. E
24. D

PT 13, Game 1
1. D
2. B
3. C
4. E
5. B
6. D

PT 13, Game 2
7. E
8. E
9. C
10. C
11. C

PT 13, Game 3
12. B
13. A
14. E
15. D
16. B
17. E

PT 13, Game 4
18. E
19. C
20. A
21. A
22. D
23. C
24. E

PT 14, Game 1
1. B
2. A
3. E
4. B
5. D
6. C

PT 14, Game 2
7. E
8. A
9. B
10. C
11. E
12. A

PT 14, Game 3
13. D
14. D
15. D
16. D
17. B
18. E

PT 14, Game 4
19. B
20. A
21. C
22. B
23. B
24. C

PT 15, Game 1
1. D
2. B
3. C
4. A
5. D
6. A

PT 15, Game 2
7. D
8. A
9. E
10. E
11. D
12. E
13. A

PT 15, Game 3
14. D
15. E
16. C
17. A
18. B
19. E

PT 15, Game 4
20. C
21. C
22. B
23. A
24. A

PT 16, Game 1
1. D
2. E
3. A
4. E
5. C
6. D

PT 16, Game 2
7. E
8. B
9. C
10. E
11. C
12. B

PT 16, Game 3
13. D
14. B
15. A
16. A
17. E
18. A

PT 16, Game 4
19. D
20. E
21. A
22. C
23. A
24. C

PT 17, Game 1
1. E
2. E
3. B
4. B
5. D

PT 17, Game 2
6. D
7. C
8. B
9. E
10. E
11. E
12. B

PT 17, Game 3
13. E
14. D
15. D
16. B
17. B

PT 17, Game 4
18. A
19. D
20. E
21. C
22. C
23. B
24. B

PT 18, Game 1
1. C
2. D
3. D
4. A
5. C
6. E

PT 18, Game 2
7. D
8. A
9. B
10. D
11. B
12. E
13. C

PT 18, Game 3
14. C
15. C
16. A
17. C
18. E
19. A

PT 18, Game 4
20. E
21. D
22. B
23. E
24. B

PT 19, Game 1
1. B
2. E
3. C
4. E
5. D
6. D
7. C

PT 19, Game 2
8. B
9. C
10. A
11. A
12. C

PT 19, Game 3
13. C
14. E
15. C
16. A
17. B
18. A
19. B

PT 19, Game 4
20. E
21. A
22. C
23. D
24. A

PT 20, Game 1
1. A
2. A
3. D
4. A
5. B

PT 20, Game 2
6. A
7. E
8. B
9. A
10. A
11. C
12. E

PT 20, Game 3
13. C
14. D
15. C
16. E
17. E
18. D

PT 20, Game 4
19. E
20. C
21. D
22. D
23. B
24. C

PT 21, Game 1
1. C
2. B
3. B
4. C
5. A
6. C

PT 21, Game 2
7. D
8. A
9. A
10. B
11. A

PT 21, Game 3
12. D
13. D
14. B
15. E
16. E
17. A

PT 21, Game 4
18. B
19. C
20. B
21. A
22. E
23. D
24. E

PT 22, Game 1
1. D
2. C
3. E
4. B
5. E
6. B
7. B

PT 22, Game 2
8. B
9. B
10. D
11. B
12. B
13. A
14. A

PT 22, Game 3
15. E
16. D
17. C
18. E
19. A

PT 22, Game 4
20. E
21. E
22. E
23. E
24. D

PT 23, Game 1
1. B
2. D
3. B
4. C
5. D

PT 23, Game 2
6. C
7. E
8. E
9. E
10. B
11. B

PT 23, Game 3
12. C
13. A
14. D
15. C
16. B
17. A
18. B

PT 23, Game 4
19. D
20. D
21. B
22. E
23. C
24. A

PT 24, Game 1
1. D
2. A
3. A
4. B
5. C

PT 24, Game 2
6. A
7. B
8. C
9. E
10. A

PT 24, Game 3
11. B
12. A
13. D
14. B
15. E
16. A
17. D

PT 24, Game 4
18. E
19. E
20. E
21. E
22. D
23. C

PT 25, Game 1
1. B
2. B
3. D
4. E
5. D

PT 25, Game 2
6. C
7. A
8. B
9. E
10. B
11. E
12. E

PT 25, Game 3
13. C
14. A
15. D
16. C
17. B
18. C

PT 25, Game 4
19. E
20. D
21. A
22. A
23. A
24. D

PT 26, Game 1
1. C
2. B
3. A
4. D
5. E
6. A
7. D

PT 26, Game 2
8. C
9. E
10. A
11. C
12. A

PT 26, Game 3
13. D
14. D
15. B
16. B
17. E
18. C

PT 26, Game 4
19. B
20. D
21. A
22. A
23. A
24. E

PT 27, Game 1
1. E
2. E
3. C
4. C
5. D
6. B

PT 27, Game 2
7. B
8. E
9. C
10. D
11. A
12. C

PT 27, Game 3
13. D
14. A
15. C
16. A
17. E
18. B
19. E

PT 27, Game 4
20. A
21. B
22. E
23. A
24. D

PT 28, Game 1
1. B
2. E
3. E
4. B
5. C

PT 28, Game 2
6. D
7. B
8. C
9. B
10. A
11. B
12. D

PT 28, Game 3
13. D
14. C
15. B
16. B
17. D
18. D

PT 28, Game 4
19. D
20. E
21. A
22. C
23. E

PT 29, Game 1
1. D
2. C
3. A
4. B
5. B
6. C

PT 29, Game 2
7. D
8. E
9. E
10. E
11. B
12. B
13. C

PT 29, Game 3
14. A
15. E
16. C
17. C
18. A
19. D

PT 29, Game 4
20. E
21. A
22. B
23. D
24. E

PT 30, Game 1
1. D
2. A
3. C
4. D
5. B

PT 30, Game 2
6. D
7. A
8. A
9. D
10. C

PT 30, Game 3
11. B
12. A
13. B
14. E
15. B
16. A

PT 30, Game 4
17. B
18. C
19. C
20. D
21. A
22. A
23. D

PT 31, Game 1
1. E
2. B
3. D
4. C
5. A
6. C

PT 31, Game 2
7. E
8. E
9. A
10. D
11. A
12. A
13. C

PT 31, Game 3
14. C
15. B
16. A
17. E
18. A

PT 31, Game 4
19. B
20. D
21. A
22. E
23. D

PT 32, Game 1
1. C
2. D
3. B
4. A
5. D
6. B

PT 32, Game 2
7. C
8. A
9. C
10. D
11. A

PT 32, Game 3
12. A
13. E
14. A
15. E
16. C
17. C
18. D

PT 32, Game 4
19. E
20. B
21. D
22. B
23. A
24. D

PT 33, Game 1
1. C
2. A
3. E
4. D
5. B

PT 33, Game 2
6. D
7. E
8. D
9. C
10. A
11. A
12. B

PT 33, Game 3
13. D
14. E
15. E
16. D
17. D
18. B

PT 33, Game 4
19. B
20. D
21. B
22. E
23. D

PT 34, Game 1
1. C
2. E
3. B
4. D
5. A
6. E
7. B

PT 34, Game 2
8. E
9. A
10. C
11. D
12. B

PT 34, Game 3
13. C
14. A
15. E
16. B
17. E
18. C

PT 34, Game 4
19. B
20. A
21. C
22. A
23. E
24. B

PT 35, Game 1
1. D
2. A
3. D
4. B
5. A

PT 35, Game 2
6. C
7. A
8. E
9. D
10. C
11. D
12. D

PT 35, Game 3
13. A
14. B
15. C
16. E
17. E

PT 35, Game 4
18. C
19. A
20. E
21. D
22. A
23. E

PT 36, Game 1
1. B
2. D
3. E
4. C
5. E
6. C

PT 36, Game 2
7. E
8. A
9. C
10. C
11. A
12. A
13. B

PT 36, Game 3
14. E
15. A
16. D
17. B
18. C

PT 36, Game 4
19. A
20. C
21. D
22. C
23. D

PT 37, Game 1
1. D
2. B
3. D
4. D
5. D

PT 37, Game 2
6. A
7. B
8. C
9. A
10. B
11. E

PT 37, Game 3
12. B
13. A
14. D
15. E
16. E
17. C
18. E

PT 37, Game 4
19. A
20. A
21. D
22. B
23. B
24. C

PT 38, Game 1
1. E
2. D
3. C
4. D
5. D
6. E
7. E

PT 38, Game 2
8. C
9. A
10. B
11. A
12. D
13. E

PT 38, Game 3
14. E
15. D
16. C
17. B
18. B
19. C

PT 38, Game 4
20. D
21. A
22. A
23. B
24. D

PT 39, Game 1
1. D
2. C
3. A
4. C
5. C

PT 39, Game 2
6. D
7. E
8. C
9. B
10. A
11. A

PT 39, Game 3
12. E
13. D
14. C
15. B
16. D
17. D
18. D

PT 39, Game 4
19. C
20. A
21. A
22. C
23. B

PT 40, Game 1
1. D
2. C
3. A
4. C
5. D

PT 40, Game 2
6. D
7. C
8. A
9. E
10. B

PT 40, Game 3
11. A
12. B
13. A
14. A
15. D
16. B
17. C

PT 40, Game 4
18. D
19. C
20. C
21. B
22. A
23. B

PT 41, Game 1
1. A
2. B
3. E
4. E
5. B
6. D
7. D

PT 41, Game 2
8. B
9. E
10. C
11. E
12. A

PT 41, Game 3
13. E
14. C
15. C
16. D
17. B

PT 41, Game 4
18. C
19. D
20. A
21. C
22. A
23. B
24. C

PT 42, Game 1
1. C
2. E
3. E
4. D
5. A

PT 42, Game 2
6. A
7. A
8. C
9. D
10. C
11. C
12. C

PT 42, Game 3
13. A
14. A
15. C
16. D
17. A
18. E

PT 42, Game 4
19. A
20. B
21. E
22. D
23. D

PT 43, Game 1
1. D
2. E
3. A
4. E
5. B

PT 43, Game 2
6. C
7. E
8. E
9. A
10. D
11. A
12. C

PT 43, Game 3
13. B
14. B
15. D
16. B
17. B

PT 43, Game 4
18. D
19. C
20. E
21. A
22. C

PT 44, Game 1
1. C
2. D
3. E
4. E
5. D
6. A

PT 44, Game 2
7. E
8. B
9. A
10. E
11. D
12. A

PT 44, Game 3
13. E
14. C
15. A
16. E
17. D

PT 44, Game 4
18. A
19. E
20. E
21. D
22. C

PT 45, Game 1
1. E
2. B
3. C
4. D
5. B
6. E

PT 45, Game 2
7. A
8. A
9. A
10. A
11. C
12. E

PT 45, Game 3
13. B
14. E
15. D
16. B
17. A

PT 45, Game 4
18. A
19. A
20. E
21. C
22. C

PT 46, Game 1
1. A
2. A
3. D
4. A
5. E
6. A

PT 46, Game 2
7. B
8. C
9. B
10. C
11. B

PT 46, Game 3
12. A
13. C
14. E
15. D
16. B

PT 46, Game 4
17. C
18. C
19. B
20. D
21. E
22. D

PT 47, Game 1
1. E
2. A
3. C
4. A
5. D

PT 47, Game 2
6. B
7. A
8. B
9. C
10. C
11. C

PT 47, Game 3
12. E
13. D
14. B
15. C
16. C
17. B

PT 47, Game 4
18. C
19. E
20. B
21. A
22. B

PT 48, Game 1
1. C
2. E
3. E
4. A
5. A
6. A

PT 48, Game 2
7. C
8. B
9. C
10. E
11. D
12. E

PT 48, Game 3
13. C
14. A
15. D
16. C
17. C

PT 48, Game 4
18. A
19. A
20. A
21. D
22. B

PT 49, Game 1
1. E
2. D
3. A
4. B
5. D
6. E
7. D

PT 49, Game 2
8. B
9. B
10. E
11. B
12. E

PT 49, Game 3
13. A
14. C
15. A
16. D
17. E

PT 49, Game 4
18. B
19. E
20. B
21. D
22. C

PT 50, Game 1
1. D
2. B
3. C
4. E
5. B

PT 50, Game 2
6. E
7. D
8. B
9. A
10. E

PT 50, Game 3
11. B
12. B
13. B
14. C
15. A
16. E
17. E

PT 50, Game 4
18. B
19. D
20. E
21. D
22. A

8652576R0

Made in the USA
Lexington, KY
18 February 2011